THE 5TH (BELGIAN) SAS IN THE SECOND WORLD WAR

THE 5TH (BELGIAN) SAS IN THE SECOND WORLD WAR

CAPTAIN BLUNT'S BASTARDS

Pen & Sword

MILITARY

AN IMPRINT OF PEN & SWORD BOOKS LTD.
YORKSHIRE – PHILADELPHIA

A version of this book was previously published by Amicale Belgian SAS Vriendenkring vzw in 2016 under the title: *Des SAS au "Special Forces Group" – 75 ans de forces spéciales belges / Van SAS tot 'Special Forces Group' – 75 jaar Belgische Special Forces*

This edition first published in Great Britain in 2025 by
Pen & Sword Military
An imprint of
Pen & Sword Books Ltd
Yorkshire - Philadelphia

ISBN 978 1 03613 788 5

A CIP catalogue record for this book is available from the British Library.

Printed and bound in England
By CPI (UK) Ltd.

The Publisher's authorised representative in the EU for product safety is Authorised Rep Compliance Ltd., Ground Floor, 71 Lower Baggot Street, Dublin D02 P593, Ireland. **www.arccompliance.com**

For a complete list of Pen & Sword titles please contact:

PEN & SWORD BOOKS LIMITED
George House, Units 12 & 13, Beevor Street, Off Pontefract Road, Barnsley, S71 1HN, UK
E-mail: enquiries@pen-and-sword.co.uk
Website: **www.pen-and-sword.co.uk**

or

PEN AND SWORD BOOKS
1950 Lawrence Road, Havertown, PA 19083, USA
E-mail: uspen-and-sword@casematepublishers.com
Website: **www.penandswordbooks.com**

CONTENTS

ACKNOWLEDGMENTS

FIRST AND FOREMOST, I would like to thank my family for their support during the countless hours required to complete this project.

My gratitude goes to Colonel Tom Bilo for his confidence in my ability to put the story to paper.

I am very grateful to the authors who paved the way in spreading the word, especially Emile Genot, who published dozens of books and articles on the subjects covered in this book, and to British author Damien Lewis for his advice and encouragement.

Regretting I was unable to conduct this research much earlier, I am nevertheless immensely grateful for still having had the opportunity of talking to some veterans of the wartime Belgian SAS, who have now all passed away.

Many thanks to all who helped me during my research, many of whom cannot be fully named, especially the president, vice-presidents, secretary, treasurer, archivist and selected other members from the Belgian SAS Association, including relatives of Second World War Belgian SAS veterans, for their continuous support in the seemingly endless research of events and details related to those involved in them and their patience in having to deal with my persistent questions.

Thanks also to our active duty or retired friends from the international SAS community, without whom many questions would have remained unanswered, especially the secretary, archivist and selected members of the British SAS Regimental Association, the heritage officers of the 21st and 22nd SAS Regiment and the French SAS current successor unit, the president of the French SAS Association, and the commanding officer, regimental sergeant major and archivist of the Belgian SAS current successor unit.

Thanks to Joe and the late Mick A. for their advice on British military awards.

Thanks to Peter Verstraeten for sharing information on Belgian SOE agents and MI9.

Thanks to Professor Matthias Strohn, Head of Historical Analysis, Centre for Historical Analysis and Conflict Research in Camberley, England, for his review of German terminology.

Thanks to Colonel Harold de Jong for his clarification of issues related to the campaign in the Netherlands.

Thanks to Russ and Steve for taking the time to review the manuscript from an English language perspective.

Finally, I would like to thank you, the reader, for your interest in a highly specialised subject, a small story in a war of immense proportions, but one that hopefully will allow you to appreciate the contribution of a select group of men that gave their all for our freedom and set the example for their successors who continue to preserve it to this day.

Dirk G.
Lead author
November 2025

FOREWORD

WHEN BELGIUM WAS invaded by the Germans in May 1940, many patriotic Belgians were determined to come to England to join the fight against the Nazis. Some were able to escape from Belgium and make it across the Channel, whilst others who were already abroad travelled directly to England. The most important of these people was Edouard (Eddy) Blondeel, who had been studying dentistry in Chicago and who was determined to create a special forces unit that could operate behind enemy lines. On arrival in England, he formed the Belgian Independent Parachute Company from a deliberately widely diverse group of people, a unit that later became the 5th SAS Regiment.

Blondeel not only demanded a very high standard of physical fitness from his men, but he chose those who also displayed a high level of mental resilience and ingenuity. These qualities were to be the key to the unit's great success in the fight against a numerically superior enemy. Always operating ahead of the Allies as the Germans were driven eastwards, the primary mission of the Belgian SAS was intelligence gathering and disrupting the German defences. Between July 1944 and the end of the war, the unit suffered twenty killed and over seventy – a very high casualty rate for such a small unit. In the words of the SAS Brigade commander Brigadier Roddy McLeod, "The Belgians were splendid. They all spoke English, indeed some who had been enlisted in Canada spoke a little French or Flemish. They did what they were told, their discipline was admirable and my staff loved them. Their CO — Eddie Blondeel, was one of the best COs I have ever had to deal with…".

The 5th (Belgian) SAS in the Second World War is a well-researched book based closely on war diaries and it graphically describes the chaos and confusion of the battlefield as well as the extraordinary human qualities that are needed in war, especially during the German counter-offensive in the Ardennes. Having commanded the Belgian Para-Commando Regiment – the post-war successor to the 5th SAS Regiment – on an airmobile divisional exercise in Germany in 1991, I can attest that the Belgian special forces have lost none of their war fighting capabilities.

For those who wish to understand the relevance of special forces even amidst the complexities of modern war, this book will make a valuable contribution.

General Sir Michael Rose
KCB, CBE, DSO, QGM

PREFACE

BARELY TWENTY-ONE YEARS after the armistice of the First World War – the war to end all wars – Europe was at war again when forces of the Nazi regime overwhelmed their neighbouring countries and beyond. For almost a year, the United Kingdom was the only European country still able to continue to wage war on Nazi Germany. An unprecedented war effort ensued, fuelled by the optimism, fighting spirit and vision of the indomitable Winston Churchill. A first-hand witness of non-conventional warfare during his younger years, Britain's prime minister was a firm supporter of small-scale operations behind enemy lines, to bring back the fight to the enemy during the dark hours that Britain was on its own, unable to confront the Nazis in conventional battle on the mainland. Britain also became the safe haven for volunteers from many nations who refused to accept the defeat of their country and were eager to join the Allied cause. Most of them would end up in conventional land, maritime and air units, often in formations composed of their countrymen but integrated into the Commonwealth forces, and would later participate in the liberation of Europe, made possible after the industrial might and the mobilised human resources of the United States came into play once that country was forced to enter the war when attacked by Japan. A minority would be selected to serve in one of the several special operations units that had recently been formed in the United Kingdom.

The 5th (Belgian) SAS in the Second World War is the story of such a special operations unit. It covers the origins, training and operations conducted by a small group of men who eventually became part of the Special Air Service, originally a British unit formed by David Stirling in North Africa, but later expanded to a multinational brigade-sized entity. Part of the Belgian SAS Regiment went by the nickname 'the Bastards', which is used here to designate the complete group. It is not to be seen as a derogatory name, but rather as a sign of respect in a humourous way, a sense of humour still being considered a key trait for personnel serving in the SAS. In a more serious view, bastards they were indeed, at least from the enemy's perspective, given their determination to defeat the Nazis no matter what.

This book is a testimony to the commitment and sacrifices made by those who have been and are still serving in the SAS, a community which includes the British, French and Belgian SAS, the Greek Sacred Squadron (all carrying varying names at some point in time during or after the war), the post-war Rhodesian SAS, the Australian SAS Regiment, the New Zealand SAS Regiment and the short-lived Canadian SAS Company.

The history of the Belgian SAS is based on the manuscript for a book on the history of Belgian special forces published in Dutch and French in 2017, provided by Milo Genot, former commanding officer of one of the Belgian SAS successor units during the Cold War. His initial text has been reviewed and updated, integrating new archival materials and other publications that have become available since. The primary sources used are the original after-action reports written by those who conducted the missions.

They are not free of error, since often during operations behind enemy lines, detailed notes could not be kept out of fear of falling into enemy hands, or the operational tempo simply precluded maintaining accurate records.

Spelling errors in the source documents for names of persons or geographic locations have been modified when possible and place names have mostly been used as they applied at the time the events happened or as found on contemporary War Office maps. Names for organisations or ranks have been translated whenever possible and corrected when required, after cross-referencing with other sources. Some German, French and Dutch names have been maintained in their original language when proper translation or accurate English equivalents could not be provided. For Belgian ranks, English names have been used, since the Belgian army in the UK used British ranks and insignia, but slight equivalence differences existed between some similarly sounding ranks in Dutch or French and English, so often it is impossible to know whether a specific designation referred to the British equivalent rank or was just an English translation of a different Belgian rank. British English has been used throughout, but proper nouns designating American units have been spelled appropriately in American English. Except where used differently in quoted texts, imperial units of measure have mostly been used to maintain historic authenticity.

LIST OF MAPS

Map 1. Origin of some Belgian SAS personnel.

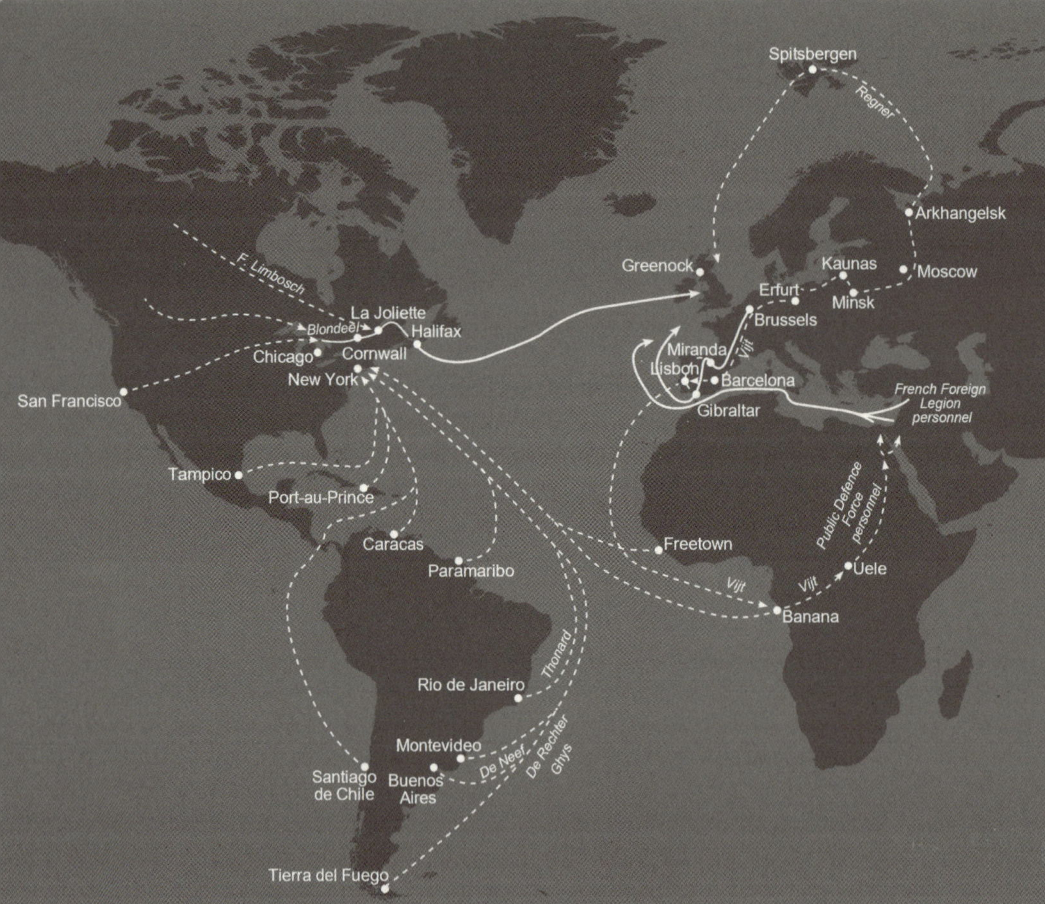

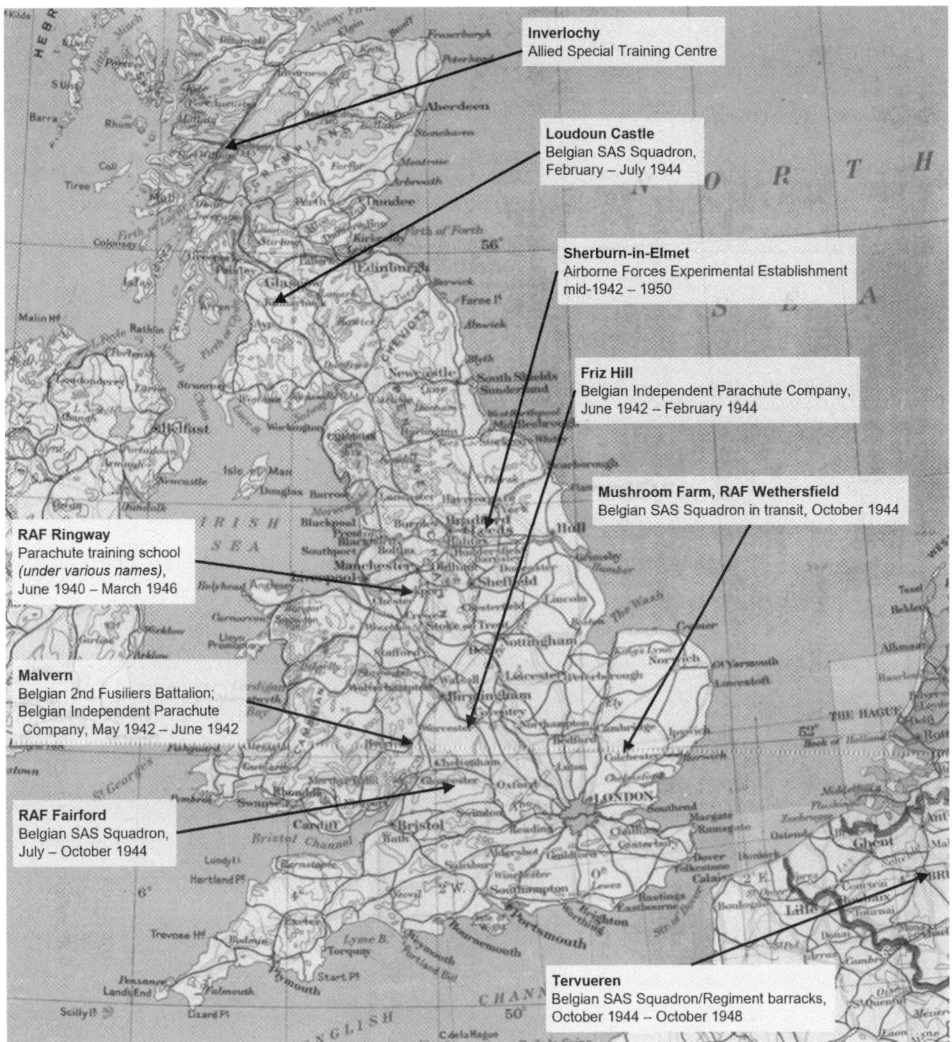

Map 2. Bases and training locations of the Belgian Independent Parachute Company, SAS Squadron and SAS Regiment, 1942-45.

Map adapted from War Office G.S.G.S. No. 4464 Europe 1:2,000,000 sheet B1 (1944)

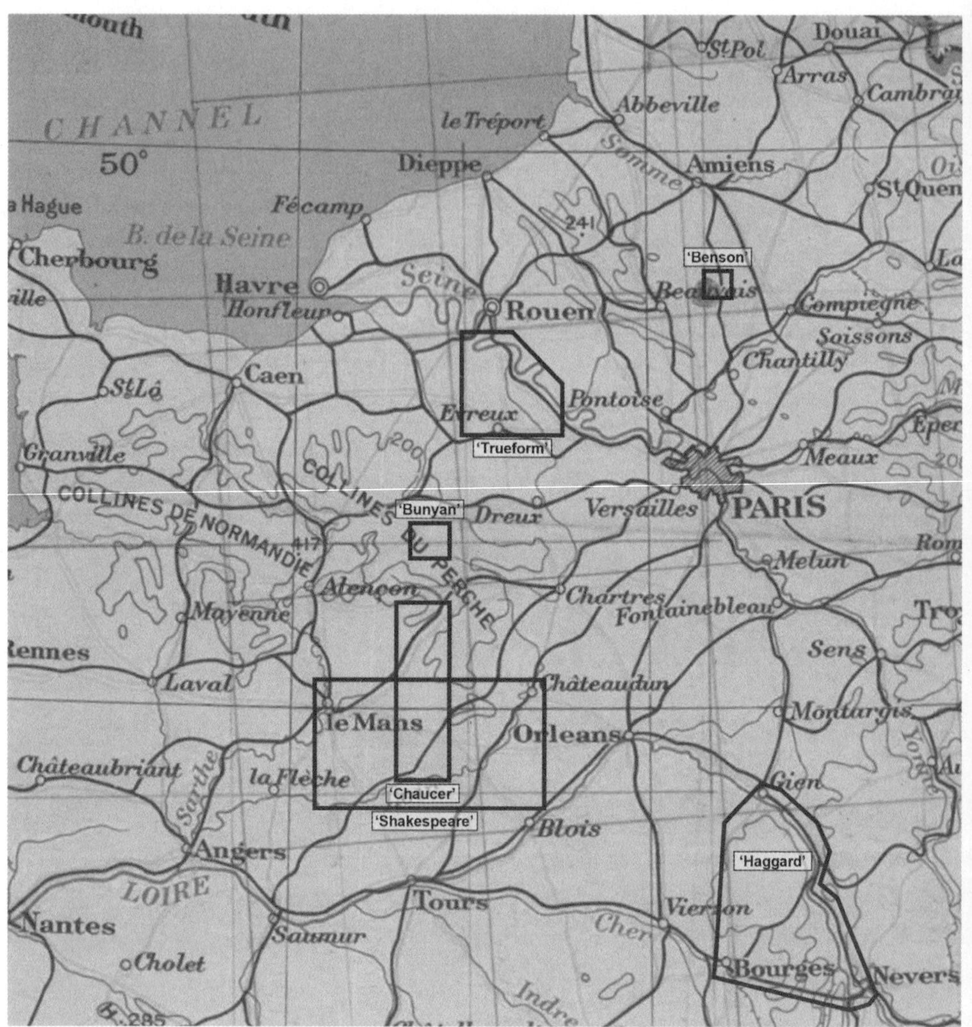

Map 3. The Normandy Campaign: operations 'Chaucer', 'Shakespeare', 'Bunyan', 'Trueform', 'Benson' and 'Haggard'. *Map adapted from War Office G.S.G.S. No. 4464 Europe 1:2,000,000, sheet B1 (1944)*

Map 4. Initial missions in Belgium: operations 'Noah', 'Brutus', 'Bergbang' and 'Caliban'.
Map adapted from War Office G.S.G.S. No. 4369 1:500,000 RAF (War) (1945) and A.M.S. M404 (GSGS 4072) 1:500,000 Europe (Air) (1944)

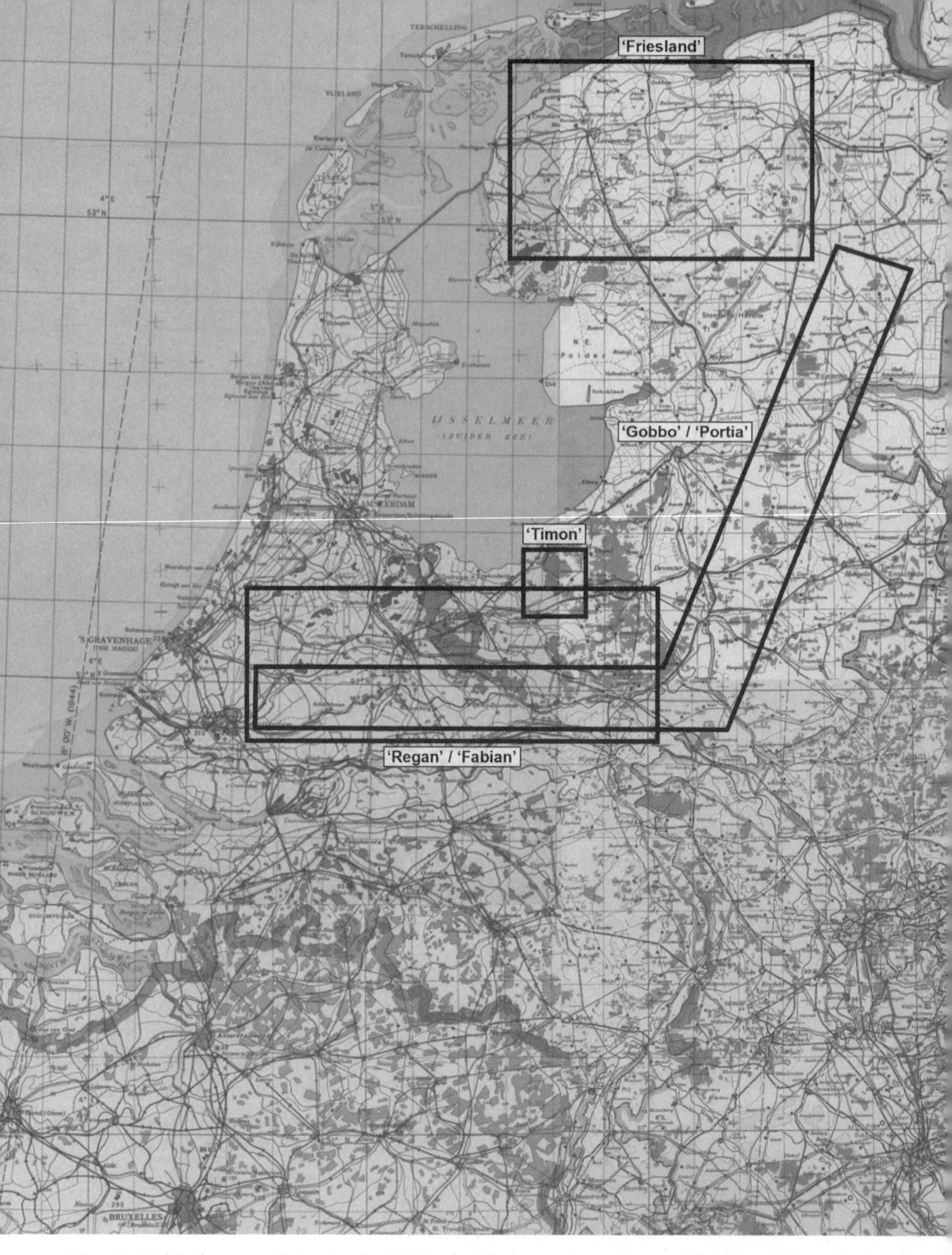

Map 5. Behind enemy lines in the Netherlands: operations 'Regan/Fabian', 'Timon', 'Portia/Gobbo' and 'Friesland'.
Map adapted from War Office G.S.G.S. No. 4369 1:500,000 RAF (War) (1945) and A.M.S. M404 (GSGS 4072) 1:500,000 Europe (Air) (1944)

Map 6. General area of operations during the Ardennes offensive.

Map adapted from A.M.S. M404 (War Office GSGS 4072) Europe (Air) 1:500,000 (1943), A.M.S. M404 (GSGS 4072) 1:500,000 Europe (Air) (1944), and War Office GSGS 4040 France and Belgium 1:50,000 (1943)

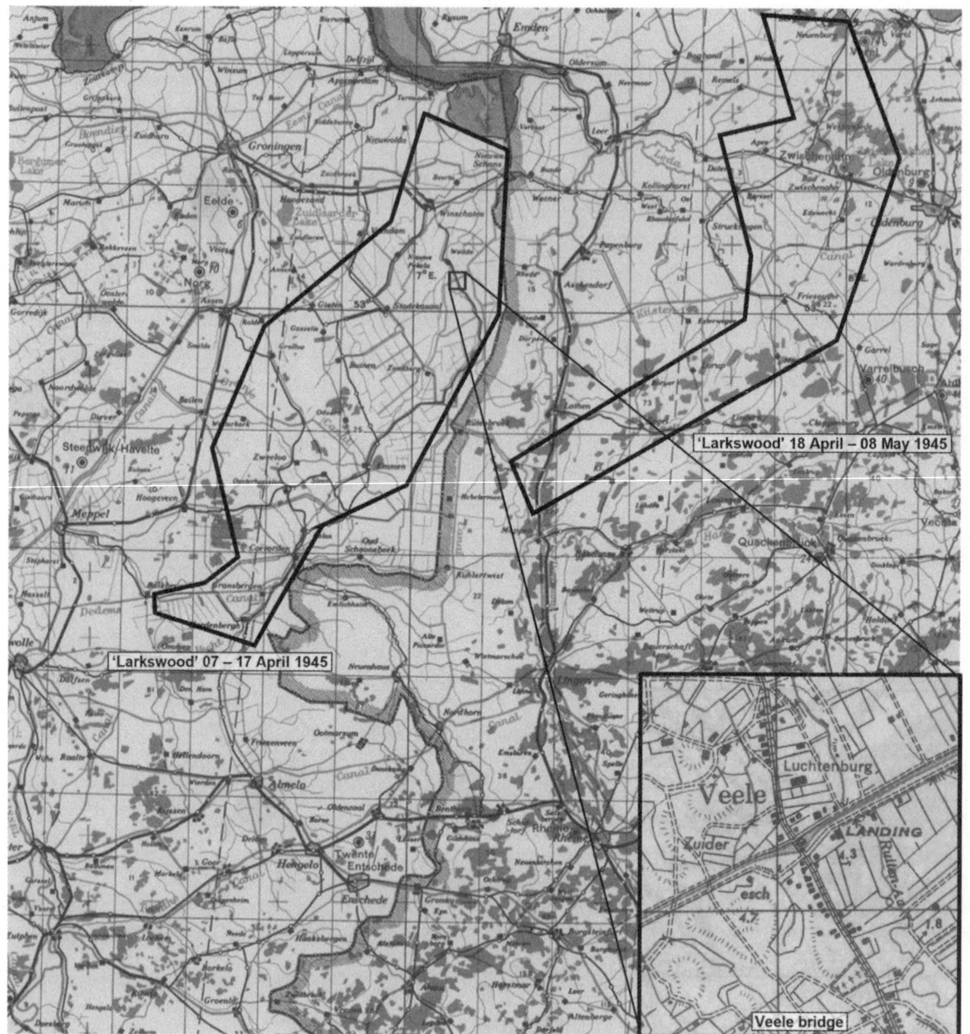

Map 7. Liberation of the Netherlands and defeat of Nazi Germany: Operation 'Larkswood'.
Map adapted from War Office GSGS 4072) Europe (Air) 1:500,000 (1943) and A.M.S. M832 (GSGS 4414) Eastern Holland 1:25,000 (1944)

ABBREVIATIONS

AAC	Army Air Corps
A.M.S.	Army Map Service
BBC	British Broadcasting Corporation
BEM	British Empire Medal
CO	commanding officer
DCM	Distinguished Conduct Medal
DSO	Companion of the Distinguished Service Order
DZ	drop zone
FFI	Forces Françaises de l'Intérieur ['French Interior Forces']
FSS	field security section
Gestapo	Geheime Staatspolizei
G.S.G.S	Geographical Section, General Staff
GHQ	General Headquarters
HQ	headquarters
IS9	Intelligence School Number 9
LUP	lying-up position
MBE	Member of the Order of the British Empire
MC	Military Cross
MI5	Security Service [formerly: Directorate of Military Intelligence - Section 5]
MI6	Secret Intelligence Service [informal designation of]
MI9	Directorate of Military Intelligence – Section 9
MM	Military Medal
NCO	non-commissioned officer
OC	officer commanding
OP	observation post
OSS	Office of Strategic Services
PIAT	projector, infantry, anti-tank
RAF	Royal Air Force
REME	Royal Electrical and Mechanical Engineers
RV	rendezvous
RVV	Raad van Verzet in het Koninkrijk der Nederlanden
SAS	Special Air Service
SHAEF	Supreme Headquarters Allied Expeditionary Force
SIS	Secret Intelligence Service
SD	Sicherheitsdienst
SFHQ	Special Force Headquarters
SOE	Special Operations Executive
SS	Schutzstaffel

Chapter One

THE FORMATION OF THE BELGIAN INDEPENDENT PARACHUTE COMPANY

Unity in diversity

"The Belgians who will form the Independent Parachute Company – the forerunner of the SAS squadron – have the most diverse backgrounds. Origin, language and vastly different training backgrounds make this unit one of the most heterogeneous of the Belgian army in the United Kingdom. This diversity ensures, however, extreme adaptability, a great deal of ingenuity and great operational resilience, a diversity that will increase the keen awareness of the common goal, i.e. participating in the destruction of Nazism and especially the liberation of Belgium and Europe. Therein lies the basis of an esprit de corps, and an unparalleled cohesion and efficiency."[1]

Among the Belgians who responded to the call for resistance by the Belgian government in exile in London and who volunteered to subsequently serve in the parachute company, were refugees and escaped prisoners of war, but also seasoned fighting men from the French Foreign Legion, graduates from the *Force publique* ('Public Defence Force') of the Belgian Congo, veterans of various other organisations such as the Special Operations Executive (SOE), as well as some who already lived in the United Kingdom or on the other side of the Atlantic when war broke out. How they all ended up in Britain could fill a book, but it should be emphasised that rarely was it a walk in the park, and some risked their lives to reach the UK.

Belgian refugees and escaped military personnel

In 1940, Jules Regner was called up to serve in the 1st Regiment of Dismounted Chasseurs. Near the end of the Eighteen Days' Campaign,[2] he was taken prisoner in Eeklo and a few weeks later, he found himself in prisoner of war camp Stalag 1-A near Stablack in East Prussia. Together with other prisoners, he was put to work on a local German farm. On 26 April 1941, while delivering hay near the Lithuanian border, he took the opportunity to deceive the Germans. He recalled:

> The weather was nice and I decided that the time had come to escape. A French prisoner of war who was aware of my plan suggested accompanying me. During our work, the farmer's son told us about the Russian border. Without realising it, he gave away important information about the direction we should follow to reach it. Back on the farm, we secretly stocked up on food, putting a few bread crusts in our travel bag during the meal. When the farmer came to lock us up

> for the night, I immediately told him that I had forgotten to water the horses. He let us out again and demanded that we do this quickly. We rushed to the water pump in the middle of the yard, filled the buckets with a lot of noise, walked to the stable, picked up our rucksacks and disappeared. The darkness played in our favour. We knew that to walk eastwards and reach the Lithuanian border, we had to feel the wind on the left cheek. Not such an accurate method of orientation of course, but at 4 o'clock in the morning, we managed to see the two barbed wire fences at the border.

Jules and his companion were intercepted by sentries and handed over to an internal security service of the Soviet Union. They ended up in a company of common-law prisoners and were incarcerated, first in Kretnina and later in Kaunas. Regner recounted: "Every now and then a state official called me. I was even more surprised and confused when I met a fellow inmate who claimed to originate from my hometown Ecaussines. To support his claims, he called several street names and even gave details of a particular inhabitant. In reality, it was a Belgian in the service of the Soviet police, who questioned me in an insidious manner!"

A month later, Regner was on a train on his way to Siberia. Arriving in Mitchourin, the prisoners were housed in a castle where they could live in somewhat more favourable conditions. Jules met 140 Frenchmen including Captain (later general) Pierre Bilotte, but also a Flemish compatriot. "It was there that we were informed of the start of the German offensive against the Soviet Union on 22 June 1941", Jules explained.

The detainees were constantly kept in the dark about their fate. They left for Minsk, then Smolensk, made a detour around Moscow and ended up in Vologda, where they met Poles who had been imprisoned there since 1939. They were subjected to communist propaganda and every day the *Pravda* was read to them. The food got worse and worse:

> The deterioration was probably due to rumours that units were being raised in France and Belgium to fight with the Germans on the Eastern Front. Fortunately, better news would come. General de Gaulle and the Belgian government in London had declared their alliance with the Soviet Union to fight against the Nazis. One day I was called to the camp director who proposed to me...to return to Belgium to help organise the resistance with the communist Independence Front or to join the Belgian troops in Great Britain. I chose Britain; my Flemish friend preferred to extend his stay in Russia. Despite my research after the war, I heard nothing more from him since.

Regner had several possibilities to return to the homeland, including the trans-Siberian Railway, or by travelling via Iraq. A third possibility, which Regner eventually chose, was to take sail to Spitsbergen in a ship departing Archangelsk. In Spitsbergen, the British had launched an operation to destroy the coal mines and Russians needed to be repatriated. "With five Belgians, we were going aboard the *Empress of Canada*. After a short stop in Spitsbergen, the ship docked in Greenock, Scotland, on 10 September 1941."

On the quay, a Belgian officer waited for the survivors from the Soviet Union, an event that caused a lot of curiosity. A press conference was organised, during which their many experiences and impressions were recounted. Then Regner was screened at the 'Patriotic School' and was finally able to join the forces: "After a stay in the 'Patriotic School', a few days later, I was conscripted into the Belgian Forces in the United Kingdom. Supported by my experiences and with the deepest desire to be part of a special unit, I volunteered for the Belgian parachute unit in 1942. My peregrination to England eventually took more than sixteen months!"[3]

Much later, his superior, 1st Lieutenant Gilbert-Sadi Kirschen, had nothing but praise for Regner:

> Which Jules Regner should I introduce here? The 1940 soldier who, at the beginning of his stay in a Stalag in East Prussia managed to reach the border of the Soviet Union, moving through forests and swamps? The extraordinary athlete in England who jumped from the horizontal bar with a perfect somersault? Or the paratroopers' sergeant who, acting upon orders from his superiors on 18 September 1944, crossed enemy lines and outsmarted German patrols to reach a burning Arnhem, searching for Major General Urquhart, the commander of the 1st British Airborne Division? No, Jules Regner was different and was much more than just one of the bravest soldiers of the last world war. He was a gentle and good man, always careful not to hurt anyone, who avoided what was mean and narrow-minded and who was open to everything that was correct and beautiful. He was an artist who smiled at the world he loved and depicted it with a swift and firm pencil stroke.[4]

Another interesting escape story is that of René Krins.

> For some time, the idea had been haunting my mind that I had to try to get to England. There one could still live freely – which I missed – and there one could continue the struggle for the liberation of Europe. I left my native Verviers by bicycle on 10 May 1941, at 8 o'clock in the morning and with 50 Belgian francs in my pocket. I slept in sheds and after two days I reached the border and began my journey through France, first in the occupied part, then in the [non-occupied] Vichy part.

Krins was halted by German sentries and was sent back. However, a farmer came to his aid and the next day he managed to travel by train to his aunt in Paris.

> After three days I crawled back on my bicycle in the direction of Bordeaux. I was still sleeping in barns, because with my 50 francs, I had no other choice. Having arrived in Bordeaux after more than 1,000 kilometres [620 miles], I was dead tired, hungry and thirsty. I walked into a café to have a drink and rest. The manager immediately understood my situation and advised me to cross the demarcation line[5] in the vicinity of Langon. After a good night's sleep, a meal and having sold my bicycle, I moved on. The next day I crossed the demarcation line with a little more money in my pocket and took the train to Toulouse. There, unfortunately, I got arrested by French gendarmes.

Then began his stay in Vichy prisons. He spent two weeks in a youth camp, then in another camp in Puy-l'Evêque, where he worked on a farm. However, his French boss was not satisfied and sent him back to the camp. On 14 July 1941, he and a few friends laid flowers at the monument to the fallen of 1914 and sang the 'Brabanconne' (Belgian national anthem) and the 'Marseillaise' (French national anthem). Krins was considered ill-disciplined and guilty of work refusal, so ended up in the Vernet concentration camp, where he met Raymond Godfroid[6] and another Belgian. They decided to escape but had to postpone their plan twice before they managed to crawl over the barbed wire fence without attracting the attention of the guards:

> We knew that we had a night and part of the morning before the guards would ascertain our escape; so we marched through the fields to Toulouse. Arriving at the Belgian Office in Toulouse, our compatriots first wanted to hand us over to the authorities in Vichy. Godfroid became furious and thanks to his reaction, they put us in touch with a Montauban man who accompanied us to Palavas-Les-Flots, where a group under the command of a certain major Branders helped evaders and escapees to cross the Pyrenees.

After a month's rest, during which they hid in a villa on the beach, the long-awaited day arrived. The three men went to the railway station of Montpellier and made contact with a resistance leader of the *Groupe Zéro*. They boarded a train to Perpignan. During the journey, their counterfeit French papers were checked by gendarmes, but nothing suspicious was noticed.

> We then followed a large tunnel, at the end of which a Spaniard was waiting to smuggle us over the Pyrenees to Spain. At a certain moment, however, he left us, while giving us instructions so that we could continue towards the British consulate in Barcelona. We were left to ourselves and continued our journey along mountain paths. By the time we reached the Figueras railway station to take the train, we were exhausted and fell asleep while waiting. Our awakening was a disappointment: members of the *Guardia Civil* asked us for our papers.

The three men had no Spanish documents. They had thrown away their French papers andpretended to be British and Canadian. From Figueras, they were taken to the prefecture of Barcelona and questioned, then locked in the basement of the building, where they were crammed into a cell with all kinds of individuals.

> After additional interrogations, we were transferred to a prison in Barcelona. Several weeks later, we were moved to other prisons in Irun, Lerida and Saragossa, before ending up in the Miranda de Ebro concentration camp. This camp was comparable to the French one; however, here we lived with the hope that one day we would be released because since we pretended to be Canadians, the British consul would be allowed to visit us. Having investigated the matter, the latter declared to the Spanish authorities that we were British subjects. We were being fed very poorly, but thanks to an employee of the consulate, Miss Freda Moore[7] (who was to become our godmother), we periodically received a food parcel. The hygiene was terrible. We had to deal with diarrhoea and were full of vermin. At times, our morale was very low!

After some time, the Belgians were taken to Madrid, accompanied by members of the British embassy. Finally, they got on a train that should bring them to safer places.

> ... It was impossible to sleep during those first nights. The beds were too comfortable and to sleep, we ended up lying on the floor. But we had the luxury of being able to take a bath.
>
> It was quite a sensation when we found ourselves on the Rock of Gibraltar, between army soldiers and naval personnel, waiting for a troop transport to England. At last the ship we had been expecting docked and after eight days at sea, we reached the port of Greenock in Scotland. There we took the train to London, all the way being guarded. We knew that upon arrival we would not be released and would be held in a place called the 'Patriotic School', and be questioned by the intelligence service. I was interrogated for a whole day by a Brit who knew the town of Verviers and everything that had happened there, as well as I did. After a few days of relaxation in London, I went to the Belgian embassy in Eaton Square and enlisted in a Belgian parachute unit. A year had passed since my departure from Verviers.[8]

The Miranda de Ebro camp also left certain impressions on Emile Debefve:

> After our wanderings through France, the Pyrenees and our imprisonment in Spain, we were convinced that the day of our liberation was near, for we were now officially Canadian citizens. After arriving at the camp, we were asked a few questions, after which we were united with other 'Canadians' who spoke with a Brussels or Liège accent. Personally, I suffered most from the total lack of hygiene. We were plagued by lice, fleas, in short by all kinds of pests, the inevitable companions of places that lack constant maintenance. Once a week, the camp was visited by the British military attaché or his deputy. Each time this was automatically followed by the release of some prisoners who then went to the United Kingdom embassy. The United Kingdom with its overseas territory of Gibraltar has a common border with Spain. For this reason, the Spanish adopted a policy of relative neutrality, which varied according to the success of operations in North Africa. From Miranda, the men were transported to Gibraltar to board a ship that would take them to Greenock. There they were placed in quarantine in the 'Patriotic School', a place where one tried to unmask enemy spies.[9]

Belgians from the French Foreign Legion

Several legionnaires also joined the parachute unit at the end of May 1942. They were mostly young men who had fled from Belgium two years earlier and ended up in the Sainte-Marthe camp near Marseille, as prisoners of the French Vichy government. To buy their freedom, they had been forced to sign a five-year contract with the Foreign Legion. They ended up in French Vichy units in overseas territories and later joined the forces of General de Gaulle. Major Louis Legrand was sent to the Near East to request the French to rescind the contract of these men and to allow them to join the Belgian forces in Great Britain. As a result, at the beginning of 1942, many legionnaires would arrive in England. However, many of them would be disappointed upon arrival, once they found out that the promises they had been made came to nothing. They had been told, among other things, that once in England, they would be accepted with the rank of warrant officer. Not only was there no promotion, but many also had to renounce the rank they had in Syria, Dakar, Eritrea or Abyssinia. They were hardened and experienced fighters, yet they had to undergo a full training programme again. Some among them opted to join the Belgian troop in the No. 10 (Inter-Allied) Commando. A dozen, however, decided to join the Belgian parachute unit: Georges Ratinckx, Jean Lox, Florent Grétry, Ferdinand Hendrickx, Théo Clamot, Jacques Goffinet, Rene-Gaston Geldof, René Balsat, André Bouillon, Pierre Polain[10] and Albert Meisch.

Veterans of the colonial Public Defence Force

Warrant Officer Charles Vijt was among a group of veterans of the colonial *Force publique* ('Public Defence Force'). When he joined the parachute unit, he already had a successful military career behind him. His testimony is therefore important. From 1936 to 1939, after his studies at the military pupil schools of Safraanberg and Aalst, he attended courses at the Military Institute for Physical Education in Brussels. He intended to become an instructor, but the war interfered with his career. During the German invasion of May 1940, he served in an artillery unit. At the time of the capitulation, he was taken prisoner and ended up in Stalag IX, a prisoner of war camp in Erfurt (Germany). After helping several French prisoners escape, he meticulously prepared for his own escape:

> Barbed wire separated me from an area that was lit up at night. With extreme caution and in the dark, I managed to get through this area, which wasn't easy... Once this obstacle was behind me, I followed a wall that led to the light. I put socks over my shoes and left pepper behind, to prevent any dogs from following me...so I stood a few metres from a sentry. As he moved away, I discreetly leapt to within a metre of the illuminated area. At the moment that the sentry, who was still in the illuminated area, came back in my direction, I pressed myself against the wall, which was in total darkness. The sentry's look was continuously directed towards the right-hand side, more specifically to the inside of the station. When he made a half turn to the right, I followed him closely to the end of the illuminated zone, where he turned left, so that he could always keep his eyes on the inside of the station. During this turn to the left, I performed a muffled jump and disappeared into the darkness.[11]

Vijt, having worked there, was familiar with the Erfurt station to be able to make a safe escape. He walked the 15 miles to Gotha station on foot. There he jumped on a train to Cologne and ended up in Aachen. His knowledge of German was very useful. To cross the border, he covered the last few miles on foot and finally arrived in Brussels on 16 October 1941. In the capital, he went into hiding with his aunt. But the hardships of the last few months had weakened him considerably. He was also diagnosed with a pleural effusion. He was first hospitalised at a hospital in Uccle, then in the sanatorium of Buizingen, where he recovered for nine months. It would not occur to the Germans to look for him there. With extraordinary willpower, he devoted himself to physical rehabilitation. He had only one goal: to join the Belgian army in Great Britain. At the beginning of November 1942, he crossed the border with France. He went to Paris and Bourges and on 11 November, he crossed the demarcation line. He then moved on to Vichy, Périgueux, Carcassonne, Limoux, and Montpellier and reached Montauban, where he managed to get in touch with a Belgian evasion organisation, but was arrested by French police, together with a fellow countryman. With the solemn promise to return to the North, the two men were released. In reality, they stubbornly maintained their plan to cross the Pyrenees. Barely arrived in Spain, they fell into the hands of the *Guardia Civil*, yet were helped by two Spanish gendarmes to reach Barcelona, for which Charles paid them with his watch. At the British consulate, they linked up with a Belgian who helped them traverse the rest of Spain. When crossing the Portuguese border, they were stopped by the police and detained. The Belgian embassy was informed of their arrest and contacted them. Vijt then stated his intent to join the Royal Air Force (RAF), but his application was refused because he was married and had children. The Belgian embassy finally decided to have him join the Congolese *Force publique*. Together with a dozen Belgians, he left the European mainland on board the *Mouzinho* and headed for Banana (Belgian Congo). He was promoted to warrant officer and assigned to a group of three artillery batteries stationed in Uélé. He quickly adapted to this new colonial military environment and gave physical training lessons to Europeans and Congolese soldiers, until he was sent to Egypt to serve in a Belgian expeditionary corps in the Middle East. Vijt recalled:

> When the corps was disbanded in 1944, I was able to return to the Congo; however, the campaign for the liberation of Europe was already underway and I wanted to take part in it. I heard about the SAS paratroopers and was prepared to commit myself to this Belgian unit. I got my travel orders for Great Britain and twelve days later I disembarked in Glasgow. I joined the first batch of Belgian volunteers in Leamington Spa. These had just arrived from liberated Belgium. According to the usual standards in this unit, I was downgraded to trooper and I got the chance to attend the parachute training. When I arrived at Leamington Spa railway station in my beautiful uniform of warrant officer, there was a big guy with a red beret waiting for me, dressed in a camouflage vest with SAS wings, khaki trousers with a huge pocket on the front and equipped with a revolver and a dagger.[12] I had to swallow: I was standing here in front of a member of the SAS. The big guy introduced himself: "Sergeant First Class Krolikowski, good afternoon, Sir." This was accompanied by a peculiar salute that Kroli had kept from his time in the armoured forces. I answered his salute. "Allow me, Sir", he continued, taking my suitcase and carrying it to the jeep. "Please take a seat, Sir, we are leaving." In the jeep I felt a lot better, my dream was coming true; I was going to join the paratroopers. But a sudden U-turn put an end to my thoughts. Kroli asked: "Scared, Sir?" "No, Sir." The jeep entered the camp at full speed and braked abruptly. The tyres screeched... "Did you get a fright, Sir?" "No, Sir." Kroli took my suitcase and shouted, "Follow me on the double!" and ran to a hut where he reported, "Sir, from now on you are a trooper, and responsible for this room." "Yes, Sir!" I changed my clothes and five minutes later I was standing in front of four instructors: sergeants

> first class De Rechter, Crèvecœur, Parmentier and Kroli. "Tomorrow, an hour of gymnastics, an hour of running, one hour of obstacle course and one hour of tactical exercises." Before handing over the command to a colleague, the instructor asked after each exercise: "Are you tired?" My answer that followed was always: "No, Sir!" I admired their fair play, their enthusiasm and their training methodology.[13]

For their part, and impressed by his toughness, his dynamism and his enthusiasm, the instructors quickly made friends with Vijt, who became increasingly well accepted by his superiors, his colleagues and, later on, his subordinates.

Members of services for clandestine operations

Several members of the future Belgian SAS Squadron also fled from Belgium after the outbreak of hostilities but first joined other organisations carrying out operations in occupied Europe. In this group are, among others, father Robert Jourdain, Jean Cassart, Georges d'Oultremont, Robert Feremans, Jacques Van Broekhuizen, Rene Van Haezendonck, Raymond Holvoet, Etienne Gailly, Regner de Wykerslooth and Arnaud de Montpellier.

Cassart was a striking figure with a history that defies all imagination. This officer of the Belgian army graduated from the polytechnic department of the Royal Military Academy and was assigned to the artillery. In 1936, he completed the general staff course. Then he was assigned to the 3rd Aviation Regiment, where he conducted 500 flying hours by day and 100 by night. On 3 April 1939, during one of these flights, he was the victim of an accident, which forced him to sit idle for six months of mandatory inactivity. During his military career (1937-1940) he also enrolled as a student at the Free University of Brussels and obtained the title of engineer in aeronautical engineering, a licence in economic and financial sciences and a licence in political and administrative sciences. On 5 October 1939, he returned to the artillery, in the meantime having been promoted to captain, and took part in the Eighteen Days' Campaign. After the capitulation of Belgium, he went into hiding to avoid ending up as a prisoner of war in Germany. Two months later, he reached Switzerland by bike, crossed the non-occupied part of France and made contact with some French intelligence personnel. He worked under the pseudonym 'Metrat', derived from a French captain who disappeared in 1940 and whose papers he had been using since the beginning of 1941. Between October 1940 and March 1941, Cassart carried out three missions in Belgium for the *2ème Bureau français* (French intelligence). In April, he went to North Africa and on 31 May he appeared in London, where he tried to gain admission to the RAF. However, he was declared unfit because he wore spectacles. Nevertheless, he was recruited by the SOE. On 11 August 1941, he was ordered to get in touch with resistance groups in Belgium and to train saboteurs. On 3 October, he and a radio operator parachuted into the neighbourhood of Jalhay without ever having made a training jump. As such, Cassart can be considered one of the first parachutists flown in from the United Kingdom to make contact with the resistance.[14]

He managed to make several contacts. On 23 November he chaired a meeting in Antwerp with the most important leaders of the resistance. He provided them with financial support, distributed sabotage material and gathered important information for London. On 8 December, he and his radio operator went to an agreed location in Neufchâteau, to be picked up by a Lysander[15] of the RAF. He was betrayed but escaped in the nick of time. Five days later, he was arrested in Brussels by the *Gestapo* and imprisoned in the Saint-Gilles prison. On 28 January 1942, after an attempt to escape, he was transferred to Aachen, and then sent to Berlin, where he arrived on 21 September 1942. His trial started on 14 September 1943 before the *Oberreich Kriegsgericht* in Charlottenburg. At the moment when his verdict was about to be pronounced, he saw another prisoner going to the toilets without surveillance. He also asked for permission, locked himself in, crawled through a small window into the adjoining corridor leading to the exit and, posing as a staff member of the courthouse, greeted the sentry with a loud "Heil Hitler" and disappeared into the city.

> The first day I walked 40 kilometres [25 miles]. In the evening I was in Potsdam, tired and tormented by thirst. I arrived at a level crossing and in the half-darkness, I heard French voices... Deportees, to whom I told my story gave me German marks in exchange for my watch. The next morning I walked a short distance and two days later I took the train, and on 29 September 1943 I arrived in Fléron in Belgium, where I hid for three months to regain strength.

From Belgium, he would follow the classic route to England: France, Spain, and Gibraltar and would arrive in London on 24 January 1944. His two-year absence meant that he was presumed dead and British authorities wanted to investigate. They decided to lock him up in Guildford in a so-called luxury prison with a 'special regime': "In England, the 'intelligence service' vetted me", he said. "Two months under the supervision of an officer who found me unbearable. Interrogations and counter-interrogations followed each other... In the end my incredible story was accepted. I was released and... congratulated..."[16] Because Cassart was compromised as an SOE agent, he would later be assigned to the SAS Brigade headquarters.

Another extraordinary character is Raymond Holvoet, alias 'Henderson'. In October 1940, at the age of 16, Holvoet was a member of the underground press group *La Belgique avant tout* (Belgium before anything else). In Kortrijk, he was responsible for editing and preparing stencils. The magazine appeared periodically in 500 copies until 13 February 1941, when the *Geheime Feldpolizei*[17] arrested some group members. Holvoet was warned and decided to evade to England, together with six comrades. His family had no idea where he had gone. Later they received news from Lourdes... Raymond's group (which also included Roger Carrette and Henri Nieuwenhuyse) took the train and travelled via Tourcoing, Lille, Paris and Angoulême to Mont-de-Marsan, where a priest assisted them to cross the demarcation line between occupied France and Vichy-France. On the way, Urbain Deprez also joined them. On 30 June, Holvoet went to Irati, at the foot of the Pyrenees. He crossed the Spanish border but was arrested in Ochagavia by the *Guardia Civil,*[18] on 3 July. Via prisons in Güesa and Pamplona, he subsequently ended up in the Miranda de Ebro camp. Thanks to the intervention of the British consul, he was allowed to leave the camp and was brought to Gibraltar. On 15 March 1942, he finally arrived in England, where he was enlisted into the Belgian army on 2 April. Jean Temmerman testified:

His comrades will always remember the boy with blushing cheeks, who was a talented Flemish writer. After fleeing from Belgium, he arrived in Gibraltar in early 1942. He reacted enthusiastically to the news that a Belgian parachute unit was being established in Great Britain. This news was incorrect or at least premature, because, although some [Belgian] agents had already been parachuted and some Belgians [from the army in exile] had already jumped, it should be noted that the Independent Parachute Company would only be established on 8 May 1942. The freed Belgians, while waiting for a ship in Gibraltar, used their free time to remain in good physical condition.[19]

He eventually joined the Belgian Independent Parachute Company, but from 1 June 1942, he attended SOE training and obtained his parachute qualification on 11 September. He was appointed radio operator for Operation 'Griffon-Badger'; his task was to provide the radio link between England and Belgium. On the night of 13-14 February 1943, he was parachuted, together with Lieutenant Gauthier, into the province of Liège in Belgium. In May 1943, during a meeting with members of the resistance, the Germans discovered their hideout. Of those present, only the two SOE operators escaped, through a basement window. At the beginning of July, Holvoet returned to the hiding place and arrived back in England, now with the help of an organised network. His comrade was not so lucky: he was caught by the Germans in Paris and eventually ended up in Dachau concentration camp. In early 1944, Holvoet was promoted to sergeant while serving in the SOE, but because he decided to transfer to the Belgian SAS Squadron, he immediately lost his rank.

Count Georges d'Oultremont MBE, MM, another former special operations agent, joined the SAS squadron in 1944. His son recounted:

In May 1940, my father participated in the Eighteen Days' Campaign with the 2nd Mounted Chasseurs. Taken prisoner on 28 May, he escaped on 1 June. At the end of the year, he joined the *Secours d'hiver* (Winter aid), doing a considerable amount of work helping families without food or heating. Bored by office work, he joined the ranks of the *Volontaires du Travail* (Work Volunteers), whose task was to give work to teenagers to prevent them from being sent to Germany for compulsory work. By mid-1942, he left the organisation, which had been infiltrated by the enemy, and joined the *Aide aux Enfants des Prisonniers de Guerre* organisation (Aid to the Children of Prisoners of War). In February 1942, under cover of the A.E.P. and the *Cantine Suédoise*,[20] where he was working in parallel, he joined the *Comète* network, which helped evade downed Allied aircrew members to reach Great Britain via France, the Pyrenees, Spain and Gibraltar, where he was an international guide between Brussels and Paris for eight months. Having become too well known to the *Gestapo*, he escaped from Belgium via the *Comète* network in December 1942 with two other members and arrived in the UK on 13 January 1943. During his three-day stay at the Patriotic School, he expressed his suspicions about a so-called Dutchman who had accompanied them from France; he turned out to be a German spy. On 20 January, he joined the Belgian Forces in Great Britain and spent several months training at the training centre of the Belgian forces in Great Britain, in

Leamington Spa. Airey Neave then proposed him as a recruit at the Belgian *Sûreté de l'Etat* (State Security), in London, for MI9/IS9, which he joined on 31 July 1943. He was trained by SOE, obtained his parachute wings at Ringway on 3 August and joined MI9/IS9, where he was trained as a clandestine operations officer specialised in the extractions by Lysander and 'M.T.B.' (motor torpedo boat) of Allied airmen shot down in occupied countries. On 7 November 1943, he was dropped off by Lysander 2 kilometres [1.25 miles] southwest of Selens in France, on Operation 'Ormonde', where he was acting manager of the Possum evasion network. At the end of December 1943, the Possum network came to a tragic end after being denounced. On 10 February 1944, he escaped from France via the SOE network *Lorrain Cruze* and was arrested in Pamplona (Spain) and placed under house arrest until 20 March. He reached London on 9 April, was re-trained by MI9/IS9 and sent on a mission to extract airmen from Fréteval Forest near Bayeux in Normandy, on 30 June, from where he returned to Britain on 26 July. On 26 August 1944, he joined the Belgian SAS Squadron at Fairford, where he remained until the end of the war.[21]

Belgians responding to the call of the Belgian government in exile

Finally, there are all those who responded to the ministerial decree, issued by the Belgian government in exile in London, which stipulated that compulsory military service applied to all Belgians living in the non-occupied territories. Several groups would join the Belgian parachute unit: a group that fled from Belgium after the Eighteen Days' Campaign and then joined the Belgian unit being formed in Tenby, in addition to those whose parents stayed in Britain, and others yet who would come from North America. In February 1941, twenty-eight volunteers presented themselves at the Cornwall military camp in Ontario (Canada). Among them was 1st Lieutenant Blondeel, who, thanks to a scholarship, was completing his studies for a doctorate in dentistry in Chicago. He was allowed to return to his unit (the 7th Artillery Regiment) in July 1940, but the outbreak of hostilities on 10 May changed his plans. It was only in September 1944 – during SAS operations – that he would return to Belgium.

Freddy Limbosch, an agricultural engineer, had emigrated to Canada in 1938 and ran a farm in Ontario. Roger De Neef was a well-known cyclist during the Six Days of Buenos Aires. Paul Thonard, who worked as an engineer in Brazil, took part in the battle of Houthulst (near the Yser) as a 2nd lieutenant in the artillery during the First World War. Since he did not possess any document in Canada that could prove the rank he had held in 1918, he had to start from scratch in the military hierarchy. In England, he was awarded the rank of warrant officer. Private First Class Leo Van Cauwelaert spoke several languages, which allowed him to command the group of Belgians who spoke English, French or Spanish. He performed this task until the arrival of the officers. This group did not sit back but started practising British drills and marches, but the number of rifles and rounds was limited. On 8 April, the group left the camp in Cornwall and moved to Camp de la Joliette in Quebec (Canada). Joseph Ghys, who had been in Argentina for some time, joined the group. By June 1941, they were 186, under command of 1st Lieutenant Blondeel, in Halifax (Canada). On 30 June 1941, the group reached Greenock (Scotland) and then travelled on to Malvern where the 2nd Fusiliers Battalion was formed.[22]

Blondeel commanded 'A' Company. Ghys recalled:

> When the Canadian troops arrived, a band and a welcoming committee awaited them... For us Belgians...nothing, except two officers sent by the Government in London. The first thing they asked us to do was to line up in two rows according to language: on one side the [Dutch-speaking] Flemish, on the other side the [French-speaking] Walloons. On the advice of Blondeel we all replied that our language was English. Our two contacts, who had not expected such a response, were stunned.[23]

Initial parachute training

In November 1941, the War Office requested that each British or foreign combat unit make available several men who, after special training, could then be entrusted with 'special tasks' in the occupied territories. The Belgian Minister of Defence was asked to provide twenty soldiers – two officers and eighteen other ranks – who were suitable to attend this unusual training. These men were to assemble in a training centre on 11 January 1942. The first group, selected by Major Charles de Cumont from the ranks of the 1st Fusiliers Battalion, was commanded by 1st Lieutenant Jacques Wanty and 2nd Lieutenant Marcel Leclef. The training programme was shrouded in secrecy and the men were completely ignorant of the fact that they had to become paratroopers. Of the twenty selected, only eight would eventually get their parachute qualification on 17 January 1942, after completing five jumps.[24]

The jumps were conducted with the standard British Type X parachute. It was a British design, developed by combining the technology of the Irving Air Chute Company and GQ Parachute Company. Contrary to the Americans, who had a reserve parachute in addition to their main one, British – and hence Belgian – parachutists were not equipped with a reserve parachute.[25]

The first officially acknowledged Belgian paratroopers were Lieutenant Marcel Leclef, Sergeant Robert Schils, Corporal Albert Lesage, Lance Corporal Pierre Pus and privates René Pietquin, John Budts, Constant Barette and Verelst.[26]

Schils described the training:

> When Major de Cumont had to select the initial eighteen men, he had no problem finding them. After all, they all wanted a more exciting existence and wanted to fight the enemy as soon as possible. When we arrived at the school in Ringway, we realised it would be a hard, difficult training. From the moment of our arrival, we were spared nothing: neither the ground exercises ('rollings') nor any of the acrobatic stunts or the crawling exercises... At midnight, we were finally allowed to our room! The next day at 6 o'clock in the morning, the circus started again: running, flexibility exercises, weapons knowledge, etc... At the end of the day, we were a shadow of ourselves and the fact that we were still standing was only thanks to the miracle of willpower! In these circumstances, we were to make our first jump. That morning I was rather worried. I saw ambulances come and go without stopping between the camp and the hospital. The ground was frozen, hard as concrete, and I knew that the platoon of our Polish friends

was almost decimated by the jumps of the previous day. Consequently, I was not very talkative when boarding the Whitley[27] bomber – which we called the 'flying coffin' – with my comrades. I thought that my parachute would never open! After all, I was lucky. I touched the ground unscathed. However, the final balance was a real disaster! Many of us were taken to the hospital and after each jump, we could take stock of the sobering status sheet.[28]

As the first parachute course came to an end, Leclef made a report for the commanding officer (CO) of the 1st Fusiliers Battalion, in which he stated:

> At the end of the 'parachute course', which in fact is not a course at all, but a succession of tests with the sole purpose of obtaining the parachute qualification, it is necessary and even unavoidable to take stock of the situation, which will show that just like for all similar foreign units, the Belgian candidates need a preparatory training of several weeks. Out of the twenty candidates – who all seemed perfectly suitable – there were: ten wounded; some are still in the hospital, others were able to continue their training; one refusal to jump; five refusals to jump after the second jump, due to airsickness (in reality, I think these men were exhausted and on the verge of a nervous breakdown); in total, seven men [excluding Leclef himself] were able to complete the tests and got their qualification. It is certainly thanks to the efforts of the instructors who made a special effort to give us in a few hours as much preparation as possible, often even until late in the evening, that we had no more accidents. In reality, a trained man would only get hurt by accident.
>
> According to the guidelines given to me by the British instructors, the preparatory training should consist of: (a) a thorough medical examination; (b) progressive and continuous physical training; (c) theoretical lessons and demonstrations related to parachute safety; practical training with the harnesses and on drills for the different types of jumps; each participant must have full confidence in his parachute and must know that, if he uses it in accordance with the rules, he will not be in any danger; this cannot be learned in one day; (d) theoretical lessons and practice in regrouping on the ground, by day and by night; knowledge by all of all weapons, assault tactics, defensive tactics, orientation, map reading and showing initiative; part of this programme can be covered in more detail once jump qualified; (e) arrangements must be made with a nearby airfield for candidates to get flight familiarisation and help them to assess altitude and drift.[29,30]

2nd Lieutenant Limbosch learned the necessary lessons from the failure of the first group and had a complete set of training devices made in Malvern. He was responsible for the methodical training of twenty volunteers of the second group, now from the 2nd Fusiliers Battalion. They conducted their basic parachute training during the week of 22-28 February, and eighteen men received their parachute qualification. Blondeel was full of praise:

> This success raised morale at all echelons. The favourable report about the group that walked out of Ringway's No. 1 Parachute Training School speaks

> volumes: “One of the best Allied teams we ever had” and was a tribute to the qualities of the leader, F. Limbosch. This report gave him a solid reputation. At the new recruitment effort that followed, all the men of ‘A’ Company, except two, volunteered. F. Limbosch proposed the battalion commander have this company in its entirety start the parachute training and effectively created a unit within the battalion specialising in this new domain while at the same time retaining its cantonments, its services and its support personnel, who, although not jump-qualified, provided the unit with well-established logistic support. The proposal to conduct specialised training as a parachute unit while remaining an infantry company in the 2nd Fusiliers Battalion was accepted and enthusiastically supported by the second-in-command of the battalion, Major J. Thise. The veterans were thus reunited under the command of F. Limbosch, who would, among other things, train the new group of candidates and prepare them for the jumps.[31]

On 15 March, a third group, originating from the 1st Fusiliers Battalion and trained by Leclef, went to Ringway. At the end of the week, all but two were awarded their jump wings. On 26 April, the fourth group started the course, which included Captain Blondeel, and everyone succeeded.[32]

These successes and the contagious enthusiasm let the Belgian government support the formal establishment of a parachute company, as had been proposed several months earlier. With a letter dated 27 April 1942, Undersecretary of State for Defence Henri Rolin, informed the inspector-general of the Belgian armed forces, the commander of the army, and the director-general of the Belgian Ministry of Defence, of his decision to establish an independent parachute company as part of the army. He specified that the new unit was to be organised in accordance with war establishment No. 10/127/1, that a commander had to be designated immediately, and that every section of the company could be commanded by an officer.[33]

On 8 May 1942, Major Jules Thise presented his ‘A’ Company of the 2nd Fusiliers Battalion to Rolin, who recognised it as ‘officially established’. But the War Office, which designated the unit as ‘D (Parachute) Company, 2nd Battalion, Belgian Fusiliers’, did not share the Belgian point of view. The company would have to wait until July 1942 to be allowed officially to adopt the designation ‘Belgian Independent Parachute Company’.[34]

Chapter Two

TRAINING FOR WAR

IN JUNE 1942, the Belgian Independent Parachute Company left Malvern to take up residence in the castle farm of Friz Hill. In the words of one of the original unit members,

> The Friz Hill camp was hidden in an extremely picturesque corner of Warwickshire, a county with many old castles in between ancient parks, sparsely dotted with woodland and bathed in medieval silence. The camp was 12 kilometres [7.5 miles] from historic Warwick, whose ferocious noblemen were among the main protagonists of the War of the Roses, 15 kilometres [9 miles] from Leamington Spa, which was one of the most elegant of towns, and 10 kilometres [6 miles] from Stratford-upon-Avon, where the traders ensured that the tourists overpaid for the honour of shopping in Shakespeare's birthplace. Friz Hill certainly deserved the nickname 'end of the world'.[1]

The atmosphere in the Friz Hill quarters could be described as a strange mixture of satisfaction, camaraderie and anxiety. Satisfaction, because the paratroopers were all volunteers who had attended a demanding training programme and were impatient to be deployed on operations. Camaraderie, because, although they faced a tough challenge for which enormous efforts would be requested from them, they believed they belonged to a class apart. Anxiety, because everyone lived far from home, received little news and feared the consequences for their relatives of the German occupation.

The company counted some 120 men. At the start of June, half of them were parachute-qualified, and their number continued to grow as more of them were to undergo parachute training in the subsequent months. Passing the required medical and physical tests and the parachute course was the condition upon which non-badged personnel who had been assigned to the company could stay in the unit.[2]

On 11 July 1942, Major Thise suffered a severe injury when hitting the ground during his first parachute jump, fracturing his pelvis and resulting in months of hospitalisation.[3,4] His second-in-command, Captain Blondeel, temporarily took command of the company. Ten days later, the company paraded in London on the occasion of the Belgian national day, wearing a maroon beret[5] in public.

Gradually, the company was organised and equipped. In general terms, the company consisted of a company headquarters (HQ) and three rifle platoons. The company HQ, the administrative platoon and the HQ platoon – which were initially grouped into a single entity – integrated a wide range of supporting capabilities, such as mortar and anti-tank detachments, a signals detachment with telegraphist-signallers and despatch riders, a motor transport section, quartermaster functions, physical training instructors and parachute riggers. Later on, a separate provisional training platoon was added to take responsibility for bringing candidates up to the required training standard. Since the company was a rather new type and, in a way, an almost experimental unit, flexibility was maintained and changes to the organisational structure and the names of their entities occurred regularly.[6]

However, some existential problems were already emerging for Blondeel:

> At the end of 1942, Colonel J. B. Piron, tasked with the reorganisation of Belgian ground forces, called me to his headquarters to tell me that the government had committed a grave error by allowing the establishment of the parachute company, which by the way was not in line with the traditions of the Belgian army, that the employment of such a unit had never been taught at the Belgian Staff College, and that for these reasons he had decided to disband the parachute company, divide her into three parts and use each part as a separate reconnaissance unit. I decided to ask the chaplain, Jesuit Father R. Jourdain, to see Prime Minister Pierlot. He knew the Prime Minister well because, on the latter's initiative, he had been parachuted into Belgium in 1941 to assess the local authorities' intentions towards the German occupation.[7] Jourdain had to ask the Prime Minister to summon me, which he did. I asked the minister what his reaction would be when I had to inform my men "that the government has made a serious mistake, that during training, we had suffered two deaths and a lot of wounded, that all of this was in vain, that everybody's hard work during the past year, the brilliant results that had been achieved, were all a waste of time and effort."
>
> I continued: "Minister, what I am being asked, I cannot do. I would lose the confidence of my men, I would lose face and the government along with me." Pierlot thanked me and said, "I will think about this". The following week, Colonel Piron paid us an unexpected visit. I expressed my surprise at not having been informed of this honour. I told him: "Colonel, we will not deviate from what an ordinary day looks like for us." In fact, in our stores, he counted the number of socks, inspected the underside of the kitchen tables, etc. He turned everything upside down. Afterwards, it seemed he hadn't found anything that was not in line with regulations, because I learned that he had told a few folks that we were a good unit.
>
> Then I was informed that General Victor van Strydonck de Burkel,[8] commander of the Belgian forces in the United Kingdom, would visit us. On this occasion, we organised the splashiest programme for him: wine being offered, signing of the golden book, etc... In the end, the general took me aside and asked: "Blondeel, why don't you want to be part of Colonel Piron's 1st Group?" I replied, "General, I don't want anything. The authorities must decide. I only ask that I don't have to communicate this decision to my men. It would be too painful for me, a denial of all the efforts made to satisfy the government's wish to create an elite unit. It would also be an enormous psychological shock for all my comrades. I fear, on the other hand, that the shock would be so great that we might have to increase the number of military prosecutors." The general collected his thoughts and to my utter surprise he replied: "You are polite, Blondeel." As a good soldier, I took care not to refuse anything, nor to express my indignation in an explosive way, but in a calm, quiet manner, I presented

the authorities with a mirror, so that they could take a good look at themselves and would take their own responsibilities. Later, I learned that van Strydonck had told Piron: "Don't insist, because you would have led a hedgehog into your group." They left us alone and we continued our training.[9]

Airborne training continued and for some, it meant participating in events run by the Airborne Forces Experimental Establishment at Sherburn in Elmet, near Leeds, where they jumped from different types of aeroplanes, even from Horsa gliders.[10,11]

But airborne training was hazardous duty… On 19 April 1943, the unit suffered its first casualties. During a daylight test flight to study the physiological effects of flying, such as air sickness, Etienne Battaille and Florent Depauw were the only passengers aboard Wellington[12] DF 743 from the No. 22 Operational Training Unit, RAF, based at Wellesbourne Mountford, when the aircraft crashed at Staple Farm, Withington, in cloudy conditions, killing both soldiers, along with one British and four Canadian crew members.[13] Battaille, a Walloon, and Depauw, a Fleming, were close friends and had been serving together in the French Foreign Legion in Algeria. Blondeel honoured both men, describing them as excellent soldiers who would continue to serve as an inspiration and example.[14]

The summer of 1943 saw several combined training events with the British 3rd Parachute Brigade. Blondeel spent a few days at the brigade from the end of July,[15] and in August the company was informed it would participate in a series of nighttime exercises with the 8th Parachute Battalion from early September.[16] The culminating event was a 50-mile night march with arms and small packs, which was completed by all.[17] But no matter how useful this training was, there seemed no prospect of being integrated into a British airborne division. Blondeel had to face reality when he learned that a battalion would be welcomed but a company was too small a contribution to be of any value to a large conventional airborne formation.

Being small, however, would also bring opportunities for employment in less conventional operations. Already months before the very existence of the parachute company, Brigadier Gubbins from SOE had suggested to Belgian Prime Minister Pierlot to train a force of some 200 parachutists to 'represent the advance guard of the landing forces' to cooperate with the armed resistance groups in Belgium once the invasion of mainland Europe materialised.[18] However, relations between the SOE and the Belgian government in exile were at a low by August 1942,[19] and this option would not be pursued.

From 22 November 1943, the company attended the course at the Special Training Centre at Inverlochy (Fort William), in the Scottish Highlands.[20] Its four-week training programme covered guerilla warfare, with an emphasis on demolitions (especially calculating explosive charges), river crossing, organising lying-up positions, survival techniques and pistol shooting at short range, among others.[21]

The first group to discover the centre's training approach was ordered to put on their exercise clothes and obtain information to conduct an area familiarisation tour. While running behind the instructor, they encountered a river and saw the instructor jumping into the ice-cold water and swimming to the other side... Once across, the Brit apologised for forgetting to tell them that every activity was done on the double and always in a straight line, regardless of the obstacles that were ahead. Josy Déom confirmed: "The assault course at Inverlochy was, without doubt, the toughest the paratroopers would encounter during their training in Britain."[22]

Blondeel received an excellent course evaluation report, which contained the following assessment: "An officer for whom we soon developed a liking and respect. In the British Army, he would probably be a Battalion Commander. The Parachute Company is fortunate in having an officer of this ability and calibre to lead it."

The Belgians seized every opportunity to attend specialised training with the Brits, including intelligence and security courses, mortar shooting, urban combat, mine awareness, night operations, etc.

Also, for the mascot of the Belgian company, the stay with their British colleagues was a memorable event. Temmerman recalled: "The unit had adopted a little monkey and named him 'Emile'. He became the mascot of the company and went everywhere with it throughout its training. We already had a zoo consisting of dogs, cats and a poached rabbit. A monkey would not spoil the atmosphere at all. After all, Emile was only a small monkey of 30 to 40 cm, not a chimpanzee or an orangutan." Emile had a favourite companion, Deprez, who fed the animal and had a certain affection for it. The monkey was given to him by a certain sailor who had brought it from Africa but wanted to get rid of it. During his stay with the 6th Airborne Division, the mascot fell into 'enemy' hands, to the despair of the company and his friend Deprez. A few days later, the company commander was informed that the unfortunate monkey was behind bars at a local police station. Being the rightful owner, Deprez presented himself at the station and Emile was released, but only after Deprez reluctantly paid two shillings a day to cover the cost of feeding and caring for the monkey. He was quite astonished and thought: "What the heck, if one is captured during an exercise, one has to pay to be released... where are we going?"[23] The mascot would remain with the unit until it started operations in France in July 1944. According to some, Blondeel was not fond of the animal and found a place for it in a zoo, where Emile died shortly afterwards.

Blondeel received few if any direction from his higher command in London. They seemed to rarely move around and to be poorly informed about what was going on. At the end of February 1943, Blondeel had been part of a group of fifteen men from the company who had been designated to attend a course on fighting in built-up areas and in early March, the company had taken part in an exercise in an urban environment.[24] When the visit of a Belgian general officer was announced, Blondeel organised a demonstration to show him their newly-acquired house-to-house fighting skills. While street-fighting techniques were discussed in various contemporary British tactical pamphlets, it was unknown in the pre-war Belgian army. When the visiting general officer observed the paratroopers jump from one roof to another and enter buildings through doors and windows, he suddenly shouted: "But Blondeel, you are training your men to become burglars!"

When Belgian journalist Charles d'Ydewalle visited Friz Hill, he was impressed by the prevailing *esprit de corps* and spontaneously confessed to Blondeel that the unit reminded him of a commandery of the Templars. The paratroopers were indeed a close-knit group. Officers and non-commissioned officers (NCOs) lived side by side with their men, sharing their joys, their disappointments and their difficult moments. This team spirit was expressed most strongly when lorries brought them back to the camp upon returning from leave. They sang 'Home Sweet Home' in unison and expressed their joy at returning 'home', where they would be reunited with their comrades and bosses.

During breaks in between long training sessions, some soldiers played card games, trying to gain some extra money. The unlucky ones who lost their meagre pay in the process felt forced to sell pieces of equipment to pay their debts. The NCOs and privates conducting this type of nocturnal recreational activity did so in an abandoned nearby chicken coop under candlelight. When the officers got word of the games, which were banned by British regulations, they decided to act. One night, those at the spot were caught red-handed and the money on the table, £60 in all, was confiscated. This then considerable amount of money was used afterwards to build a library. Blondeel decided that the first book to be purchased would be *How to Overcome a Gambling Addiction.* It is unlikely, however, that these measures put an end to unauthorised recreational activity.Temmerman described the leave:

> The paratroopers could enjoy a ten-day leave period every three months. In the beginning, this was also the rule in Friz Hill...with seven francs paid per day... How could one afford to make a trip and where would one go? However, the financial situation would improve. Travel tickets were free during leave, one just had to mark the destination on the train ticket. Some took advantage of this system to explore areas ranging from the far south of England to the northernmost part of Scotland. One even managed to cover some 8,000 kilometres [5,000 miles] in less than a year. On top of that, when the soldiers were on leave, the state no longer had to provide them with food, but the company staff came up with the idea of issuing them the equivalent of the unspent meal cost in money, a decision that rendered the leave issue even less hard to deal with. Concerning the destinations...through the creation of a holiday home in a district of London, some people had the opportunity to stay in the capital. The prices had been reduced; however, certain reasonable obligations were also imposed, such as the rule to return no later than 2300 hours, or the requirement to register in advance for meals. Some soldiers, however, didn't feel bound by reason during their leave and disliked any constraint, no matter how small. Other destinations were possible. A dedicated British lady was creating an institution to find 'war godmothers' for the Belgians and, thanks to her efforts, many could stay to relax in a British family. One of them, who had expected to settle down in the quiet company of three people – the godmother, whose husband was in the forces, her old mother and another elderly lady – experienced an unpleasant surprise when he was met at the railway station by the godmother who proposed him to drive immediately to a warehouse where three wagons loaded with potatoes were waiting. Upon arrival, the lady explained that these wagons had to be unloaded quickly, otherwise she would have to pay taxes. Our leave pass holder would therefore spend the majority of his leave carrying tons of potatoes; gruelling labour, even for a trained parachutist. He was exhausted when he returned to Friz Hill, where, upon his arrival, he heard the captain say to someone "The problem with these permits is that they totally break the rhythm of the physical exercises. The men abruptly lose all habit of exerting themselves, they just let themselves go during those ten days."[25]

In times of food shortages, the Belgian self-reliance ensured they significantly improved their daily food rations. When noticing a pigpen in one of the outbuildings at Friz Hill, Limbosch, who was an agricultural scientist by training, assumed that ten young swine could be fed with the kitchen waste. When later slaughtered one by one, their number would decrease as they grew. A British Army regulation reportedly stated that, if a unit kept cattle, it had to inform the military authorities, and after each slaughter, the regular daily meat ration would be reduced. The Belgians kept ten animals and once all ten pigs had been slaughtered, due to some mathematical error, one was left, which, once big and fat, provided an excellent meal of sausage, pressed head and roast, intended for those who were unlucky enough not to get any leave on Christmas Day 1943.

The new year brought some exciting news. Blondeel recalled:

> On returning from an exercise in Friz Hill in January 1944, we received the visit of two representatives of the intelligence office of the Belgian Ministry of Defence [namely Captain Hardy Amies, head of SOE's 'T' section, which dealt with Belgium and Luxembourg, and 1st Lieutenant Idesbald Floor from the Belgian *Sûreté de l'État*[26]]. They came with the intention of recruiting a dozen paratroopers for a special service entity. They were promised the sky: ranks, operational employment...and to me, they said, "You can keep the rest as an SAS unit." Once again, I sent Padre Jourdain to see the Prime Minister to request a meeting with him. We ended up handing over eighteen men, five of whom were valuable, while being happy to get rid of the thirteen others. As compensation, the Prime Minister allowed me to recruit thirty-five new volunteers from [Colonel] Piron['s 1st Group]. With the help of a selection team (consisting of a physician, an interviewer, a physical training instructor and someone to conduct psychological tests), we recruited thirty-five men out of a hundred candidates.[27]

On 8 February 1944, Major Thise officially turned over command to Captain Blondeel. Temmerman summarised Thise's personality: "The first commander of the unit, a kind of 'father of the regiment', brought the authority of a hero of 1914 and 1940. Volunteering to jump by parachute just like his men despite his age, he received a spinal injury, which finally forced him to leave the company to which he gave much more than perceived by some who admired his successor."[28]

The official ceremony was attended by Colonel Piron, who afterwards addressed the troops during a drink in the canteen, declaring: "And now, gentlemen, it is all about being disciplined!" Faces turned pale and silence fell. At the moment Colonel Piron got ready to leave, Padre Jourdain intervened with a loud voice: "Colonel, had the soldiers not been disciplined, they would have thrown you through the window!" "How dare you!", burst out Piron, "I forbid you to speak to me like this and advise you to take care of your flock!" "This is my flock", replied the chaplain, calmly, "because I am here to keep up the morale of the men!"[29] The incident was closed...

The change of command also marked the end of the era as a conventional parachute unit. The company now entered a transition period towards a new, even more demanding role as a special operations unit.

Chapter Three

JOINING THE SPECIAL AIR SERVICE BRIGADE

The Belgian SAS Squadron

In mid-February 1944, the Belgian parachute company moved to Loudoun Castle, an old castle that had been inhabited by the Campbell clan, located near Galston (Ayrshire) in Scotland. The castle had been renovated over the years and was nicknamed the 'Windsor Castle of Scotland'. For over a century, it had been inhabited by the Abney-Hastings family. In 1941, around the time the British Army requested to use the castle, it was badly damaged in an accidental fire. Its silhouette, however, would continue to dominate the immense surrounding park. Around forty huts in the vicinity of the castle had been constructed of wood and corrugated iron, which is where the Belgians would be accommodated. It was much closer to the training centre at Inverlochy, where new groups from the unit were still being sent for training.[1]

Around the same time, the unit was incorporated into the Special Air Service Brigade and was renamed 'Belgian Special Air Service Squadron'. In the newly-formed multinational brigade commanded by Brigadier Roderick McLeod, it joined two British regiments (1st SAS and 2nd SAS) and two French regiments (3rd SAS (aka *3ème Bataillon d'Infanterie de l'Air (3e BIA)*, later renamed *3ème Régiment de Chasseurs Parachutistes (3e RCP)* in French), and 4th SAS (aka *4e Bataillon d'Infanterie de l'Air (4e BIA)* later renamed *2ème Régiment de Chasseurs Parachutistes* (2e RCP) in French))[2]. In line with the sequential number designations within the brigade, the Belgian SAS unit would also be referred to as the '5th SAS'.

The exact date the unit came under command from the SAS Brigade is hard to ascertain and correspondence going back to at least 17 February 1944 referred to instructions from the 'HQ SAS Troops', as the brigade HQ used to be designated in official documents.[3]

The move and the unit's anticipated new role were accompanied by enhanced operations security measures. While the daily orders provided the address in nearby Kilmarnock for supporting administrative tasks, care was taken not to explicitly mention the new location, which was simply referred to as the 'new cantonment'. Orders from the SAS Brigade HQ stated that incoming mail through the field post office should be addressed to '1 Belgian Ind. Para Coy Home Forces' (a plausible and convenient cover name), that no mail was to be dispatched from civil post offices or posted in civil boxes and that telegrams could be dispatched from civil post offices provided no name of office of origin was used by the post office.[4]

On 29 February, Blondeel issued the communication that the company would be reorganised to be able to function as an SAS squadron. The message included a simplified schematic table of organisation (i.e. organisational structure) that had been approved by the (unspecified) 'higher authorities', with the provisional name '1st Belgian SAS Squadron', and mentioned that the actual order of battle (i.e. the allocation of names to each position on the table of organisation) would be determined later on. The table of organisation showed a squadron HQ, an HQ troop, 'No. 1 Troop' and 'No. 2 Troop', the latter two each consisting of a troop HQ and four sections, each composed of two six-man squads which could be split into two-man teams. On the administrative side, with the transition of the company to a squadron, the designation 'private' for the lowest-ranking personnel was replaced with 'trooper'.[5]

Four days later, the unit was notified that it would undergo an administrative inspection by the brigadier on 10 March. The squadron passed the initial test and on 14 March Blondeel relayed an extract of McLeod's remarks to his troops that:

> The B[riga]de Com[man]d[er] is fully satisfied with the administration of the unit which is first class. The general cleanliness of the camp, and the arrangements in the Q.M's [quartermaster's store], armourers, M.T. [motor transport], offices, etc. were more than satisfactory. He considers that the interior economy of the unit under your command is at present the best in the S.A.S B[riga]de and he wishes to congratulate you and the unit under your command on the high standard that has been achieved. He would be grateful if you would inform all ranks accordingly.[6]

At their new site, the SAS members now honed their skills to master the tactics of operating in small teams while isolated behind enemy lines, such as conducting night ambushes with mines and anti-tank grenades, establishing lying-up positions and operational bases, evading capture, escaping if captured and how to train resistance fighters. They gained an in-depth knowledge of the German army and learned how to handle prisoners. The squadron also trained its own signallers and became familiar with new equipment, such as Eureka.[7] Medical training was also an important subject; every man was issued with a medical kit, and each operational section had a medical orderly equipped with a comprehensive medical pack.[8] 1st Lieutenant Van der Heyden summarised the training as follows: "The unforeseen was always around the corner, so we prepared for the unforeseen!"[9]

During this period, important changes were implemented. Parachute jumps were rarely conducted by Whitley bombers anymore, but mostly by Stirling,[10] Albemarle[11] or Halifax[12] bombers instead. Since collective containers with individual equipment were sometimes hard to find quickly, the men were now also being trained to use an individual kitbag attached to the leg when jumping.[13]

On 26 March 1944, the brigade organised a demonstration in which three teams of six men had to jump from an aeroplane as fast as possible, with a kitbag attached to their leg. The two Belgian teams ended first and second and Déom, whose team cleared the aircraft in four seconds – a second faster than Devulder's team and two seconds faster than the 1st SAS team – was designated to accept a bottle of whisky offered by the brigade commander to the winning team. McLeod was clearly pleased with the Belgians' performance, informing Blondeel that "I should like to congratulate you and the men who jumped on the remarkably fast time. Well done!"[14]

This result, in addition to the successful participation in other field training events, as well as the discipline prevalent in the unit and the strong personality of Captain Blondeel, ensured that the Belgian squadron was well regarded by the brigade.

Meanwhile, the new organisation was being implemented. The former rifle platoons were amalgamated and replaced with two troops: 'A' Troop (replacing the initial name 'No. 1 Troop'), with Van der Heyden, Debefve and Ghys as officers, and 'B' Troop (replacing the initial name 'No. 2 Troop'), with Limbosch, Renkin and Kirschen as officers.[15,16] At the request of the brigade commander, two officers – newly assigned to Blondeel by the Belgian Ministry of Defence in London – were detached to the brigade HQ: Major Etienne Delelienne became liaison officer and Major Cassart planning officer. Interestingly, both outranked Blondeel.[17]

The commanding officer

Most who knew Captain Blondeel appreciated his official appointment as CO and spoke only with praise of him. His peers regarded him as a very respectable man, purposeful, a hard worker, always setting a good example and having the characteristics of a leader. During his interim command and afterwards as CO, and with the assistance of extremely competent officers and NCOs, he was able to provide his men with highly effective training programmes. His strong personality instilled a military spirit characterised by camaraderie, self-discipline, a sense of individual responsibility and the willingness to fight. In his view, to command was first and foremost to persuade. He created a personal command style in which he gave maximum initiative to his subordinates, but mercilessly removed those who did not play by his rules or showed a clear lack of team spirit. He would transform the unit into an instrument capable of fulfilling its assigned tasks and would make the best use of the training facilities offered by the Brits, while ensuring his subordinates further developed their brainpower as much as their physical abilities, always keeping in mind the military dictum that sweat saves blood, but brains save sweat and blood.

Temmerman, still a trooper at that time, later humorously described his commander:

> Without much effort, Captain Blondeel achieved the title of 'greatest intellectual'. With a great love for new scientific developments, he used all his spare time to expand his knowledge. The light on his desk was on until deep into the night. On his table, books piled up. For eighteen hours a day, his brain was running at full speed. For the remaining six hours and during his sleep, he subconsciously recalled the day's emerging problems and came up with a solution. His manner of behaving and his language were with the utmost distinction. His lively and cheerful spirit made his conversations both instructive and entertaining. He always had kind words for those who approached him and the many stories of events and adventures that he was able to tell, kept the audience on the edge of their seats.
>
> During working hours, however, his communication skills dropped below freezing point and he had the kindness of a coarse fibre.[18] His sharp eyes immediately detected any abnormality in military affairs and provoked a series of quick and dry questions, speaking with a strange metallic voice, piercing the ears of the guilty whose answers became more and more hesitant. Once

the infringement had been discovered, stigmatised and punished, the captain showed what harm had been done to the unit due to the error of the wrongdoer (whether it was a poorly maintained rifle or getting up too late), leaving behind an individual who was more stunned than regretting the consequences of an insignificant offence.

The captain's eloquence was often noticeable in the morning during the ceremony of raising the flag. Chin forward, hands crossed behind his back and slightly balancing on his foot soles, he knowingly commented on some topics related to airborne doctrine or reminded us of certain regulations. Since no one was supposed not to know the law, he accurately explained the instructions in English, French and Dutch, ignoring the sun that congested his men or the snow that gradually covered them. During certain hours of relaxation, the boss turned into a charming, cheerful and pleasant companion. His surprisingly well-developed knowledge was unique and enabled him to soundly discuss the most diverse subjects. He managed to associate the most unpleasant aspects of military life with reasonable considerations, something his men had never expected from him. Obsessed with statistics, this engineer-dentist was not afraid to play the piano or to create a work of art with the soul of an artist.[19]

Another description is the one given by Jean Delhez:[20]

This man showed character and, taking into account the events of 1940, he succeeded in leaving his mark. Far from hiding behind a hierarchical system or disciplinary regulations, he tackled the problems head-on. In England, he had to deal with difficulties caused by an obstructing bureaucracy like any other, but overcame every obstacle in order to allow his unit of specialised paratroopers being employed behind enemy lines. He felt strengthened by his own enthusiasm and willpower.[21]

General Montgomery's pre-D-Day visit

On 22 April 1944, General Montgomery inspected the SAS troops. The entire brigade was assembled near Loudoun Castle. Montgomery met the commanders of the various units[22] and talked to the men of the brigade. When inspecting the Belgians, he first exchanged a few words with Captain Blondeel and then looked at the troops, apparently looking for ribbons on their chest. To his surprise, he noticed that only Padre Jourdain, the squadron's chaplain, had been decorated, having been awarded the Order of the British Empire after his mission in Belgium in 1941.[23]

On 15 May 1944, the squadron adopted its final organisational structure before the start of its operations. The training of the sections was more and more aimed at independent operations, especially at night. The squadron now conducted weekly field training exercises in Scotland, which inevitably started with a night jump.

The Normandy invasion

In his memoirs, Blondeel recalled the situation at the start of D-Day:

On 5 June, at around 10 pm, I was in my office when the telephone rang. When I took the call, a heavy voice said: "Rustigate". I was staggered, because that code

> word meant that the invasion of the continent had begun. Indeed, I learned that Major Bourgoin's battalion, some 700 Frenchmen in all, had been parachuted into Brittany during the night of 5-6 June, in order to contribute to the deception of the Germans about the exact location of the invasion. In addition, from 6 June onwards, some small British teams were [to be] parachuted in the eastern part of Normandy. And we...were still waiting.[24]

While the Allies landed in Normandy, the Belgians once more were to conduct field training exercises. They bitterly regretted not having been committed to the fight. Aware of their growing impatience to go into action as the battle raged in Normandy, Brigadier McLeod paid them a visit. He explained to them that the Belgians were intended for operations in Belgium, but that the RAF assessed the frontline as being too far away from the Belgian border for safe insertions to be feasible, so they would have to wait.

Blondeel provided an overview of their capabilities at that time.

> They did indeed have twenty-four operational teams, equipped with signalling kit, weapons and equipment, that were able to wreak havoc behind enemy lines. In order to be prepared for every eventuality, during the years of waiting, I had been devoting my time:
>
> • figuring out all the possible types of training, in accordance with a maximum of potential mission profiles;
>
> • training specialists in all possible branches of the art of warfare;
>
> • compensating for our numerical inferiority, by ensuring a high level of quality in our education and training;
>
> • creating an open mindset that was welcoming innovation, with the desire to master it thoroughly and as quickly as possible, accepting endless rehearsals as a condition for a perfect performance, in the end allowing us to detect each individual's strengths and weaknesses, and then to draw the necessary lessons to be learned, in a sense absorbing the conscious into the subconscious, in short, creating the right responses when dealing with danger and the unexpected.
>
> By forging the esprit de corps while overcoming common challenges, we ensured that each man had great confidence in himself, in his team and in his superiors, guaranteeing fewer losses in operations, rendering the latter 'easy', compared to the 'demanding hardship' experienced during training.[25]

During his command, Blondeel was assisted by excellent officers. In one of his books, Temmerman described the officers he had known for more than two years when he was a trooper:

> Lieutenant Radino, with his skills as a sharpshooter, had had an eventful and adventurous past. He gave practical advice, ranging from how to quickly present a pistol from a holster to the best method to catch game.
>
> Doctor J. Limbosch could easily have hidden in his infirmary. However, he jumped like all the others and followed up on the company's health situation.

The nutritional system of concentrated food he refined for missions behind enemy lines was adopted by the Allied units.

His cousin, Lieutenant Freddy Limbosch, who was an agricultural engineer who came over from Canada, and was energetic, tireless and a remarkable leader, never stopped organising the most diverse field exercises. If the title of chief instructor had existed, he would rightfully have held it.

Lieutenant Debefve,[26] always calm and quiet, proved to be as courageous in 1944-45 as he was during the 1940 campaign with the 2nd Carabineers Battalion, for which he was awarded the War Cross, and when evading to Great Britain afterwards. He led his platoon[27] with a gentle hand but always managed to have it do what he requested.

Another active-duty officer and former evader, Lieutenant Van der Heyden[28] vigorously commanded the most hard-to-handle troops. The former legionnaires of his platoon behaved like angels compared to the 'Mirandese', his former fellow inmates in Spain, and eager to join the fight rapidly. After each training exercise, Van der Heyden succeeded in patiently discussing and analysing their training with his men.

Kirschen, an advocate and now intelligence officer, was logically put in charge of the staff troop, mainly manned by mortar crews and signallers. The former lawyer was considered one of the best SAS operators during operations in France and Holland.

The much younger Lieutenant Renkin passed all sporting events with exceptional ease. This jokester, who was also an excellent illustrator, taught any observer to distinguish the make of a tank using a quick caricatural sketch.

Padre Jourdain accomplished his work as a chaplain with dignity and kindness. For instance, he encouraged vocations...to become a paratrooper. Because, although he never spoke of it, everyone knew that at the age of 47, he had jumped into Belgium as part of a secret mission. Together with Holvoet and Cassart, he was the only one in the Belgian SAS Squadron who had conducted an operational jump between 1942 and early 1944, while serving as an agent for special services.[29]

In the face of such examples, the NCOs could not bring disappointment, and they did not. Many patiently complemented the work of their superiors.

Chapter Four

THE BELGIAN SAS IN NORMANDY

Insisting to join the fight

Blondeel was annoyed by the decision of the Belgian government in exile. He recalled:

> I learned that certain Belgian circles in London opposed our dropping into Belgium. To put things in order and to clarify the situation, I went to London. I failed to unravel the issue; everyone was passing the responsibility on to someone else. Later, I learned that the opposition originated from the 2nd office of the Ministry of Defence [i.e. the intelligence staff], which was responsible for the operations of the Secret Army in Belgium, as there was a fear that we would interfere too much with their activities. Even sending small teams of instructors intended to teach the resistance how to use the parachuted weapons and equipment, was refused. A regrettable attitude, for afterwards we learned about their severe lack of skills in this regard. Tired of having to wait and lacking new field training exercises, we were allowed by General Koenig, commander of the Free French Forces, to parachute into France, to somewhat temper our impatience.[1]

Almost two months after the invasion of Normandy, the Belgians were still waiting to be deployed on the mainland. In the meantime, field training exercises resumed, but in July Blondeel granted his men a few days' leave, trying to let them deal with the situation resulting from their restless desire to go on operations. At that very moment, the CO got the long-expected call:

> I received the message that I had to keep three sections on stand-by. One of them would have to be made available with immediate effect. So I started preparations for the first five-man team that would have to join the transit camp in Fairford, where orders would be issued. It had to consist of an officer, two signallers, someone able to cypher and decipher messages and one additional trooper. I thus informed Radino and told him: "We leave immediately with a jeep; the four men will follow by lorry afterwards." After about 50 kilometres [31 miles], the left front wheel of our vehicle hit a pole on the side of the road with full force and I was ejected from my seat in the back, ending up on the verge of the road, fortunately without injury. I noticed that the driver had been thrown through the windshield and had deep cuts on his cheeks. Radino was half unconscious and groaned... Later it turned out that he had a fractured shoulder. I immediately notified our base to have another officer designated: I suggested to task Lieutenant Ghys, who had to return from leave, and specified that Lieutenant doctor Limbosch had to join the hospital to see the two wounded. I waited for the lorry transporting the men. When it arrived after an

> hour, I gave a first briefing to the team in the back of the lorry, emphasizing the highly classified nature of this information. As the driver had not eaten anything yet, I suggested I took the steering wheel for a few kilometres. When we passed through a village, a distracted cyclist suddenly appeared from a side street and collided with the lorry. A new mandatory delay as the police investigation cost us another two hours. Needless to say that I was impatient... Finally, we reached the transit camp. Fortunately, the jump had been postponed until the next day.[2]

While Kirschen was on leave at the Mont Royal Hotel in London, he received a message from Debefve with the request to return to Scotland. Thinking he was dealing with a practical joke from his friend, he carelessly spent another night in the hotel, but early in the next morning, however, he recalled being woken up by a telephone call from Loudoun Castle: "So, Lieutenant Kirschen? Are you ready to depart? We are waiting for you in Scotland. You immediately have to select the men who will join you on operations. Since this is an intelligence gathering mission, you will need a second-in-command, two signallers and two other men." Kirschen replied: "Give me Corporal Barette as second-in-command, and I would also like to take Regner with me. With regard to the signallers, we'll see at the camp who's available." "Excellent, you will be leaving for Scotland this evening. We have reserved you a seat on the train", came the reply.[3]

The transit camp

To assemble and prepare the teams that were to deploy on operations, the SAS Brigade had set up a secret transit camp in Fairford, in the south of England. It was surrounded by barbed wire and was heavily guarded. Those who entered were only supposed to leave it in the back of an aircraft towards occupied Europe. Kirschen described some atmospherics from the camp at a later point in time:

> The transit camp at Fairford gave a taste of the apocalypse: the turbulence of uniforms from a multitude of Allied nations in close proximity of each other and multiple languages being heard. The Scots tested their weapons by shooting one over the head. The French checked their radios or donned their parachutes. Norwegians, flat on their bellies, studied their maps. Men were leaving for France, others returned, telling stories of adventure.[4]

The Belgian SAS Squadron left Scotland for good to be at Fairford. All teams were accommodated in tents. The British, French and Belgians had a building that served as a briefing room. To maintain secrecy, information could not be shared between teams. They received detailed mission briefings and were handed out topographic maps of their area of operations. They carefully examined aerial pictures from their allocated drop zone (DZ) and the surrounding area with a stereoscope, to assess the relief in the area. They were provided with a code book, intended for encrypting radio messages. They were issued with small arms and equipped according to the nature of their mission. The Belgian SAS operators were issued with new identity papers with British or Canadian names, to prevent any reprisals against their families in Belgium in case they were captured.[5] Thus, Debefve was called 'MacBef', Limbosch 'MacLean',

Kirschen 'King', Blondeel 'Blunt', etc. In addition, some wore a higher rank, to give them more authority when dealing with indigenous resistance groups.

The first three missions were harassment and interdiction operations. Their actions on the objective during the execution would consist of two phases. In the initial phase, their task was to gather information about German convoys moving along three avenues of approach, Paris – Normandy in the north, Paris – Le Mans in the centre and Orleans – Bretagne in the south. In a subsequent phase, they would harass the enemy by attacking troops, transports and supplies in the same areas, aiming at hastening his withdrawal.

On 28 July, 31 July and 3 August, advance parties led by Ghys (Operation 'Chaucer'), Debefve (Operation 'Shakespeare') and Kirschen (Operation 'Bunyan') respectively,[6] would be dropped with four or five men each, to reconnoitre their areas of operations and prepare the arrival of follow-on groups, which would consist of elements about fifteen men-strong and be led by Van der Heyden ('Chaucer'), Limbosch ('Shakespeare') and Déom ('Bunyan') respectively.

Upon his arrival at the transit camp, Blondeel went to see Brigadier McLeod. He then waited for the arrival of Ghys, Debefve and Kirschen to give them a detailed briefing, the content of which is covered in Kirschen's post-war book:

> Captain Blondeel had always impressed me, but never as much as at this moment... Yet I knew the look from his blue, stern eyes, his uncompromising appearance, his commanding posture, his impressive personality. What impressed me that day was his voice, a slightly muffled voice that I had never heard before. He would have been mad at me if he had had the slightest awareness that I had noticed the emotions that made his voice tremble in a way that was hitherto unheard of. For Blondeel made an enormous effort to remain absolutely calm and unmoved! He was a man of duty and his duty that day, for the first time ever, was to send the boys he had gotten attached to, day after day, for two years on end, behind enemy lines in harm's way. That is why this day he was very more abrupt and bitter than usual. "Blondeel is an idealist," we used to say smilingly during the months of training, to explain intransigence, his emphasis on discipline, and his stubborn refusal to accept any form of compromise. While saying this, each of us knew that our squadron would never have become this cohesive and enthusiastic unit, had it not been headed by Captain Eddy Blondeel, a meticulous and methodical man, strict and full of faith. Slightly leaning on his desk, he looked at us one at a time, at Ghys, Debefve and at me, while explaining to us the broad outlines of the operations plan:
>
> "The task of the three of you will be to conduct surveillance of enemy movements along a few major avenues of approach and to designate potential objectives for air attack. As the Allies are currently attacking Normandy, it is extremely important to know what the Germans are doing, in which direction they are withdrawing and to which sector they are sending reinforcements. Study the map carefully, I'll show you the three main roads on which you will operate:
>
> • the southern route is the one that connects Orléans with Brittany

• the central route is the Paris – Bretagne avenue of approach
• the northern route runs from Paris to Normandy.

The first group to be dropped is the one from Ghys whose departure, as you know, has been postponed by 24 hours. You will probably wonder why the three groups are not commencing their operations simultaneously. The reason is that we have encountered some problems related to the [parachute] landings. As regards the first operation, the brigadier and I are of the opinion that it should not be a 'blind' drop, but that you require a reception committee on the ground, provided by the local resistance. Despite all our efforts, we have only succeeded in identifying a single reception committee, which operates in the area of the southernmost route, which also has a drop zone, called 'Caramel'. Ghys, you will jump on 'Caramel' tonight. You will make contact with the resistance and you will move immediately to the north. You will need three days to cover the distance that separates you from the central Paris – Bretagne route. Once on the spot, your immediate priority will be the preparation for Kirschen's arrival. You will transmit to us the coordinates of a suitable area."

He then turned to Debefve: "As far as you are concerned, the concept is very simple. Within one or two days from now, you will jump on the 'Caramel' drop zone and start conducting your mission immediately."

Finally, he turned his seriously looking face towards me, and continued: "With regard to you, Kirschen, you will wait here in the transit camp until Ghys lets you know that everything is ready to receive you. Once in France, you will carry out the mission on the Paris – Bretagne avenue of approach, some 50 kilometres [31 miles] northwards towards the region of Paris-Normandy."[7]

Insertion of the 'Chaucer', 'Shakespeare' and 'Bunyan' advance parties

Captain Ghys,[8] Staff Sergeant Klein, corporals Marcel Demery and Daniel Demoor and Trooper Albert Petit took off from an airfield[9] in the vicinity of the transit camp on 27 July at 10:39 pm. The first operation of the Belgian SAS carried the code name 'Chaucer'. Captain Blondeel carefully noted the time when the aeroplane of Ghys' team took off, fully aware of the historic significance of this moment when the first members of the Belgian army departed to the fight in Normandy.

In the plane that was on its way to the area around La Chartre-sur-le-Loir (in the Sarthe department), the men crouched against the wall, trying to find the most comfortable position, despite the strain of the parachute harness pulling against their shoulders and the large and heavy kitbag held between their legs. Suddenly, the sound of machine gun fire could be heard over the roar of the engines. This immediately woke up those who had partially dozed off. "Do not panic, it is the machine gunner in the back of the plane who is testing his weapon over the sea", shouted the British dispatcher. Around one o'clock in the morning, they received the order to strap their kitbags to their leg and belt.[10] When the green light went on, the dispatcher, instead of the familiar "go", shouted "good luck", while assisting to push the heavily burdened jumpers out of the plane, as they were struggling to quickly follow each other.

During the descent, the heavy weight of the kitbags attached to the leg of each man became an issue. The extension line of two kitbags could not hold the weight and made the bags crash, while the lines of the other three could not be released, resulting in two men having a sprained ankle on landing, which would hinder the team throughout the operation.

The team quickly regrouped. A group of French resistance fighters waited for them on the ground and took them to a sheltered place, where they could rest for a few hours under their protection. The aircraft then circled and made a second pass, dropping twenty-four containers, three with the SAS team's equipment, the remainder containing supplies for the resistance.

Ghys recalled the moment:

> After us, a considerable number of containers were dropped. Given the late hour, we quickly understood that despite the help of the resistance, we would run out of time. However, we had been told that to cover such an eventuality, the parachute canopies were made of camouflage fabric, so we decided to use them to cover some of the containers. The night was pitch black and it was difficult to work, we could hardly see what we were doing. At the crack of dawn, I crawled out of my sleeping bag and went to take a look at the edge of the forest. I noticed huge red spots on the drop zone. Mistake...our containers were dropped with parachutes intended for the infantry. The colour had to ensure they could be recognized and retrieved quickly.[11]

Once Captain Blondeel learned from the returned pilot and dispatcher that the dropping went according to plan, he returned to the transit camp and wrote a message for his squadron:

> To all members of the squadron, greetings. I am now in a position to reveal to you that your comrades were the first Belgian soldiers who reached the western theatre of operations, ready to strike the enemy in the heart. I am sure that they will accomplish their assigned task in an honourable way, thus contributing to the reputation of the Special Air Service regiments, which the enemy, after bitter experience, has learned to fear and to respect. I know how much all of you are looking forward to following in their footsteps and joining them in the hunt for the hated enemy. At this historic moment for us, I see myself obliged to repeat the already often given advice: be patient, stay in good shape for the fight, because the day will come when you too have the opportunity to realise your expectations and live up to the SAS motto 'who dares wins'.
>
> Captain E. Blondeel
> Commanding the Belgian Squadron[12]

In their temporary bivouac area, Ghys' team used the day of the 28th to bury the containers and stay in contact with the local resistance, who promised to return with a guide to assist them with their infiltration towards their objective area near Nogent-le-Rotrou. On the 29th, there was still no news from the guide, so the decision was made to start the infiltration to the north. Assisted by two resistance fighters, Klein managed to get in touch with a veterinary surgeon, who provided them with valuable information to reach the zone. He warned them to avoid the Vibraye Forest, which was believed to be occupied by German troops. The information was immediately transmitted to England and would force the team to make a detour.[13] Slowed down by the two injured, the team moved to the Bois de Merceries, where it stayed for the day. On 30 July, the Belgians contacted a farmer, who guided the team to a forest south of Saint-Calais during the night. He also gave contact details from a relative living in Nogent.

The early infiltration stages were not without problems. Temmerman, who was not at the scene but had first-hand access to those involved, described how the team was still moving during early daylight to make up for the time lost, when the men were looking for a lying-up position (LUP) and had to cross a river. As they had been taught during their training, they stripped and made a buoyant raft to keep their clothing and equipment afloat and dry. They were hardly across when they narrowly escaped detection by an enemy motorised column. During another incident, Petit had a neglecting discharge when the barrel of his submachine gun hit his foot, fortunately without anyone getting hurt.[14] Neither incident was mentioned in the official after-action reports.

On the 31st, the team observed only a very slight enemy presence in Saint-Calais and moved to another wood during the night.[15] The next day, when readying themselves to resume their movement, Klein's ankle was swollen to the point that he could no longer put on his boot.[16] Ghys decided to spend the night at the same location and take a day's rest. He recalled: "This was probably the right decision because Klein's injury got better, but he still delayed our progress! On 2 August, Petit managed to recover two bicycles from a farmhouse, this new acquisition greatly facilitated the transport of our equipment. That same day, a rabbit got entangled in a trap set out by Klein, which modified our menu, which until now had consisted of canned rations."[17] The team moved to a wood some 7 miles northwards and reached a wood some 3 miles southwest of Saint-Bomert the day afterwards. The two bicycles enabled the men to transport their kit, especially the heavy radios and the generator.

After advancing very cautiously, the Bois de la Grève [forest], northeast of Saint-Bomert, was reached on 4 August. During the next two days, the team came into contact with local residents and conducted reconnaissance operations on the main roads around Nogent, during which a suitable DZ for the follow-on force was identified. Operations with the local resistance could lead to tense situations, as witnessed by Ghys:

> On 6 August, we were hidden in a forest close to Nogent-le-Rotrou, waiting to link up with resistance fighters, when suddenly we heard the sound of engines. We saw an enemy lorry approaching, driven by a wildly gesticulating man in a German uniform, who was arguing with the man next to him, who also wore a uniform. More surprised than impressed, we held our fire, fortunately… They were two French resistance fighters who had put on German uniforms to join the rendezvous point.[18]

On 7 August, the Germans occupied the Château de la Grève. Petit was fired upon when reconnoitring the site. Later, he went to Nogent wearing civilian clothes.[19] During the night, the team moved to a wood south of Nogent, conveniently sited for nocturnal observation of the main roads and in close proximity to points of contact in Nogent. The team observed and reported a disorganised retreat by the enemy. On 8 August, Klein, disguised as a farmer, went to Nogent and its main road to the northwest up to Berd'huis. He noticed that a large proportion of German vehicles was moving by day while being marked with red cross symbols, even ammunition transports and armoured troop carriers. The same day, orders were received to prepare the DZ for the follow-on force, necessitating the suspension of observation posts (OPs) for two nights.[20]

For Operation 'Shakespeare', Captain Emile Debefve,[21] 2nd Lieutenant Charles Mathijs,[22] Sergeant François Siffert, and lance corporals Albert Mestdagh, Alexander Vandermeeren and Roger Carrette were to be dropped as the advance party on the same DZ as the first reconnaissance team. However, contrary to what was planned, the team was inserted – from a British Albemarle bomber from No. 295 Squadron of the RAF – on DZ '*Tornade*' (Tornado), near Dissay-sous-Courcillon,[23] south instead of north of La Chartre-sur-le-Loir. They landed around 1:15 am on 31 July.[24] The team quickly occupied an LUP in a forest northeast of the DZ. When trying to establish radio communications with England, the signaller noticed that only the emergency frequency could be used since some radio crystals were damaged. Fortunately, he was able to initiate communications, and on the night of 3-4 August around midnight, a new drop[25] delivered Trooper Rene-Gaston Geldof with the required replacements.

Communications on the primary frequency resumed and a message was sent containing information about the presence of wagons loaded with nitroglycerin in Château-du-Loir, as well as the presence of *Gestapo* agents and 400 *miliciens*.[26] The SAS Brigade HQ subsequently directed the team to move to DZ 'Caramel' as quickly as possible.

Debefve recalled his arrival in France: "The reception by the French resistance was cordial. Nevertheless, we could not count on any effective form of assistance, except for food, which, however, was always accompanied by a significant bill. In two to three days, it was impossible to set up an efficient intelligence network without the help of the local population. And that help was lacking."[27]

Since DZ 'Caramel' was to the north across the Loir river,[28] the team started to move immediately after nightfall. Debefve wanted to avoid enemy contact before the arrival of his follow-on party, so he took a route that avoided urban areas, infiltrating through fields and using cover whenever possible, taking particular care not to disturb any dogs that might give away his team's presence. In addition, he was somewhat concerned about the sign left by their footwear, anxious that the Germans would be able to track them down easily.

While continuing to make cautious progress during the night of 5-6 August, they arrived at the Loir, but the nearby bridge was guarded. The signaller objected to crossing by swimming, not so much for himself but for the radio, which was very sensitive to humidity. The dilemma was rapidly solved with the discovery of a small boat nearby. Arriving in the vicinity of La Chartre-sur-le-Loir around 2 am, the team contacted the local resistance and made preparations to receive the reinforcements with Sergeant Déom, planned for the next day. They established a bivouac in a small forest and received word from local sources that throughout the night, trains full of ammunition were leaving the Villiers railway station towards Le Mans and that they usually remained at the station for several hours before departing again. Debefve, extremely careful as usual, sent out two men to check the accuracy of the information, but they ran into some Germans, exchanged fire, and were forced to abort their mission.

On 8 August, at around 9 am, having gathered information all night long, the team was resting in some bushes, when gunfire suddenly erupted less than 1,100 yards away. The team leader decided not to get involved so as not to jeopardise the planned night drop. Later, they found out that about fifty German soldiers in a farmhouse 500 yards from their position had been attacked by French resistance fighters.

Operation 'Bunyan' started with the insertion of the advance party consisting of Captain Gilbert-Sadi Kirschen,[29] Corporal Constant Barette, Lance Corporal Jules Regner and troopers Joseph Moyse, René Pietquin and Jean Geysens in the woodland area east of Mortagne. Since Ghys' team – which had two injured – had not managed to arrive in time to secure a DZ, and the insertion couldn't be postponed, it was decided to conduct a 'blind' drop, i.e. without a reception committee on the ground. The planned DZ, 'Toffee', was located near Les Menus. The drop was conducted by an Albermarle of No. 297 Squadron of the RAF, on 4 August[30,31,32] at around 00:45 am. Most landed well, but Geysens had a violent landing, causing him to limp slightly. First, the equipment dropped in the pannier had to be distributed and the pannier hidden. The parachutes were recovered, stored in bags, and hidden in the middle of a wheat field.[33] The precious equipment would likely bring a pleasant surprise during harvesting, as the canopies could be used to make clothing.

The six-man team had landed some 8 miles northwest of the intended DZ, near the Le Noyers farm a mile west-north-west of the centre of Marchainville.[34] The two signallers, Moyse and Pietquin, recovered the S-phone[35] but had problems carrying the device, so suggested hiding it in a hedge and retrieving it the evening before the reinforcements would arrive, since it was planned to be the same DZ. The team then left the site, silently moving in single file in a northerly direction. After a while, Kirschen slowed down. He did not recognise the surroundings he had carefully studied on maps and aerial pictures during mission planning and preparation. At a crossroads, a sign indicated La Fortinière in one direction and Marchainville in another. No reference at all to Senonches, Les Menus, Fontaine-Simon or Neuilly. They occupied their first LUP in the Cherencey[36] Forest. Around noon and without worrying about some isolated gunfire that occasionally could be heard, the signallers moved to a more remote location to set up their radio set to establish radio communications with England. It was oppressively hot and Regner was sent out to the forest to fetch water. He returned after two hours and reported having discovered some ruins that might be of interest. Kirschen decided to use the building as a cache, leaving a spare radio set, batteries, food ration boxes, ammunition and several maps at the site. Towards the evening, the team was split to gather information. Regner went east, and Barette and Pietquin took a westerly direction. Regner, other than bringing back bread, eggs, and the information that a pork roast awaited them in a nearby farm, also reported the presence of numerous Germans in the vicinity of an ammunition depot, north of the forest. Barette and Pietquin returned with vague promises of assistance, given to them by two young residents of the area. Meanwhile, Kirschen managed to make an appointment with French Captain Bignon and was soon able to pinpoint the location of the ammunition depot in the Cherencey Forest. The team stayed in the same forest but moved to another LUP.[37]

On 5 August, Regner – wearing a borrowed suit – conducted a reconnaissance of DZ 'Toffee', as this might still be suitable for future use. Meanwhile at the base, messages related to the German depot were exchanged and info on the presence of some hundred German lorries at Ferté-Vidame was obtained from Captain Bignon. The target of opportunity was reported to England at once and immediately bombed but was missed by some 200 yards. While most likely a coincidence unrelated to the report, the near-simultaneousness of the radio message and the attack nevertheless did not fail to impress the French resistance fighters.[38] Attempts to report the battle damage assessment failed initially, as subsequent communications could only be established again on 6 August.[39]

That day, Kirschen was told by Lieutenant Jérôme Levesque,[40] a young local resistance leader, that the night they landed, a load of weapons had already been dropped to supply the resistance. He reportedly wondered why the SAS team had not jumped on the same DZ, just before this aerial resupply, as this would have allowed them to directly link up with the resistance, saving time in the process. Fortunately, the officer would willingly provide many services to the Belgians in the future.

The next day, Barette and Geysens conducted a reconnaissance of the Longny Forest, with the intent of establishing a new base. Throughout the day, the radio was still functioning well and during the last radio contact, an extensive message was received, announcing the airdrop of the planned reinforcements and a request to specify the DZ that would be prepared. Since it was now too dark, the message could only be decoded at dawn the next day.

On 8 August, the suitability of DZ 'Toffee' – physically reconnoitred by Regner three days earlier – was confirmed to the brigade HQ. With the reply came the code letter that would serve as the ground-to-air recognition and authentication signal for the approaching aircraft: the letter 'W'.

Kirschen, Moyse, Levesque and another resistance fighter, all in plain clothes, rode a bicycle to the DZ. Regner took a small vehicle to retrieve the S-phone, while the remainder was given a rendezvous (RV) in the Longny Forest, where they should link up the next morning.[41]

Arrival of reinforcements

On 8 August, while the advance parties were carrying out their reconnaissance missions, Blondeel briefed the follow-on groups in the transit camp at Fairford. Several maps were hung up in the briefing room. In front of him was a three-dimensional scale model representing the area of operations. On a large table, aerial photographs and a stereoscope were available. Sitting or standing around the briefing aids, the men were waiting to receive their orders. Holding a few sheets of paper and a stick, the squadron commander addressed them in a dry tone. Every time he mentioned a place name, he calmly indicated the location on a map so that everyone could absorb the information. Below is a summary of Blondeel's briefing:

Ground

The 'Chaucer' team will encounter small hills, lots of hedges, stretches of grassland, cornfields, and rocky heights.

The 'Shakespeare' team will find itself on a plateau descending towards the Loire valley and will encounter hedges and fields. Part of the terrain is rather unfavourable, consisting of flat terrain over the entire length of the valley. There is no lack of water.

The 'Bunyan' team will operate in the area of la Perche, with grassland, fields surrounded by hedges, oak forests and lakes, and in an area with steep slopes north of the Huisne river, with deep valleys and wooded hills and flattened peaks.

Enemy
We have no precise information about his exact intentions. There is little train traffic. All the intelligence we have available comes from our reconnaissance teams. No significant enemy air activity has been reported. You have seen the front line, but it is announced that the Americans have reached Le Mans.

The enemy is moving out of Brittany in a disorderly manner. Elsewhere, he is withdrawing eastwards in a more or less organised manner.

Mission
Each combat group will

- harass the enemy without ceasing and by all means to turn his withdrawal into defeat;
- make maximum use of the firepower of the Royal Air Force by reporting targets by radio;
- let me know what the resistance is capable of and keep me informed of its movements.

The tasks are therefore to attack and inform, avoiding any prolonged regular combat with the enemy.

You will avoid large concentrations of resistance fighters around your positions, and for offensive actions, you will employ only those you can really trust, and under your command.

Drop zones
'Chaucer': southwest of Dreux.
'Shakespeare': north of Tours.
'Bunyan': north of Bercé Forest, near Longny.

Movement
Embarkation for departure to the airfield at 18:45 hours.

Each team will be transported by two Stirling planes, each carrying ten containers with supplies.

Boarding of the planes at 21:30 hours.

Flight to Caen, then towards the dropping zone.

Estimated drop time: 02:00 on 9 August

The reconnaissance teams will provide a reception committee.

On landing, regrouping in accordance with the orders of the team leader; burial of parachutes.

Armament

Rifle with scope; two automatic weapons per section, four per group.

Depending on the instructions of the commander: no. 36 grenades, Lewis bombs.

Method

To be determined depending on local information and observations.

For example: shooting at troop convoys; blocking traffic by means of tyre busters;[42] derailing trains; attacking and destroying small isolated outposts; taking out sentries; setting fire to supply dumps.

Intercommunication

We have made arrangements with your signallers with regard to procedures, call signs and operating instructions. From time to time, we will perform authentication procedures to make sure it is not the Germans who are using your transmitters. We will also sometimes resort to asking indiscreet questions and we might ask your signaller to state his date of birth or the name of his girlfriend.

Recommendations

Applying strict discipline, staying on one's assigned position, always placing sentries near positions or a base, setting up a guard post in the vicinity of your position or base, speaking in a muffled voice, reconnoitring quick evasion routes, avoiding farms; when attacking, using the mortar and pestle method, concentrating large numbers, but using ammunition sparingly and for demolitions, using plenty of explossives. You will be recovered after link-up with Allied forces who will pass through your positions. Use your SAS credentials to join the army staff, and then return to England, to take part in new operations.

Next, the captain covered the service support section of his orders. The audience remembered that a flask of rum would be issued to the team leaders, that two bicycles would be loaded in a container and that the mail would be parachuted. For local purchases, everything would have to be paid for. The team leaders would be issued with money for this purpose. Many must have been surprised when actions on prisoners were covered: "Avoid taking prisoners; if you do, blindfold them and give them an injection so that they sleep for four to five hours and leave the site. To this end, use the small morphine syrette from the medical kit." No one had come up with this idea, except the captain, who had studied medicine.

You must administer first aid to all the wounded, put them at ease and, as far as possible, ensure that they will be seen by a local physician in a secure site.

> Beware of venereal diseases. No contact with women during the mission! Do not consume any alcohol; the rum is only for medical purposes. Cover any open wounds immediately with sulfamide powder. As far as contacts with the population are concerned: distant and polite. Avoid villages. No written information about the inhabitants to prevent reprisals. Trusted agents: in principle, the teacher and the priest. No political discussions. And, I repeat: pay for everything. All that remains is for me to issue you the money. To begin with, 100,000 French francs for each team leader. You will be provided with more if and when required.[43]

After the detailed briefing, the men returned to their tents to load their magazines with ammunition and fill their pockets and kitbags with lightweight equipment. Personal documents were removed and left behind and radios were tested.

The reinforcement for Operation 'Chaucer' consisted of Captain Raymond Van der Heyden,[44] Staff Sergeant Denis Devignez, sergeants Jaques Goffinet, Georges Ratinckx and Pierre Polain and troopers Jacques Hambursin, Jacques Gilson, Alfred Becquet, Marcel Chauvaux, Ferdinand Hendrickx, Théo Clamot, Urbain Deprez, Charles Lemaire, Jean Demery and Willy Deheusch.

On the evening of 8 August, the 'Chaucer' advance party arrived at the DZ and placed the signal lights. Around 1 am on the 9th, the sound of engines could be heard, and the signal lights were lit. But as the noise grew closer, the team suspected it to be a German plane, so Ghys decided to switch off the lights. The plane loitered above their position, then disappeared. Some fifteen minutes later, another aircraft approached the DZ. The team turned the lights back on and watched the stick[45] being dropped at an extremely low altitude from Stirling LK510 from No. 196 Squadron, RAF.[46,47] The parachutes barely had time to open, and all landed outside the marked DZ, with the kitbags still attached to their legs. Devignez's back was seriously injured and he remained unconscious on the ground; three others had minor injuries. Before daybreak, most of the accompanying equipment and supplies were recovered and hidden, but one of two bicycles could not be found. The party subsequently withdrew to the woods with as much ammunition as they could carry, as well as the wounded.[48] Petit was tasked with establishing contact with a resistance group. He rode a bicycle to Nogent-le-Rotrou, but on his way, he was stopped by four Germans who were determined to confiscate his bicycle. Even though he was wearing civilian clothes, one of the Germans noticed his unusual boots and wanted to search him. Petit reacted immediately and jumped back, took a No. 36 grenade from his pocket, threw it in the middle of the group, went down, jumped up after the explosion, took his bicycle and rode to a nearby concealed position. Having observed stretcher-bearers coming to the aid of the four wounded Germans, he resumed his movements and eventually managed to get into touch with the maquisards.[49] During the night, patrols were sent towards the roads from Nogent-le-Rotrou to Authon and to Beaumont-les-Autels respectively. On the former, six armoured vehicles were observed, including one identified as a Tiger tank.[50]

On 11 August, Van der Heyden intended to move by day towards a crossroads in the Huisne river valley some 8 miles southwest of Nogent-le-Rotrou, assuming that

German forces were still conducting a retrograde manoeuvre in this area against the advancing American forces. He linked up with Ghys' team at Les Hérissières, some 3 miles south of Nogent-le-Rotrou and was informed that a resistance group was attacking the Germans – some thirty in total – who were still in Nogent-le-Rotrou. Almost simultaneously, the Belgians received a request for support by the resistance group, so Van der Heyden changed his plan, linked up with the maquis near the town and sent a reconnaissance party forward, only to find the disorganised band withdrawing. While leaving the town themselves during the night, the Germans placed mines on the roads. The next day, Ghys' team rendered safe some sixty mines, quite a delicate task – three were found to be booby-trapped.[51] In the meantime, Van der Heyden's team tried to cut off the German withdrawal, laying ambushes along two roads north of the town.[52]

On 13 August, Klein interrogated some German prisoners, who all confirmed the state of disarray of the German forces. Their main concern, however, was the ability to surrender to regular forces and not to the resistance. When American ground forces reached the town on 14 August, all access roads had been cleared of mines, so they could enter the town safely.[53]

Temmerman described the problems that emerged immediately after the liberation:

> The population was hungry for justice, if not revenge. They demanded the arrest of the enemy's collaborators. In most cases, the traitors and supporters were obvious, due to their attitude during the occupation or by their behaviour during the withdrawal of the German troops. Nevertheless, some Frenchmen loudly protested their innocence, referring to witnesses, and declared to be the victim of conspiracies, fuelled by jealousy. The resistance fighters were worried. Having fought against a dictatorship, they now didn't want to become involved in arbitrary arrests, let alone install a regime based on terror! One of them suggested using the parachuted SAS troops who knew how to lay ambushes, how to get into contact with London, who could handle rifles, grenades, pistols, submachine guns, anti-tank weapons, who could clear mines and who could interrogate German prisoners of war. Because the SAS men were not local natives, their perceived impartiality would be well accepted. But the Belgians refused to play judge, prosecutor or referee. The French were reluctant to accept their advice to lock up those suspects that might have caused trouble, rather for their own safety, to treat them well and wait for the return of the French authorities, which would be imminent.[54]

On 15 August, the teams of Ghys and Van der Heyden joined the HQ of the American 3rd Army and returned to England shortly afterwards.

After the operation, Van der Heyden regretted not having been dropped two weeks earlier and not having been equipped with jeeps. However, the reported presence of SAS troops in several locations seemed to have had a significant psychological effect, potentially hastening the German withdrawal. There seem to have been rumours about the presence of 150, 200 or even 300 'Canadian and Belgian paratroopers' in the region and some Germans reportedly disabled their weapons in Nogent, while *Wehrmacht* army troops clashed with SS troops in Condée. In the area around Nogent-le-Rotrou, between Le Mans and Chartres, the Americans encountered no German resistance whatsoever.[55]

During the night of 8-9 August, Debefve and his men waited for their reinforcements for Operation 'Shakespeare' at DZ 'Caramel'. Around 1:30 am, they heard the sound of an aeroplane,[56] and shortly afterwards, parachute canopies could be seen in the air. Two men suffered minor injuries upon landing.[57] Debefve walked towards a silhouette in the night and met Freddy Limbosch, to the surprise of both men. It immediately became clear that a mistake had been made. Instead of Sergeant Déom's team, the one commanded by Limbosch had landed. Limbosch already identified a lesson: "The team leaders should compare their maps with those of the pilots before take-off. Look at me now, standing here with maps of another region in an area I have not studied." "Doesn't matter", Debefve assured him, "I'll get you a Michelin map. They are better than the British maps anyway."[58]

The reinforcements consisted of Captain Freddy Limbosch,[59] Staff Sergeant Georges Verberckmoes, Corporal Charles Sas and troopers Victor Debuf, Alphons Peere, Henri Derath, Jean Switters, Maurice De Serrano, Andre Marginet, Jean Veroft, Lucien Goessens, Leonard Roegist, Emile Lorphèvre and René Krins.

Most of the day was spent trying to find the party's nine containers among the many more that had been dropped for the resistance and to distribute the equipment and supplies and hide the containers. Limbosch managed to find transportation, and in the evening, the group went to La Chartre-sur-le-Loir, trying to find fuel. The town was now all but left by the Germans, but no fuel could be found. By 10:30 pm, the party left the town, moving to the northeast, to lay an ambush near St-Calais on the main road between Le Mans and Orléans. On the outskirts of the town, a German lorry was encountered and halted. Contrary to the trigger-happy maquis in their area, the Belgians proceeded with caution, as any lorry could very well be one from the resistance or even be part of the advancing American forces. A German disembarked from the lorry and found himself facing Carrette, one of the lead scouts of the Belgian patrol. Both opened fire simultaneously. Carrette was killed, and his opponent was wounded and subsequently killed by the resistance. The same night, Roegist was wounded in the leg during a firefight with the occupants of a German vehicle, who were all killed.[60] With the death of Carrette,[61] the Belgian SAS mourned its first killed in action.

During the day of the 10th, the party moved to Cogners and Montoire and found that German forces had mostly withdrawn from the area between Saint-Calais and Montoire.

On 11 August, the 'Shakespeare' team conducted a link-up with the vanguard of the American ground forces and left for Le Mans in the evening. Meanwhile, in Hotel Moderne in Le Mans, British Major Airey Neave,[62] who belonged to MI9, the department of military intelligence responsible for evasion and escape activities, was planning a delicate operation. Neave was trying to find more than 150 evaders, half of them escaped aircrew members from the US Army Air Forces, who had regrouped in the Fréteval Forest, some 50 miles east of Le Mans, to return them to Britain. But the XV US Army Corps, which had to leave Le Mans, heading for Alençon (to close the Falaise pocket), had no spare assets available. Four officers and thirty-four men of the British 2nd SAS, who had moved from Brittany, entered the courtyard of the hotel. Neave asked Captain Greville-Bell, who had been awarded a Distinguished Service Order (DSO) for operating with Italian partisans behind enemy lines almost a year earlier, for his cooperation. That evening, the Belgians in turn moved into the hotel.[63] A signal was sent to the SAS Brigade HQ to obtain approval to take part in the operation to rescue the evaders. Approval being granted, Limbosch spent the next two days exchanging information with the G2 (intelligence) staff section of the 3rd US Army, while a multinational party including Debefve conducted a route reconnaissance towards Châteaudun.[64] The latter revealed that some villages were still occupied by the Germans, but also that the route was feasible, especially when protected by some fifty SAS troops.[65]

Buses and lorries would be provided by the French Forces of the Interior (FFI)[66] to transport the recovered isolated personnel, but hardly anything in working order could be found. Eventually, buses and trucks were reluctantly provided by the Americans and the mixed maquis-SAS column – some 100 men and at least a dozen vehicles – left Le Mans towards Fréteval Forest, on the morning of 14 August. Several hours later, they returned with 132 rescued personnel from the US, the UK, New Zealand, Canada and Poland, as well as a few prisoners picked up along the route. Some twenty other survivors had decided to continue evading on their own prior to the arrival of the rescue force.[67]

This rescue mission, known as Operation 'Sherwood', marked the end of Operation 'Shakespeare' and on 17 August, its participants were back in Britain.[68]

On 8 August, night fell, and Kirschen was happy that he would welcome his friend Limbosch with the reinforcements for Operation 'Bunyan'. In the early hours of the 9th, aircraft engines could be heard, and lights were lit. Moyse displayed the 'W' Morse code signal in the direction of the aircraft. Ten men could be seen jumping, then, on the next run, five more, followed by equipment containers.[69] The insertion by Stirling LJ925 of No. 196 Squadron had gone smoothly.[70]

The reinforcements consisted of three sections of five men: Sergeant Josy Déom and troopers Jacques Levaux, Joseph Levaux, Laurent Boch and Daniel Rossius, Sergeant Roger Parmentier and Corporal Ivo Brasseur and lance corporals Hector Breuze, Jean Thévissen and Jean Quirain and Sergeant Jules Crèvecœur with troopers Marcel Moreau, René Balsat, André Bouillon and Henri Flips.

Kirschen described the link-up with the reception committee:

> I turned to the nearest newcomer and heard him ask "Where is Lieutenant Debefve? I have instructions for him."
> "Debefve? He is at Le Mans, some 100 kilometres [62 miles] away. What are you doing here? You're not one of my troop…and where is Lieutenant Limbosch?"
> "Lieutenant Limbosch…he's in the other plane", the reply came.

After a rather confused explanation, Kirschen realised that Limbosch's group was to reinforce Debefve, and was also confronted with two injured. Brasseur had a fractured foot and Breuze had a fractured leg, caused by landing on their kitbag. Levesque woke up a farmer in the vicinity, who provided a cart to transport the heavy containers and allowed his farm to be used to hide the equipment and the wounded. Parmentier,

Quirain, Bouillon and Flips remained with the wounded. Kirschen designated an RV for the following night for the remainder of the follow-on team, about 9 miles to the northwest, at the pond of Boustières, in the forest of Longny and appointed Regner – who arrived late with the S-phone – as their guide.[71] First, he had to take the group to the Porcherie Forest before dawn.[72] Kirschen then returned by bike to the remainder of the advance party in the Longny Forest, together with Moyse, but failed to link up with Barette's party. In the meantime, around 3 pm, a doctor arrived at the farm and brought Breuze to the hospital, disguised as a refugee.[73]

Regner guided Déom's group, who moved cautiously, amazed by the amount of German troops operating in the wooded area. At any sound or suspicious movement, a scout was sent ahead, while the main body was mentally preparing for the fight and to break contact quickly. They advanced slowly and at dawn Sergeant Déom decided to move into a concealed position and wait until the next night. He recalled: "At the end of this day, the men only thought about drinking. It was hot and we were completely dehydrated. At 8 pm, it was not completely dark yet, but we had to move on because we were going to become crazy."[74] The group left its position and followed a road. Suddenly, the squeaky sound of moving metal could be heard. "A tank", someone whispered. "No, a less heavy vehicle, but on tracks anyway", replied another. They plunged into a ditch, ready to fire. A German soldier on a bicycle without tyres passed by while he was singing loudly to cheer himself up. Smiling, they let him pass. Why would they burden themselves with a prisoner?[75]

During the night, the planned link-up with Déom's group – guided by Regner – did not materialise; Kirschen could find no one at the RV.

On the morning of 10 August, Parmentier left his hiding place to move the containers to a barn, using two horse-drawn carts covered with straw and each hiding two men. Three hours later, he arrived at his destination and waited for further instructions from Captain Kirschen. Around 10 pm, a German convoy of about 150 men, twenty lorries and several armoured vehicles halted at the farm. The party remained stuck, as the closest group of Germans was only 15 yards away.[76]

Throughout the day of the 10th, Kirschen was becoming impatient and wondered why Barette and Regner were not at the agreed RV in the forest of Longny. He had been wandering around this forest with Moyse for two days. They were exhausted and encountered one problem after another. He saw only one possibility to put an end to this game of hide-and-seek: send a message to his HQ in Britain to let his men know they had to join him as soon as possible in the vicinity of the Boustières pond. To call London, however, a radio was required. Barette was the signaller normally carrying the radio set. Kirschen and Moyse departed to the ruined house to collect their spare radio set, stimulated by Benzedrine[77] tablets to keep them awake after forty hours without sleep and burdened by the weight of their packs, while jumping into ditches each time they heard a German lorry approaching. Unfortunately, there was a new setback upon returning to the forest of Longny... The radio that had been retrieved with much effort from the cache was useless. No matter how much they turned the crank handle of the hand-operated generator, Britain kept repeating: "I can't hear you..." Moyse had to return to the cache to recover spare lamps and by the end of the day, the radio had been repaired.[78]

During the night of 10-11 August, Déom and his men finally arrived near the Boustières pond. Since there was too much enemy activity, Regner was sent out to the actual RV location, while Déom and the remainder of the team waited in a secure concealed position. Regner recalled: "I was overheated, tired and my feet were in bad shape. I blew the special signal whistle we had been issued but got no reaction. Kirschen was not at the RV! I sat down on the shore of the pond and plunged my feet into the cool water. Seconds later, I had to pull them back out: they were covered with leeches. Instead of waiting any longer, the idea came up to go to the farm of my friend Simon."[79]

A few days earlier, Regner had met Simon, a member of a local resistance group. During one of their activities, both halted at a farm to have dinner. When they were about to start eating their meal, some Germans knocked on the farmer's door, asking to join them for dinner. Regner and Simon were wearing civilian clothes and pretended to belong to the farm. "One of the Germans spoke good French", recalled Regner.

> Before we sat down at the table, we argued and he told me that when the war would be over, he would teach the French German lessons. Then he asked me from which region I originated. I told him I came from the north of France. "That I could hear", the German proudly replied. Then we sat down at the table. I had slipped my Colt .45[80] inside my belt, but when I sat down, I felt the pistol slide up against my abdomen, with the result that it nearly fell out. I pretended not to feel well, grabbed my belly with both hands and rushed to the toilet, to properly adjust the position of my weapon. I had no fear for myself because the safety catch of my weapon was not even on, and the Germans would not have had time to react. But I feared for the security of the civilians, against whom retaliatory measures would certainly have been taken afterwards.[81]

On 11 August, contact with the higher HQ was established and messages to facilitate the link-up with Barette's and Déom's groups were sent. They now knew the RV location would once more be confirmed to the others, provided they had good communications with England as well. While Moyse was listening to the BBC, Kirschen looked over his shoulder and suddenly noticed an armed German soldier looking at him, some 11 yards away. "Moyse, a Jerry, watch out!" shouted Kirschen. With the headset firmly pushing against his ears, Moyse could only hear the radio. A kick from his boss alerted him. The lieutenant drew his handgun and fired at the same time the German soldier fired his gun while going down to take cover. Moyse quickly returned fire and both men broke contact, running away at full speed. Out of sight, they assessed the situation. The German was most probably trying to augment his soldiers' rations, as Kirschen noted that his leg had been struck by round projectiles intended for a different kind of game. They then carefully returned to recover their radio set, before the enemy had the chance to search the scene of the incident. Again, radio contact was established with England, requesting to cancel the RV to avoid Déom's team running into an area under enemy surveillance. Kirschen then asked to bomb the site where a German convoy had been spotted in the forest, which was executed by the RAF in the afternoon. He hoped to neutralise some of the Germans searching the area. His leg hurt and he was hungry, noting that the food in the emergency rations was far from sufficient. Above all, he wondered how to link up with his men. Simon, the farmer they had met before, was thought to possibly be aware of Regner's whereabouts. The two men took advantage of the night to knock on his door. Simon did not look surprised and indeed knew where to find Regner.[82]

At the farm where Parmentier's group was hiding, two Germans were moving towards his position around 9 am on the 11th, when he gave the order to abandon their hiding place. One by one, all managed to quietly evacuate, carrying weapons and ammunition, but leaving their rucksacks behind. After a five-hour journey, they found shelter on another farm.[83]

Regner could be contacted and he led Kirschen to Déom's group on the 12th. En route, they suddenly noticed two silhouettes. It turned out to be Barette and Pietquin. Nearby, the remainder were laying up in the forest, except for Parmentier and his men, all eager to get into action.

They could finally start their harassment operations, together with local resistance forces. Three groups were formed, commanded by 1st Lieutenant Kirschen, Sergeant Déom and Sergeant Crèvecœur respectively. Levesque's maquisards were organised in two groups of five to six men. All groups were ready by 10 pm.

During the night, Déom and the maquisard group with Levesque encountered two German batteries near the Sainte-Anne crossroads. They were pinned down and needed three hours to break contact. A round, its origin unknown, caused an ammunition lorry to explode, killing several Germans.

The other maquis party, tasked to operate on another road from Marchainville, blew up a German staff car using a No. 82 grenade,[84] commonly known as Gammon bomb.

Kirschen and Regner placed tyre busters on the road from Longny-au-Perche to Marchainville, which stopped a convoy on which Regner threw a Mills grenade, after which both men moved to another location and emptied their carbines on a German horse transport. When their supply of ammunition and tyre busters was exhausted, they decided to quench their thirst in a roadside creek.

Meanwhile, Barette and two men (the other element of Kirschen's split team) ambushed a lorry on the same road, using their Sten guns.[85]

Crèvecœur and his men conducted operations on the road from Marchainville to La Lande. They destroyed an air defence half-track using a Gammon bomb, which killed the occupants. They also placed tyre busters, but without success. After their withdrawal, they noticed movement in the woods and opened fire. It turned out they had hit Regner, who got a small arms round in the leg. Initial medical care was provided and Regner was evacuated to a farm, the reluctant resident of which was ordered to take care of the wounded man. Regner refused to be given morphine to manage his pain but was given sulfanilamide tablets to prevent wound infection. Kirschen then went to inform Simon, who promised to try to bring a doctor to treat Regner.

Back in their patrol harbour, on the afternoon of 13 August, Déom's men regrettably learned what had happened, but all were happy they had had the chance to put their SAS training into practice. For most of them, these night attacks were their baptism of fire and the successful completion of their operations, so far, instilled new confidence. Kirschen summarised the results: "two tracked vehicles carrying ammunition and six German lorries destroyed, enemy killed and wounded, a tracked vehicle on fire, peasants claimed having seen seven bodies being retrieved from it. Time lost for the Germans and confusion in their ranks!" They then planned their operations in the same – now familiar – area for the next night.[86]

Meanwhile, Sergeant Parmentier was becoming impatient. He had been waiting for orders for three days now. He put on civilian clothes and returned to the farm where the containers were hidden but found it occupied by Germans, who came and went throughout. On 13 August around 9 pm, he managed to enter the farm, where he found a message awaiting him: "RV tomorrow at 2 pm at 7 kilometres [4.3 miles] west of your position to contact Captain King," with a request to bring arms, including a Bren gun,[87] ammunition and explosives.[88]

During the night, while trying to find targets to attack, Kirschen received word that the Germans had evacuated Longny. The groups led by Crèvecœur and Barette and one of the resistance groups had nothing to report either, but Levesque and Déom had more success the next morning.

Levesque had been informed that the withdrawing Germans had installed a dump with some 30,000 litres of petrol in the Château de Miserai.[89] Déom and his team followed Levesque. The nine men (six Belgians and three maquisards) took positions at the two exits of the park and an ultimatum to surrender was issued. The Germans jumped into their vehicles and attempted to leave. Levaux threw a phosphorus grenade on one of the vehicles and at least three Germans who exited the vehicle were believed to have been killed by Tommy guns. Those in two other vehicles disembarked and fled into the woods, leaving weapons and equipment behind.[90]

The same morning, around 11 am, Parmentier and his team departed for their RV. They arrived around 1:50 pm, but found no sign of Kirschen. Around 4 pm, he got into contact with an FFI member, who reported that six Germans were hidden in a farmhouse. He went to investigate with his team, but upon arrival, the enemy had already gone. Around 5:30 pm, he finally linked up with the remainder of the SAS party. Half an hour later, he left with a few others to the Sainte-Anne crossroads, and fifteen minutes afterwards, two Germans were killed in a hotel. Their bodies were moved to the base, where Parmentier reported to Kirschen.[91]

In the afternoon, as soon as Kirschen was informed of the result of Levesque's and Déom's combined effort, he had the castle secured to ensure that the fuel could be given to the advancing Americans. Defensive positions were organised around the castle and patrols sent out. In Marchainville, Crèvecœur's three-man team threw a Gammon bomb when encountering an amphibious vehicle. The grenade touched the vehicle but exploded too late to have any effect. Déom's team was sent to the Sainte-Anne crossroads, together with Parmentier, whose team managed to kill two Germans as already mentioned. Kirschen himself went to Longny and finally got his buckshot wounds treated by a doctor. He also visited Regner, who in the meantime had been hidden in the town while recovering from his gunshot wound.

On the morning of 15 August, Kirschen heard rumours that an American column was on its way to the Sainte-Anne crossroads and went to meet them. He found them on the road to Marchainville, exchanged information and returned to the castle to assemble his men by noon. A ceremony was held, followed by a lavish meal, after which Kirschen said goodbye to Levesque and departed to Longny.

For the next three days, Kirschen and his men drove through France in a captured German lorry, halting on a number of occasions, such as at the HQ of Lieutenant General Patton's 3rd Army, making arrangements for the evacuation of Brasseur and Breuze in the process. They arrived in Arromanches on the 18th, handed over their lorry to two maquisards, embarked, and arrived in Newhaven the day after. They were reunited with Blondeel and granted five days of leave.[92]

Operation 'Haggard'

That the Belgian SAS did not encounter too many problems during their first operations was partly due to their knowledge of French, which greatly facilitated contacts with the local population. On the other hand, certain British SAS elements reportedly had some difficulties in establishing indispensable contacts with the local resistance networks. For Operation 'Haggard', an operation conducted by 'B' Squadron, 1st SAS, two Belgian SAS signallers were attached. Since both also spoke French, it would help the Brits to deal with the language issue. Holvoet and Temmerman were summoned to the briefing room, where they were greeted by Captain Jean Dulait, Blondeel being absent at the time. Dulait told them: "You are both ordered to leave with a British squadron that has insufficient signallers. I do not know what the mission is, nor do I know the date of departure." He continued: "Here are your British identity papers. Please hand in your photographs and personal documents in the office. But first of all, go and present yourself to the major commanding 'B' Squadron of the 1st SAS Regiment. Before you do, sew your stripes first. Because for the duration of the operation, you will be – and he was looking at the bigger of the two – corporal, and you – while he addressed the other one – lance corporal."

Holvoet was promoted to acting corporal and Temmerman to acting lance corporal. The lance corporal found it difficult to reconcile himself with the state of affairs. He would have liked to become corporal too, just like his friend, not out of vanity, but because the corporal's chevrons were wider and therefore easier to sew on... Besides, those huge Vs on each sleeve were very ugly, he thought. Even worse, the marks would still be visible when the chevrons had to be removed afterwards, so it could fuel the perception that he had been degraded. After searching a bit, both men met Major Eric Lepine, 'B' Squadron's officer commanding (OC). He sent them to a sergeant major who preceded them to an unoccupied tent. Temmerman was not impressed, but eager to get into the fight: "We were poorly housed, miserably fed, without sanitary installations worthy of the name, but were almost looking forward with enthusiasm to the idea of living in even worse conditions. We are ready, we had waited long enough. Let us now be employed, the sooner, the better!"[93]

'B' Squadron was to establish a base in the area between the Gien – Bourges road, the Bourges – Nevers road and the Loire river between Gien and Nevers, from which small parties were to cut enemy communications, carry out sabotage operations, hamper enemy movement and report on enemy movements and troop concentrations. An advance party was to be parachuted west of the Ivoy Forest,[94] to be followed by the main body a few days later.[95]

After the briefing and the meticulous preparation of their equipment, the two

Belgians found themselves at the airfield, accompanied by five Brits: their chief, a blond colossus of a lieutenant, with four men. An officer of the US Army Air Forces joined them and informed them that the group would be split in two. Arriving at the B-24 Liberator[96] bombers, the jumpmaster, seemingly surprised and pointing to their kitbags, asked them: "What are you going to do with that?" "Jump with it, of course, we've always trained this way", the British lieutenant replied. "I don't want you to get stuck in the gap above the drop zone. I will drop your packs after you have jumped", the American replied, "Just look at that gap...,[97] you will have enough trouble getting out quickly with the parachute on your back. I will attach a parachute to each bag and don't worry, I won't forget to drop it." Holvoet from his side clearly showed his unhappiness with having the misfortune of being dropped by an American crew. The Americans apparently did not have the best reputation; they were suspected of having rather relative notions of precision when dropping paratroopers over the site where they should land. In this case, he thought, it would not be a surprise if they dropped their passengers 50 kilometres [31 miles] from the intended zone, that they dropped their jump bags in a lake, and that their colleagues in charge of dropping the second half of the team would drop them at the other side of France.[98]

On the night of 9-10 August,[99] the two planes were on their way to drop the seven[100] men that constituted the advance party of Operation 'Haggard' on a DZ along the western edge of the forest of Ivoy, near Bourges. After flying for about two hours, the green light went on. "Go!" the jumpmaster shouted. The lieutenant pushed himself up with both hands and jumped through the aperture in the aircraft floor, followed by the corporal and the lance corporal. Within three seconds they had left the plane. Temmerman recalled:

> The clean air was welcome after this stay in an overheated and dark fuselage with the smell of oil and petrol. The parachutists balanced gently, overlooking a wooded area. The ground or at least the dark strip that was supposed to be the ground, quickly came closer. They made a soft landing and after rolling in the grass, they ran around their parachute, in line with what had been taught, to bring down the canopy so that they would not be dragged along. Apart from the light of the signal fires, the darkness was complete. The countryside and the forests bathed in peaceful tranquillity. The plane made another pass and dropped three containers that looked like their kitbags, in addition to six other containers which, upon hitting the ground, disturbed the atmosphere of total quietness.[101]

From a corner of the forest, several silhouettes quickly ran towards the containers. Temmerman, carrying his folded parachute under his arm and his pistol in his hand, made his way to the place where the shadows had appeared. On the way, he stumbled over an obstacle, which he recognised as his kitbag. He opened the bag, took out a carbine, put his pistol back into its holster and was relieved to see it was indeed his kitbag, which was intact, while the radio set had not been damaged. A little further on, a noise sharpened all his senses. He silently switched off the safety catch of his carbine and observed through the darkness. A few metres from him, a man stood upright. "Who is there?" the paratrooper whispered, first in English, then in French. "You are undoubtedly one of the Belgian parachutists?" a voice replied. "It's fair to say so", the signaller said, his finger on the trigger. "Yes, I know", the voice continued. "It is a secret. But I am the only one who knows about it and I am not telling anyone about this. I am the chief of resistance. Your comrades are over there behind the hedge."[102]

Despite Holvoet's pessimism, the jump went well, and the men had been dropped at the right site. After regrouping and assuming that they were complete, the Belgians again heard the sound of aircraft engines. Now a Jedburgh team[103] was being inserted,[104] whose mission and destination they did not know.

A cart pulled by two farm horses then brought their equipment to a farm, the owner of which was a member of the French resistance. They were generously fed. Afterwards, they left the area, followed a path that crossed a watercourse, entered the forest and proceeded cautiously and without making any noise, until they reached a small house in the middle of a wasteland area. Holvoet, who had drunk a glass of local liqueur with the farmers (in the mistaken belief that the colourless drink was water), seemed to show more and more signs of fatigue and Temmerman helped him carry his equipment. The team decided to halt at the house. The resistance fighters who were accompanying them continued their way and the SAS party, after having established a guard duty roster, got into their sleeping bags. The first man on the watch installed himself on the roof of the cottage. The next morning, contact with England was established.[105]

The main party, with Major Lepine, was parachuted in on the night of 14-15 August. Half the men were dropped too low, without time to properly release their kitbags, and the other half was dropped too high, landing 2 miles from the DZ. Three men were severely wounded. Lepine established his base in the Ivoy Forest, from where the British squadron launched its operations to create havoc behind enemy lines, together with the resistance. Ambushes were laid, railways were cut and some 120 enemies were killed and over twenty vehicles destroyed. But success came at a price: Corporal Wilkinson was killed in a firefight and three men were wounded, while the maquis also had casualties.

In addition to their job as signallers, the two Belgians were used as interpreters during the numerous contacts of the British with the French resistance. The major had forbidden them to take part in the harassment operations, but because they insisted, he finally allowed one of them to participate, providing the other remained at the base. This allowed Holvoet to participate in a sabotage mission against a railway, the destruction of which had been ordered by London. Back at the base, however, he was tired and in a rather bad mood: "It was far", he explained to his comrade. "It took us forever to reach the actual objective. The tracks were rusty, and between the sleepers there was plenty of vegetation; I wondered why such a long distance had to be travelled when there were several railways in the vicinity." He took a few hours' rest, while his friend sent the message that the railway tracks had been destroyed at the planned site. The next morning, Holvoet was on duty when the reply came in: "Bravo, but the line has been out of service since 1899. With apologies for our mistake."[106]

The two Belgians, like the Brits, had the pleasant surprise to receive their – censored – mail by parachute, during resupply drops. To Temmerman, it was almost surreal: "It's a strange impression: being cut off from one's comrades of the SAS Squadron, having little or no news of the general course of operations, having absolutely no idea when exactly we would be going back to England or Belgium and suddenly being in front of a stack of letters reminding us of the existence of a distant world."[107]

On 4 September, they learned that Brussels had been liberated. Paradoxically, when their relatives lived in a region occupied by the enemy, they were training in a free country; now that their relatives had been liberated, they found themselves in an area occupied by the Germans.

Throughout the long operation, during which they had to send plenty of messages, the two signallers remained extremely cautious, often moving frequently to deploy their antennas to avoid being located by German radio triangulation units.

In the first half of September, German Major General Botho Henning Elster had negotiated a surrender with more than 19,000 men to American Major General Macon's 83rd Infantry Division. Elster was the territorial commander of German forces in the Mont-de-Marsan area in southwest France and following the Allied breakout in Normandy and the landings in southern France on 15 August, he was ordered to evacuate his forces back to Germany. His column, which included the 159th Infantry Division, navy and air force units, police and civilian administrative personnel, moved north to Poitiers, before turning to the east. His retreat being blocked by advancing Allied forces and fearing reprisals for his own atrocities in the past, he started negotiating. The French resistance played a major role in the surrender, but, in addition to Lieutenant Magill and his intelligence and reconnaissance platoon from the American 83rd Infantry Division, British special operations personnel, including Captain John Cox (Jedburgh team 'Ivor') and Major Tommy McPherson (Jedburgh Team 'Quinine'), were also involved in a delicate movement of German troops through an area with intense resistance activity before they were finally interned by American forces.[108] Temmerman described the implications:

> The German general gave the signallers a lot of work. First of all, the movements carried out by his column had to be reported daily. And then, before laying down his weapons, he wanted to have the guarantee that his retreat would have been cut off [to justify his surrender towards his superiors]. The major wasn't sure, but London confirmed that it was impossible to retreat to Germany. A prisoner was released to inform the general of this reality and the aviation gave a demonstration of its firepower on the main roads, not without firing on some vehicles of the resistance by mistake. Impressed, the general announced his decision to surrender, but not to the resistance, only to regular American or British troops. Upon being informed, the staff in London reminded the SAS party that they were part of the regular British Army and that therefore they had to deal with the German general's issue. This had little effect on the Major who telegraphed to his superiors that the general had 18,000 men with him while the parachutists were only around sixty. However, the staff, to whom this seemed a negligible detail, ordered the parachutists to take care of the general and his forces, to have them follow a precise route towards Blois, where the Americans would set up a large cage, and to conduct continuous jeep patrols along the German column. The French for their part were far from happy when

they found 'their' prisoners being handled by the British, who themselves didn't appreciate the radio reports announcing the capture of 18,000 Germans by the Americans in the vicinity of Blois.[109]

Operation 'Haggard' ended for the two Belgians on 15 September. They wished to be able to drive to Brussels and spend a few days with their relatives. A message from London informed them that an aeroplane from the RAF was going to pick them up at the Briare airfield. They said goodbye to the British, with whom they had been working for over a month. The sergeant major of the unit escorting them to the airport wished them a good journey. Before saying goodbye, the Belgians asked him: "Where in fact are you going now?" The sergeant major seemed to hesitate for a moment and, closing the door of the aircraft door, replied: "To Brussels!" Slightly disappointed that they could not accompany their British friends, they consoled themselves with the thought that they must have been very important, since a plane was sent from England to pick them up.[110] In his after-action report, Major Lepine added a note of thanks to the Belgians, mentioning Holvoet and Temmerman as "two of the best signallers I ever had".[111]

Operation 'Trueform'

At the end of July, after several weeks of hard fighting in which little ground had been gained, the American 1st Army under Lieutenant General Bradley succeeded in breaking through the German lines around Saint-Lô, in the western half of the Normandy frontline, when Operation 'Cobra' was launched. Along the eastern half of the frontline, German forces were kept fixed by the British 2nd Army under Lieutenant General Miles Dempsey and the Canadian 1st Army under Lieutenant General Harry Crerar, preventing the Germans from withdrawing forces to reinforce their positions in the southwest. On 1 August, the American 3rd Army was activated, commanded by Lieutenant General George Patton. The advance of American forces was spectacular and by 13 August, their forces were enveloping the German forces – mainly the 7th Army and the 5th Armoured Army – to positions just south of Argentan, 14 miles southeast of Falaise. The Germans now held a front to the west, north and south that became increasingly hard to hold and started withdrawing their forces to the east.

Given this situation, the SAS Brigade planned to parachute teams west of the river Seine in the area between the Mantes – Conches line in the north and Mantes – Dreuin the southeast and bounded by the river Risle in the west, over two nights between 16 and 18 August. Ten men would be provided by Lieutenant Colonel Mayne's 1st SAS, forty would be provided by Lieutenant Colonel Franks' 2nd SAS, and sixty-two would be provided by Captain Blondeel's 5th SAS, with Franks being appointed as overall force commander. The task of this composite force was to harass the enemy, with a priority on the destruction of petrol tankers and dumps, as it was believed the Germans were short on fuel and interference with their petrol supply might result in tanks being discarded.[112] The operation was planned on short notice, so secure DZs could not be guaranteed.

The Belgians were divided into six groups. Party 1, 2 and 3 consisted of five men each. Party G, H and M, consisted of eleven, sixteen and fifteen men respectively.

Party 1

The young 1st Lieutenant Heilporn, whom his subordinates had known as a corporal before attending a British officer school, wanted to carry out his mission perfectly, in order not to jeopardise his promotion and to prove to his old comrades that he was worthy of his new rank. Part of his team was Staff Sergeant Schils, a career NCO with an impressive service record, Corporal Georges Patyn, not very talkative but effective, Lance Corporal Victor Vivey, who was the youngest, and Lance Corporal Albert Claessen, one of the longest serving in the unit, together with Schils and Patyn.

On the morning of 17 August, the party landed near Saint-André-de-l'Eure and Pacy-sur-Eure on an unplanned DZ. A kitbag got lost. The team set off to the south of Boisset-les-Prévanches, where locals informed the men that the Germans had not left any petrol dumps behind. No traffic could be observed on the road between Saint-André-de-l'Eure and Pacy-sur-Eure, but explosions could be heard in the direction of Evreux. They found out the Germans were destroying stockpiles and the airfield. Throughout the day of 18 August, Heilporn sent a patrol to the main road to lay an ambush and scatter tyre busters, but only tanks were seen, impervious to tyre busters and small arms. The team moved on to the forest of Mérey, to the north of the village of Bretagnolles.

On 19 August, a patrol sent out towards the main road was unable to do much while the area was illuminated by a burning petrol storage tank that the RAF had set on fire. On 21 August, rain delayed the reconnaissance operations. In a village,[113] the team was fired upon, but lacking automatic weapons, could not return effective fire and had to withdraw. On 22 August, the arrival of the Germans forced them to evacuate their hiding place in a barn and on 23 August, they contacted elements of the vanguard of the American army.[114] Schils described how the chaotic, rapidly changing situation, almost turned into a drama:

> We were dropped too late, in the sense that the German troops still in the Falaise pocket would like nothing better than to surrender. On the other hand, several groups were dropped without being given an accurate description of their area of operations. I remember one day we noticed a soldier along the road. We thought it was a German who was mining the road. We opened fire. At the same moment, the Germans also fired on the poor men. Only then did we realise that it was Ravet from party 'H'. Fortunately, this mistake had no nasty consequences.[115]

Party 2

Party 2 consisted of Sergeant Henry Verschuere, Corporal August De Belser and lance corporals François Hellegards, Karel De Belser and David Kowarski.

On 17 August, the team jumped from the same aeroplane as Party 1, Stirling LJ873 of No. 620 Squadron, RAF.[116] Verschuere landed in a forest in the vicinity of party 1's DZ but could not find any member of his group during the night. Only the next morning he came across another team member. The two men decided to attack the enemy traffic between Evreux and Pacy-Sur-Eure. Tyre busters augmented by plastic explosives stopped three lorries, upon which they opened fire. The result of this action was unknown due to the darkness. No fuel storage sites were found, but in addition, they cut at least fifteen field telephone lines. The information gathered – the destruction of a railway tunnel by the Germans, the presence of White Russian troops in Saint-Germain-de-Fresney, etc. – could not be forwarded because a radio was lacking. On the 23rd, the two men were picked up by American forces and subsequently reunited with their teammates.[117]

Party 3

Party 3 consisted of Sergeant Maurice De Vulder and lance corporals Franciskus Huybrecht, de Saint-Guillain, Camiel Verfaillie and Jan Vos.

Early on 17 August, the men were dropped by Stirling LJ865 of No. 620 Squadron in the Saint-Just Forest and had great difficulties assembling; several were missing. The team moved to a wooded area east of Saint-Marcel during the night. On 18 August, De Vulder contacted the local FFI head, who led the team to an abandoned farm along the main road to Gaillon, during the next night. On 19 August, an initial reconnaissance could not identify any petrol dumps. An ambush was laid at night, but no vehicles showed up. A day later, still nothing was found. The team moved north and occupied an LUP in a small wood. On the 21st, it was raining hard and they stayed in the wood, moving once more to another wood the following night. On 22 August, they were forced to stay in the wood due to heavy artillery fire but managed to find a cave in which to shelter. The next day, they again experienced heavy artillery fire but were finally picked up by American forces in the afternoon of the 23rd.[118,119]

Meanwhile, de Saint-Guillain had landed in a forest but had to wait till dawn to bring down his parachute from the trees. He then tried to find any teammates and found Vos, with whom he continued the search for the others. In the evening, after contact with a civilian warning them about the presence of Germans nearby, both men split up again. A new civilian contact brought de Saint-Guillain into contact with a farmer, who fed him and helped track down the others. They found two and enabled him to link up with Vos and Huybrecht in the morning of the 21st. At midnight, de Saint-Guillain had a meeting with Visée and Pus from party H. On 22 August, the three men left tyre busters on the road from Fresney[120] to Boisset-les-Prévanches. Again, at midnight, they intended to link up with Visée and Pus at the same RV, but the latter were unable to make it due to the large number of enemy troops in the area. On the evening of 23 August, the three men came into contact with American ground troops, who agreed to recover them an hour later. In the meantime, they had to pack their kit. At that time, they noticed three Germans coming out of the forest and called to them to surrender. The Germans refused and opened fire. The Belgians returned fire. Vos wounded a lieutenant, who was taken prisoner, but died afterwards.[121]

Party G

Party G consisted of Major Delelienne, warrant officers Rudolphe Groenewout and Arthur Delagaye, staff sergeants Maurice Flasschoen and Jacques Doome, officer candidates José Tinchant and Daniel Pécher, Corporal Jean Gigot,[122] troopers Jules Fraix, Alphonse Delsaer and Jean Lox and six other ranks from the British 2nd SAS.

On the evening of 17 August, Party G was taken to Stirling EF322 of No. 299 Squadron, RAF. The aircraft was deemed unserviceable, but the flight proceeded without difficulties. When airborne, Delelienne, who could have remained at the brigade HQ as liaison officer but volunteered to participate in operations, contacted the pilot. He returned from the cockpit, reassuring his team it would be dropped on the briefed DZ. Without warning, the red and green lights went on. It was shortly after midnight. The first two jumpers did not immediately exit the plane since the lack of prior warning caused a slight hesitation.[123,124]

Delelienne, a former cavalry officer serving in the 2nd Lancers Regiment during the 1940 campaign, estimated he had to jump first, although the commander was normally in the middle of the stick. As a consequence, he was completely isolated after his landing on the ground. He barely had time to get up when he saw two guns pointing at him. He had landed on top of an armoured patrol and was captured immediately. He was taken to a German officer who mumbled something along the lines of "shoot him!" Using his torch, the officer took a closer look at him and then told him in English: "You participated in the 1936 Olympic Games of Berlin." Delelienne made a gesture that could mean both an affirmation and a denial. The German then continued in French: "You were a good rider and a loyal opponent...which saves your life."[125] He was sent to Germany and spent the rest of the war in Oflag[126] 79 in Braunschweig.[127] The members of his group, who carried out searches around the dropping zone, would only learn in 1945 what had happened to him.

The other team members were also highly dispersed around the DZ. In addition, the drop took place over a mile north of Amfreville-la-Campagne, at about 9 miles from the intended DZ.[128]

Delagaye was the second to jump. He hurt his arm when he collided with an equipment bag and landed on a fence, injuring his left leg. At the time of the landing, shooting was going on and flares were lit. About 100 yards further in the forest, he noticed Germans but did not see a single teammate. He searched for more than two hours, but to no avail, and hid in a bush for the night. The next day, he could not move either his arm or his leg. Afraid of being discovered after a German had almost run into him, he moved to another location, where he hid until 22 August, when he contacted a farmer. The latter told him that the villagers had seen four men digging in their parachutes but did not know what had happened to them. Delagaye remained in hiding until the arrival of the first Allied troops, to whom he passed on information about the enemy, which he had obtained from the French.[129]

Groenewout searched for his comrades for more than an hour. Finally, he found Doome and Delsaer. A mile from the DZ, they ran into Flasschoen. He was wounded in the leg and had only his .45 pistol,[130] his kitbag having become detached upon exiting the aircraft and smashed. During the day, the team hid at some hundred yards from the village of Amfreville-la-Campagne. In the evening, the men left their LUP but could only advance some 3 miles due to the condition of the wounded. Nevertheless, during their move, they managed to destroy two lorries on the road between Amfreville-la-Campagne and Villettes early on the 19th. That morning, they got help from a farmer, who agreed to take the four men in his cart, hidden under the hay. To gain time in reaching the originally planned DZ, the team moved through the woods by daylight.

Arriving at a plateau, they came across a petrol dump protected by anti-aircraft guns, as well as SS troops. A German opened fire, forcing them to withdraw. When contact was broken, Flasschoen and Delsaer were missing.

The two others, not having found their missing comrades, moved on towards Saint-Aubin-d'Écrosville, where they arrived after midnight on 20 August. The village was crowded with convoys and the team contacted a farmer, who kept them in hiding in the loft of a farm occupied by Germans. On 22 August, they retrieved their packs which had been abandoned in the wood. Next, they destroyed two enemy lorries, but were subsequently asked to refrain from further action, for fear of reprisals, and linked up with American forces on 23 August and returned to Arromanches the next day.

Tinchant had a normal landing. Once his parachute doffed, he removed his kitbag and recovered his rifle and bergen, disposed of his parachute and moved to cover. On his way to the tree line, he came across Pécher, who had lost his kitbag – the sling having broken – and been knocked unconscious during a hard landing. Moving on, both men bumped into a sergeant and three troopers from the 1st SAS, and later on, they found Fraix and Lox. The men hid in the forests of Saint-Amand-des-Hautes-Terres. At dawn, they set out to reconnoitre the area and encountered a woman who informed them that plenty of Germans with armour were around; they could observe some as close as 650 yards from their position. Later that day, a boy served as a guide to accompany them to the forest of Elbeuf, north of Mandeville. Not having been given an RV and their radio set being incomplete and damaged, precluding any contact with the remainder of their party, the decision was made to conduct the mission on their own.

On 18 August, a reconnaissance was conducted in the direction of Saint-Germain, to find a suitable area to set up a base for Tinchant's group. When darkness fell, they set up base in a wooded area on a hill north of Saint-Germain-de-Pasquier. During the night, the group was split in three to harass the enemy. On the roads between Neubourg and Elbeuf, plenty of German transport could be observed. After midnight, the Germans tried to ease the burden on the main road by deviating convoys through the road from Louviers to Elbeuf. Two groups each managed to stop and set fire to a lorry.

On 19 August, civilians reported dense German traffic on the road between Louviers and Elbeuf and a secondary road between La Saussaye and Saint-Pierre. The same night, Tinchant and Pécher set fire to two lorries in a railway tunnel under a road, preventing the latter's use and obliging the enemy to use an already congested main road. On the way back to their base, they fired on two more lorries loaded with troops but had to break contact when reinforcements arrived.

On 20 and 21 August, no significant actions were possible, due to heavy German troop concentrations near their LUP. On the 22nd, the frontline came closer, and the Germans were withdrawing in a somewhat disorderly fashion. A day later, patrolling was resumed and in Saint-Cyr-la-Campagne some thirty prisoners were taken, mostly Poles and Russians. There was contact with advancing American ground forces on the road from Neubourg to Elbeuf, and afterwards some more prisoners were taken.[131]

Party H

Party H consisted of Staff Sergeant Pierre Pus, sergeants Jacques Levaux, Marcel Visée and André De Rechter, corporals Marcel Engelen and Maurice Ongena and troopers

Roger Natengel, Alexander Lamiroy, Albert Ravet, Emile Delvigne, Robert Laurent, Philippe Machiels, Georges De Block, Dieudonné Frison, Henri Bonne and Bernard Kowarski.

Having been dropped by Stirling LJ835 of No. 196 Squadron on 18 August[132,133] after midnight near Saint-Germain-de-Fresney, 2 miles from the planned DZ, the stick was widely dispersed. In addition, several kitbags containing signal equipment, two Sten guns and an M1[134] carbine were lost during the descent. Helped by information provided by civilians witnessing the presence of troops in the area, it still took more than twelve hours to reassemble most of the stick.

Reconnaissance activities and information provided by local sources showed that the anticipated petrol dumps were not present anymore. German forces were still present, though; some 200 Germans with some thirty-five vehicles were reported in a nearby chateau, as well as a tunnel used as an ammunition dump, guarded by some twenty *Waffen-SS* troops with light machine guns and dogs.

During the night of 18-19 August, an ambush was laid, with tyre busters placed on the road. After three hours, the party withdrew. From information reported by an American HQ, it was learned that at the moment two lorries with enemy soldiers were about to cross each other; both were stopped by tyre busters. Assuming they were being ambushed by troops in front of them, the occupants of one lorry opened fire on the second lorry, whose occupants returned fire. Fifty-two Germans were reported killed.[135]

On the night of 19-20 August, one element scattered tyre busters on the road from Saint-André-de-l'Eure to Pacy-sur-Eure. Lorries parked on a farm were reported by farmers but could not be attacked as they were heavily guarded. However, the next day they were shelled by the Americans.

On the night of 20-21 August, a group moved to the road from Saint-André-de-l'Eure to Ivry and cut communications on the road between Mousseaux-Neuville and Fresney. They reached a farm called 'Ste-Marguerite', where they were able to contact Frison, Bonne and Kowarski.[136]

The next day, local farmers informed the Belgians that the Germans estimated some 150 paratroopers were operating in the area. The SAS party once again placed tyre busters on a couple of roads but had a narrow escape when a German lorry ran into their position at the same moment and opened fire on Delvigne, Ravet, Natengel and Laurent with a lorry-mounted machine gun. They withdrew to the relative safety of the forest and shortly afterwards heard a bang after a tyre buster destroyed the tyre of a German lorry, which crashed into an isolated building. An hour later, an enemy despatch rider on a motorbike also became the victim of a tyre buster. Upon observing that the road was also used by civilians, Pus decided to have the remaining tyre busters removed.

On the morning of the 22nd, Lamiroy, who was posted as sentry, observed some ten Germans approaching the Belgian position. The Belgians opened fire. More Germans arrived, but at the same time, they were being shelled by American mortars, dangerously close to the Belgian position, which was only separated from the enemy by yards. The Belgians had no losses and managed to link up with American troops around noon, effectively ending their mission.[137]

Party M

Group M consisted of Captain Jean Dulait, 2nd Lieutenant Paul Thonard, Staff Sergeant René Mombel, sergeants Andre Stevens, Franciscus Van Uffelen and Freddy Emonts-Pohl, corporals Michel Mas and Albert Meisch and troopers Jacques Oosters, Gustave Flasschoen, André Houet, Henri Sougnée, Arthur De Lison, Roger Nizet and Jean Hébette, as well as Corporal Burton, a 2nd SAS signaller.

In the late evening of 17 August, the party boarded its assigned aircraft, Stirling LJ821 of No. 299 Squadron,[138] after being directed twice towards the wrong one. Since the navigator found it impossible to conduct an accurate drop in two passes, the drop had to be conducted in a single pass. The parachute insertion – at an excessive speed and too high above the ground – took place close to the village of Surville, to the southwest of Louviers, in the early morning of the 18th.[139]

Thonard, the second-in-command of Party M, had finally been promoted. At 48 years, he was the oldest of the unit. Going through a tree, he scraped his left leg and bruised his knee, but using his owl whistle, he managed to assemble his five-man team in about forty minutes. Stevens also had a badly bruised knee, while Meisch was hanging in a tree 15 feet above the ground and had to be helped by De Lison. Both their parachutes were stuck in trees, and it took two hours to recover them. Since the soil was too hard to dig, parachutes and kitbags were hidden in ferns. Sougnée, from another team in Party M, joined Thonard's team.[140]

Elsewhere on the DZ, Nizet had problems with the harness of his parachute, which did not unbuckle. Fortunately, De Lison was close and managed to help resolve the issue. Both men then noticed an unfolded parachute and found Hébette lying on the ground with his leg injured by the extension rope of his kitbag. At dawn, Nizet and De Lison reconnoitred the surroundings but found no familiar landmarks. The most urgent thing now was to hide and find a doctor who could take care of their wounded comrade. A haystack provided initial shelter but proved far from adequate. When a farmer approached their position, he was halted by Germans. Nizet held his weapon ready to fire and thought: "If they discover us, they will not get away with it, but what's next?" Fortunately, the Germans passed without noticing them. In the evening, Nizet knocked at the door of a farmhouse and aimed his pistol at the chest of the man who opened the door. He was lucky; the man was the mayor of the village and, more importantly, the father of the local resistance chief, and agreed to house the wounded Hébette.[141]

Some six hours after landing, German voices were heard at Thonard's location, as a party moved in to settle down for the day, some 15 yards west of the SAS team. Thonard tried to reconnoitre the eastern side of his position but almost ran into two Germans walking down a forest track. He followed them for some 50 yards and discovered about fifty others at the northern edge of the wood. Later that morning, a P-38[142] circled overhead and opened fire into the forest, triggering a reaction of a German anti-aircraft battery about 250 yards southwest of the SAS party.

In the evening, Thonard contacted three civilians, who confirmed the presence of an anti-aircraft battery at Surville, with twenty-six Germans, while reporting a twenty-man static signalling unit along the Le Neubourg – Louviers road and huge numbers of Germans in the forest of Acquigny. More importantly, they denied the presence of petrol dumps in the area.

On the 18th, there was still no news available from the other teams in Party M. Throughout the night, lorries, horse carts and a few tanks could be heard moving, although it was too dark to observe anything beyond 10 yards. The next morning, Thonard prepared his team to move south to search for petrol dumps on the Evreux – Louviers road along the Eure river.[143]

Meanwhile, Dulait had landed close to the village's water tower and linked up with four members of his team within half an hour. The plan for the immediate assembly was for two out of three teams to link up around Mombel, who was carrying a luminous ball, but the latter found himself isolated on the DZ. Mombel had fled from Belgium to join the fight, but being far from fit at nearly 40, he learned he was not suited for combat, so he ended up as the unit's secretary. For almost two years, however, he trained hard during the evenings, conducting long marches and other exercises, until he was declared fit to conduct jump training. Only weeks before this operation, he received his jump wings. He contacted an inhabitant of Surville, changed into civilian clothes to conduct reconnaissance activities on his own and would join the remainder of his party on the 21st.[144]

The pre-arranged RV was also useless, since the party was not dropped on the correct DZ. After camouflaging their parachutes, Dulait and his men set off west and arrived in a wood by the next morning. One man was sent out and contacted a farmer, who supplied the team with water and food. In the afternoon of the 18th, the team was visited by Mr Darce, a British agent operating from Acquigny. Valuable information was gained and the agent relayed messages to the SAS Brigade HQ through his channels. During the night, an ambush was sprung on the Louviers – Neubourg road, resulting in four German lorries being damaged, causing four to five hours of traffic delays.

On 19 August, Dulait saw three men from Mombel's team joining his group and found out that Sougnée – whose leg had been injured on landing – was now hiding with local citizens. During the night, Dulait reconnoitred an ambush site on the Louviers – Neubourg road; tyre busters were placed.

The next day, radio contact could still not be established, but the farmer who provided the team with food also handed over a message from Thonard. In the late evening, Thonard's team, including the wounded Sougnée, linked up with Dulait.

On 21 August, De Lison was able to get his hands on a civilian soldering iron and repaired the radio, in time for the next scheduled communications window. Dulait – wearing civvies – visited the wounded Hébette and was satisfied to see he was in good hands. He then contacted Captain Delas, a resistance chief, who advised him to move north, allowing for better ambush sites, but also to minimise exposure to civilians. It had started to rain heavily and on the night of the 22nd-23rd, Dulait's group moved towards Saint-Lubin, near the edge of the wood, some 2 miles west-north-west of the centre of Louviers, where they sheltered in a hayloft and established contact with Britain, sending observation reports.[145] The hiding place was a location "where one had not seen Germans for four years". The next morning, however, some twenty-five Germans arrived and asked the farmer some hay for their horses, not noticing the discreet radio antenna above the courtyard. The hay being located where the Belgians were hiding – and watching the discussion through the cracks of the plank floor –

the farmer energetically repeated "échelle kaput" ("ladder inoperable"), which finally discouraged the Germans to insist, after which they departed.[146]

On the morning of the 23rd, Thonard conducted a reconnaissance of a new LUP and fractured a rib in the process. In the afternoon, Dulait, aided by the resistance, reconnoitred a supply dump and a heavy battery and was able to observe the intact bridges in Lanvier. In the evening, his team moved to the new position in a brushwood, reconnoitred earlier by Thonard. On the 24th, Dulait's team blew up an ammo dump and cross-checked confusing reports on the Allied advance and German withdrawal, while another element took two prisoners. A day later, a link-up with American forces was conducted and seven more prisoners were taken. On the 26th, the team left the area and was back in Fairford three days later.[147]

On 29 August, all elements who took part in Operation 'Trueform' were assembled at the Fairford camp. Although the operation was carried out after a very rapid preparation, with mainly 'blind' drops and therefore considerable risks, it nevertheless contributed to the creation of a climate of insecurity among the enemy. It also gave the Belgian SAS the opportunity to operate in enemy territory and provided them with additional experiences, on top of those they had gained from their training in Scotland.

The wounded – limited in number – would need several weeks to recover.

If any results were achieved, it was thanks to their initiative and adaptability to the local circumstances. During the debriefing, lessons were identified. The after-action reports showed that there was a feeling earlier employment might have been much more beneficial, as the Germans had already withdrawn most of their forces, while there was a lack of information on the Allied advance. Kitbags were deemed too heavy and the limited number of automatic weapons was seen as a deficiency.

Operation 'Benson'

Three weeks into August, Allied intelligence assessed German intentions as withdrawing from the Seine river towards Belgium, possibly making a temporary stand on the Somme river. It was desirable to have as much information as possible regarding the enemy withdrawal. On 25 August, the SAS Brigade tasked the Belgian SAS Squadron to insert a team in the area southeast of Compiègne to report on enemy movements and dispositions.[148]

Originally, Operation 'Benson' was to be commanded by Cassart, but in the end the brigade chose to send him to the Belgian Ardennes, a region he knew very well. Kirschen was selected instead.[149] He would be accompanied by troopers Bouillon, Flips, Moyse and Pietquin, and Lieutenant Franck, a French inhabitant from the area. The team was to be dropped on the night of 27-28 August, preferably on a DZ north of Estrée-Saint-Denis with a reception committee on the ground or otherwise blind on another DZ. Their task – derived from the higher command's instruction – was to gather information on enemy dispositions and movements in the area between Compiègne, Senlis, Soissons and Villers-Cotterêts.

Late on 27 August, the six men boarded Stirling bomber LJ896 of No. 299 Squadron, RAF.[150] Remembering the confusion on the previous mission, Kirschen compared his map with the data of the Australian aircrew, and everything seemed aligned. His only concern was that the aircrew was under strict orders from the RAF not to conduct a 'blind' drop. In the early hours of 28 August, during a thunderstorm, the team was parachuted in the vicinity of Saint-Just-en-Chaussée, between the Somme and Seine rivers. When assembling, certain problems emerged: Kirschen had trouble with his kitbag and sustained a hand injury during the descent; Moyse sprained his ankle in a hollow road; Flips landed on his kitbag and injured himself on the barrel of his carbine; and Franck had an injury to his foot. It was pitch black-dark and there was no sign of the reception committee, so Kirschen was forced to leave their pannier and the twenty containers that had been dropped for the resistance. A signpost showed that the team had landed some five miles northwest of the planned DZ, so Kirschen presumed the pilot had mistakenly believed the blinking light of an abandoned train to be the marking light of the reception committee.[151]

Marching east, the team – slowed down by the injured – came across Valescourt and found a far from ideal hiding place between a dozen trees. With half his party unable to walk any distance, Kirschen suggested his HQ to work on the Paris – Amiens road, which the team had under direct observation. At noon, contact was made with some farmers and shortly afterwards with local resistance leaders. They informed Kirschen that the containers had been recovered and provided information on an anti-aircraft artillery battery at the Montdidier airfield and on German road movements.[152] Kirschen was approached by a resistance fighter suggesting he move to a better hiding place: "Why don't you try the basement of La Folie [The Maddness]?" "La Folie, you say?" Kirschen replied. "This is the name given to this barn because it was used by couples in love. The entrance is hidden behind bushes. I can take you there this evening."[153]

Laying on the damp floor that night in a cellar that smelled of mould, the men regretted they had left their sleeping bags in England to lighten their load. At 5 pm, radio communications with brigade HQ were established; the team received authorisation to operate in the area where it is was located and sent the info received by the resistance earlier in the afternoon.

On 29 August, doctor Caillard dropped by to treat Moyse's ankle and other smaller injuries. The man was calm and quiet. Before examining the wounded, he put down a small piece of paper and said:

> I think this might interest you. Yesterday, at the crossroads of Saint-Just-en-Chaussée, a German officer was directing military traffic. He made every vehicle stop, checked his map, and pointed out the route to follow. Since this intrigued me, I watched him for a few minutes. At a certain moment he suddenly wiped the sweat from his forehead and went into the café to drink a glass of red wine. I followed him and saw him putting his map on the table. While he paid no attention, I copied the map. This is my sketch: this is the coast along the Channel and this line is the Somme.

"But that's great, doctor!" Kirschen replied. "What you have there is the overview of all the German divisions on the Somme! All the numbers of the divisions, the sectors of the divisions in front, the numbers of the reserve divisions and even the location of the army headquarters."[154]

The sketch covered the area from Abbeville to Saint-Quentin. This valuable information had to be reported to England as soon as possible. Just at the moment the signallers were finishing the encryption of the message to be sent, however, a German self-propelled gun appeared at the barn and its crew was surprised by the SAS team. Flips and Bouillon opened fire with their automatic weapons. The Germans took cover behind a wall and set the barn on fire with incendiary rounds. Flips and Bouillon then chased the Germans and fired some rounds, while Kirschen, Moyse and Pietquin dismantled the radio set, hid it in a ditch and withdrew to the neighbouring fields. Franck, who was not at the barn, joined Flips and Bouillon, but was shot in the arm. Flips and Franck were then able to link up with Kirschen, whose party remained hidden in haystacks for the remainder of the day. Temmerman described the uncomfortable situation:

> Each paratrooper chose one of the straw bundles and crawled towards it to hide. The bad smell of damp straw was sometimes replaced by the smell of smoke coming from the burning barn. There it was too hot, here it was too humid. The rain fell on the straw, ran down the stems, infiltrated between the collar and the neck, and ran down the back. Now and then, a large raindrop splashed on the face. The straw prickled the hands, the cheeks, and the neck! The night, slow to arrive, brought only partial improvement. Stacked cubic bales of compressed straw provided a less precarious shelter than the sheaves. A careful reconnaissance showed that the Germans occupied the village in force. Dinner consisted of a few biscuits and vitamin-enriched sweets.[155]

The next morning, Kirschen returned to the barn and found Bouillon, who had remained hidden in a small wood. As no Germans were seen, Moyse retrieved the radio set to finally transmit the important message on the German dispositions. Establishment of contact was difficult, but finally succeeded. It was a long message: 125 words, all sent twice to be sure it came through, while London interrupted them several times to ask for additional repeats.

At the end of the afternoon, maquisard Lucien came to check and bring food and was happy to find the team more or less unharmed. But some Germans showed up and took positions close to the barn, disrupting their meal. They quickly returned to the previous day's hiding place to spend another night in the rain.

On 31 August, some sunshine brought improvement. Radio contact was established around noon and Moyse smiled after decoding a message that came in, relaying the personal congratulations from Brigadier McLeod for the information transmitted. The team witnessed an artillery duel and noticed the Germans started to withdraw quickly.

On 1 September, Kirschen's team moved into Saint-Just-en-Chaussée, where they linked up with American forces. Kirschen recalled:

> This was the liberation and the city experienced an eruption of joy. Everywhere we were well received, celebrated, people overwhelmed us, kissed us. We went to Saint-Just to see Franck, who had been staying in the mayor's house and who was recovering from the wound to his arm. Drinks, ceremonies, speeches. I luckily managed to repeat the speech which I had delivered in Longny a fortnight ago and which still was applicable. In a German lorry, filled up with petrol given to us by the Americans, we drove to Paris.[156]

On 3 September, the team was ordered to return to England. On their way to Normandy, Regner, still recovering from his wounds, was visited. The latter accepted with joy the offer to leave with his comrades. On arrival in the port of Arromanches, the embarkation officer recognised Kirschen, whom he had met on 8 August, at the end of Operation 'Bunyan'. "How so, you haven't left yet?" he asked in amazement. Kirschen smiled and left it at that. [157]

The operations in France having been concluded for the Belgian SAS Squadron, the unit had been blooded and almost all its operational personnel had participated in at least one operation, some in two. Many of them would see operational deployment again, in Belgium or the Netherlands

Chapter Five

VANGUARD OF THE ALLIED ADVANCE INTO BELGIUM

WITH THE GERMANS WITHDRAWING rapidly following the Normandy breakout, it was expected that Belgium could be liberated soon. From mid-August, the Belgian SAS Squadron would start conducting operations on its occupied national territory, in support of the Allied advance.

Operation 'Noah'

On 15 August 1944, Stirling bomber number EF296 of No. 620 Squadron of the RAF was ready to embark its passengers at Fairford. These included Jedburgh team 'Andrew', two French officers from SOE's 'RF' section and nine members of the Belgian SAS Squadron: Captain Renkin, Sergeant Krolikowski, two signallers, lance corporals Fernand Noël and Philippe Gérard, and lance corporals Albert Bogaert, G. Casier, Claude de Villermont, Jean Mal and Armand Maréchal.[1] For all of them, it was their first operation with the SAS.

In line with what had been planned by the brigade HQ, Renkin's party was to be dropped in the French Ardennes, where he had to organise a base from which to conduct operations, and to prepare for the arrival of reinforcements, to have an SAS force ready at short notice to enter Belgium at the appropriate time. Working on his own responsibility, Captain Blondeel had issued the additional order for Renkin to establish contact with the Belgian resistance across the border.[2] Renkin also received a mysterious little package from Blondeel and carefully stowed it away in his clothes.[3]

In the early hours of the 16th, after a very bad flight, shaken by heavy wind gusts and with a disturbed stomach as a result of the turbulence, Renkin and his team were dropped on DZ 'Astrology' in the French Ardennes, near Les Vieux Moulins de Thilay, less than a mile from the Belgian border. The team exited the aircraft at about 1,150 feet above ground level, and Renkin landed almost a mile from the DZ. Two men lost their kitbag during the descent.

Resistance fighters provided a reception committee, but rain and wind reduced the visibility of the small ground-to-air signal fires. After dropping the SAS team, the fires were extinguished. Renkin believed that the five others had returned to England and that at least part of their equipment containers had remained on board.[4] Unbeknownst to him, however, the others had been dropped 'blind' during another pass over the – now unmarked – DZ, and later linked up with the same resistance group as the SAS party.[5] "The area is not safe, hide in the woods. A guide will pick you up", a resistance fighter told the team. Leaving Krolikowski on the DZ in an attempt to find their missing equipment and assisted by their guide, the team marched towards the French resistance base, over 10 miles away. Upon their arrival, the men were exhausted. One of the lance corporals, who had started medical school before joining England, wondered why it was possible that men who had been training for years to conduct long marches could be so tired after only a few miles. He attributed this phenomenon to mental stress caused by waiting at the airfield and in the plane, conducting a parachute jump, as well as the excitement associated with carrying out a first operation and the fact that they had returned to the continent.[6]

Renkin established contact with 'Prisme', the *nom de guerre* of Lieutenant Colonel Jacques Pâris de Bollardière,[7] commander of the 'Citronelle' inter-Allied liaison mission, whose twelve-man group had been parachuted in the Ardennes, the advance party on 12 April 1944, followed by the main body on 5 June, to organise and equip the maquis along the Franco-Belgian border.[8] After a warm welcome by Prisme, Renkin explained his intention: "I should meet the chiefs of the Belgian resistance." Prisme agreed: "Perhaps you have not noticed, but when you were walking in the woods, you were in Belgium." He explained that both French and Belgian resistance groups operated along both sides of the border since the Germans in both countries belonged to different territorial organisations and didn't conduct any cross-border operations. He then added: "You will easily be able to meet the leaders of the Belgian resistance, one of their liaison officers happens to be here." The liaison officer, Van Bilsen, noticed that the French language of the Canadian captain had a slight Brussels accent. For his part, Renkin discovered Flemish intonations in the voice of the resistance fighter from the Ardennes. Both were correct. Renkin would certainly have been surprised to learn that the first Belgian resistance fighter he met had once been a member of the pre-war Verdinaso movement, and thus a supporter of the 'Dietsch Empire' consisting of the Netherlands, Belgium, Luxemburg and the Flemish-speaking part of northern France. The liaison officer assured him that he would inform his group leader about the presence of 'Canadian' paratroopers.

On the night of the 16th to the 17th, Renkin, accompanied by Krolikowski and de Villermont, left the French camp to carry out a mysterious mission. As ordered by Blondeel, they were going to leave a pouch in which a Belgian flag was stored, together with a written message, which they buried near a large oak. The next day, the group sent a radio message to England: "Flagpost E.Z." At his base in Fairford, Blondeel read the message and was satisfied: "The inscrutable expression 'Flagpost E.Z.' was clearly mentioned. Neither the staff of the brigade nor those who had to decipher the message knew its meaning. But the captain knew in this way that one of his officers had penetrated Belgian territory and had symbolically buried a Belgian flag, kind of, in short, 'retaking possession' of the national territory."[9]

On 17 August, Renkin met Captain Jacques, Prisme's intelligence officer, and both discussed the feasibility of establishing an intelligence network. A day later, Renkin conducted reconnaissance activities around the camp, to get familiar with the surroundings.[10] On 19 August, it was reported that a direction-finding vehicle had been spotted close to the camp. This proved quite annoying since the team could only use two different frequencies to send messages by radio, so frequent changes to avoid detection were close to impossible. The same day, Renkin handed over command to Krolikowski and left the base to contact the local Belgian resistance, together with de Villermont.[11] For the next two days, Renkin and de Villermont visited installations and DZs, accompanied by 'Grégoire', *nom de guerre* of Lieutenant Daniel Ryelandt, commander of Group D of Sector 5 of the Secret Army.[12,13]

Renkin noted the Belgian camps were small, each containing fifteen to twenty persons. He found better camp organisation and discipline compared to the French camps but also had some concerns: there was a lot of movement without using cover, fires were abundant, and the resistance fighters lacked training, including small arms training. It seemed that many were willing to fight, but that the majority preferred simply to remain hidden. The visits were conducted during daylight, since the Germans posted standing patrols at the most important crossroads for the night, making movement in the dark too risky.[14] During the journey, a resistance fighter asked Renkin about the submachine gun he was carrying.[15] The officer was armed with a Patchett,[16] belonging to a limited test series.[17]

On 22 August, the two men returned to the French camp and Renkin decided to establish his own camp for security reasons. He believed that the French resistance fighters talked too much and he had no confidence in them, except in their commanders.[18] In the meantime, according to Lieutenant Louis Barthélemy, commander of Group C of Sector 5 (operating in the Gedinne-Beauraing area), Krolikowski and a trooper arrived at his camp, guided by Jules Dubucq, Barthélemy's liaison officer, on the 21st, and left again in the morning of the 23rd.[19]

On 23 August, the SAS team established its new base at some 300 yards from a Belgian camp and 800 yards from the French camp.[20] The camp carried the code name 'Ruanda',[21] being sited within the triangle of the Secret Army camps with code names 'Bobandana', 'Uélé' and 'Katanga'.[22] The same day, Belgian resistance fighters attacked a German lorry on their initiative but got into trouble when a strong German bicycle-mounted patrol counterattacked. French maquisards came to the rescue and eliminated the Germans, but not without casualties. The SAS team helped care for the French wounded. Renkin assessed the action as reckless since the frontline was still about 150 miles away.

The next day, Renkin was attending the funeral of a French officer in the French camp when shooting started. Around 100 Germans, supported by 3-inch mortars, attacked the camp, but Renkin managed to return to the Belgian base. Although the Belgians had positioned themselves in all-round defence, it quickly became clear that they were surrounded and outnumbered. Renkin decided to evacuate the site, and despite the heavy weight of their bergens, Krolikowski and Mal found a way out, optimally using the terrain to allow the team to slip out of the encirclement. They moved north and halted for the night.

On 25 August, exhausted from their narrow escape and hungry due to the lack of food for over a day, the men were recovering. Krolikowski provided them with a decent breakfast, thanks to a farmer he knew. They also managed to find a guide, with whom they joined a Belgian resistance camp.[23] Most likely, it was the site manned by Barthélemy (Group C), who remembered they arrived around 5 pm,[24] while Ryelandt (Group D) also confirmed the location.[25]

In Fairford, Captain Blondeel was impatient to take part in the operations himself:

> On 25 August, I went to see Brigadier McLeod and asked him to allow me to join Renkin's section to organise an operational base. At first, he refused,

arguing that the commander of the unit should be located in Fairford, where the decisions were made, that he should not risk his life and that his subordinates could perfectly execute the mission without him. I answered sharply, that, if I was not allowed to conduct an operational jump, I would lose face with my men, that I was sufficiently confident I could avoid any reckless action, taking into account the excellent training that we had received in the SAS. The brigadier suddenly realised that I wanted to be dropped into Belgium and exclaimed: "But Belgium is forbidden territory." I answered him naively "Well, I hadn't noticed." With a small smile on his face, he then told me "We will suppose, I didn't know either."[26]

The SAS signallers in the Ardennes received the news of the upcoming arrival of Captain 'Blunt' and Renkin started preparations for the parachute insertion of his CO. Blondeel recalled his operational jump on DZ 'Gordits'[27] from Stirling 995 of No. 295 Squadron, RAF:[28]

I was finally dropped on the night of 28-29 August at 02:35, north of Rienne and east of the road Rienne-Vencimont, between a wooded massif and the road, along with six men: sergeants Georges d'Oultremont, Jacques Van Broekhuizen and Roger De Neef, Corporal Rene Van Haezendonck[29] and troopers Jean Bernard and Florent Grétry. What an emotion at the moment of the jump. German tanks passed a few hundred yards from the area, but this didn't disturb us. I landed without any problem. The whole team of Renkin was present to receive us, along with men from the resistance who carried my rucksack and weapons and led me into the woods, towards a tent lit by a candle. A sleeping bag and a cup of coffee were waiting for me. Even the best travel agency couldn't give you a better welcome! Very quickly we fell into a deep sleep while resistance fighters took care of our security.[30]

d'Oultremont, Van Broekhuizen and Van Haezendonck had joined the SAS only recently, but were among the most experienced, having been deployed as SOE agents before.

d'Oultremont described his integration into the SAS and his arrival in Belgium:

After a few days of shopping in London, I was allowed to present myself at the Belgian parachute unit and was sent to the transit camp of Fairford. Since I was back in the Belgian army, I got my rank of sergeant back and had to give up my rank of lieutenant in the British Army. Upon my arrival, I introduced myself to Blondeel, who received me with a kind but dry welcome. He asked me which area in Belgium I knew well and then told me I could stay in the camp, but that I shouldn't think that, because of my past in the special services, I would be allowed into his unit, since many with a similar history found themselves superior to others! Felling disconcerted, I was led to a tent, where I met very congenial men. I had a bad night, as my tent didn't survive the stormy wind. The next day, I met Padre Jourdain, with whom I quickly became friends. I shared my disappointment and fear that, since several groups had already been dropped behind enemy lines, I would easily be forgotten in Fairford, being unknown in the unit and not having trained with them. However, fortune favoured me – Padre Jourdain had talked to Captain Blondeel, who became interested when he learned I knew the Condroz and the Ardennes well. I was called to see the captain, who told me that I had been accepted and I should prepare myself to be dropped with him into Belgium, the following evening. I was intensely happy and back in my tent, I handed out the six shirts on which I had spent a lot of money at Harrods a week earlier.

The famous cyclist De Neef became my instructor for the next twenty-four hours. He explained to me how to jump out of a Halifax through the door and I was allowed to choose my weapon. I selected the M1 carbine, which I preferred over the Sten, and never regretted my choice. The next day, I prepared my backpack and took care as much as possible not to take any useless stuff. In the evening, before we took off, Blondeel shouted: "No need to tell you, since you're good paratroopers, that the grenades should go into the bottom of the bag." I didn't say anything, but these words kept resounding in my head during the whole trip until the final jump.

Despite some enemy anti-aircraft fire, the flight went well and when the light turned green, we all made a perfect exit from the aeroplane. Around 02:35 hours, the plane reached the DZ and answered the recognition signals. Lights that were carefully shielded from the sides, were turned on. The plane returned and dropped seven men. Grétry injured himself on the knee upon exiting the plane. The others made a good landing except for me, who hit my head. It was a very clear night and I was admiring the sky and the stars. Too bad, because I didn't hear my bag hit the ground and two seconds later, it was my turn, hitting the Belgian soil with my head backwards, so hard that I noticed flashes of light and thought my grenades were exploding! But despite this concussion, I quickly got up, surrounded by members of the Secret Army who were waiting for us; among them, Gendarmerie[31] major Postal, in uniform, Doctor Stercx from Gedinne, majors Barthélemy and Delsaux, veterinarian Vincent and Lieutenant Verbois. I was happy, but for three days I was left with a splitting headache from my hard landing.[32]

Renkin and the maquis retrieved the equipment containers from the DZ, which took about four hours. While Blondeel moved toward a maquis camp – containing supplies stored in numerous small dumps – around 1,000 yards from the DZ, Renkin and his signallers stayed behind to ensure communications with England. Later that day, Blondeel's party moved to the camp where 'Captain Toussaint' (*nom de guerre* of Lieutenant Barthélemy) had his HQ, in a hard-to-access thickly wooded area at a site known as 'Barbouillon', on the d'Aursis[33] brook, 1 mile southeast of the church of Vencimont and just north of the Ruisseau de Felleuwe brook. It was one of several small camps used by Toussaint's maquisards, each accommodating seventy to eighty persons. Blondeel found Group C's overall strength to be at around 300 and noticed order and good camp discipline in Toussaint's HQ, which included a sabotage section, a liaison section, a defence platoon and administrative personnel. Toussaint agreed to take care of administrative support for the SAS party and to provide guards.

Together, they discussed how best to report information on enemy movements and looked into suitable sites to lay ambushes. At that time, the Secret Army had not been authorised to commence offensive operations yet and since reprisals had to be avoided, ambush sites were selected at reasonable distances from villages. A stretch along the Malvoisin – Vonêche road was chosen to conduct a first trial.

On 30 August, Renkin returned to Toussaint's camp and Blondeel sent a message to the commander of Sector 5 asking him to make arrangements for a meeting with the zone commander. Training was initiated on the use of tyre busters and Gammon bombs, as it appeared that the maquis ignored the use of many items with which they had been supplied by the British.

On 31 August, the commander of Sector 5, Lieutenant Count Harold d'Aspremont-Lynden, arrived at the camp and approved the planned operational schemes. He also complained about the shortage of arms and equipment for the 2,000 troops under his command. Blondeel promised to inform the British authorities and provided sergeants d'Oultremont and Van Broekhuizen as liaison elements to the sector commander. Around 4 pm, Blondeel was notified that Debefve's party would join them during the night. Since the previously used DZ was now considered unsafe, another one had to be selected. Around 6 pm, Krolikowski and two maquisards laid an ambush using tyre busters, but with explicit orders not to open fire, since the Belgian SAS was still not supposed to operate on its national territory. Three lorries were stopped, making the road impractical for two hours. Observation showed that the Germans were replacing the flat tyres, so it was decided to augment the tyre busters with plastic explosive charges during future iterations, so the axles would be damaged as well.[34]

In the evening, a reception party under the command of Renkin prepared DZ '*Buffle*' (Buffalo)[35] where the third group was to be parachuted. The reinforcements were commanded by Captain Debefve and consisted of three squads, sixteen men in total. The first squad consisted of Sergeant Déom, Corporal Gaston Heylen and troopers Rossius, Boch and Joseph Levaux. The second squad consisted of Sergeant Goffinet, Lance Corporal Lemaire and troopers Becquet, Hambursin and Gilson. The third squad consisted of Sergeant Ratinckx, Corporal Deprez, Lance Corporal Clamot and troopers Chauvaux and Hendrickx. The group took off in three Halifax bombers (two from No. 298 Squadron and LL328 from No. 644 Squadron, RAF).[36] After a calm flight, the planes arrived over the DZ but had some difficulties in identifying the ground-to-air signal, so had to search for a while before seeing the DZ marking. The parachute drop took place somewhere around 1:15 to 1:40 am on 1 September. The party was widely dispersed and most men landed in the trees. It took all night to assemble and by 8 am, they were found by the maquis.[37,38,39] Some containers were lost and it turned out Deprez fractured his leg while still in the air, a static line from a pannier having caught his foot.[40] Debefve's party was led to Lieutenant Questiaux's camp, where they met Captain Blondeel. Next, they moved to Toussaint's camp, where they linked up with Renkin's party in the evening. Hambursin and Rossius were still missing.[41]

The fact that the brigade agreed to send reinforcements implied to Blondeel that there was no objection to conducting offensive operations, for which these reinforcements were intended in the first place.

The following night, Krolikowski's party, using tyre busters reinforced with plastic explosives disguised as horse dung, ambushed a lorry and a staff car in the same place as the day before. A dozen Germans were killed and documents were captured, which would later be handed over to American intelligence. Two Germans were wounded and taken care of by civilians in Malvoisin. The two wounded were hoping to surrender soon to the arriving Allies, but their superiors decided otherwise, having them evacuated back to Germany instead.

On 2 September, the two missing men from Debefve's party turned up in the camp.[42] Debefve, Krolikowski and three other Belgians conducted a reconnaissance and assessed the results from Krolikowski's attack the previous night. They were hardly at the ambush site when a thirty-man bicycle-mounted patrol appeared, followed ten minutes later by a second thirty-man patrol. Debefve's party withdrew and heard a vehicle convoy on the road. During the night, new ambushes were laid, one by Goffinet's and Ratickx's squads in the woods on a T-junction along the road between Haut-Fays and Gedinne, the other by Debefve and Déom's squad at a T-junction 2 miles northeast of Gedinne along the road connecting Vonêche and Bièvre, but no further enemy traffic was seen.

To attack the enemy far from their camps and villages, the SAS detachment was required to carry out long approach marches. In the afternoon of 3 September, Goffinet's squad was sent to operate on the Gedinne – Beauraing road. Debefve, who remembered well how his friend Limbosch had acquired a lorry during Operation 'Shakespeare', set off with Déom's and Ratinckx's squads to fetch a lorry from Louette-Saint-Denis. At less than a mile from Gedinne, the presence of a few Germans with a lorry was reported by the wife of a resistance officer. Debefve's men entered Gedinne and saw the lorry but were discovered by the enemy, who started a firefight. Several Germans were cut down by Bren gun fire; the remainder fled in the lorry at full speed. It now seemed there were approximately fifteen Germans in the village, with about fifty horses; the latter ran away as soon as the shooting started. Debefve decided to avoid the village and continue to Louette-Saint-Denis, where he managed to find a lorry in fairly good condition. They returned to the camp while avoiding Gedinne. In the evening, maquis sources notified the presence of around 100 Germans surrounding Gedinne, with armoured cars present on the roads, and ambushes laid on the road used by Debefve. Meanwhile, Goffinet laid an ambush on the road between Gedinne and Beauraing. He had seen several armed vehicles passing by, but having no anti-armour weapons, decided to attack anything that would present itself anyway.

At 3:30 pm, an armoured car appeared. Goffinet threw a Gammon bomb in front of the vehicle, while Lemaire opened fire with his Bren and attacked the vehicle from the rear, hitting a fuel can, which exploded and killed four occupants. Two hours later, the same team ambushed a convoy of four vehicles about two thirds of a mile south on the same road. The second vehicle was brought to a halt with a Gammon bomb thrown by Goffinet. Lemaire killed or wounded the four occupants and then shifted fire to the first vehicle, although it was able to escape. Goffinet threw another Gammon bomb on the third vehicle, which was also fired upon by Lemaire's Bren. The lorry caught fire and exploded over 400 yards away. The occupants of the fourth vehicle chose to flee, leaving their vehicle behind, which was subsequently destroyed by a Gammon bomb. During the team's withdrawal, a lorry arrived, presumably to recover the wounded. Goffinet waited to open fire until the Germans got back into their lorry, but many remained hidden in ditches. Eventually, Lemaire hit the lorry with his Bren gun, causing the ammunition aboard to explode, after which the team withdrew to its camp.[43]

The same afternoon, Renkin's party laid an ambush on the road from Gedinne to Wellin. The team was organised into several sub-elements, consisting of an observer (in the direction of the anticipated enemy approach), a man to throw Gammon bombs, a Bren gunner, two men with submachine guns and a three-man cut-off element. At around 6 pm, having waited for three hours, a lorry showed up. It was attacked and when the SAS party withdrew, twelve soldiers of the *Waffen-SS* and nine *Gebirgsjäger* (Alpine infantry) remained dead.[44]

Meanwhile, the resistance sector chief had received the order to start offensive operations. Blondeel's two-man liaison team and some twenty-five resistance fighters ambushed two lorries transporting twenty men each on the road between Rochefort and Ciergnon. A reconnaissance team sent out the next day reported that ten corpses were found and twenty wounded had been evacuated to Rochefort.[45]

On 4 September, Renkin's party was less successful. An ambush was laid on the road from Wellin to Haut Fays, but only tanks and armoured cars passed by. These were not suitable targets since no anti-tank weapons such as PIATs[46] or bazookas[47] were available.[48] Also Goffinet's squad had no luck as nothing happened at their ambush site along the road from Vonêche to Pondrôme. A team commanded by Ratinckx repeated the night ambush from two days before on the Gedinne – Wellin road. They used No. 75 grenades[49] and tyre busters to stop a small convoy. Several vehicles were destroyed and twenty-one Germans were reportedly killed and fifteen wounded.[50]

Since Blondeel had received a signal from brigade HQ to contact the Secret Army's zone commander at all costs, he left his camp in the evening, together with Bernard, his batman, Déom, who knew the area well, and a maquis guide. With Germans moving around on the roads, they had to keep to the woods. Moving fast with minimal equipment, they halted shortly at a maquis base after midnight and continued to the sector HQ, which they reached at 6 am the next morning, only to find no sign of the zone commander, almost infuriating Blondeel. After some sleep, a message was sent out to the zone commander to notify him of Blondeel's arrival and to ask for his intentions. While waiting for a reply, Blondeel instructed the maquis in the use of grenades and laid an ambush on the Ciergnon – Rochefort road from 9 pm till 5 am the next morning, but no enemy were attacked. Several fighting patrols sent out during daylight only encountered armour or heavily protected convoys. The lack of anti-tank rockets severely limited their options. No. 75 grenades were of little use since they could easily be spotted and Gammon bombs required good cover very close to the objective.[51] Goffinet's squad, however, attacked a *Panzerkampfwagen IV* tank when springing an ambush in the morning, possibly at the same ambush site where they spent the night. The tank stopped when seeing No. 75 grenades and started firing. A crew member standing in the turret was hit and a Gammon bomb was thrown, which killed a crew member and wounded another one. The tank drove on for a while but was eventually abandoned beyond Vonêche.

Still on the 5th, Debefve received a message requesting him to arrange the reception of two jeeps and ten men on DZ '*Buffle*', a mile from the Rienne – Hargnies road. While fierce combat was taking place between Germans and Americans in the French town of Hargnies, Debefve moved to the DZ on foot, accompanied by Heylen, Levaux, Toussaint and a guide. Some three quarters of an hour before reaching the spot, when coming out of the woods, his party was surprised by a command to halt, almost immediately followed by fire from automatic weapons. Throwing themselves to the ground, Debefve shouted the password, and the fire stopped at once. They had run into a resistance party. By 11:30 pm, they had reached the DZ, which was guarded by around 200 resistance fighters, the Secret Army having received the order to permanently occupy the '*Buffle*' area three days earlier.[52,53]

Minutes before midnight, the first aircraft – a Stirling bomber – dropped Padre Jordain, Captain[54] Jean Limbosch (the unit's medical officer), Ongena and Frison. In the air, Limbosch encountered difficulty releasing his kitbag and decided to drop it completely from about 60 feet. The entire party, along with their twenty-two containers and three panniers, landed in the woods. Limbosch landed on top of a pine tree and struggled to get down but finally managed to do so without too much trouble. He felt relieved finding his kitbag with most of his medical kit stowed inside in two US Army haversacks and was happy his careful packaging had minimised damage to the medication bottles. Following contact with Debefve, the party marched to a resistance camp about 5 miles away, where Limbosch contacted the local maquis doctor, noting the resistance's lack of preparedness to handle severe casualties. Upon finding Deprez, Limbosch immobilised his fractured lower leg with a wire splint and made arrangements for his later evacuation by American ground forces.[55]

Around 2:30 am on the 6th, two Halifax bombers – one from No. 298 Squadron and LL309 from No. 644 Squadron RAF[56] – arrived over the DZ and dropped Sergeant Van Uffelen, Meisch, Bonne and Trooper Edgar Vieuxtemps with two jeeps, twelve containers and four panniers. The jeeps, which had been dropped using four parachutes per vehicle, were rapidly removed from their cradle and made operational, firmly impressing the resistance, and by 5:30 am, the DZ was vacated, after which the party moved to their camp without incidents.[57,58]

Meanwhile, the town of Hargnies was taken by American ground forces but lost again following a German counterattack, then taken again. When they retook the village, the Germans killed women and children and set fire to the buildings. On the Belgian side of the border, no enemy convoys were observed on the roads, but *Panzerkampfwagen IV, Panzerkampfwagen VI* (Tiger) tanks and armoured cars were reported on the roads connecting Gedinne, Rienne, Vencimont and Wellin, while some thirty *Panzerkampfwagen* IV and VI tanks remained in Gedinne. During the night, Rienne was liberated by the Americans, who linked up with Debefve's party in Gedinne on the afternoon of the 7th.[59]

The same day, Renkin's party linked up with American forces after a narrow escape the day before, when on their way to Gedinne they had been surrounded by approximately 1,000 Germans and had to hide for six hours while enemy search parties came as close as 30 or so yards before they were able to return to their camp.[60]

In the meantime, Blondeel had still been waiting for news from the Secret Army's zone commander. On 6 September, he received word that the *Waffen-SS* had torched the village of Navaugle and, hoping to intercept the Germans, he laid an ambush northeast of the village, without result, however. Another ambush was laid in the pouring rain during the night of 6-7 September, again without any result. Back at the sector HQ, there was still no news from the zone commander. Blondeel's party was about to get some sleep when they learned that 1,000 Germans with armour and artillery were resting in Mont-Gauthier, where they had arrived the previous evening. Assuming the enemy would soon resume movement to the east, a daylight ambush was prepared on the road between Mont-Gauthier and Haversin. Blondeel was joined by the two sergeants of his liaison team and by d'Aspremont-Lynden and three Bren gunners. While the ambush was still being established, a German car with four men approached and surprised the Belgians. A Gammon bomb was thrown on the vehicle, which continued for some 50 yards before coming to a halt. The only survivor of the car fired with an MG 34.[61] Fire was returned with a Bren gun, which had a stoppage after a few bursts. Blondeel's men started to outflank the German machine gunner when a small lorry appeared. A resistance machine gunner panicked and left his position, allowing the vehicle to escape. Shortly afterwards, a column of some fifty well-camouflaged vehicles, including armoured cars and 150 mm guns, passed by, but any attempt to attack it would have been suicidal. Later, a solitary lorry appeared and was destroyed along with its occupants, which included two *Waffen-SS* officers. A site exploitation was conducted and documents were found which were later handed over for further examination. When several armoured fighting vehicles arrived, the party withdrew through the woods to its base, noticing blind machine gun fire before the last German vehicles left the area by sunset.

On 8 September, American ground forces were close to the sector HQ and a messenger reported that the zone commander was at an unknown location. Blondeel decided to return immediately to his camp. The sector commander gave him a ride and he was reunited with his men in Gedinne, now in full control of the 4th American Infantry Division. An American colonel contacted at the first command post he encountered saw no possible employment for the SAS men but asked for an interpreter. Van Haezendonck was made available to help him out. Having received a signal from brigade HQ urging him to meet with the zone commander and with Major Fraser,[62] Blondeel again planned a renewed attempt to establish physical contact. Assuming it far too dangerous to send his entire 'Noah' party along the roads barely under the control of American ground forces, he decided to first conduct a jeep reconnaissance on his own, assisted by a guide, while moving in the direction of the operations 'Brutus' and 'Bergbang' areas of operations (see below).

On 9 September, Blondeel left with the sector commander in his jeep driven by Bonne, intending to reach the area of Fisenne (10 miles northeast of Marche-en-Famenne), where the zone commander had last been reported. The jeep was unable to cross the Ourthe river, though, as all bridges had been blown and German forces occupied the eastern bank in strength, so Blondeel returned to Haversin, where the sector commander had established his new HQ.

Another attempt was made on 10 September. The sector commander's uncle volunteered to act as a guide, fully knowledgeable of the fact that he risked being shot when captured as a non-combatant. This time, the jeep managed to ford the Ourthe near Hampteau and no German presence was observed. Upon reaching Fisenne, Blondeel learned that the zone HQ had been dispersed, but that the zone commander was at Amonines, a few miles to the south. After some detours and some very rough going to avoid roadblocks and mines, Blondeel finally managed to meet him. He also found 2nd Lieutenant Mathijs, Corporal Demery and Barette, all assigned to Operation 'Brutus', as well as Major Fraser. Major Bastin requested Blondeel assist in mopping-up operations to clear the area from German pockets. Blondeel agreed to start operating from his present location, moving to the east, while at the same time planning to collect and refit his personnel who had been overrun by the advancing Allies in a camp in Chevetogne. This would apply to Operation 'Brutus' personnel since those on Operation 'Bergbang' were out of reach, the area separating him from theirs being too dangerous to cross in light vehicles.

Blondeel set off toward Bois de Saint-Jean,[63] a forest to the northeast of La Roche-en-Ardenne, where the remainder of the 'Brutus' party was located, and ran into the spearhead of American forces on the road from Samrée. Reunited with Captain Dulait, Blondeel was informed that Trooper Lox had been killed and Officer Cadet Tinchant wounded in an engagement shortly before.

On 11 September, Lox was buried and Tinchant was evacuated by ambulance. Blondeel held a meeting at the zone HQ and planned the establishment of new camps in the area, but received orders from brigade HQ to return to England with his men. In the confusion caused by rapidly changing orders and the dispersal of personnel, some of the written instructions issued by Blondeel were misinterpreted and a group of resistance fighters – possibly under the impression they had been recruited by Blondeel – presented themselves at an airfield in Brussels and were sent to England by error, later causing quite some administrative issues.

The next day, Blondeel left Gedinne by jeep towards Pessoux, Namur – where he crossed the Meuse over an American pontoon bridge – and on to Brussels, where he met Renkin at the central police station, which served as RV. Their return to England had been postponed till the next day.

On the 13th, Blondeel learned about the loss of Freddy Limbosch (see below). The group departed from the aerodrome at Evere towards Fairford, where the aircraft landed in the early evening.[64]

Operation 'Brutus'

On 31 August, Mathijs was tasked to proceed to Belgium to establish liaison with the commander of Zone V of the Secret Army and to pass on instructions to Captain Blondeel related to the employment of his troops in Belgium, as had been agreed upon between the commander of the SAS Brigade and Special Force Headquarters (SFHQ).[65] The Belgian SAS Squadron was to be employed under the overall operational command of the commander of the Secret Army's Zone V, but detailed local command arrangements had to be agreed upon between both parties. The squadron's general task was to hinder the German withdrawal through Belgium by any means, either independently or closely integrated with the local resistance.[66]

On the night of 1-2 September, having taken off from Fairford, Mathijs' team was inserted on DZ '*Sophocle*' (Sophocles), over 3 miles southwest of Durbuy and less than a mile southeast of Somme-Leuze. He was accompanied by Barette and Demery and by British Major Hugh Fraser from the GHQ Liaison Regiment's squadron attached to the SAS Brigade. The reception committee, provided by the Secret Army, was well organised and contact was rapidly established with Lieutenant Dambois, a liaison officer from Zone V. The party was taken to a shelter near the DZ to spend the rest of the night.

In the late morning, the group moved off to a wood a mile north of Erezée. After an uneventful 15-mile march, Mathijs met Major Bastin, the Secret Army's zone commander, and arrangements were made to link up with Captain Blondeel, which would prove unsuccessful in the short term.

On 4 September, the four men moved at night to a wood less than a mile southeast of Amonines, close to Bastin's HQ. A signal was sent to England requesting to drop three jeeps and their drivers at the '*Sophocle*' DZ.

The next day, Mathijs and a liaison officer from the Secret Army were on their way to DZ '*Zèbre*' (Zebra), east of Bois de Saint-Jean and 2.5 miles east of Samrée, when they noticed lights and vehicle noise near the DZ's location. Assuming the DZ was in German hands, they returned to their base. Their assumption proved correct when the day after, reports came in that the DZ was now occupied by a German artillery battery. But Mathijs was also informed that a jeep and personnel had been dropped over a mile from the planned DZ.[67]

The '*Zèbre*' DZ site, a large open field, was surrounded by plenty of woodland, which provided cover once the DZ was cleared and was also used to hide resistance fighters, as many young men were assembling at areas designated by resistance leaders, hoping to be armed quickly through supply drops, to take part in the final fight against the occupier. The Germans, however, had selected the same site for use by the *Lehr- und Versuchsbatterie* (Training and Experimental Battery) 444, which had been tasked to conduct the very first operational employment of the V-2 ballistic rocket. Well away from major roads, the area had the required characteristics to provide concealment for the large and vulnerable logistic convoys and the vast amounts of protective troops associated with this highly complex system and was within range of Paris, the planned target. Following a failed launch attempt on the 6th, the battery and its large force protection package moved further east. An alternate site a mile east of Sterpigny was identified, still behind the 7th Army's frontline, which had moved from the Meuse to the eastern bank of the Ourthe on the night of 7-8 September. From this location, two rockets were launched on the morning of 8 September, one of which probably disintegrated at high altitude, while the other impacted near Paris, killing and wounding dozens.[68,69]

On 5 September, Company Sergeant Major Delagaye departed from Keevil aboard Stirling LJ888 of the RAF's No. 196 Squadron with his squad, which consisted of Visée, Tinchant, Pécher, Mombel, Geldof, Lox, Gigot and Clasen.[70,71] Reaching their destination early on the 6th, the aircraft circled for over half an hour since no signals could be seen at the DZ. Then some lights were observed, and the stick was dropped. All landed in the trees, and voices were heard all around. It turned out to be the maquis. With their help, the men regrouped, and soon the containers were found, but only in the afternoon, and the party was accounted for. Clasen was found injured. While the containers were being collected, Delagaye set out to look for a suitable base site and found a jeep and some containers in the middle of a wood. A camp was established at this location, the security of which was improved in the evening by placing tyre busters connected to Lewes bombs[72] on the neighbouring roads to prevent any surprise. When informed of upcoming drops on two separate DZs, Delagaye split his force between DZ '*Zèbre*' and DZ '*Mulet*' (Mule), but both groups returned the next morning, as no planes had been seen.

On 7 September, the jeep was prepared for operations. Delagaye continued setting up an information network and sent out a mixed party of SAS and Secret Army personnel to arrest some collaborators in Chabrehez, who were subsequently handed over to the *Gendarmerie*. Being without a radio set, Delagaye used the maquis' channels to request sending a new set, as well as supplies for around 250 men from the resistance.[73] Meanwhile, Mathijs received a message that Blondeel was unable to link up. His orders were then sent by a runner, but later it turned out they were never received by the squadron's CO.[74]

On 8 September, patrols were conducted from Delagaye's base along the roads and in a small farm near the Bois Saint-Jean Castle, a patrol was attacked. Three resistance fighters were wounded in their legs, the remainder running away. Assisted by the maquis doctor, the SAS men dressed their wounds and arranged for their evacuation.[75]

A new parachute drop being announced, Mathijs went with a Secret Army officer to see the party at DZ '*Zèbre*', but no resupply drop took place, which was a big disappointment for the 200 Secret Army members waiting to be armed. The next morning, he returned to Amonines and ran into a German artillery position which opened fire at 300 yards without inflicting harm. At 5 pm, troops from the 1st SS Armoured Division *Leibstandarte Adolf Hitler* reportedly arrived in Amonines[76] with tanks. Mathijs' radio set was inoperable, but his signallers were able to keep in contact with England through another set.[77] Patrols from Delagaye's base continued throughout the day. Four Germans were happy to surrender, and an escaped Russian prisoner of war and an Australian navigator who had bailed out a month earlier linked up with the SAS detachment.[78]

In the night, further reinforcements would arrive. At RAF Tarrant Rushton, Captain Dulait, Groenewout and De Lison boarded Halifax LL309 of No. 644 Squadron, while Schils, Doome and Fraix embarked on Halifax LL224 of No. 298 Squadron. Each aeroplane also carried a jeep, six containers and three panniers. Dulait's team was dropped around forty minutes after midnight on or very close to DZ '*Zèbre*', followed over half an hour later by Schils' party.[79,80,81,82,83]

Dulait got into contact with Lieutenant Nizet from the Secret Army and made arrangements for upcoming reconnaissance and offensive operations and the anticipated link-up with American ground forces. He was informed that the latter were now at Hampteau, Somme-Leuze and Maffe and that the bridge at Salmchâteau had been destroyed.[84] Also, Amonines had now been reached by an American reconnaissance patrol. Mathijs contacted the Americans around 9 am.[85] In the afternoon, Dulait, who was conducting a reconnaissance to find a suitable position for his jeep, was warned that a German armoured car had detonated a mine placed at the crossroads southwest of Chabrehez, while skirmishes had occurred with some of the sentries posted by the Secret Army, one of whom had been captured. Dulait drove to the crossroads to check personally but found no sentries. Leaving his jeep in the woods, he continued on foot along the road to Chabrehez but was shot at by well-camouflaged Germans. He assessed the enemy was trying to infiltrate the woods. Concerned that the nearby DZ might get compromised, Dulait issued quick orders to organise defensive positions at the edge of the wood. He would occupy the crossroads with his jeep and a few men, Nizet's men and three SAS men would take positions to his right. Dulait's jeep fired from different positions to bind the enemy, while looking for an opportunity to conduct a flanking movement to attack the Germans.[86] Delagaye had been urged to come to the Bois Saint-Jean Castle at once. On arrival, Delagaye's party was tasked with moving through the woods to chase the enemy. Upon approaching the edge of the wood, the Germans, with a strength equivalent to two platoons, opened fire with machine guns, 20 mm guns and rifles. The clash lasted for an hour and a half, after which the Germans withdrew towards the Samrée – Vielsalm road. When the calm returned, Lox was found dead, having a back and neck wound, while Tinchant was wounded in the back. A search of the site revealed multiple first field dressings and later the Belgians were told several dead bodies and wounded had been found in the wood. Later that day, Blondeel joined the 'Brutus' party and met Mathijs and Fraser.

On 11 September, after Lox's funeral, Blondeel and Dulait left and Delagaye brought his men to the castle while waiting for further orders.[87]

Mathijs and Barette conducted a night patrol with two American jeeps on the Marche-en-Famenne – Aywaille – Liège road to collect information for the zone commander. The previous night, the CO had agreed that Mathijs' party would stay at the disposition of Fraser.

On 12 September, Mathijs and Fraser went to DZ '*Zèbre*' to link up with Dulait. Mathijs was given command over two jeeps and their crews and went to Malmédy, where he would link up with Fraser. One jeep broke down in Salmchâteau and had to be towed by an American reconnaissance unit. Inspection revealed the engine had to be replaced. De Lison was ordered to stay with the vehicle and Mathijs continued with the other jeep and two men and conducted a reconnaissance to Bütgenbach.[88]

Meanwhile, Schils went with a resistance fighter to Wibrin to fetch rations for the group. On his way back that evening, he was taken prisoner by seven Germans coming out of a wood near the Wibrin – Bois Saint-Jean road but managed to escape in the early hours of 13 September. He reached the camp in the morning and set out again to search the woods, but nothing was found. On the return journey, a tyre was punctured and Schils was thrown out of the jeep and sustained injuries to the arm and leg.[89]

Still on the 13th, Mathijs returned to Amonines, but could not find De Lison and his jeep on the way back.[90]

Meanwhile, on the 12th, Delahaye had been visited by Lieutenant Mac Davies, from the GHQ Liaison Regiment, with instructions to leave the castle and report at once to Major Hardwicke[91] of the 21st Army Group in Brussels. Since the maquis had left, and being without transport, Delahaye requisitioned a lorry and came back to pick up his men when he met Dulait. New orders were given: the party would leave the next day, pick up almost a dozen resistance fighters in Haversin and return to Brussels.

In the city's central police station (in the town hall), written instructions were waiting and, in the evening, Dulait ordered a move to Evere airfield. The group missed the plane, however, but was flown back to England a day later.[92]

Mathijs was still in the field. The same evening, he went to DZ '*Diane*' to collect a supply drop with weapons, but a farmer told him the aircraft had passed over ten, minutes before his arrival. He returned to Amonines and reported to Fraser and the zone commander.

On 15 September, Mathijs, Fraser and their wireless team moved to Brussels, where orders were received for Mathijs' return. Fraser and the wireless team were to stay in Belgium. Major Hardwicke was then contacted to arrange Mathijs' flight to England, which happened on the 19th. Mathijs was happy with the performance of the resistance as far as he had been able to observe when dealing with their HQ. Despite an acute shortage of arms, it was very well organised; their liaison was excellent and plenty of information had been provided. But he also found that his mission could have been more useful if they had been inserted a week earlier.[93] Also, Fraser was full of praise for the Secret Army. Although he considered Zone V's organisation over-centralised to the point that it restrained the initiative of local commanders, he nevertheless found it an efficient organisation and he admired the Ardennes' inhabitants' courage, determination and loyalty. He was very critical of the lack of sufficient help by the governments of the free world, given the atrocities the poorly equipped resistance – and population – were facing.[94]

Operation 'Bergbang'

By the end of August 1944, the SAS Brigade anticipated a German withdrawal behind the defensive positions of the *Weststellung*, for which the bulk of their forces would move through Belgium. While Operation 'Noah' was to be launched as soon as possible, another operation, code-named 'Bergbang', was a 'be prepared to' mission that could be initiated if and when the conditions would warrant it. It had to be planned in detail in advance, so as not to waste any time should its execution become necessary. The aim was to disrupt the German lines of communication between Belgium and Germany and to hinder the German withdrawal. The general scheme of manoeuvre consisted of the insertion of a reconnaissance party, its reception arranged by either SFHQ or a reception committee from Operation 'Noah', or, as a last resort, by a blind drop, to reconnoitre suitable base areas, after which a follow-on party would join them to conduct offensive operations. As the situation on the ground might develop quickly, the plan had to be flexible and a contingency in which all parties were to be dropped simultaneously in small groups, had to be taken into account.[95]

On the night of 1-2 September, the reconnaissance party, consisting of Cassart, Demoor (signaller), Deheusch, Quirain[96] and Thévissen was flown in. The insertion DZ was located in Solwaster and a reception committee had been anticipated. Since it was only about a mile from the German border,[97] it was agreed that a blind insertion would not be acceptable, and the DZ near Somme-Leuze, which was also used for Operation 'Noah' would serve as an alternate DZ. In the event, no signals could be observed on the primary DZ, so the team was dropped at a rather high altitude in a bright moonlight, at the alternate DZ about an hour after midnight. Having landed near a road on which lorries were driving, Cassart was happy to find out his team's insertion had not been noticed. He rapidly found Demoor and Thévissen but could not find the others. While looking for their teammates, they almost ran into a German bicycle-mounted patrol, which silently passed behind a hedge about a yard away without using lights. At 5 am, the search was suspended, to be resumed an hour later. By 8 am, they learned from a farmer that the others were safe, although Quirain had hurt his leg upon landing. The farmer brought them into contact with the local resistance.

The next day, it rained, which it would continue to do throughout almost the entire operation. Dressed in plain clothes, Cassart cycled to Mormont, about 13 miles away, to contact the commander of Zone V of the Secret Army and 2nd Lieutenant Mathijs (who was on Operation 'Brutus'), but they turned out to be absent for several days. A signal was sent to brigade HQ to pass on information and to request supply drops at Louveigné and Bronromme and arrangements for Secret Army reception committees were made.

On 4 September, Cassart prepared an ambush to capture a German vehicle, since he wanted better mobility. Just as his men were occupying their positions, Lieutenant Pierre Dambois of the Secret Army told him he had found a vehicle and would drive them to where they had left their equipment along an allegedly fast and safe route. However, in Petite-Somme, on a small road north of the road from Barvaux to Somme-Leuze, at a spot some 600 yards southwest of the Château de Petite Somme, the group bumped into a fifteen-man enemy column with four vehicles and was taken by surprise. Cassart managed to warn those who were about 50-100 yards behind, but Dambois was killed and Cassart, who was still in civilian clothes and now unarmed, having given his weapon to a wireless operator a few minutes before, was taken prisoner. He was beaten and several times threatened to be killed, but played dumb, pretending not to know anything of these 'bandits'. During a search, all his belongings were taken, even his spectacles. He was transported to a police station in Durbuy to be interrogated. On their way, they passed the village of Septon, where his convoy was attacked by the resistance. Cassart was taken to the cellar of a house but managed to escape through the roof some fifteen minutes later. He was lucky: throughout his ordeal, he noticed wounded uniformed resistance fighters being murdered. After travelling through the woods, he arrived at a farm guarded by the resistance, where, after having proved his identity, he was pointed in the right direction to join his team, with which he was reunited an hour later.

On 5 September, signals were exchanged with brigade HQ and in the afternoon the party set off for Bronromme, which they hoped to reach the next day. Their guide, however, made a mistake along the route, while the cross-country movement was initially conducted at about two thirds of a mile per hour, despite having left their heavy kit behind, except for the radio. Radio contact with England was not without difficulty. From around 8 am on the 6th, the signaller tried to send messages on the emergency frequency, then again at 10 am on the primary frequency, and several hours were spent decoding incoming messages, seriously hampered by unfavourable light conditions. The team crossed the Ourthe south of Sy and had to halt at 5 pm to listen to the radio. Again, trying to decode messages proved problematic. When it got dark, the team sheltered in an isolated farm, where the men could dry their clothes, have a meal and get a few hours' sleep. Shortly after 2 am the next morning, a new and excellent guide led Cassart's team to the maquis of Chapelle Saint-Roch, covering 4 miles in under an hour. Half an hour later, another guide accompanied the team straight to Harzé and before sunrise the team reached a woodland area around the Amblève river and contacted the maquis of Quarreux, in time for its next communication window at 10 am. Atmospheric conditions were still bad, though, and only fractions of messages came through. Cassart also realised that England had no better reception of his messages either. Being asked what he was doing, it was tempting to reply he was taking some leave, but he did not want to waste the radio's batteries. During the day, a German column passed at about 100 yards away, possibly to verify whether the Quarreux bridge could be blown. Nothing happened, but it interrupted the radio transmissions as the radio set and its antenna had to be dismantled. In the evening, Cassart was informed that a reception committee was ready at the Bronromme DZ for the night, but he was also surprised to hear that on the night of 5-6 September, a group had been dropped. He had no idea where they were nor how to find them.[98]

Meanwhile, in Britain, Van der Heyden and the men who remained became increasingly impatient and found the long wait hard to endure. Finally, on 5 September, the next team would be inserted. It consisted of Van der Heyden, Crèvecœur, Emonts-Pohl, Maurice Flasschoen, Polain, Jean Demery, Marcel Moreau, Balsat, Delvigne, Oosters and Mas. During the pre-flight briefing with the aircrew, the DZ location was checked. The intent was to drop the team near Bronromme. It took off from Tarrant Rushton in a Stirling bomber in the evening. Shortly before the drop, the aeroplane had to conduct evasive action when encountering German fighter aircraft. The team got ready but had to wait while the aircrew tried to identify the anticipated DZ marking. None was found and Van der Heyden was asked whether he preferred to return to England. He had no intention of doing so and requested a blind drop a few miles away, just in case the Germans were occupying the pre-planned DZ.[99] In reality, the team landed to the west of Höfen, 1 mile south of Monschau, in Germany. The medical orderly and the signaller were injured. A pannier containing Gammon bombs exploded and three other containers were lost.

In the early hours of 6 September, the containers were hidden, and reconnaissance patrols revealed they had jumped over Germany. By 9 am, however, the containers were discovered by the Germans, who searched the woods until 5 pm, firing at random. Mas got separated and was discovered by a German, whom he reportedly killed, but was able to rejoin the group. The decision was made to move west towards Belgium on a compass bearing; no maps were available. In Kalterherberg, they narrowly avoided running into a German patrol. Afterwards, they passed through a row of concrete 'dragon teeth' anti-tank obstacles and saw guard towers from which messages were exchanged in Morse code. Thanks to the bad weather, they passed unnoticed. By 2 am the following morning, the team had to take a break, several men being exhausted.

The day of 7 September was spent in the woods. Running out of food, the men had to revert to their emergency rations. At night, movement through woodland and marsh areas was resumed and by the end of the night, a busy road could be observed. A patrol sent out during daylight on the 8th allowed the team to pinpoint its position.

Tyre busters were laid on the road, which was crossed at night, and in the morning of the 9th, the team was back in Belgium, where it contacted civilians in Solwaster. Van der Heyden started setting up an information network and in the afternoon his party ambushed a staff car and a lorry on the Sart – Francorchamps road. A counterattack was mounted against the Belgians and Flasschoen and Demery were slightly wounded. The Germans subsequently cleared the wooded area but without success. Their HQ located at Sart left for Germany afterwards. In addition to the wounded, three others were sick, one of whom had malaria while another was exhausted. Two parties were recruited from the resistance and Crèvecœur took a group to the Jalhay – Belle Croix road, while Van der Heyden took the other one to the Sart – Francorchamps and Spa – Francorchamps roads. They had nearly run out of ammunition when Sergeant Pus' party was dropped almost on top of them.[100]

Upon hearing an approaching aircraft and hoping for a drop of long-awaited supplies, the Secret Army element manning the area had lit signal fires, likely letting the pilot believe he had reached the correct DZ. In reality, Pus' party, which consisted of twelve men, was dropped on DZ '*Xénophon*', far from its intended DZ at Bronromme. Most men landed in the trees, but Mas was able to link up soon with Van der Heyden, who immediately integrated the reinforcements into his own team.[101,102,103]

On 10 September, containers were recovered, but one was lost when the Gammon bombs it contained exploded. Several parties were sent out. One was sent to Spa, where they met an American reconnaissance unit, which they provided with information on the ground and German dispositions. A maquis party was sent to a bridge to capture German sentries believed to guard it and brought two German vehicles back to base.[104] A third party, commanded by Pus, was sent to lay an ambush along the road between Baraque Michel and Jalhay. When Pus and Peere were at the point of conducting a reconnaissance, they were challenged by two Germans. They shot them, but, noticing they were surrounded by several small groups, they withdrew. Less than a mile to the southwest, Pus' party ran into a group of some seventy Germans but got away safely. After a break to rest and check their weapons, the men moved on. Some ten minutes later, Pus noticed that a man was missing, but no one was able to tell him what had happened. Confident that he knew the RV, Pus moved on.

The next day, his party went out to the Jalhay road again but still had no news from the missing man. Being overrun by American forces, they helped them clear the woods and took ten prisoners which they handed over in Jalhay.[105] The same day, Crèvecœur's party laid an ambush on the road from Solwaster to Germany, without much result.

On 12 September, Van der Heyden got word that German tanks were at Bronromme. Moving off with their four captured vehicles, mechanical failure had them stranded in Spa that night. He then learned that all action had ceased and proceeded to Brussels the next day.[106]

In the meantime, Cassart, who was in the Amblève valley, learned that Sprimont was now in Allied hands and decided to shift his attention to the southeast. On the 9th, there was a lot of radio traffic, but again, the quality was bad and mostly a waste of time. Around 5 pm however, an important message was announced for 7 pm. It turned out five aircraft were expected that night, three of which were carrying equipment

astle farm of Friz Hill in 1942. *(E. Blondeel)*

Captain Blondeel during training in Britain. *(Pegasus Museum Diest)*

arachute company standing
n formation at Friz Hill. Note
he Belgian flag painted on the
eft on some helmets.
E. Blondeel)

Belgian paratroopers at Friz Hill wearing British battledress with British rank insignia. On the righ sleeve, the British parachute qualification badge and a Belgian flag can be seen. Headgear consiste of a maroon beret with a metal Belgian lion cap badge. Note the general issue British steel helme carried by the second man from left, which would be replaced later on by a different model designe for airborne forces. *(F. Van Haezendonck)*

Close combat training at Friz Hill. *(Pegasus Museum Diest)*

arachute training using a construction to replicate the exit hole in the floor of a bomber. *: Van Haezendonck)*

arachute training. The proximity of trees indicates that this was most likely not a parachute jump ut a ground training session designed to learn the drills to handle the parachute after landing, specially procedures to overcome windy conditions. *(Belgian Armed Forces)*

Jules Regner on top of the gymnastics bar during physical training. *(Belgian Armed Forces)*

Andre Stevens giving a lecture on the Sten gun at Friz Hill. *(Private collection)*

ean Lox behind a Bren gun at Friz Hill.
Private collection)

River crossing training. *(Belgian Armed Forces)*

Field training exercise near Inverlochy, Scotland.
(F. Van Haezendonck)

Belgian paratroopers during training. They wear a Denison smock, various elements of the British 1937 pattern webbing, the airborne troops helmet, A-frame bergen and Lee-Enfield rifle.
(F. Van Haezendonck)

Log physical training at Inverlochy.
(Belgian Armed Forces)

Obstacle course training at Inverlochy. *(Belgian Armed Forces)*

Willy Deheusch and Emile Lorphèvre manning a 3-inch mortar during training. *(Private collection)*

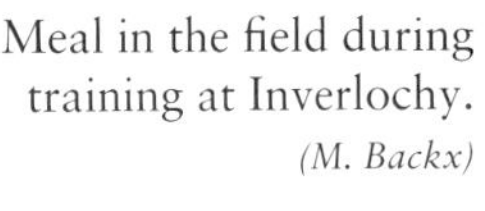

Meal in the field during training at Inverlochy. *(M. Backx)*

Group picture during training at Inverlochy. *(Y. Brasseur)*

Roger Natengel and Alexander Lamiroy in front of Loudoun Castle, Scotland. *(Y. Brasseur)*

Jeep in front of Loudoun Castle. Standing in the back of the jeep is Raymond Holvoet. *(B. Otté)*

Belgians with British instructors at Inverlochy. *(Y. Brasseur)*

Albert Mestdagh with monkey Emile, the unit's unofficial mascot for a while. *(Van Haezendonck)*

Kirschen's team with French locals in the Longny-au-Perche town square during the conclusion of Operation 'Bunyan'. *(J-V du LAC de FUGÈRES)*

An S-phone as used during operations in France for communicating with aircraft. *(Private collection)*

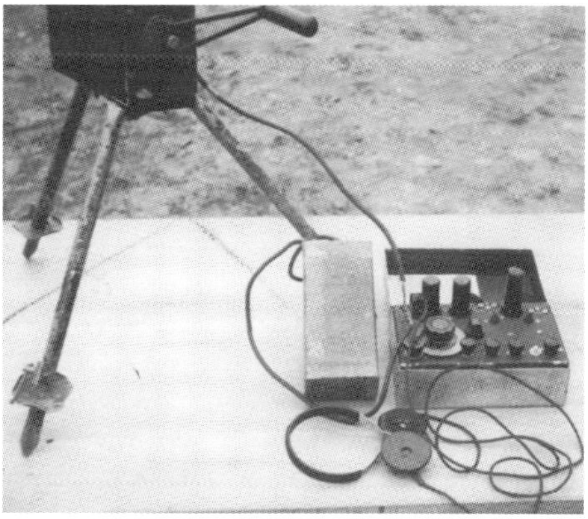

Sketch showing the Geman dispositions behind the Somme river. This high-value information obtained by the resistance was reported to the SAS Brigade HQ by Kirschen's team during Operation 'Benson'. *(Pegasus Museum Diest)*

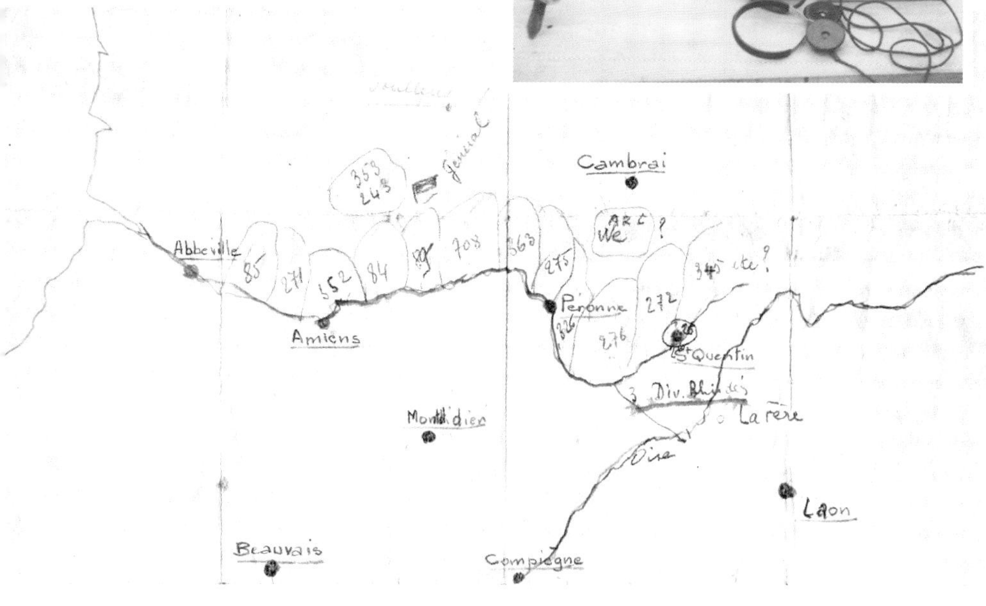

Belgian SAS jeep at Beauraing during Operation 'Noah', September 1944, with Trooper Edga Vieuxtemps behind the steering wheel and Sergeant Franciscus Van Uffelen behind the Vickers I machine guns. Both had been dropped with their jeep by a Halifax bomber. *(E. Blondeel)*

Warrant Officer Rudolphus Groenewout (left) and Trooper Arthur De Lison (in the jeep) talking to a clergyman during Operation 'Brutus', September 1944. They were part of a team that had been dropped with their jeep by a Halifax bomber. Note the sawn-off bars of the radiator grille, a practice initiated by the British SAS in North Africa to improve radiator cooling. *(J. Temmerman)*

Captain Blondeel on a short family visit in Brussels, at the end of Operation 'Noah', on 12 September 1944, having been separated from his wife and two daughters for more than five years. *(ANPCV)*

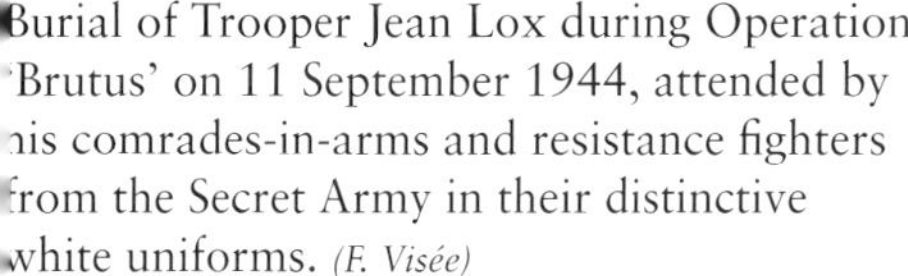

Burial of Trooper Jean Lox during Operation 'Brutus' on 11 September 1944, attended by his comrades-in-arms and resistance fighters from the Secret Army in their distinctive white uniforms. *(F. Visée)*

Belgian SAS party during Operation 'Bergbang', September 1944. *(J. Temmerman)*

Ambush layout shown in an Operation 'Noah' report. The ambush would be sprung by throwing a Gammon bomb. A primary Bren gunner provided enfilade fire, a second one was on standby, and additional light machine guns might be used. Two 2-man protective parties would put No. 75 grenades across the road once the ambush had been sprung and were to block enemy reinforcements. Along the enemy flank, men with Gammon bombs or bazookas were to engage the enemy. Behind them, men with M1 carbines and No. 36 grenades were to cover their withdrawal. The action would not last longer than a minute, after which the patrol was to withdraw to a pre-arranged RV. *(Belgian SAS Archives)*

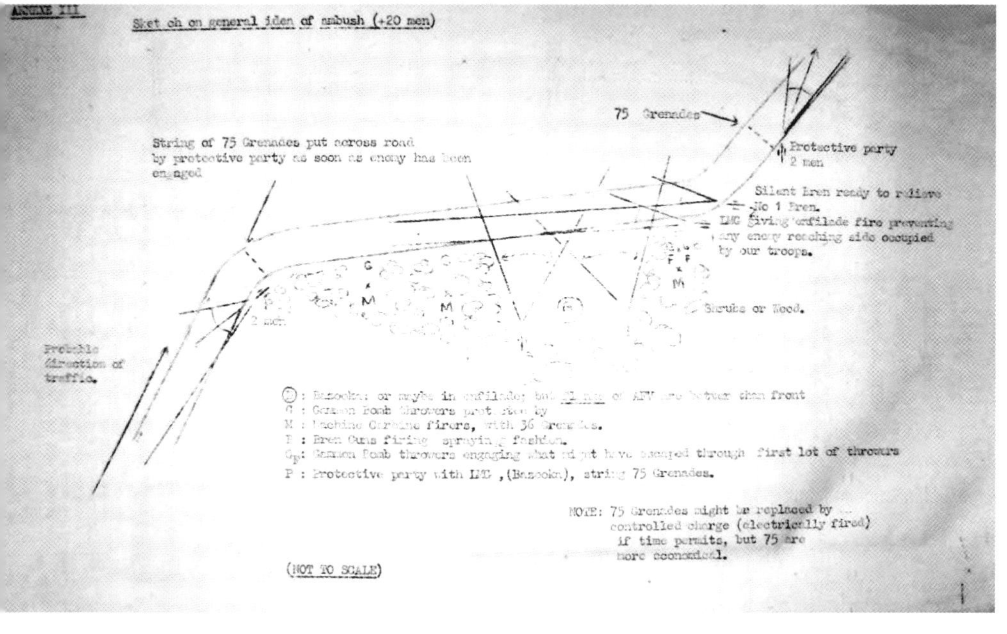

Belgian SAS personnel who conducted Operation 'Gobbo', including Operation 'Friesland' Back row (L to R): Corporal Daniel Demoor, Warrant Officer Rudolphus Groenewout Corporal Gaston Heylen; front row left to right: Sergeant François Siffert, 1st Lieutenant Emile Debefve, (then Lance) Corporal Joseph Levaux. *(J. Temmerman)*

'A' Troop jeep in Givet, before starting their patrolling activities along the Meuse river. *(B. Otté)*

Jeep maintenance during the Ardennes counteroffensive, with 1st Lieutenant Van der Heyden behind the jeep in the forefront. Note the armour plate at the back, the extended range fuel tanks in the rear compartment, the frontal armour plate with armoured glass and the drum magazines for the Vickers K machine guns attached to the bonnet. The tyres are fitted with snow chains for driving on snow-covered roads in icy conditions. *(M. Backx)*

'roopers Laurent ßoch and Daniel Rossius with jeep at the ßelgian SAS quadron's HQ ı Froidfontaine. *M. Backx)*

ßelgian SAS jeep nd 15-cwt lorry ı the Ardennes. Note the body rmour worn by he dismounted ıan in front. *M. Backx)*

'A' Troop patrol test-firing its Vickers K machine guns. Note the frontal armour plate with armoure glass and the drum magazines on the bonnet, the sawn-off bars of the radiator grille and the capture German helmets in front of the jeeps. *(B. Otté)*

'A' Troop jeep test-firing its Vickers K machine guns. Note the extended-range additional fuel tank to the side of the gunner. *(M. Backx)*

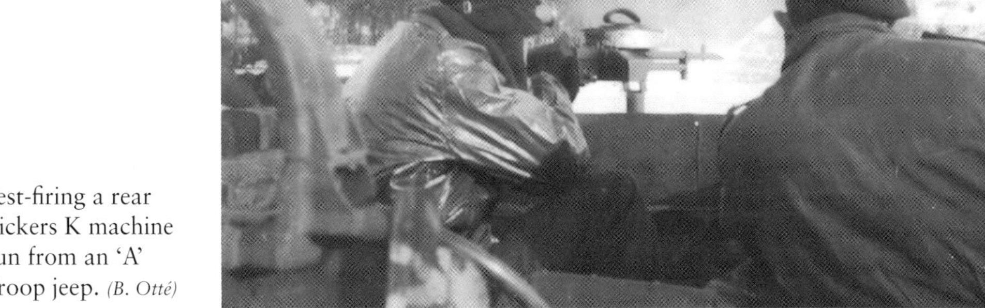

Test-firing a rear Vickers K machine gun from an 'A' Troop jeep. *(B. Otté)*

'roops wearing ewly-issued white now camouflage uits. *(B. Otté)*

'he victims of the ande massacre. *Ministry of Justice)*

The remnants of 1st Lieutenant Renkin's jeep after being hit by a German gun in Bure. *(Renkin family)*

Belgian SAS jeep bringing in a German prisoner of war. Note the simplified painted SAS logo on the front of the jeep and the single Vickers K machine gun on the driver's side. *(B. Otté)*

German prisoners of war in the Ardennes. *(B. Otté)*

A Belgian SAS patrol bringing in German prisoners of war in the Ardennes. *(Archives 40-46)*

Belgian SAS jeeps during gruelling winter conditior in the Ardennes. Most of the men are seen wearing white snow camouflage suits. *(B. Otté)*

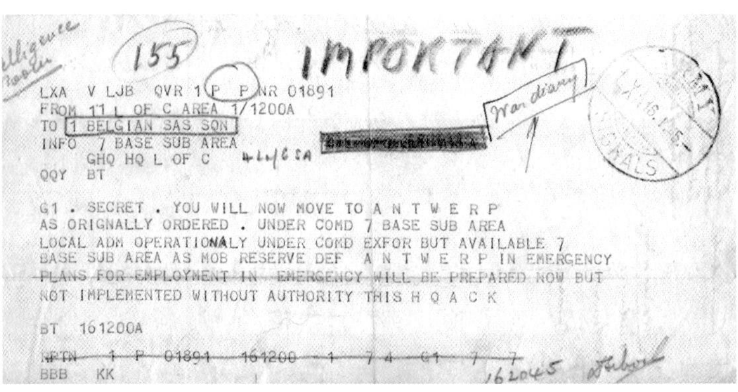

155 IMPORTANT

LXA V LJB QVR 1 P P NR 01891
FROM 11 L OF C AREA 1/1200A
TO 1 BELGIAN SAS SQN
INFO 7 BASE SUB AREA
GHQ HQ L OF C
QQY BT

G1 . SECRET . YOU WILL NOW MOVE TO A N T W E R P
AS ORIGNALLY ORDERED . UNDER COMD 7 BASE SUB AREA
LOCAL ADM OPERATIONALY UNDER COMD EXFOR BUT AVAILABLE 7
BASE SUB AREA AS MOB RESERVE DEF A N T W E R P IN EMERGENCY
PLANS FOR EMPLOYMENT IN EMERGENCY WILL BE PREPARED NOW BUT
NOT IMPLEMENTED WITHOUT AUTHORITY THIS H Q A C K

BT 161200A

NPTN 1 P 01891 161200 1 7 4 G1 7 7
BBB KK

War diary

162045

Message to the Belgian SAS Squadron from the HQ 11th Lines of Communications Area, one of the rear-area logistic support organisations of the 21st Army Group. It shows the typical style and length of messages for sending orders or reports *(E. Blondeel)*

Non-armoured Belgian SAS jeep during rear-area security operations in Berchem, Antwerp, with Corporal Michel Mas behind the steering wheel and Sergeant Count Georges d'Oultremont to his right. *(M. Backx)*

Belgian SAS jeep during rear-area security operations ir Berchem, Antwerp. *(M. Backx)*

and supplies for the resistance. The Allied advance had now reached Theux, to the northeast, while the bridge at Marteau, 3 miles away, had been blown by the retreating Germans. The rapidly changing situation would influence the DZ selection, but by the time the message was decoded, it was too late to reply. Cassart was concerned that the small number of resistance fighters at the Bronromme DZ would be insufficient to absorb the large amount of goods to be dropped, while he assessed that any capability to train the maquisards in the use of the new equipment was largely non-existent. The first aircraft appeared shortly after 11 pm and dropped a team commanded by Heilporn, who had eleven men with him, together with fourteen containers, two of which were destroyed, their parachutes not having opened, four landing far away and four others never to be seen again. Another plane arrived but apparently could not see the DZ marking lights.[107] This was probably the aeroplane carrying Pus' team, who would conduct a blind drop, as described above.

During the night, Cassart made arrangements to prepare Heilporn's team for combat, while the maquis needed the whole night to recover their containers dropped by the other aircraft but ignored by Cassart. Departure on the 10th was set for 1 pm. Cassart used the remaining time to search for the missing containers. Around noon, he heard shots being fired all around and returned to the site at once. He ordered two men to dismantle and hide the radio set and moved in the direction of the noise. He encountered Heilporn, who explained to him what had happened. Small arms had been distributed at will and a resistance fighter could not resist the temptation to fire his new Sten gun at a passing German vehicle on the road to Desnié, despite the warning from his friends to hold his fire. The Germans deployed troops and fired randomly into the woods. The resistance acted similarly and around 1,000 rounds were fired. Cassart made sure he kept his men together and moved between small bushes, hoping to surprise enemy elements along the tracks. The Germans finally withdrew, having suffered a dozen killed. The resistance lost five men, and an American airman was killed as well. An enemy gun had been captured and a lorry had been destroyed by a bazooka operated by Deheusch. At Bronromme, three farms had been torched. Cassart's team moved to Desnié but found no one willing to open his door, so the team went back to Quarreux for the night.

The next morning, American armour appeared, indicating the operation was about to end. Looking for transport, Cassart was happy to meet Mister Legrand of Stoumont, who offered him to use his car from the next day.

On 12 September, Heilporn contacted the nearest American authorities, while Cassart returned to Bronromme, only to find his equipment dump having been pillaged. An RV at the Hotel des Fagnes in Spa was arranged, after which Cassart went to find Heilporn, gave him the same RV, and went on to Somme-Leuze to recover their kit. After recovering a broken-down lorry at a ford at Petithan, Cassart hit a tree when the brakes – affected by staying in the water – failed to work. He made arrangements to recover the lorry, met Major Bastin and then returned to Spa. No one was left and Cassart contacted the maquis of Forêt, where dozens of resistance fighters had been brutally murdered by the Germans only hours before the liberation. Finally, Cassart arrived in Brussels on 18 September. Two days later, he met Major Hardwicke and returned to England the day after.[108]

Operation 'Caliban'

The liberation of Antwerp on 4 September provoked an instantaneous reaction by the German high command to prevent an Allied breakthrough in the lightly occupied area between Antwerp and Maastricht. *Generaloberst* Kurt Student, commander of the 1st Parachute Army – hardly worth that name – was tasked to organise a defence behind the Albert Canal. Using precious time provided by what the Germans assessed as an unexplained hesitation in the Allied advance, Student hastily built his force, mostly understrength, remnants of, or ad hoc formations. His main force included the LXXXVIII Army Corps, consisting of the 719th Division (which had to abandon its defensive positions on the Dutch coast) and some miscellaneous smaller units to hold the line from Antwerp to the west of Hasselt. On the corps' left flank, a Dutch SS battalion occupied the Hasselt bridgehead, flanked on its east by two replacement and training battalions from the *Hermann Göring* Division, also transferred from the Netherlands. The bridges over the canal were blown, except the one at Beeringen. Meanwhile, further reinforcements, including the 6th Parachute Regiment, a battalion from the 2nd Parachute Regiment, the 7th Parachute Division and the 176th Division, were being rushed from Germany to the frontline by train and would arrive by 6 or 7 September.[109,110] In the area behind the Albert Canal in the northeast of Belgium, in the Province of Limburg, another operation was conducted by the Belgian SAS Squadron, code-named 'Caliban' and aimed at cutting enemy lines of communication west of the river Meuse.[111]

On the night of 5-6 September, twenty-six men were dropped by parachute behind enemy lines in front of the advancing Allied ground forces. They were organised into two groups: a section commanded by Captain[112] Ghys, which had a reconnaissance mission, and three sections commanded by Captain[113] Freddy Limbosch, intended to conduct sabotage and harassment operations.[114] The air insertion was conducted by two Short Stirling bombers from the RAF's No. 196 Squadron. Stirling LJ810 contained Ghys' section and one of Limbosch's sections (Ghys, De Vulder, Klein, Siffert, Delsaer, Petit, Hellegards, Vivey, A. De Belser, K. De Belser, B. Kowarski and Vandermeeren[115]). Number LJ848 contained Limbosch with his other sections (Limbosch, Verberckmoes, De Rechter, Melsens, Sas, De Serrano, Switters, Marginet, Veroft, Goessens, Debuf, Vos, Engelen and D. Kowarski).[116,117,118]

The planned DZ[119] was located less than 3 miles south of Peer and over 2 miles west of Meeuwen. The aircraft took off from Keevil around 10:45 pm. The flight was uneventful, but the crew of Limbosch's plane had some difficulties finding the DZ. For almost an hour, the stick had to remain on action stations, the jump being imminent. Around 1:40 am on the 6th, the aircraft released its load. All fourteen men had a good landing, although slightly dispersed, while three containers were lost. The remaining were collected and hidden in a wooded area a few hundred yards to the south, together with the men, except for De Rechter, who was missing and would join the next day. It turned out they had been dropped more than a mile east of Meeuwen, almost 4 miles east of the planned DZ. Limbosch and another man went to the latter, hoping to link up with Ghys, but no one could be found. Meanwhile, reconnaissance operations were conducted in the vicinity, revealing plenty of traffic.[120]

Ghys' stick was dropped to the northwest of the intended DZ, on top of some farms. Delsaer was badly injured by a container while leaving the plane and had to be evacuated to a farm. Klein was injured by the sling of his kitbag, which landed in a tree and Ghys had a sprained ankle. All containers were brought to a small wood northeast of the DZ, with the help of a farmer. A base in the wood was organised and contact with the local resistance was established. Doctor Verschuere, a resident from Peer, came to look after the wounded and stayed with the team throughout the operation. During the night, Devulder's squad was sent out on a reconnaissance patrol, and Melsens squad – part of the other group – managed to establish contact with Ghys party.[121]

At the site of Limbosch, ambush patrols left around 7:30 pm. Limbosch, two Belgians and four escaped Russian prisoners[122] took positions along the road of Bree to Gruitrode; Verberckmoes with a teammate and two Russians covered the road from Helchteren to Bree; De Rechter's squad operated on the road between Peer and Bree. All teams were in position by nightfall. The Germans somehow discovered Verberckmoes' party and for an hour, they swept the road with a car and three lorries, firing machine guns and forcing Verberckmoes' team to stay in cover. When the calm returned, the team placed tyre busters on the road, but nothing else happened and by dawn, the team withdrew to its base. The other parties did not see a single vehicle passing by.[123]

Ghys obtained regular updates on enemy troop movements, which were sent to his HQ. In the morning, four of his men destroyed a German car, killing a major and an NCO. He decided to cease all offensive actions, though, when he received word that the Germans had taken twelve hostages in Peer, threatening to execute them if anything happened again near the town.[124]

Now that Ghys' group had been located, Limbosch decided to move with his men to the former's LUP, leaving the Russians behind. Movement was conducted by squad, first Limbosch with Verberckmoes' squad, followed by De Rechter's and Melsens' squads. The infiltration was slowed down due to the presence of Germans in the area and De Rechter was ordered to proceed to Ghys' position as soon as possible.[125] He arrived in the evening. As reports came in notifying the arrival of the first British tanks in Helchteren, Ghys sent two men towards the town to contact the liberators and provide them with all the information he had at his disposal. One man came back with a request from the colonel in command to provide regular info updates from the next morning on.

On the morning of 8 September, the remainder of Limbosch's group arrived at Ghys' location. The decision was made to ambush the road from Peer to Bree during daylight hours since few Germans appeared to be still in the area. Impeded by his ankle injury, Ghys left an hour before the main body, leaving Klein – who could not walk at all – in charge of the LUP. De Rechter and another man were sent to Helchteren with the latest information but would not be able to return. They would remain with the lead British units, assisting them as guides and interpreters. Soon after reaching the Peer – Bree road, numerous German reinforcements were observed moving west, mainly parachute and *Waffen-SS* units too strong to attack. Limbosch called off the ambush and informed the vanguard at Helchteren, while requesting guidance on how to best assist the advancing forces. Ghys stayed near the road during the day and sent information back to the base by runner, where Klein received frequent and accurate updates from the well-organised network of the White Brigade.[126] That evening, it turned out Limbosch had not returned to the camp.

On 9 September, heavy fighting was reported at Helchteren. It became impossible to cross the frontline and the information flow from the White Brigade was severely interrupted. During the day, ambushes were laid by Melsens' squad, resulting in a destroyed lorry and six enemy casualties. There was still no news from Limbosch; it was assumed that he and four others had remained with the advancing Brits. Eager to join the fight, resistance leaders from other areas in Limburg came to visit the SAS party, requesting arms supplies. The HQ in Britain sent messages with instructions to establish a DZ for the party's own resupply, but owing to the use of a wrong one-time pad,[127] not all communications passed well. A reception party was sent to the DZ anyway and waited between midnight and 2 am the next morning, flashing recognition letters to two planes circling above.

On 10 September, ambush patrols were sent to the roads between Bree and Helchteren and between Bree and Peer. Melsens' squad reportedly killed and wounded at least fifty Germans when an artillery battery moved into the position of their ambush site. All available weapons were fired from point-blank range into the lorries packed with personnel. During the withdrawal, Melsens was killed and Sas was wounded in the arm.

On 11 September, British armour was reported at Peer and Ghys decided to meet them on the road from Peer to Linde. He was also informed by a local that the body of a British officer was lying in the heather at Heide-Huiskens near Linde. He went to the spot and found the body of Limbosch.

The local population had also suffered during the battle involving very fanatic *Waffen-SS* soldiers and German paratroopers: dozens were murdered by the Germans in Hechtel and Helchteren.[128]

The exact events surrounding the final moments of Limbosch have been the subject of speculation. According to Bernard Kowarski and Temmerman, Limbosch insisted on joining the British lines on his own, accompanied by a guide.[129] According to Temmerman, the guide went by the name of Reckers and around 4 pm, Limbosch and his guide came across a small, isolated farm, after which Reckers, who was walking in front, suddenly noticed five Germans in a machine gun position. He warned Limbosch and after checking his map and observing a railway, the latter continued towards a small river along a trail, having given an RV (the crossing of the river and the railway) to the guide. At around 4:30 pm, bursts of fire were heard by the guide, who quickly returned to the small farm and requested a change of clothes. Upon finding Limbosch's body a couple of days later, several impacts were observed in the chest, and his weapon was found next to him, without any remaining ammunition.[130]

The assumption that Melsens was killed having run out of ammunition was the accepted version in several sources, but eyewitness accounts of civilians who had seen Melsens shortly before his death and had found his body afterwards revealed a somewhat different version. They recalled that Melsens was part of a group of four conducting a recce, during which he had left his men in a covered position while proceeding on his own when the remainder of an already partially deployed

German artillery battery coming from the direction of Meeuwen arrived at the site. Almost certain to be discovered and not wanting to risk Melsens being cut off, the SAS party's Bren gunner opened fire, and a firefight ensued. Later on, plenty of empty brass cases were found where Melsens had had his last stand, but his Sten gun, pistol, belt, M3 knife, compass and a loaded magazine were also discovered. His body was found in a different location, though, leading to the belief he might have been captured, disarmed, evacuated and afterwards either summarily executed or shot when trying to escape.[131]

On 17 September, with parts of Belgium still under Nazi control, the Allies launched Operation 'Market Garden'. They intended to cross several major water obstacles and conduct operations north and east of the Rhine to liberate the Netherlands and attack the industrial heartland of Germany. However, the operation did not reach the planned objectives and resulted in a far longer occupation of the Netherlands, where the Belgian SAS Squadron was also conducting operations in Nazi-occupied territory.

Chapter 6

WORKING IN NAZI-OCCUPIED TERRITORY IN THE NETHERLANDS

BY MID-SEPTEMBER 1944, the Allies had liberated most of France, Luxemburg and Belgium. In the north, Field Marshall Montgomery's British 21st Army Group was advancing towards the Netherlands, while General Bradley's American 12th Army Group had reached the Belgian-German border and the area of Lorraine along the French-German border, and General Devers' 6th Army Group was advancing towards the southern part of the Alsace along the Swiss border. In Belgium, the northern parts of the provinces of Antwerp and Limburg were still under German control. Meanwhile, most of the Scheldt estuary, including the northwestern corner of Flanders, was still occupied, which precluded the use of the port of Antwerp, although the port itself had been captured almost intact, in large part thanks to the assistance of the Belgian resistance.

On 10 September, General Eisenhower, the supreme commander of the Allied expeditionary forces, met with Montgomery in Brussels. He explained the condition of the Allied supply system and their need for the early use of Antwerp. He also believed it possible that with airborne assistance, a bridgehead over the Rhine in the Arnhem region could be seized, after which the Walcheren peninsula could be cleared to open the Scheldt and accelerate the logistic build-up, while only minor operations would be carried out along the remainder of the broad front. Montgomery was very eager to attempt the seizure of a bridgehead north of the Rhine and was allocated Lieutenant General Lewis Brereton's First Allied Airborne Army to plan for his operation, which would carry the code name 'Market Garden'.[1]

During Operation 'Market', one British and two American airborne divisions and a Polish parachute brigade would capture and hold the crossings over several waterways in the Netherlands: the American 101st Airborne Division was to secure the bridges from Eindhoven to Veghel; the American 82nd Airborne Division was to secure the bridges from Grave to Nijmegen; and the British 1st Airborne Division (with the Polish 1st Parachute Brigade attached) would secure the Rhine bridge at Arnhem. Meanwhile, during Operation 'Garden', the British 2nd Army commanded by Lieutenant General Dempsey and led by Lieutenant General Horrocks' XXX Corps, would advance through a narrow corridor to relieve the airborne forces.[2] The start date for the operation was tentatively set for 17 September.

Operation 'Regan' – 'Fabian'

A few days after his return from France, 1st Lieutenant Kirschen was eager to join most of his friends still on operations in Belgium. On 10 September, at the brigade HQ at Moor Park, in Rickmansworth, Hertfordshire, he learned that most Belgian SAS parties had now been overrun by the advancing Allied ground forces and discussed future operations with Major Shaw. During lunch, Brigadier McLeod congratulated him on his results in Operation 'Benson' and informed him of an upcoming operation for his team.[3] He was going to be sent to the Netherlands. His team would be dropped by parachute on a DZ where a reception committee would be waiting. Kirschen had become quite sceptical about the feasibility of being dropped at the right location with a reception committee on the ground. Checking for contingencies, he was given an address and a Dutch phrase that would authenticate them, after which they would be brought in contact with the local resistance. McLeod valued the Belgians because (as a unit) they spoke Dutch, French and English. But Kirschen's team, which included Regner, Moyse and Pietquin, was composed of French native speakers, and operating in enemy occupied territory in the Netherlands would prove to be a linguistic challenge for some. They expected to be deployed for two weeks at the most.[4]

The tasks of Operation 'Regan' (which was later renamed 'Fabian') were to gather information on enemy movements in the Netherlands, especially on roads leading east and southeast from Utrecht, and to identify V-2 rocket sites and transports. Only the first task was included in Kirschen's initial instructions, which he received on 12 September; the additional task was only added just before his departure.[5] The operational employment of V-2 ballistic rockets, which started in the first half of September 1944, against London and cities in France, was a major concern for the Allies, since mobile launch systems were used and there was little that could be done to counter the V-2 once in flight.[6]

Since the reconnaissance mission's success relied on the ability to report the information gathered, two radio sets were carried to provide some redundancy. An RBZ receiver set[7] was also carried. Weapons were to be used for self-defence only. Each man carried a Colt .45" pistol, two carried an M1 carbine, one a Sten gun and one a Thompson[8] submachine gun and plenty of grenades were available.[9] In addition to their equipment, twenty-four containers with arms for the Dutch resistance were to be dropped.[10]

The team departed from RAF Keevil in a Stirling bomber of No. 299 Squadron and was parachuted at DZ 'Bertus' near Nijkerk around midnight on the night of 15-16 September.[11,12] A reception committee from the *Raad van Verzet in het Koninkrijk der Nederlanden* (Council of Resistance in the Kingdom of the Netherlands), RVV for short, was waiting and assisted in collecting the equipment. Kirschen was welcomed by several members of the RVV: 'Piet Weluwe', a local brigade commander, 'Lange Jan' (Jan Thijssen),[13] the division commander, and 'Roelof' (Roelof van Valkenburg), who would liaise between the RVV and the SAS party. An intelligence network was set up, using the well-organised messenger service of the RVV.[14] Many messages were to be hand-carried by Bep Labouchère, Roelof's fiancée, who habitually cycled 30-50 miles a day to convey messages while serving as a courier for the resistance.

On 17 September, Operation 'Market Garden' started. It rapidly became clear that multiple unexpected problems popped up which especially affected the Arnhem area. Inadequate radio sets caused issues for inter-unit communication between most units of the spread-out 1st Airborne Division, while the divisional HQ signals and the GHQ Liaison Regiment's team had trouble contacting England.[15] The communications breakdown added to the anxiety for those who had to wait impatiently for situation reports, including the Auxiliary Territorial Service women assigned to the SAS HQ, who had no choice but to stay at the now almost deserted Moor Park golf course where, shortly before, truckloads of cheerful airborne troops whose courage they respected so much had departed from the location which was also the site of Lieutenant General Frederick Browning's I Airborne Corps HQ.[16]

Two days into the battle, Kirschen received a message from the SAS Brigade HQ requesting him to send a man to Arnhem to re-establish communications between the 1st Airborne Division HQ and the HQ of airborne forces in England. Regner was designated.[17] Although he did not speak Dutch, it was an obvious choice since Moyse and Pietquin were signallers.[18] He would be accompanied by Leen Timmers of the Dutch resistance and both travelled on bicycles in civilian clothes, carrying handguns. Around noon on 20 September, they followed the road from Veenendaal to Bennekom. The volume of German traffic was such that they decided to abandon their bicycles and continue on foot to cross the wooded area between Bennekom and Renkum, where they noticed a continuous stream of German forces going east, while captured British airborne troops were being evacuated to the west. The local resistance advised the men to leave their identity papers behind and gave them forged ones in return. They crossed the Rhine by ferry, blending in between a group of refugees, and managed to obtain two bicycles on the southern riverbank. In Driel, they contacted the local priest. No Germans were seen. Regner tried to locate British troops, but fire from the north bank forced him to remain in cover. That night, he met a British airborne captain and four men in the priest's house and asked for their assistance. The officer promised to return and pick him up once his assigned task was completed.

Regner went out to reconnoitre the river again but noticed an enhanced German presence firing towards the northern bank. Being downstream from Arnhem, he could not swim across since the current was too strong. He waited for the British captain until the morning, but the latter did not come back, so he decided to move on to the east to find an upstream location to cross. Moving through Elst, to avoid German troop concentrations along the Rhine, he found an even stronger German presence. He contacted the resistance but had a lot of trouble proving his identity. After two hours of interrogation, the resistance finally agreed to help, but when asked to bring him to Arnhem, his request was refused outright, since the city was now in firm control of the Germans.[19] Although most of the bridges had been taken intact by the Allies, including those at Eindhoven and Nijmegen, the Rhine bridge in Arnhem could not be seized. Only the north side of the Rhine bridge was held, by a force under the command of Lieutenant Colonel John Frost, CO of the British 2nd Parachute Battalion. Despite a heroic defence, the defenders were forced to surrender after three days when their ammunition ran out. The rest of 1st Airborne Division, under the command of Major General Roy Urquhart, succeeded in maintaining a small perimeter in Oosterbeek, north of the Rhine, but faced constant pressure from the *Kampfgruppe Von Tettau*, consisting of regional defence and training battalions quickly thrown together under command of *Generalleutnant* Hans von Tettau (director of operations and training of the Armed Forces Commander Netherlands),[20] the 9th SS Armoured Division *'Hohenstaufen'* under the command of acting divisional commander *SS-Obersturmbannführer* Walter

Harzer and the 10th SS Armoured Division *'Frundsberg'* under the command of *SS-Brigadeführer* Heinz Harmel. Both SS divisions, although seriously understrength, had arrived in Arnhem to refit a few days before the Allied operation had been launched.[21]

All the resistance could do to help Regner was to show him the way to the south. He crossed the Waal river by small boat and reached the Allied lines. On the evening of 21 September, he was debriefed by Captain Duvivier at the British XXX Corps HQ at Malden. A day later, Captain Strut sent him back further south. On the way, Regner got caught in the German counterattack at Veghel to cut off the Allied corridor but eventually arrived in Brussels without further difficulties.[22]

As the advance of the ground forces was slowed down and it became clear there would be no timely link-up with the 1st Airborne Division, the remnants of the division withdrew south of the Rhine during the night of 25-26 September. Only a quarter of the initial force succeeded in being safely evacuated, having held out for nine days despite the promise of being relieved after two to four days.[23]

Meanwhile, Kirschen received his first information about launching sites and transport methods of the V-2 rockets. A resistance group from a neighbouring province also kept him informed on the positions of artillery batteries and HQs on the Rhine front in the Arnhem area. His main challenge was now to identify the essential information and to summarise it to keep his messages as short as possible. Piecing together the German dispositions, he asked his HQ to send him pigeons, so more elaborate information could be provided.[24]

Having spent the first few nights in several temporary locations, Kirschen's team was moved to a farm near Barneveld, where a chicken coop had been furnished for them to stay.[25] Although the soldiers were trained to stay in the field, the thin woodland area in this region was different from the dense forests of France and unsuited for clandestine LUPs. The safest option seemed to stay in barns.[26]

After the failed operation in Arnhem, numerous soldiers and airmen who had been cut off and had not been evacuated with the main body of the remnants of the 1st Airborne Division, or who had been captured by the Germans and later escaped, started to get into touch with the Dutch resistance. Roelof brought Flight Sergeant Wood, RAF, and Lieutenant Donald Olliff,[27] Royal Army Medical Corps, to Kirschen's location.[28] Olliff was in charge of a group of about thirty medical orderlies who were hidden in the woods.[29,30] Instructions were requested from the brigade HQ, who replied they would have to wait patiently. Shortly afterwards, two more evaders were brought in: Major Leo Heaps, a Canadian serving in the 1st Parachute Battalion, and Sergeant Alan Kettley, Glider Pilot Regiment. They wanted to get back to the Allied lines at once and Kirschen facilitated their movement back to friendly lines, first guided by an RVV messenger to cross the Rhine at Wijk bij Duurstede, then handed over to the *Knokploegen*, another Dutch resistance organisation, to cross the Waal river at Tiel.[31] Before they left, Kirschen managed to get a resupply drop in which broken-in and well-fitting civilian boots for Heaps were delivered since he had lost his when trying to cross the Rhine and been given a pair of undersized boots when captured.[32] After his return to Allied lines, Heaps was introduced to Airey Neave and got an offer to work for IS9[33] in the Netherlands. In England, Urquhart gave his consent when personally interviewing Heaps, who was the first evader known to have come back to Britain. Heaps returned to Brussels and reported to Neave.[34]

More and more evaders showed up and Kirschen contacted Major Digby Tatham Warter, 2nd Parachute Battalion, who took charge of them and planned to work with the resistance in support of the expected Allied advance. The route via Wijk bij Duurstede and Tiel was only occasionally used and Kirschen sent Lieutenant Ronald Adams, 156th Parachute Battalion, to facilitate movement along this route, where he met Captain Peter Baker from IS9, who had been sent into occupied territory for the same purpose but would be captured later on.[35]

Towards mid-October, the situation of the evaders changed significantly when instructions from London were received through Kirschen that the Allies had no intention of renewing the offensive during the winter. The suggestion to lie low and hide in the Dutch countryside through the winter months was not accepted as a feasible course of action by the evaders, who now numbered around eighty in and around Ede alone, with dozens more elsewhere, and would all have to be hidden and fed for several months, posing an enormous strain on Dutch families. Lieutenant Colonel David Dobie DSO, CO of the 1st Parachute Battalion, was selected to try to reach the Allied lines to explain the evaders' circumstances and plans.[36] He was one of the last to use the aforementioned individual evasion route successfully.[37] To assist in taking care of the evasion efforts, Dutch 1st Lieutenant Abraham 'Martien' du Bois (code-name 'Ham') and Belgian SAS Squadron signaller Raymond Holvoet (code-name 'Bacon'), both former SOE agents borrowed by MI9, were dropped in Kirschen's area.[38] Holvoet was captured soon, but du Bois was able to work with Kirschen and apart from their reporting tasks, also arranged drops of uniforms, arms and equipment for the evaders.[39]

In the meantime, the Dutch underground provided Kirschen with the location of the HQ of Student, commander of the 1st Parachute Army. A message was sent to London, and on 12 October, Typhoons[40] from No. 124 Wing RAF, operating from the B78 airfield in Eindhoven, attacked and severely damaged his HQ at the Wisch Castle in Terborg, forcing Student to relocate. His new location, a villa in the town of Dinxperlo, 25 miles east of Nijmegen, was again found by the resistance and relayed to England. Ground attack missions by Typhoons from the same wing were launched on 6 and 8 November and on 10, 11 and 15 December, but each time, unfavourable weather conditions prevented mission execution.[41,42,43,44,45]

The issue with the British evaders was still far from resolved, but the planning had become much easier once it was discovered that the Dutch resistance had access to a telephone line between Nijmegen and Ede, which proved a welcome alternative to Kirschen's radio set. The phone line was believed to be secure and allowed Tatham Warter to get into direct contact with Neave and Fraser, who would also be assisted by Dobie to help plan a mass crossing. Many organisations were involved in the planning and execution of this complex operation, which would be named 'Pegasus I'.

From the morning of 22 October, resistance guides led the evaders, dressed as Dutch civilians, to an RV in the woods west of Renkum, where they changed into their uniforms smuggled in by the resistance and then continued at night towards the Rhine on their own, where they were ferried to the south bank by British army engineers, protected by American paratroopers. Some 138 persons were rescued, mainly British military, but also service personnel from other nations and Dutch civilians.[46,47] But many more were still on the run, and from the end of October, plans were made for another attempt to exfiltrate personnel from occupied territory, called 'Pegasus II', for which Neave again relied on Kirschen to relay messages to London.[48]

Since Kirschen realised the military situation had changed completely and he would not need two signallers for the now extended stay of his team, he got approval from his HQ to send back Pietquin, who was exfiltrated towards friendly lines by the resistance.[49] Kirschen was very security conscious and kept those who knew his location to a minimum,[50] but gossip started to spread and knowing that 'Bacon' had been captured, it was decided to relocate near the end of October. Kirschen and Moyse were moved to a new location[51] and would again hide in a chicken coop. They were fortunate to have done so since the *Sicherheitsdienst*[52] (SD) raided their former hideout a few days later. On All Saints' Day, however, the chicken coop caught fire and all equipment and supplies were lost. Their spare radio set was hidden around Barneveld, but the code book had been destroyed by the fire. After requesting a new code book in an uncoded message, the replacement was included in a resupply drop to 'Ham', after which Kirschen's team could resume its work. Since explosions caused by the fire had attracted too much attention, both men had to move again. They went to a country house in Maarn, then stayed for a week in a villa near Doorn, after which they returned to the house in Maarn,[53] the home of Vera Hoogewegen, which was also used as an HQ of the RVV.[54] Their work was becoming exceedingly difficult, as the Germans arrested and tortured leaders and messengers of the resistance.[55]

Thijssen was arrested, probably around 8 November. He did not reveal much but mentioned he had been in contact with 'Captain King' and gave the address of his hideout in Scherpenzeel, knowing it had already been vacated a long time before.[56]

On the night of 18 November, Operation 'Pegasus II' was executed, but it failed after a German patrol was encountered, several men were killed, and the parties scattered. Only a handful made it across the Rhine.[57]

Around the third week of November, Kirschen sent a message to his HQ mentioning that ten manned torpedoes were being manufactured in the Jongerius factory in Utrecht, aimed at being used for an attack on the Waal bridge at Nijmegen.[58] The warning was not idle: attacks to destroy the bridges over the Waal at Nijmegen had already been conducted by German navy special forces combat swimmers, but without success and new attempts would follow indeed.[59]

At the beginning of December, Kirschen was informed that his task was considered completed. He had to propose a replacement for du Bois, who had been arrested, and Dignus 'Dick' Kragt, known under his field name 'Frans Hals', was designated to be in charge of the evaders.[60] Kragt was working for IS9 and had been working with Kirschen and 'Ham', who relayed his messages since he had lost his own radio set when parachuted in the Netherlands in June 1943.[61] To assist Kragt, Jean Temmerman, another signaller from the Belgian SAS Squadron, was to be parachuted to replace 'Bacon', but several attempts failed. In addition, a couple of resupply drops did not work out as planned and arrived in German hands. Most of the time this month was used in trying to organise the escape of Brigadier John Hackett, commander of the

4th Parachute Brigade, who had been severely wounded at Arnhem.[62] Kirschen came up with two plans to get him out: one was a pick-up by light aircraft, the other to go down to the Rhine and be picked up by a patrol from the southern bank of the river. Hackett had to wait for a few more weeks, however, before being evacuated after a journey by bicycle and canoe in a bitterly cold winter.[63]

Early in the new year, Kirschen was ordered to exfiltrate back to friendly lines. An attempt to use the old Wijk bij Duurstede to Tiel route failed. The area of Tiel was now a restricted area from which civilians had been forcibly evacuated by the Germans, putting a lot of pressure on the resistance and forcing the evaders to move back to their country house in Maarn. Kirschen and Moyse finally managed to use another route and left for Rotterdam on 12 February. The continuation of their journey was further delayed by organisational problems and by an unfavourable moon. On 12 March, they moved to Zwijndrecht, and on the night of 13-14 March they were transported by boat between Sliedrecht and Lange Zwaluwe, bypassing the marshy Biesbosch, after which they proceeded to Vught where they met Major Fraser. After nearly six months in hostile territory, they were back in friendly lines.[64]

Operation 'Timon'

Shortly after his return from Operation 'Haggard', Holvoet volunteered to be sent to the Netherlands, together with du Bois, assigned to the Dutch *Bureau Bijzondere Opdrachten* (Special Missions Office), a secret organisation established by the Dutch government in exile in the spring of 1944. Both men were tasked with facilitating the evasion of Allied personnel stuck behind German lines on behalf of MI9 (see above).

They were dropped during the night of 16-17 October on a DZ near Boeschoten, close to Garderen.[65] A reception committee, which included Kragt, was waiting on the ground and had much trouble recovering the two dozen containers that were dropped with the two men.[66] Assisted by headteacher van den Bovenkamp and Nol Burger, Holvoet and du Bois went to a hideout at a house in Garderen named 'de Ruif', which was owned by Dr Joop Kruimel, an orthopaedic surgeon from Utrecht. In the afternoon, they were visited by Kirschen and Roelof to conduct a meeting. In the evening, du Bois went to Nol's house, while Holvoet stayed with Huber, whose house was located close to Kruimel's.

The next morning, Germans searched Nol's house, but found nothing suspicious, du Bois being well hidden. A few days later, du Bois relocated to the Wester Wetering in Ede, a large farm with hidden spaces used by the resistance.

Around 23 October, the hideout at Kruimel's house, although well concealed, was accidentally revealed by a careless young occupant to a passing German *Feldgendarmerie*[67] patrol, resulting in the house being searched and burned down. Since Holvoet was hiding in the immediate vicinity, it was deemed unsafe to stay, so he was urgently moved by the resistance to the farm of Berend van Looijengoed in Houtdorp.

On 26 October, an incident in which a suspected traitor was eliminated by a Dutch resistance group, and the body subsequently sloppily disposed of, led to the discovery of the corpse by the *Feldgendarmerie* on the next day. The investigation resulted in the detention of two persons and during their interrogation, the name of van Looijengoed was apparently mentioned as a diversion. This in turn led to the Germans visiting van Looijengoed's farm, where Holvoet and a Jewish girl who was hiding at the same location were caught unawares. Holvoet, using his English name 'Henderson', claimed to be an evading British paratrooper who had landed near Arnhem. On his way to the police office, Holvoet escaped but was shot in the thigh and captured again. From 27 October, he stayed in the infamous Willem III barracks in Apeldoorn. Repeatedly interrogated, he feigned not speaking Dutch and clung to his cover story that he was a regular British paratrooper.[68]

With Holvoet arrested, the Belgian SAS Squadron received a request from the brigade HQ to provide a signaller who spoke Dutch and was willing to operate in civvies. Temmerman volunteered and got approval to replace Holvoet. From the squadron's new location, the Two Lions barracks in Tervueren near Brussels, he moved to the brigade HQ in England, where he met Major Shaw on 19 November. Before taking a definitive decision, Shaw first consulted with Kirschen to make sure the latter did not need a signaller and by 2 December it became clear Kirschen would manage without an additional one, but the agent who had been working alongside Holvoet would gladly accept the offer, so preparations were made to provide Temmerman with the appropriate clothing, false identity papers, etc.[69]

After Holvoet's arrest, du Bois continued planning for Operation 'Pegasus II', but also tried to save Holvoet's life. He told Kirschen that he believed he could bribe a high-ranking German who might consider having Holvoet treated as a prisoner of war. Kirschen suspected a set-up and informed the SAS Brigade HQ. On 4 December, having received the brigade's order for an immediate breakdown of the negotiations, since it was believed du Bois would put himself in danger, Kirschen sent a messenger to inform him of the decision, but it was too late: du Bois had been deceived and was arrested.[70] He tried to escape, but was shot in his leg and transferred to the Lunteren hospital. Around Christmas, he was moved to Velp. Later attempts to pay him free were in vain, while plans to assault the prison to liberate him were deemed unfeasible.[71]

Meanwhile, Temmerman's insertion had been postponed multiple times due to bad weather. Around mid-December, he took off in a Stirling bomber, only to return a few hours later, fog along the Dutch coast preventing the pilot from finding his route.[72] A few weeks later, during a second attempt, the pilot circled about half an hour above the DZ but could not see any signals on the ground and returned to base.[73] A third and final attempt was made around mid-February. When comparing maps during the pre-flight brief, Temmerman was surprised to see the aircrew had maps from Norway, while the crew was not expecting a passenger. Temmerman, in the end, boarded the right aircraft and, after an uneventful flight, waited for some forty minutes to jump. The DZ was not considered safe, and the aircraft returned, conducting evasive action and flying at low level to prevent attacks by German fighter aircraft.[74]

On 24 February 1945, Holvoet was moved to a Dutch-controlled detention facility in Almelo, where the Dutch staff assisted him where possible, within the limits allowed by the SD.[75]

On 8 March, du Bois was executed by the Germans at the Woeste Hoeve farm,[76] between Arnhem and Apeldoorn, together with 116 others.

On 2 April, Holvoet was moved to a prison in Zwolle commanded by *SS-*

Hauptsturmführer Joseph Rauch. According to a Dutch policeman and collaborator detached to the SD, two of Rauch's subordinates, *SS-Untersturmführer* Walter Bartels and *SS-Hauptscharführer* Willy Mönnich, proposed Rauch dispose of their prisoners, since the Allies were approaching. In the presence of wine, it apparently came to a vote to decide who would be released and who would be killed, after which their death list was forwarded to their higher command level, to request formal approval for their planned action, which was provided shortly afterwards.

On 10 April, ten prisoners were transported to the Katerveer ferry site, lined up along the IJssel river and shot. All but one, including Holvoet, were killed and fell into the river. Jean Lemarche, a Belgian citizen living in the Netherlands, had managed to loosen the rope with which his hands were tied behind his back and let him fall into the river just as the shots were fired. He swam away, was fired upon and wounded, but managed to escape. Holvoet's body washed ashore at Wilsum on 25 April.[77]

On 4 April, prior to the executions at the Katerveer, six others from the Zwolle prison had already been murdered by the SD, over a mile to the south at the other side of the river. They included Buunk (who had been working with Debefve, see below), Dr Dirk Eskes (who had been working closely with Thijssen, Kruimel and Burger) and Sergeant John Austin (the British wireless operator of Jedburgh team Dudley).

Possibly, all names of those eligible for execution were already known as soon as 2 April, based on a list provided to Rauch by his higher command, containing the names of those 'no longer required for their investigations' and there is reason to believe that *SS-Obersturmbannführer* Hans Kolitz, head of staff department IV (dealing with resistance and counterintelligence activities) of the *Sicherheitspolizei und Sicherheitsdienst*[78] in the Netherlands, was personally involved in the decision-making to commit the war crimes.[79]

Operation 'Portia'/'Gobbo'

After the British 2nd Army's failure to establish a bridgehead north of the Rhine, a Belgian SAS team was inserted near Westerbork, in the Drenthe Province, some 80 miles behind the frontline, on 26 September. The team consisted of 1st Lieutenant Debefve, Sergeant Siffert, corporals Demoor and Heylen, Lance Corporal Joseph Levaux and Sergeant Rudy Blatt, a German-born Jew who had been serving with the Dutch troop of No. 10 (Inter-Allied) Commando who was attached as an interpreter and liaison with the resistance.[80,81,82,83] The operation carried the code name 'Gobbo', a change from the original name 'Portia'. It was a reconnaissance mission first, but the intent was to expand it into a harassment and interdiction mission later after being reinforced by additional troops. The drop took place around 1 am, after an uneventful flight, besides the occasional anti-aircraft fire. Despite the low dropping altitude, no one was hurt, thanks to the drenched soil. A reception committee was waiting on the DZ and led the team to a farm. The Dutch were very excited to see the first Allies in uniform and expected to be liberated in a matter of weeks. So did Debefve. The next morning, he met several resistance leaders from the Drenthe, Groningen and Friesland provinces: Mr Beckers, from the *Knokploegen*, Dr Van der Bosch, from Assen, and Mr de Boer, a commander of the *Ordedienst*, another resistance group.[84] Since early September 1944, the *Nederlandse Binnenlandse Strijdkrachten* (NBS) (Dutch Interior

Forces) had been established by royal decree, grouping the (previously independently operating) officially recognised resistance groups, although these groups (*Knokploegen, Ordedienst, Raad van Verzet*) were only designated by name in a rather informal way on 18 November.[85] With the help of the resistance, Debefve started setting up his intelligence network. In the evening, the team moved to an isolated farm near Orvelte, which would become its base till the end of November.

The intelligence network paid dividends and allowed Debefve to report on multiple aspects of the German occupation: troop movements, road, rail and water traffic, pictures from fortified areas and the airfield at Leeuwarden, layouts of defensive positions, V-1 launch sites, recruitment facilities between Nieuwe-Schans and Groningen, vehicle parks, ammunition supply dumps and the HQ of Seyss-Inquart[86] at Beilen. He also requested locks to be bombed to lower the water level in areas inundated by the enemy. At the request of brigade HQ, pictures and layouts were hand-carried by trusted agents from the resistance but it was unclear to Debefve whether they ever reached their destination.

Debefve found the Dutch underground quite dispersed but well organised, especially in Friesland, slightly less so in Drenthe and Groningen. Their main activities were to collect information and conduct hold-ups on banks and supply offices to help out the resistance, especially railway personnel. The Dutch resistance in the area was poorly armed and hardly trained to use weapons, so Debefve requested resupply drops in Friesland, Groningen and Drenthe to deliver small arms, but also asked for four instructors to train the resistance.

Enemy security forces were noticeably present and included German and Dutch troops of the *Waffen-SS* and personnel from the SD, the so-called 'green police' (i.e. *Ordnungspolizei*)[87] and the *Landwacht*, a Dutch auxiliary police force collaborating with the Germans. Often, they were looking for potential labour, so it was rare to see men under 50 in public. The flat countryside with hardly any cover and the abundance of waterways – which often included 2-3-yards-wide ditches flanking the road – made it hard to move unnoticed, let alone get away quickly when needed. The few small woodland areas were searched regularly by the Germans, but also the fair number of isolated farms did not escape their attention.[88]

Near the end of October,[89] Siffert was sending a message when the team's lookout noticed some thirty SS troops on bicycles making their way to their farm. The team quickly packed their equipment and went into its hiding space, deep into the straw. The farmer and his family were able to get away, but a young farm worker was caught and was brutally interrogated but refused to tell anything of use. From their conversation, it was understood that the Germans were looking for a weapons dump. Upon finding some traces of digging, they found some food tins with English text on them, so they intensified their search and found the aerial, as not enough time was left to dismantle it. Under duress, the young man told his interrogators that six Englishmen had been at the farm but had already left. The team was not discovered, but it was a close call. As the Germans stayed at the farm during the night and an even more thorough search could be expected the next morning, Debefve's team prepared to evacuate the site. Around 11 pm, having just descended from their hiding space, two German sentries inspected the barn, shining a torch through the open-door opening. Fearing they had been discovered and their weapons ready to fire, the men saw the two Germans turn back and managed to slip out of the barn and leave the farm unnoticed, leaving most of their kit behind, except for a radio receiver.

They marched south, hoping to reach the Overijssel Province. For eight days, they moved during the night – in British uniforms but posing as a German patrol – and rested in woodland areas during the day. They were constantly wet and starving, happy to eat the odd plant root or to find some sustenance at the occasional farm they encountered on their way. The survival situation caused a lot of interpersonal tension. At the end of their ordeal, they found shelter on a farm near Ommen and were put into contact with the local resistance. Initially, both parties were quite suspicious, especially when the 'Brits' talked with a very strange accent, but all issues were soon clarified.[90,91,92]

The team was brought to the vicinity of Vroomshoop and met 'Fopkonijn'[93] (code name of Ben Buunk), who worked for the Dutch *Bureau Inlichtingen* (Intelligence Office) and had been trained by the British Secret Intelligence Service.[94] Debefve stayed for a week at the same location while planning his next moves. For security reasons and to augment his team's reporting capacity, Debefve decided to split his team. A signal team consisting of Siffert and Heylen was sent to Kloosterhaar, while Debefve moved with another signal team (Demoor and Levaux) and two civilians to a caravan outside Vroomshoop, keeping in touch with the other team – 10 miles away – by courier. Blatt, with whom Debefve seemed to have an uneasy relationship, was dismissed from his tasks and put at the disposition of Major Henk Brinkgrave, the Dutch officer of Jedburgh team 'Dudley', which had been dropped in Overijssel a week prior to Operation 'Market Garden'.[95,96] Using Buunk's link with England, new radio sets were requested, but the SAS Brigade HQ had not understood Debefve's intention and a few days later only a single set was dropped. Despite the setback, the team was now able to continue its reporting task. During the next three weeks, plenty of information became available, including V-2 launch site positions, but Demoor had plenty of trouble getting through.

Compared to the northerly provinces, the resistance in Overijssel was better armed, but suffered a lot from the increased activities of German security forces, especially the *Gestapo* and SD, and arrests were rife.

After three weeks, the radio set was moved to Siffert's location for security reasons. On the evening of 4 December, Debefve's party noticed Germans and feared their caravan was surrounded. When a German officer opened the door, he came face-to-face with Debefve, who shot him with his handgun. Other Germans replied with automatic weapons, hitting both Debefve's and Levaux's right hand. The caravan's light was destroyed, and a window was crushed, through which the team could escape in the dark. Running for their lives, the men split up. Debefve met Levaux at the fence around the property and after a while they ran into an NCO from the *Marechaussee*,[97] who provided them with an alternate address, urging them to leave the area since German patrols were searching the village's streets. About an hour later, they reached the house of a teacher and dressed their gunshot wounds. Afterwards, they were moved to a farm where they had the company of six American airmen and where a doctor looked after their wounds the day after. According to villagers, Demoor was safe, but the two civilians had been caught. Debefve's team was now compromised, since the Germans had their pictures, but their uniforms, food and most of their equipment had been well cached and was not found. It would be retrieved later by the resistance.

Following this incident, Debefve received a message authorising his team to join the Allied lines on its own. In the meantime, reports to London were still being sent, now being helped out by Buunk, their code book having been lost. New code books sent by the SAS Brigade HQ to Buunk around mid-January got lost again on their way to Debefve.

Between December 1944 and early February 1945, Siffert's team had been able to work uninterruptedly for five weeks, having been hidden in the morgue of a cemetery. For Debefve, on the other hand, it became increasingly difficult to operate. Hiding places had to be changed regularly whenever someone was arrested who knew his location. After a while, almost everybody who had been in contact with Debefve had been detained, leaving him no choice but to ask for assistance from brigade HQ.

In the early days of February, Debefve was told by the resistance of Almelo to go to Heeten and contact 'Joop', who had been tasked by Major Fraser to exfiltrate his team. Together with a Norwegian pilot, they travelled hidden in a hay cart and arrived in Heeten, where they were picked up by Joop a week later. Since the resistance was short on bicycles, six were stolen from known collaborators and accompanied by two *Marechaussee* escorts, the party rode to Vorden, where they were picked up by a lorry to be driven to Hummelo. They stayed for a week at Enghuizen Castle, where they observed field training exercises from two German parachute battalions that were based in the area. A week later, they crossed the IJssel near Giesbeek, after which they cycled to Barneveld for over 30 miles.

Ten days later, they moved on but were forced to take a detour when they found all bridges over the canal in their area guarded by Germans. Finding no unguarded bridge, they finally risked crossing one further west without incident, after which they followed the Lek river for a few miles, which was crossed by canoe during the night. A member of the resistance had a neglective discharge and the round went through Levaux's arm. The team then moved on to Sliedrecht and was picked up by boats during the night of 17-18 March, navigating on the Waal for four hours between German positions, before finally reaching the Allied lines.

Operation 'Friesland'

As requested by Debefve, another team was tasked with training the resistance in the northern part of the Netherlands. On 5 October 1944, Groenewout was informed he had been selected for the mission.[98] He was to be accompanied by three commandos of No. 2 (Dutch) Troop of No. 10 (Inter-Allied) Commando: Willem van der Veer, Robert Michels and Nikolaas De Koning.[99] Technically, the mission may have been part of Operation 'Portia/Gobbo', but most Belgian sources consider it as a separate operation referred to as Operation 'Friesland'.

On the night of 8-9 October, before departing, Groenewout asked the Halifax pilot first to drop the personnel at 350 and to drop the containers afterwards at 150 feet. This would avoid too wide a dispersion of the containers in an area where large water-filled ditches and canals were prevalent. At the DZ near Veenhuizen, however, the requested altitudes were inverted, resulting in serious injuries to Groenewout, who did not have time to release his kitbag and landed in the trees. He needed assistance, and when a member of the resistance reception committee showed up after quite a while, Groenewout nearly shot him since the man was wearing his Dutch police uniform, not dissimilar to a German one. The Dutch resistance party was somewhat short in numbers to retrieve the twenty-six containers but behaved in a very disciplined way – no torches, no cigarettes, no noise.

While recovering from his injuries, Groenewout hid in Veenhuizen for several days and two of the Dutch left the site to operate in different areas. The remaining Dutchman and Groenewout were transported by car to Oudega, where contact was established with the regional and district resistance leaders, after which both men went their own way to assist various resistance groups.

For security reasons, the regional resistance HQ was moved to Swichum. Groenewout joined the town by bicycle and started his first week of giving weapons instruction. For the next seven months, he moved to different locations, teaching about 700 men, who in turn were supposed to pass on their skills to others. Since Groenewout could not take any notes that might have fallen in enemy hands, accurate details of his journey are not available, but from memory, he recalled having taught at Bolsward, Finkum, Dokkum, Tijn, Heerenveen, Dronryp, Tersoal and Hempens.

Movement by bicycle between locations was deliberate and slow, as often, wide detours had to be made to avoid checkpoints. Five times he was nearly caught by the enemy, and twice he had to throw his bike in a body of water and run away across the fields. Staying for any time longer than a week at the same location was considered risky. Much more than the Germans, Groenewout feared loose talk by locals. Operating in plain clothes, he chose to carry his .45" pistol at all times, preferring to fight it out instead of getting arrested, which would entail a certain death. He did not want to rely on his false identity papers, which would not have survived close scrutiny, being antedated but containing a recent photograph on which he was visible in the same clothes he wore during operations.

His courses were usually given at farms, to groups of up to thirty persons, and covered how to operate rifles, Sten guns, Bren guns, hand grenades and explosives. They required a lot of coordination with local groups, but logistic and organisational problems often complicated his task as weapons were not always available at the time and place they were required. Apart from the short time frame to conduct training at the same location, perhaps the most important shortcoming was the lack of practical marksmanship training. Since attacks by the resistance were supposed to be conducted at night when aimed fire became even more challenging, tactics were adapted to counter the detrimental effect of the lack of training: only surprise attacks would be conducted, in which a maximum volume of fire would be developed, lasting no longer than three to four minutes, after which the resistance party would disappear into cover, regardless the results of the shooting. But not just *how* to fight deserved Groenewout's attention, the *when* and *why* being more important in the end. Only targets providing a clear military advantage when neutralised would warrant an attack. While many resistance fighters were good patriots and eager to fight, they often underestimated the savagery of the Nazis and their invariable reprisals against the civilian population.

Groenewout was also confronted with other realities of working with resistance groups. Different entities sometimes had differing views or interests and leadership issues seemed to become more important as the liberation became nearer. Resistance members that had been inactive for years suddenly emerged and competed with leaders who had been on operations and taken a lot of risk.

From early February 1945, Groenewout's identity was compromised due to a house search leading to the arrest of top resistance leaders and lots of documents falling into German hands. At Hempens, his last residence, where he stayed for about seven weeks, Groenewout extensively trained a group of some fifteen men belonging to the *Knokploegen* and joined them on operations when the signal to do so was given. Two days later, Leeuwarden was liberated.

On 22 April, Groenewout linked up with the 3rd Canadian Division near Heerenveen and returned to Tervueren, near Brussels, two days later.[100]

Chapter Seven

THE BELGIAN SAS SQUADRON IN THE BATTLE OF THE ARDENNES

THE ILL-FATED OPERATION in Arnhem caused some delay in the capture of the approaches to the port of Antwerp, but also the excessive rain slowed down the Allied advance throughout the autumn. By the end of October, the South Beveland isthmus was liberated by British and Canadian forces, and in early November, an assault on the Walcheren island was conducted, in which the Belgian troop of No. 10 (Inter-Allied) Commando participated. From mid-November, Montgomery's 21st Army Group undertook an eastward drive and cleared out the last German pocket west of the Maas river, despite the difficult country and the approaching winter conditions. The Commonwealth forces could hardly be reinforced, as few units could be spared from the Mediterranean theatre or elsewhere, but American reinforcements continued to arrive from the United States. In the third week of October, Lieutenant General William Simpson's 9th Army was moved from the Ardennes and brought into line north of Aachen, in the north of Bradley's 12th Army Group. From mid-November, the 1st and 9th armies renewed the offensive toward the Rhine, but progress was slow, as the 1st Army became involved in dense woodland fighting in the Hürtgen Forest, which favoured the defender. By early December, the banks of the Rur river were reached, but an immediate assault was not possible since the far side could be flooded using the dams under German control.

Meanwhile, Patton's 3rd Army made good progress in the Saar region, bridgeheads were established across the Moselle river north of Metz, and after mid-November, the German border was crossed. More to the south, extensive fortifications slowed its advance, which had to be suspended as logistical support could not keep up with the vast amounts of artillery ammunition required.

Further south, Devers' 6th Army Group advanced across the Vosges mountains and reached the Rhine in the Strasbourg area, although the Germans managed to maintain a large pocket west of the Rhine around Colmar.

Priority was given to attacks in the vicinity of the Rur dams in the north (under Hodges) and the Saar area in the south (under Patton). Available forces were concentrated in those areas, and by the end of November, the badly stretched condition of Allied troops caused constant concern. For some time, no more than four divisions covered a front of some 75 miles in the Ardennes between Trier and Monschau. This was a definite risk that was accepted to allow for the continuation of offensive operations to the extreme limit of the Allies' ability before the arrival of further reinforcements from across the ocean.[1]

Reorganisation in the autumn of 1944

Following the departure of Kirschen's and Debefve's teams to the Netherlands, Captain

Blondeel returned to Belgium. He tasked Dulait to set up a small base at the Saint-Jean hospital near the Boulevard Botanique, where the squadron's excess equipment and supplies, such as the jeeps that had been parachuted, could be stored. In Brussels, Blondeel ran into Major General François Temmerman. When Temmerman asked about his son Jean's whereabouts, all Blondeel could tell him was that he was on operations in France. Upon hearing the SAS Brigade's decision for the Belgian squadron to move to Belgium, Temmerman pointed out the potential availability of barracks at Tervueren which were being used as temporary accommodation for families of arrested collaborators. Blondeel went to visit the Two Lions barracks and received approval from higher authorities to evacuate the few remaining families.

Having taken care of the most urgent issues in Brussels, Blondeel returned to England, where his squadron was in the process of making arrangements for its re-location from Fairford to Mushroom Farm at RAF Wethersfield in Essex, as an intermediate base awaiting its subsequent move to Belgium.

Blondeel met Brigadier McLeod and learned it would be most unlikely for SAS troops to be parachuted into operational areas in the foreseeable future, so it was decided to adapt to the new situation by transforming the Belgian SAS Squadron as soon as possible into a reconnaissance unit equipped with semi-armoured jeeps. The squadron was to pick up thirty-five jeeps at Bicester and to re-equip to fit its new role. Five additional jeeps were to be recovered in Brussels, where the armour for all forty would be provided.

An advance party, consisting of over a dozen NCOs and troopers, commanded by Sergeant d'Oultremont, was sent to Belgium in three lorries. They carried the parts for the five jeeps to be converted and had to assist Sergeant Henri Lecluyse, who, as a skilled carpenter, had been designated to work against time to prepare for the arrival of the squadron in the new barracks. Contact with England was maintained by two signallers at Tervueren.

Around that time, Blondeel was informed by the Minister of Defence that he had to double the size of his unit. For this purpose, he set up a recruitment office in the so-called King's House, a neo-gothic building at the Grand-Place. Candidates came in by the hundreds and to make a fair selection, they were subjected to psychological and medical tests, followed by an interview to probe into their motivation.[2]

One of the recruits, Christian Van Melle, gave his impressions on his first contacts with the SAS squadron at a time that Blondeel was in Brussels:

> Everything started in a small room of the King's House on the Grand-Place of Brussels. We were asked to enter and immediately found ourselves in front of an impressive personality in military uniform. Wings and rank insignia made it clear to me that we were dealing with a parachute-qualified officer. The maroon beret on the table in front of him confirmed my thoughts. Even before he had spoken a word, his penetrating gaze, his energetic features, his willpower, his pronounced chin and his height made a tremendous impression on me. Captain Blondeel introduced himself. In a few short sentences, he covered the issues related to recruitment, selection and training. He seemed interested in my past as a scout leader and the Hebertism[3] course which I had attended. But when

he learned that my great aunt had been his language teacher at the *Deutsche Schule* in Ghent, he became animated. He stood up and told me that my relative had given him quite a fright during his school years. His finger pointing in my direction, he declared he would revenge himself on me, after which he straightened himself even more and burst into laughter! At this stage of the interview, the attitude of our future colonel had a double effect on me: first of all, I shrunk on my chair; secondly, it slowly dawned that although he wanted to take revenge, I would be allowed to participate in the entrance tests.

> Following my private conversation with 'Captain Blunt', I found out that my brother had started the series of interviews first, waiting at the door since 05:30 hours. He avoided the scene referring to our great aunt, but he had to do his utmost to prove that his physical abilities compensated for his young age. He was also allowed to participate in the entrance tests. Next, there were the actual tests in the Two Lions barracks in Tervueren. When seeing the doctor, I didn't feel uncomfortable weighing only 57 kg for my height of 1.76 m, but he reassured me. The psychological screening seemed rather funny. For physical tests, which we carried out in different groups, I seemed to remember that the group to which my brother and I belonged – under the supervision of Sergeant Goffinet – consisted of ten candidates at the start, but at the end, after a jump from the 4-metre-high wall of the former vegetable garden of the Dukes of Brabant, only my brother, myself and a third candidate, whom I never saw again, made it to the finish.

> When the tests were completed at the end of the day, all candidates were assembled in the courtyard. Sergeant Goffinet called out the names of the candidates who had passed. I remembered very well that the first names that were called out were those of the warrant officers from our colony, followed by the names of some career personnel and finally, my family name. My brother and I, of course, had the same surname and therefore I asked Sergeant Goffinet something like: "Which of the two, Sir?" That question caused a threefold reaction: first, we were scolded for addressing him as 'sir' instead of 'sergeant'; then he informed us that if he called our family name, it meant both of us, finally, after we had done some kind of Indian dance to celebrate our selection, we were asked if we found ourselves in a circus and were summoned to rejoin the ranks.[4]

Of the new candidates, thirteen were awarded their parachute wings at Ringway on 12 October and seven more on 9 November.[5]

Some of the new arrivals originated from various entities of the Belgian armed forces in the United Kingdom and the Middle East, but the majority of these reinforcements were young men recruited in Belgium after the liberation. They included four members of the *Force publique* of the Belgian Congo, who had crossed the desert in vehicles towards Egypt. Since they were extremely knowledgeable in all aspects of vehicle mechanics and maintenance, they formed the core of a new maintenance section. While expanding its manpower, the squadron was in full transformation and dispersed over several locations throughout October and November.

On All Saints' Day, tragedy struck when Major Robert 'Bob' Melot, a Belgian serving in the 1st SAS and a close friend of Mayne, was killed during a jeep accident while on leave in Brussels.

Melot was a First World War veteran who had earned the Croix de Guerre as a Belgian army aviation pilot. Living as a cotton merchant with his wife in Egypt during the inter-war years, he was fluent in Arabic and had an intimate knowledge of North Africa; skills he had put to good use after he had been commissioned in the British Army, serving in intelligence while working with the Secret Intelligence Service, the Long-Range Desert Group and the SAS, which he later joined, eventually becoming Mayne's intelligence officer, assisted by Mike Sadler.[6,7,8] He had won a Military Cross for intelligence work behind enemy lines and had survived wounds in the abdomen and legs by a grenade in North Africa and a gunshot wound through the chest in Italy.[9,10]

Despite the ongoing unit expansion, there were also some renewed existential threats. In the mind of some high-ranking officials, the squadron's existence was no longer warranted, given their assumption that no one would need to be parachuted anymore for the remainder of the war. Since the squadron participated in the First World War armistice parade on 11 November, Blondeel gave clear guidance for the conduct of his men: when the detachment's heads were turned to the right to salute the dignitaries during the march-past, every individual was to pick one person and look straight into his eyes for the entire time. Padre Jourdain, who 'coincidentally' happened to be behind the spectators, heard the positive reactions, especially the statement that 'this' must not be disbanded.[11]

On 10 December, Blondeel went to England together with Squadron Leader Patrick Smith, an RAF liaison officer attached to the SAS Brigade HQ, to inspect the training centre in Leamington Spa, to discuss future employment with the SAS Brigade and to settle some administrative issues related to the troops' pay with the Minister of Defence. He was due to be back in Belgium on 18 December.

Halfway through December, the Belgian SAS Squadron's order of battle was as follows: squadron command group and HQ (seventeen men); HQ troop, consisting of a signals section (eight men), motor transport section (fifteen men), quartermasters section (eighteen men) and reconnaissance section (seventeen men); 'A' Troop (forty-eight men, sixteen jeeps); 'B' Troop (thirty men, ten jeeps); training centre at Campion Hill (Leamington Spa, Warwickshire) (seven instructors, who had left Tervueren at the end of November, and sixty-two men in training on the pre-parachute course, the actual parachute course still being completed at Ringway with British instructors); training centre at the barracks in Tervueren (three instructors and sixty-three men in basic training); a liaison detachment with the 21st Army Group HQ (to ensure the liaison with troops deployed behind enemy lines); two men detached to 1st SAS; ten men on operations or awaiting deployment in the Netherlands, eleven men on sick leave and two men in captivity.[12]

One of those on sick leave was Dr Limbosch, who suddenly suffered from a stomach ulcer and had to be admitted to hospital, but Blondeel knew an old hand from the athenaeum in Ghent, Doctor F. Sevens, a highly competent surgeon and former SOE agent, who enthusiastically accepted to lead the squadron's medical team.[13]

Surveillance and reconnaissance patrols along the Meuse and to Marche-en-Famenne

On 16 December 1944, the German army launched a large offensive, under the code name Operation '*Herbstnebel*' (Autumn Fog). The plan was for three armies to attack through the Ardennes between Monschau and Echternach to capture Antwerp, while driving a wedge between the Allied army groups. The ultimate aim was to cause a divide between the Brits, Canadians and the Americans, forcing them to engage in separate peace talks with Germany. *Generalfeldmarschall* Gerd von Rundstedt, the supreme commander of German forces in the West, had been left out of the planning process and, together with *Generalfeldmarschall* Walter Model, commander of Army Group B, was one of several senior German commanders who understood that Hitler's plan was far too ambitious, but proposals for a limited, more realistic plan in which American forces would be enveloped east of the Meuse river, were dismissed.[14]

In the north, the 6th Armoured Army,[15] under *SS-Oberst-Gruppenführer und Panzer-Generaloberst der Waffen-SS* Josef 'Sepp' Dietrich, with four armoured divisions, four infantry divisions and a parachute division grouped in three army corps, and army level armour, anti-tank, indirect fire support and engineer formations, attacked along six *Rollbahnen* (axes of advance) between Monschau and Krewinkel.[16]

In the centre, the 5th Armoured Army under *General der Panzertruppen* Hasso von Manteuffel, with three armoured divisions, four infantry divisions and an armoured infantry division grouped in three army corps, and army level anti-tank, air defence, indirect fire support and engineer formations, attacked along two *Rollbahnen* between Lünebach and Arzfeld.[17]

In the south, the 7th Army under *General der Panzertruppen* Erich Brandenberger, with three infantry divisions and a parachute division grouped in two army corps, an understrength army corps containing only two battalions, and army level anti-tank, air defence, indirect fire support and engineer formations, attacked between Vianden and Echternach, protecting the southern and southwestern flank and tasked to eventually build up a defensive front along the Gedinne – Libramont – Medernach line.[18]

Apart from logistical constraints, the attack was timed to take advantage of a period of fog and low clouds, which deprived the Allies of their air superiority.[19]

The initial fragmentary and unclear reports indicated a limited spoiling attack to hinder the advance of Hodges and Patton and did not overly concern Bradley, but after a few days, more pessimistic assessments from Montgomery and alarming reports from American frontline units caused panic at the Allied supreme HQ.[20]

In the north, stubborn American resistance at the villages of Krinkelt and Rocherath limited the German advance to barely 6 miles after three days, which allowed the establishment of strong defensive positions along Elsenborn Ridge, blocking the shortest route to the Meuse. In the southern part of the German 6th Armoured Army's sector, a breakthrough was achieved in the area around Losheimergraben and Lanzerath, although its advance was already behind schedule and was hindered by the successful American retrograde manoeuvre around Saint-Vith, which also tied down forces of the German 5th Armoured Army.[21] The most significant breakthrough occurred in the latter's sector where five days into the offensive, the 5th Army had overcome most centres of resistance, the roads towards Bastogne and Houffalize being open. The stiff American resistance, however, had gained sufficient time to reinforce the crossroads of Bastogne.[22]

Montgomery had been watching the unfolding situation closely and made early arrangements to anticipate a German advance to the Meuse and prevent its crossing, ordering the British 2nd Army to redeploy its XXX Army Corps between Leuven and Namur.[23] In addition, forces including SAS troops were tasked with collecting information and preparing the defence of the Meuse bridges between Liège and Givet.[24]

On the afternoon of 19 December, Major Philip Yorke, the 9th Earl of Hardwicke,[25] liaison officer of the SAS brigade, arrived at the barracks in Tervueren where he met 1st Lieutenant Radino. Temporarily replacing Blondeel, who was in England, Radino received a warning order for upcoming operations. Eighteen armoured jeeps would be required on short notice.[26] He rejoiced at the news. In July, he should have been the first of the squadron to be dropped by parachute but an accident in Scotland had put him in hospital for several weeks, while all the others would soon find themselves on operations. Now, however, he would have the honour of commanding the squadron.[27]

Around 8 pm, a telephone call from the 21st Army Group ordered the squadron to report at an RV a mile north of Gembloux by 3 am the next morning with eighteen fully equipped jeeps and three days' worth of rations. An update was provided around 9:15 pm: the squadron was now ordered to leave with all armoured jeeps and all combat personnel and as many rations as possible. Personnel other than jeep crews would be transported by 15-cwt lorries.

The squadron was organised as follows:

'A' Troop:

- One section of five jeeps commanded by 1st Lieutenant Van der Heyden (OC 'A' Troop)
- One section of five jeeps commanded by 1st Lieutenant Renkin
- One section of four jeeps commanded by Warrant Officer Thonard

'B' Troop:

- One section of four jeeps commanded by 1st Lieutenant Radino (OC 'B' Troop and temporary commanding the squadron)
- One section of three jeeps commanded by 1st Lieutenant Romnée
- One section of three jeeps commanded by Sergeant Krolikowski
- Two 15-cwt lorries with the remaining combat personnel

At 1 am on 20 December, the unit left Tervueren and reached the RV almost two hours later, where it linked up with Yorke and an American liaison officer. The SAS liaison officer outlined the squadron's task: to check the state of the bridges over the Meuse and the troops defending them, between Liège and Givet, and to patrol the road from Liège to Givet to prevent the Meuse crossing by enemy forward elements. The plan appeared somewhat ambitious since a distance of over 60 miles had to be covered. To execute it, the squadron's subordinate units were each assigned their patrolling sector:

- Van der Heyden's and Thonard's sections, less two jeeps, between Liège (included) and Huy (excluded)

- Déom's team (from 'A' Troop) with two jeeps, between Huy (included) and Namur (excluded)
- Romnée's section between Namur (included) to Wépion (included)
- Radino's section between Wépion (excluded) and Dinant (included)
- Krolikowski's section between Dinant (excluded) and Waulsort (included)
- Renkin's section between Waulsort (excluded) to Givet (included)

The squadron HQ was to stay in Wépion, while two lorries with the squadron's reserve would stay at the RV. A dispatch rider would maintain communications between the HQ and the RV. Van der Heyden's and Thonard's sections and Déom's team were to send their reports directly to the RV, while the other sections had to send a representative to Wépion by 8 am the next morning.

At the agreed time, Romnée and Radino showed up at Wépion and a situation report was sent to the brigade's liaison officer: the original road bridge in Dinant had been destroyed, but had been replaced by a new American one, guarded by a military police platoon; the railway bridge between Houx and Anhée had been partially destroyed but still allowed personnel on foot to cross the Meuse, the few guards expected to be withdrawn soon; the bridge at Yvoir was impassable for vehicles and unguarded; the bridge at Lustin had been destroyed; two bridges over the Sambre river at Namur had been destroyed but repaired, both being lightly guarded; the Meuse road and railway bridges in the same city had been heavily damaged but repaired, with a handful of military policemen guarding them. According to a civilian guard on one of the bridges in Romnée's sector, some eighty enemy paratroopers had been dropped in the Flawinne – Malonne area, west of the Meuse near Namur. There was no news from the other sections, though.[28]

On the morning of 20 December, Montgomery was given command of the American 9th Army and 1st Army,[29] with Major General Middleton's VIII Corps being reassigned from Hodges' 1st to Patton's 3rd Army.[30] This temporary arrangement ensured that all Allied ground forces in the northern part of the salient were under one commander, while Bradley, unable to maintain adequate communications with Simpson and Hodges from his HQ in Luxembourg, could give his full attention to the operations on the southern shoulder.[31]

Back at the Belgian SAS HQ, a message from the brigade's liaison officer came in around 11:30 am, ordering it to check if the bridge at Dinant was prepared for demolition and to try finding information related to the rumour on enemy parachute drops. Radino went to Dinant and met the commander of the construction engineers, who was very reluctant to give any information, admitting, however, that there were no explosives and making clear that even if he had any, he would refuse to prepare the bridge and would only act upon the orders of the commander of the 375th Construction Engineer Regiment.

In the meantime, it was becoming clear why the other sections had not sent in any reports yet. Most had been running into trouble; some having been detained by American forces on the suspicion of being enemy disguised as Allies. According to Radino's report, American forces had captured Germans trying to infiltrate the American lines near Liège in an SAS jeep, which had probably been captured in France.[32]

Whether the information provided to Radino was entirely correct is hard to verify. At least one SAS jeep in running order had been reported captured by the Germans, during Operation 'Haggard'[33], but it would be hard to imagine that American frontline troops would have had any knowledge of even the existence of the SAS, let alone whether they would have been able to identify an SAS jeep, especially when assuming that its occupants would have been dressed in American uniforms. While the exact jeep type matters not, the reported jeep most likely operated as part of Operation '*Greif*' (Griffin), an operation relying on deception and commanded by *SS-Obersturmbannführer* Otto Skorzeny. His forces included Armoured Brigade 150 (its strength assessed at nearly 2,000 men,[34] out of the planned 3,300)[35] and *Einheit Stielau* (Stielau unit), a company-sized commando unit named after its commander. The plan was for the brigade to follow the German 6th Armoured Army's spearheads, bypass them at night and seize at least two intact bridges over the Meuse.[36] Skorzeny's forces were supposed to be disguised as Americans, but American English-speaking personnel and American vehicles and equipment were in severe short supply.[37] Lacking the required American equipment, the brigade's – mainly German – vehicles were painted green, often displaying a white five-pointed star,[38] while the few Panther tanks in its inventory had been structurally modified to resemble American M-10 tank destroyers.[39] The delay in the advance and the associated loss of surprise rapidly diminished the utility of the brigade, which was re-tasked to be used as a normal army unit only a few days into the offensive. The Stielau unit, on the other hand, was much more successful. Grouping the best English speakers, kitted out in American uniforms, and equipped with American jeeps, several teams managed to conduct deep reconnaissance and sabotage operations and to create confusion behind Allied lines.[40] This situation resulted in the Belgian SAS patrols being detained by American forces in multiple locations. Some were able to resume their tasks quickly, but others remained in American custody for prolonged periods. To remedy this problem, jeep drivers were issued with identification documents, but the bad quality of the hastily produced forms only increased the difficulties when encountering Americans.

At 6 pm, the brigade's liaison officer visited the HQ at Wépion and orders were issued to cease operations between Liège and Namur and to limit the squadron's operations to the southern sector. 'B' Troop was now to patrol between Namur (included) and Dinant (excluded), while 'A' Troop was to cover the area between Dinant (included) and Givet (included). Three sections were also tasked with crossing the Meuse and patroling east of the river during the night: Krolikowski with three jeeps on the road between Namur and Marche-en-Famenne, Romnée with four jeeps between Dinant and Rochefort, and Renkin with three jeeps between Givet and Chanly.[41]

Renkin's patrol ran into trouble, as testified by d'Oultremont:

> Just before Givet, our jeep, at the head of the column, was stopped by Americans who asked for our papers. Because a Belgian citizen from Chanly had generously served us with *péquet* [a strong local alcoholic drink], we burst into laughter. Moreover, Mas was oinking under a tarpaulin. These brave Americans immediately went into battle stations, believing a German deception or surprise attack had hit them; they alerted their comrades and in no time, we

were surrounded by ten soldiers, their guns pointed towards us, while we were laughing more and more. Fortunately, Lieutenant Renkin, who spoke English perfectly, arrived at that moment to clarify the situation. Without his prompt and effective intervention, we would probably have been shot by our Allies for attempted espionage.[42]

On the morning of 21 December, Romnée had nothing to report; Krolikowski reported having been in touch with elements of withdrawing American forces,[43] but could not obtain any useful information; Renkin had been told Luxembourg refugees – many of them armed – had been spotted in the vicinity of Chanly, but was unable to check for himself. Radino was told by the brigade's liaison officer to follow up on the Luxembourgers and went with his section to Chanly. The story was confirmed by the town's mayor: headed by a chief of a Luxembourg resistance group, some sixty-five refugees from Clervaux were now staying in Chanly and Resteigne, and some twenty more in Beauraing. Radino asked the mayor and the commander of the *Gendarmerie* of Wellin to disarm the refugees and keep them under control.

At 4 pm, the squadron was informed that an officer from the 21st Army Group would arrive at 10 pm and had to be escorted to the HQ of the American 84th Division in Marche-en-Famenne to get a better understanding of the confused situation, information that was needed urgently.

In the evening, Doome was sent out with two jeeps to conduct a standing patrol to protect a railway crossing just east of Namur. By 11 pm, the officer from the 21st Army Group had still not arrived, so – as previously agreed – Radino himself went to Marche. The two jeeps of his party made slow progress in the dark, the road being used by convoys. A lone enemy aeroplane dropped some six bombs along their route, without doing any harm to the Belgians. Marche was reached by 1:30 am on 22 December. Radino and Krolikowsli went to the divisional HQ, but no one wanted to talk to them. Both men returned to join the rest of their party at Déom's house in Marche, where two American civil affairs officers were billeted. Radino explained to them the urgency to contact the 84th's HQ; the two officers went to the divisional HQ and returned with an officer who agreed to take Radino, Krolikowski and Déom to the HQ. After checking their identity documents, the intelligence officer gave them a detailed overview of the situation of American forces in the Ardennes. When the briefing was finished, the Belgians wanted to leave the HQ but were suddenly detained, surrounded by armed guards, their finger on the trigger. Once again, Radino had to explain the purpose of their task, but to no avail. Around 5:30 am, the Americans were finally convinced the Belgians were not disguised Germans and permitted them to leave.

By now, the road from Marche to Givet via Rochefort was reportedly cut by German patrols, so it was decided to take the longer road back over Ciney. Running out of time and the weather deteriorating, the jeeps took the risk of using their headlights and by 7:30, Radino's party had arrived at the predetermined RV at Petit-Doische, on the border between France and Belgium northeast of Givet, where a Phantom patrol was waiting to receive Radino's report. The reported situation sounded bleak: the Germans were advancing to the northwest, with a spearhead identified at Hotton and another at Hamoir; the American 106th Infantry Division was cut off south of the Amblève river, and the situation south of Marche-en-Famenne was confused; La Roche and Bastogne were still under American control, however, and the Germans seemingly bypassed larger towns; and again there were reports of German paratroopers having being dropped.

At 9 am, having completed its task, the patrol returned to the squadron HQ. Blondeel had also made his way to Wépion, having returned from England to take command of his squadron. Jeep patrols continued to be conducted between Namur and Givet throughout the day but were finally regrouped at Wépion, as British armoured units and the 6th Airborne Division were in the process of taking positions along the Meuse.

At 1 pm on 23 December, the squadron left Wépion and returned towards Brussels, reaching its barracks in Tervueren by 1:15 pm.[44]

Yet the Christmas period would not allow for much rest. The squadron had to secure the communication centre of the 21st Army Group, located at the Maison Haute in Boitsfort, Brussels, as it was feared German paratroopers might attack the site. It was freezing, but the men had to stay outside in their open jeeps. Doctor Sevens diagnosed several cases of bronchitis, after which Blondeel was allowed to have his troops take turns to shelter in the Boitsfort church. The men were also allowed into the aisle of the church wearing their combat uniform to attend the Christmas mass.[45]

The perceived threat from German airborne forces was unfounded but highly understandable. Operation *'Stößer'* (Sparrowhawk), commanded by Lieutenant Colonel Friedrich *Freiherr* von der Heydte, was planned as a supporting operation by a parachute battle group that would be dropped behind American lines, to secure the vital crossroads along the flank of the German line of advance and block the movement of Allied reinforcements.[46] Its intended DZ was at the High Fens plateau near the Baraque Michel crossroads on *Rollbahn* 'A', where a link-up with the 12th SS Armoured Division would be conducted.[47] Already behind schedule due to fuel shortages, strong winds and pilot error resulted in the paratroopers being scattered over a wide area.[48] Not more than a third of the Junkers Ju 52 aeroplanes managed to drop their troops (some 300 in total) near the intended DZ, of which only half could be assembled. The remaining transport aircraft, two-thirds of the total force, did not reach their target.[49] In addition, as no radio sets survived the drop, von der Heydte was unable to communicate with any other force.[50] While the Germans' first and only nighttime combat jump of the war ended in disaster, the unintentional effect of widely scattered airborne troops and a lack of knowledge of their actual size and objectives nevertheless resulted in nervousness in the Allied rear areas.

Supporting the Allied counterattack: Operation 'Regent'

On Christmas Eve, the reconnaissance battle group of the German 2nd Armoured Division reached Foy-Notre-Dame, 4 miles east of Dinant. It would become the most westward point of the German advance. Since 23 December, the main crossing sites over the Meuse at Namur, Dinant and Givet were being defended by the British 29th Armoured Brigade (part of Lieutenant General Horrocks' XXX Army Corps), which, together with the American 2nd Armored Division, halted the German 5th Armoured Army's advance.[51]

Expecting a renewed attack in the northern sector, Montgomery wanted to ensure the integrity of the northern Allied lines, while preparing Major General Collins' VII Army Corps (part of the American 1st Army) to launch a counterattack towards Houffalize. Meanwhile, in the southern sector, Patton's 3rd Army had started its attack to the north on 22 December, led by Major General Millikin's III Army Corps. Five days later, on 26 December, the 4th Armored Division reached Bastogne and lifted the siege of the encircled city.[52] Once Bastogne was relieved, the plan was for III Army Corps to widen the corridor to provide a secure base for the 3rd Army's northeast thrust to link up with 1st Army forces east of Houffalize, cutting off the outflanked German forces to the west.[53]

On 27 December, Blondeel received a warning order to prepare for new operations in the Ardennes. The squadron had to join the 29th Armoured Brigade the next day and was likely to conduct recce operations with the 61st Reconnaissance Regiment. An advance party of two jeeps with Romnée, Delagaye, De Vulder and Ratinckx left for Mettet at 2 pm, while Squadron Leader Smith, the liaison officer, went directly to the 29th's HQ.

On 28 December, the squadron left Tervueren at 1 pm, with twenty-two jeeps, six lorries and a staff car. Mettet was reached at 4 pm, where the unit was joined by Smith. A meeting was held at the Château de Neffe, HQ of the 6th Airborne Division, whose commander confirmed the squadron would be attached to the 29th Armoured Brigade for reconnaissance duties. The squadron drove on to Froidfontaine, where accommodation had been prepared by an advance party.[54]

By now, the German 5th Army's westernmost divisions, having insufficient combat power for renewed attempts to reach the Meuse, were being pushed back. The 9th Armoured Division had to give up Humain on 27 December.[55] Two days later, the division was pulled back from Rochefort, taking positions on the high ground northwest of Wavreille. On its left flank, the 2nd Armoured Division occupied defensive positions along the line Wavreille-Bure-Mirwart.[56] Also elements from the *Panzer Lehr* Division, having withdrawn earlier from Rochefort, were in the Bure area.[57]

On 29 December, the British XXX Corps issued operational instruction no. 41, covering a regrouping of the defence in the Meuse area. The intent was for the army corps to protect all crossings over the Meuse between Givet and Huy, to hold a defensive position facing south on the line Dinant – Wanlin – Aye and to operate offensively south of the Lesse river on the general axis Givet – Saint-Hubert. The 6th Airborne Division (which had been hurriedly moved from England during the Christmas period, coming under the command of XXX Corps) would be responsible for the protection of the Meuse between Givet (included) and Namur (included), to hold the sector of the front between Dinant (included) and Houyet (included), and for carrying out offensive operations on the general axis Givet – Saint-Hubert. In addition to some other non-organic units, the Belgian SAS Squadron, the 29th Armoured Brigade and the 61st Reconnaissance Regiment were placed under the command of the 6th Airborne Division.[58]

Blondeel, Smith and 1st Lieutenant Laurent de Merkline had meetings with the units they would be working with in the days to come. At Mesnil-Saint-Blaise, the brigadier commanding the 29th Armoured Brigade welcomed the prospect that the Belgians would be able to question local civilians. At Pondrôme, the colonel commanding the 61st Reconnaissance Regiment immediately requested three jeep patrols to be made available. Three patrols from 'A' Troop were tasked.

The 'Tiger' patrol, consisting of three jeeps commanded by Van der Heyden, left the HQ of the 61st Reconnaissance Regiment at 1:15 pm, reaching Halma some forty-five minutes later and continuing towards Tellin, via Neupont and Resteigne. A mile northwest of Tellin, contact was established with a halted armoured car. Five enemy tanks were reported at Belvaux, a further mile to the north and Tellin was confirmed to be in German hands as well. During the recce, two jeeps hit each other, resulting only in material damage. A recovery lorry from the 61st Reconnaissance Regiment successfully retrieved the broken-down jeep and by 6 pm, the patrol was back at its base.[59]

The 'Panther' patrol, consisting of three jeeps commanded by Thonard[60] and augmented by an armoured car, conducted a recce to Han-sur-Lesse, driving via Halma, Sourd d'Ave, Ave-et-Auffe and Auffe. Before reaching the destroyed road bridge in Han-sur-Lesse, the presence of a German tank on the far side of the Lesse was noticed. The lead jeep immediately turned back to get out of sight. Simultaneously, Van Broekhuizen blew his horn to warn the lead vehicle of the danger, having been informed by a civilian that three tanks and some dismounted personnel were present in the town. At least three Germans opened fire on the lead vehicle, which broke contact while allowing the covering jeep and armoured car to return fire. The patrol then withdrew some 250 yards. The lead jeep had been hit in the tyre, but when its crew tried to replace the wheel, they again came under machine gun fire and, returning fire, the patrol withdrew further from the village. Five Germans with a machine gun running across an open field were fired upon; three were seen falling, the others taking cover. After informing the squadron commander of the 61st, the patrol was ordered to return.

The 'Lion' patrol was not sent out but kept in reserve.

On 30 December, three patrols were conducted. Radino's 'L for Lucky' patrol, with three jeeps, was attached to 'B' Squadron of the 61st. Starting at half eight at the Regiments' HQ, the patrol arrived at Auffe by 9:45 am, where a temporary defensive position was established, together with two armoured cars. Civilians reported that Belvaux and Han-sur-Lesse were now clear of enemy troops. The jeeps moved towards Han-sur-Lesse and Radino, Maréchal and Bogaert conducted a recce, finding the bridge destroyed and capturing two German officers that had been left behind. By 12:30, the patrol reached Belvaux, which was found empty of enemy troops, its bridge being blown. Half an hour later, Han-sur-Lesse was reached. The patrol then went back to Halma to report its findings and subsequently returned to Froidfontaine to have a meal. Back at Halma by 3:15, Radino's men were split. One element (also designated as 'L for Lucky' in the after-action report) was tasked with joining the party on the road from Tellin to Bure and to return at nightfall. This likely referred to Romnée's patrol (see below). The other element (designated as 'F for Freddy') found the bridge at Chanly destroyed and made a detour via Neupont, where sentries posted near the bridge over the Lesse reported the road to the east of the river being heavily mined. The patrol proceeded cautiously without detecting any mines, but due to the delays this caused, did not continue for much further and returned to Halma, where it reported at 7:05 pm, before driving back to Froidfontaine.

The second patrol on that day, called 'J for Johnny', was conducted by three jeeps under the command of Romnée, who had to collect information on the enemy in Tellin and Belvaux. His element was reinforced with an armoured car, three scout cars and an assault troop in two half-tracks of the 61st. Finding Tellin clear of enemy, at 3:15 pm, Romnée received orders to proceed in the direction of Bure and to reconnoitre the village. The assault troop and a scout car remained in reserve in Tellin to be called forward when needed. The remainder continued, a scout car in front and to the rear, with an armoured car and the three jeeps in between. By 3:40, the patrol found itself on the long straight stretch of road towards Bure and at some 400 yards west of the village, the scout car in front was shot at by what was believed to be one or two anti-tank guns or tanks.[61] The first two rounds missed their target. The scout car reacted by initiating a smoke screen to provide instant concealment but turned around when the wind quickly dispersed the smoke. Romnée's jeep reversed, firing its twin machine guns. The third German round stopped the withdrawing scout car, killing or wounding its crew, none of whom was seen leaving their vehicle. Immediately afterwards, the armoured car received a direct hit, setting it on fire. Two crew members were seen escaping the flames after throwing a No. 77 smoke grenade, while Vijt did his utmost to provide covering fire from Romnée's jeep, despite his narrow field of fire. Romnée located the enemy positions, including two machine guns sited near the first house at the village's western fringe. The enemy fired high explosive rounds in Romnée's direction, narrowly missing his jeep, but wounding De Jonghe. The driver was hit by shrapnel, removing part of his forearm and fracturing his elbow. The fuel tank was also hit. De Jonghe informed Romnée that he was wounded, assuming his arm had been blown off. Nevertheless, he continued reversing. Vijt fired a short burst at the enemy and Romnée jumped out of the jeep, pulled the clutch out of gear, helped De Jonghe out of his jeep, put him in the rear of the vehicle and jumped into the driver's seat himself. He then turned the jeep and drove further back, while Vijt, now lying on the jeep's bonnet, continued firing the frontal machine guns in the direction of Bure. As soon as the Germans ceased fire, Romnée stopped the jeep and put a tourniquet on De Jonghe's heavily bleeding arm. He also picked up the armoured car's wireless operator but failed to find the vehicle commander. Back at Tellin, the other two jeeps and the remaining scout car were found on the road just west of the village, where the two wounded were handed over to a local doctor.

Romnée ran into a patrol commanded by Krolikowski on its way to Wavreille. He advised Krolikowski not to start his patrol and requested guidance from the 61st, who cancelled the mission. Upon learning from civilians that a British officer who was wounded in the leg was trying to reach Tellin, Romnée's three jeeps again went forward to rescue the Brit. No enemy reaction was observed until they reached Tellin again on their way back when shelling resumed. Covered by Krolikowski's jeeps, a British foot patrol attempted to reach the wrecks that had been left behind, but the enemy's presence prevented them from reaching the scene, so they had to withdraw. Unable to advance any further, the Belgians returned to Froidfontaine.[62]

The third patrol was conducted by d'Oultremont, with four jeeps. Arrived at Libin, he was placed under the command of a British major and saw his patrol split in two. Levaux's and Brasseur's jeeps ('Panther 3' and 'Panther 5') were attached to a British patrol with three armoured cars and an assault section. At 10:30 am, they left Libin. Less than a mile on the southern road to Smuid – the first objective – the patrol was stopped by an abatis made of fir trees. While the obstacle was being cleared, others continued on foot. Upon entering the village, a German three-man patrol dispersed when they noticed they had been spotted, but no other enemy forces were seen. The bridge across the railway less than a mile to the east of Smuid was found intact but was blocked by pines interspersed with mines. A recce through the woods along the L'Homme river valley to the north up to Mirwart – the second objective – revealed the presence of booby traps on the railway that snaked along the valley. At 4 pm, the patrol was joined by the other half of d'Oultremont's party. The latter's jeeps ('Lion 2' and 'Lion 5') had left Libin at 11 am, taking a secondary road to the east-north-east towards Hatrival. They halted when entering the woods 1.5 miles from Libin to leave their vehicles and drivers behind and continue on foot with the four remaining men toward the Hatrival railway station. Finding the nearby bridge destroyed but no Germans in the vicinity, they let their jeeps catch up. On the eastern side of the railway line, the patrol had to slow down, as mines were widespread. Hatrival was seen to be strongly defended by an estimated 200-300 Germans with 88 mm guns, with a forward position on the hill a few hundred yards southwest of the village. The Belgians encountered two American patrols, who reported no enemy had been seen. Their recce finished, they returned to Libin, where they reported to the British OC and then joined the other half of their party at Smuid.

In the evening, Blondeel conferred with his officers to discuss the recent events. Based on what had happened to Romnée's patrol, he insisted that jeeps were not to leave cover when the enemy was known to be in the vicinity, preferring dismounted actions instead. Also, the large fuel tanks that had been added to the rear compartment of the jeeps caused concern. It was agreed to have them removed whenever they would be back in Brussels, as it was not possible to discard them in the field.

The last day of 1944 saw continued patrolling activities. The Belgians were tasked with conducting recces of Resteigne, Tellin, Bure, Grupont and Wavreille. Around 9 am, seven jeeps and a 15-cwt lorry with a wireless set No. 18 departed from the HQ, together with some British armoured cars, making their initial movement toward Resteigne. Information obtained from civilians indicated that Tellin was not in German hands. Leaving the armoured cars behind in reserve, the jeeps and the lorry moved on in two groups. From Tellin, Van der Heyden's patrol, consisting of 'Tiger 1', 'Tiger 2', 'Lion 2' and the signals lorry, continued to Wavreilles. Some 700 yards north of Tellin, after crossing the small Boyes river, the patrol followed a track west of the road, before joining the road again. At this point, just west of the hill on top of which stood the Notre-Dame de Bure chapel, the patrol split. 'Tiger 1' and 'Tiger 2' continued on the road to Wavreille; the others drove to the chapel.

Van der Heyden's two 'Tiger' jeeps continued to the cutting some 1,000 yards short of the village, from where part of his men moved on foot, the jeeps following behind them. The patrol encountered three tripwires with some 50 lbs of explosives and disarmed the booby trap. An unguarded roadblock was found in the town centre and some Germans with three light armoured cars were discovered in a farm. A plan was formulated to capture the Germans but was rejected by the British regiment. Van der Heyden's men then returned south to the Notre-Dame de Bure chapel, which was now under the control of the other half of his patrol.

While Van der Heyden was on its way to Wavreille, the other half of the patrol reconnoitred the area around the Notre-Dame de Bure (aka Notre-Dame de Haurt) chapel. 'Lion 2', with d'Oultremont, Oosters and Mas, moved uphill and captured a sentry outside and five Germans inside the chapel. The prisoners of war were taken back to Tellin, interrogated – revealing they were an OP party put in place the previous day – and evacuated to the regiment under the supervision of 2nd Lieutenant Van Cauwenberghe, the squadron's signals officer.[63] Luckily for d'Oultremont, the Germans seemed to have no intention of resisting, as he testified after the war:

> We left Froidfontaine (Vonêche) to cross the sector in the direction of Resteigne, Tellin and Bure. We had to discover the defensive positions presumably occupied by the enemy around Bure. At 3 km [2 miles] from Tellin, 1st Lieutenant Van der Heyden, considering the fact that my jeep was a non-armoured model, sent me to the neighbouring heights, Notre-Dame de Bure, which was supposed to be in American hands. On the heights, my two comrades, Mas and Oosters, went deeper into the forest on a recce. Left on my own, I saw a man coming from the bushes in my direction. I approached him without a weapon, assuming he was an American. To my astonishment, I noticed it was a German, his rifle on his shoulder. We were both surprised and frightened. His emotions must have been stronger than mine because immediately, he raised his hands in the air and shouted *"Kamerad!"* [friend]. I savagely shouted *"Schweinhund!"* [literally: swine-hound, used as a typical insult in German], which made him lose self-control. He dropped his rifle and followed me towards the jeep, 50 metres away, where I, very relieved, pointed the two machine guns at him. I then questioned my prisoner: *"Haben sie Kameraden?"* ["Do you have friends"] He answered, trembling: *"Nein, nein!"* ["No, no!"] However, to stay on the side of caution, Oosters decided to continue his inspection and go to the chapel 80 metres away. He heard German chatter in the chapel, entered inside with his Tommy gun at the ready and discovered six [*sic*] Germans, who surrendered. Later, guarding the prisoners was left to another group without [sufficient] small arms and to whom I gave my carbine, which I knew didn't work. I had applied too much oil, which froze at the temperature of -10° to -12°, having blocked the firing pin![64]

Afterwards, 'Tiger 1', 'Tiger 2' and 'Lion 2' were sent back to the chapel, together with a scout car and an armoured car. A patrol led by Déom descended into the valley as far as the track junction with the road leaving from Bure to the northwest, about halfway between the chapel and the town.

Going back in time, the other patrol, consisting of 'Lion 1', 'Lion 3', 'Tiger 3' and 'Tiger 4' and accompanied by a British assault section, left Tellin ten minutes past noon. Its task was to find the position of an anti-tank gun in the vicinity of Bure and to support the British assault section that would search the wooded area to the southwest of the village. The vehicles followed the road to the south from

Tellin, which quickly turned to the southeast, going uphill. Leaving the Brits behind to search the wood, they continued to the high ground and provided overwatch until they lost sight of them. Moving over the top of the hill, the four jeeps continued to the south and, at the T-junction north of the Tiène des Pôtis[65] wood, turned east to take the secondary road, going east initially, then northeast on the road towards Bure, while taking occasional halts to observe. A score of Germans running across a field towards a deep valley covered with woods was observed some 800 yards north of their observation position just east of the T-junction. Having moved on along the ridgeline, the four jeeps then turned due north, towards the middle of the southern edge of the wood a mile southwest of Bure. Now in completely open terrain, the jeeps halted halfway to observe, then moved on again, Renkin's jeep ('Lion 1', with Lorphèvre and de Villermont) taking the lead the whole time. Warned by Polain, whose rear gunner (Rossius) had noticed some movement, Renkin moved on taking a new halt at a height near the edge of the wood, while two other jeeps were providing overwatch, ready to fire. Lorphèvre dismounted from Renkin's jeep to investigate. After about 30 yards, he was fired upon and went into cover, returning fire with his submachine gun and signalling his jeep to recover him. For a couple of minutes, the supporting jeeps opened fire on likely enemy positions with their twin Vickers K guns, covering the withdrawal of 'Lion 1', who was moving downhill. 'Lion 3' (with Barette, Patyn and Regner) moved between 'Tiger 3' (with Mestdagh, Ravet and Thévissen) and 'Tiger 4' (with Polain, Rossius and Demery) but fired only a couple of inaccurate rounds. Polain gave a signal for Barette to take his position in the back of the formation again; 'Tiger 4' reversed and positioned itself on the hilltop to the south, allowing observation and providing cover to the rear. Reaching the fire position of 'Tiger 3' and 'Tiger 4', Renkin gave the signal to turn around. The three vehicles turned and continued their hasty withdrawal.

Suddenly, a gun roared. It was an anti-tank gun opening fire on the jeeps from about a mile away. The first round missed. Sitting in the back of his jeep, Lorphèvre was firing towards the woods. Then a second round was fired. 'Lion1' did not stand a chance. A fireball erupted, killing its crew instantly.

Finding themselves on open ground and unable to help 'Lion 1', the other jeeps had no option but to leave the area at full speed, firing their rear Vickers K guns. From his overwatch position, Barette's crew could not see 'Lion 1', but was horrified when it saw only two jeeps withdrawing. Still under fire, all three surviving jeeps withdrew while the last shells fell no further than 10 yards behind Barette's jeep. He assessed the gun as being a 37 mm or 50 mm gun, believing anything heavier would have resulted in shrapnel causing additional casualties.

Meanwhile, on the northern side of the town, jeeps joined Déom's patrol to engage a platoon-sized element of Germans moving from Bure towards the southwest. They were fired upon by a gun near the main road a few hundred yards west of Bure and by a machine gun positioned on a crest on the northwestern side of the town. The Belgians returned fire and withdrew, 'Tiger 1' and 'Lion 2' to the west and 'Tiger 2' north towards the chapel. During the withdrawal, d'Oultremont was slightly wounded when shrapnel caused a long, shallow graze to his head. Although in great pain and virtually blinded by the profuse bleeding, he continued driving his jeep backwards under fire for several hundred yards, bringing his men back to safety and refusing any medical aid before having been able to report back.[66] The element that returned to the chapel area handed over the coordinates of the German positions to the accompanying forward observation officer, after which the Germans were shelled. The German artillery reacted swiftly, shelling the chapel and Tellin. By 4 pm, the jeeps were back in Tellin.

Van der Heyden, with Smith and De Block, attempted to return to the scene to recover the bodies of their fallen comrades. They were shelled as soon as they left Tellin and all the woods in the vicinity now seemed occupied by German troops. By 6 pm, they were back in camp.

Even when many individuals were praised for their professional behaviour under enemy fire, New Year's Eve proved an anticlimax to conclude an eventful year. The squadron did not have much time to mourn, however, as operations would resume soon, so lessons from this fateful day had to be identified and implemented. Cooperation between jeeps was seen as a necessity and whenever there was any doubt a vehicle could pass, it was suggested it should be preceded by a foot patrol to confirm. There was also a recommendation for jeeps to be followed by a 15-cwt lorry with an assault section, which would allow carrying out short foot patrols without the need for two men of each jeep to dismount, so the jeeps' machine guns could remain manned.

On the morning of New Year's Day, Krolikowski reported at the British regimental HQ at Halma. His section ('F for Freddy'), composed of three jeeps, was tasked with conducting a reconnaissance patrol to Resteigne to check for enemy presence. A scout car with a radio was added to his patrol. Finding no enemy, the next assigned task was to move to Tellin and re-establish contact with the main body of armoured cars, contact with whom had been lost. More than a mile east of Resteigne, contact with a half-track was made on the open ground north of the Resteigne – Tellin road. Suspicious movement was seen in the bushes about half a mile north of Tellin. A reconnaissance by fire was conducted, using twin Vickers K and Bren guns, but no reaction was observed, after which the patrol continued to Tellin. At noon, the patrol was shelled by mortar fire and in the afternoon a third task was executed, to conduct a recce of the heights between Tellin and the Tiène des Pôtis woods, where the enemy had been reported. A seven-man dismounted patrol, equipped with a Bren gun and 2" mortar was sent out, which observed four enemies at the nearby crossroads (some 1,200 yards southeast of the centre of Tellin) and a roadblock around 1,000 yards southwest from the crossroads, where the road was about to leave the wooded area. On the main road going south from Tellin, the jeeps joined the patrol, picked up the men and resumed their route, going south on the road between the Bois de Bestin and the Bois de Tellin forests. Some 400 yards into the woods, the patrol encountered two men from the French SAS, after which the patrol returned to Tellin and further back to Froidfontaine.[67]

The French 4th SAS, aka the *2e Régiment de Chasseurs Parachutistes*, commanded by Major Puech-Samson, had been assigned to the American 3rd Army. One of its tasks was the establishment of liaison with the British 6th Airborne Division on the left flank of Patton's advance.[68]

Still on 1 January, another patrol was conducted more to the north. 'Panther 1', 'Panther 2' and 'Panther 3', commanded by Thonard, departed Froidfontaine at 8:15

am to receive orders at the HQ. They were attached to 'C' Squadron of the 61st and tasked with once again reconnoitring the Notre-Dame de Bure chapel. Two armoured cars reinforced the patrol. Around 9:15, the patrol was on its way to Belvaux along the small road north that eventually turned into a track. Although anticipating a German presence in the woods a mile north of Tellin, no enemy was seen. Reaching the secondary road coming out of Belvaux, Thonard left an armoured car behind to cover the patrol's rear, turned east across open country and crossed the bridge over the small Rau river. Arriving at a woodland area, Thonard sent out a foot patrol under the command of Ratinckx, equipped with a No. 38 wireless set, to check if the jeeps would be able to reach the top of the ridge overlooking the Tellin – Wavreille road, from where Thonard intended to continue on foot towards the Bure chapel. Radio communications with Ratinckx could not be established, however, so Thonard decided to follow the patrol on his own, trying to catch up. Failing to find the patrol, he decided to conduct the recce himself. Now again in exposed terrain, Thonard found himself on the receiving end of rifle fire originating from the area around the chapel and returned to the jeeps, meeting his returning patrol on his way. Before returning to Resteigne, the patrol checked out Belvaux, which was found free of enemy. The bridge over the Lesse had been destroyed but a 30" deep ford suitable for armoured vehicles was identified some 120 yards downstream. By 6 pm, the patrol was back in base.

On 2 January, two patrols were conducted. Levaux, with three 'Panther' call signs, accomplished his first task between 10 and 11 am. With a view to the upcoming Allied counteroffensive, passages for tanks over the Lesse had to be identified. Having halted some 600 yards from the village, Levaux and five others proceeded on foot and another suitable site was found, this one close to the wood north of the village. In the afternoon, a second task was conducted, for which the three jeeps were supported by three armoured cars. Again, the chapel of Notre-Dame de Bure and the village of Wavreille had to be reconnoitred. Stand-off observation revealed nothing, but three Germans on their way back from Tellin were captured. The patrol left their jeeps in a supporting position south of the crossroads half a mile southwest from the chapel and advanced with the Belgians dismounted behind the armoured cars. The chapel seemed to have been abandoned in a hurry since helmets and respirators were lying on the ground. The surroundings were observed but no indications of German presence were seen, after which the patrol returned to the jeeps. A third task consisted of a recce of Wavreille. The armoured cars in the lead, the jeeps followed 100 yards behind on the road from Tellin to Wavreille. Enemy artillery fire was observed on the chapel they had just left, indicating they had been seen. Some 400 yards from their target, the patrol halted to observe. The jeeps with their drivers were left in the bushes, while Levaux and the remainder moved on using a small track. One hundred yards from the village, they noticed a German sentry, his gun ready to fire. Levaux's party returned to the vehicles and passed on the information to the officer commanding the armoured cars. Assuming his recce mission was now completed, Levaux was surprised to see two French jeeps arrive. The French asked the British officer to attack the village. The armoured cars and French jeeps started firing towards the first houses of the village. The Germans replied and the Belgian jeeps, moving into position, also opened up. Next, the village was searched, but the enemy was found to have withdrawn. Civilians informed the patrol that a couple of crossroads had been mined. When a German tank started a counterattack, the patrol withdrew from the village, having expended an excessive amount of ammunition.

The other patrol of the day, with call sign 'L for Lucky', was led by Radino. At 8:45 am, his section with three jeeps was attached to 'C' Squadron, who provided two armoured cars. The patrol's task was to confirm a reported concentration of tanks in the woods north of Han-sur-Lesse. On the road from the southwest of Han-sur-Lesse, the vehicles halted around 800 yards short of the town. From this position near the edge of the wood, Radino, Maréchal and Bogaert conducted a dismounted recce and found the town clear of the enemy. The vehicles then moved to the town, taking defensive positions west of the bridge. A foot patrol with Radino, Van Haezendock, Maréchal, Hendrick and Vos, accompanied by a civilian guide, continued north on the road east of the river, then further east along the road to Hamerenne, a hamlet that had been abandoned by the Germans since 31 December. The patrol found evidence of abandoned OPs in the woods, as well as tank positions. Proceeding to the main road between Rochefort and Wavreille, German and American ammunition stocks were found in farms. The patrol returned to Han-sur-Lesse by approximately the same route and continued to report to the 'C' Squadron HQ in Halma, being shelled for a moment on its way back. At 4:45 pm, the Belgians were sent back to Froidfontaine.

Meanwhile, Rossius had taken the 'Tiger 4' jeep for a ride, against the orders of his vehicle commander. He crashed the jeep and was dismissed from operational duties with 'A' Troop.[69]

On 3 January, the Allied counteroffensive started on the northern flank of the salient. The VII Corps of the American 1st Army attacked from the north and made slow progress in appalling weather conditions against extremely bitter opposition. On the western edge of the salient, the British XXX Corps launched its attack with two divisions in line.[70] In the north, the 53rd (Welsh) Division would attack on the 4th. On its right flank, the 6th Airborne Division started its attack on the 3rd. The 29th Armoured Brigade with units of the 5th Parachute Brigade attacked Bure and Wavreille.[71]

The 13th Parachute Battalion had been assigned Bure as its first objective, with orders to attack Grupont afterwards. The battalion was transported towards Resteigne, where it debussed and marched for around 3 miles, through Tellin, reaching its forming-up place at the eastern edge of the wood just southeast of Bure. At 1 pm, the battalion prepared to attack, 'A' Company having to clear the village, 'B' Company providing support from the high ground and 'C' Company remaining in reserve.[72] It was the start of a gruelling fight, with adversaries finding themselves intermingled, sometimes occupying different floors inside the same building.[73] The confused fighting continued for the next days, in low-visibility conditions due to low cloud cover and snowstorms.[74]

The Belgian SAS Squadron did not join the fight but conducted two familiarisation patrols towards Tellin for Mathijs and Heilporn, both recalled from their training assignment in Leamington Spa. In the afternoon, four jeeps with Blondeel and Van der Heyden returned to the spot where 'Lion 1' had been hit a few days earlier. Finding themselves under inaccurate mortar fire, they arrived at the bodies of their three fallen comrades. The wrecked jeep had had its fuel tanks blown off by the explosion and the unit doctor's assessment showed that Renkin, Lorphèvre and de Villermont had been killed instantaneously. All that could be found on the bodies was quickly collected, but due to enemy fire, the party had to return.

On 4 January, the squadron received orders to move to Halma immediately. The unit departed in the afternoon, leaving a detachment behind under Doome's command to finish the necessary vehicle repairs at the workshop. A meeting was held at Tellin with the CO of the reconnaissance regiment. Its command post was shelled, destroying a neighbouring house, and resulting in a civilian being wounded. The operational situation overview showed that Wavreille was now in British hands and that half of Bure was occupied by friendly forces. Back in Halma, the squadron finished its billeting arrangements, while a logistical convoy arrived from Brussels, including two armoured jeeps for 'B' Troop.

Two patrols were sent out throughout the day, both being tasked with conducting a recce of Wavreille, Lesterny, the Bois de Wève woods a mile north of Bure and the bridge over the L'Homme river, to the east of Lesterny.

The 'Lion' patrol, with three jeeps commanded by Mathijs, was attached to a British patrol of four armoured cars and two sections[75] in Bren Carriers. The recce confirmed that Wavreille itself was under friendly control, but the main crossroads to its northeast was found mined, while the area between both was still within range of German direct-fire gun systems. The patrol was shelled twice, resulting in slight material damage to an unspecified number of jeeps.

The 'Panther' patrol, with three jeeps commanded by Thonard, stayed in Wavreille throughout the day, being shelled four times. Deprez and Delvigne sustained superficial injuries and two jeeps were slightly damaged.

On 5 January, eight interpreters were provided to the 61st, at its commander's request. In the afternoon, Guy van Doosselaere and Charles de T'Serclaes went to 'A' Squadron in Tellin, Jacques Leroy, Alfons Pallemans and Draps went to 'B' Squadron in Redu and Sergeant Emanuel Ryckx with troopers Renaud de Changy and Olivier Gendebien went to 'C' Squadron in Hamayde. Later in the afternoon, a new request was made, now for three sections of ten men each to be attached to British assault sections. Three assault sections were organised by the Belgian squadron and preparations were made for the next day's operations. Van der Heyden's section was assigned to 'A' Squadron, Romnée's section to 'B' Squadron and Mathijs' section to 'C' Squadron. Each one had an armed jeep, a lorry and two Bren guns.[76] Meanwhile, in Bure all German resistance had ceased by 9 pm and an hour later, the commander of the 5th Parachute Brigade ordered the village to be evacuated, starting just before midnight. The 13th Parachute Battalion had lost 189 killed and wounded to liberate the village.[77] Most of some 700 inhabitants had been able to hide in the safety of the cellars of the nearby Alumnat, a boarding school on the northern side of the village. No more than four became casualties, but 119 out of 166 homes were destroyed or badly damaged.[78]

At noon on 6 January, at the command post of the 61st Reconnaissance Regiment, orders were issued to adapt to the new situation.[79] The 61st moved its HQ to Redu, some 7 miles to the south, while its three reconnaissance squadrons moved to Transinne and Libin, a few miles to the southeast of the new HQ location. In the afternoon, difficulties with wireless communications with the SAS Brigade HQ were identified.

It was assumed to be a human problem at the brigade HQ's location. To confirm the assumption, Thonard was sent to Maissin to contact the French SAS to check if they were encountering similar problems. Squadron Leader Smith requested a Phantom officer from the 21st Army Group.

Meanwhile, Romnée's section was involved in the operations of 'B' Squadron, which was now occupying the village of Smuid. Enemy activity was reported on the railway line along the L'Homme valley.

On 7 January, Heilporn was sent to Daverdisse to reconnoitre a suitable site to set up the squadron's HQ. Around 5 pm, the order was given by the regiment to move to the new location. Romnée was still in Smuid. Mathijs was in Séchery. Van der Heyden was in Redu and had drawn a map of the Saint-Hubert Forest, helped by a local forest guard. His recce of the Tellin Forest earlier in the day revealed numerous obstacles, including mines. The snow made it hard to conceal tracks, but Van der Heyden noted this could be used to their advantage. Provided white camouflage clothing was worn, tracks could be followed towards German positions without too much risk. The busy patrol plan was not without problems, though; a lack of deconfliction between patrols in the same congested area might have resulted in blue-on-blue contacts.

On 8 January, snow blizzards hampered vehicle movements. Two additional jeeps were sent out to each patrol to replace the 15-cwt lorries. Lemaire was sent out to the French to serve as an interpreter for the days to come. Van der Heyden reported a German patrol in the northern part of the Bois de Tellin. The wood was patrolled by British assault sections and was found clear of the enemy, but German positions in Mirwart (to the east of the forest) were located. Romnée patrolled the road leaving Smuid from the west, up to 2 miles west of Smuid and found a roadblock along the route. He met a patrol from the 4th SAS, although from his report, an approximate location cannot be deduced. Clashes with the enemy had been reported in the Grande Taille forest (just west of the L'Homme valley, a mile north of Smuid) and when a prisoner was taken, questioning revealed the presence of Germans at Val de Poix, as well as a thirty-man platoon at Mirwart.

On 9 January, the brigade HQ announced that sixty arctic equipment sets would be flown in. Based on the information collected the previous day, the British section with Van der Heyden's men tried to pinpoint the German positions in Mirwart. Neither static surveillance nor recce by fire had any result. It later turned out that some twenty Germans remained in the village but were withdrawn the same night. Romnée's patrol conducted a recce of the railway bridge over the L'Homme a mile south of Mirwart. Fairly new tracks were spotted under the bridge, which was found free of obstacles. In the evening, 'B' Squadron was relieved by 'C' Squadron. 'B' Squadron moved to Séchery to rest, its HQ staying in Boucats, a mile to the east of Séchery.

On 10 January, Radino's three-jeep section was tasked with joining the HQ of the 6th Airborne Armoured Reconnaissance Regiment at Villers-sur-Lesse and to report to Lieutenant Colonel Stuart, its CO. From the regiment's HQ, he was sent to Han-sur-Lesse to report to Captain Selwick, OC of 'B' Squadron. He was ordered to report the next morning in Aye, 2 miles west of Marche-en-Famenne.

Van der Heyden's section was following up on information gained that the enemy was withdrawing and conducted a recce in the vicinity of Mirwart. The motorised patrol became stuck in the soft surface of the tracks in the woods and after several attempts, the four jeeps were left behind with Deprez and the drivers, while the eight others continued on foot. Mirwart was found almost clear of the enemy. A German from the Alsace region (an area in France which had been integrated into the Third Reich) willingly surrendered and indicated the locations where mines had been placed. On the western side of the hamlet, two more Germans surrendered. One of them changed his mind, but paid the ultimate price, being killed by Polain when trying to escape. Some fourteen others were seen withdrawing. The patrol had a narrow escape when mortar rounds fell close and continued to harass them for some twenty minutes, slightly wounding a British Bren gunner on the head. Van der Heyden praised Gérard, Polain and Boch for their behaviour in difficult circumstances.

Meanwhile, Blondeel toured the area of operations, accompanied by Romnée, passing Libin, Smuid, Redu and Séchery, while the squadron's doctor returned to Tellin to make arrangements for the recovery of the bodies of Renkin's crew. The squadron was also visited by Major Marsh, who needed to meet Squadron Leader Smith.[80] John 'Tony' Marsh was OC of 'C' Squadron, 1st SAS, and a veteran from the desert days with Mayne, having won a DSO as a captain during the ferocious battle at Termoli in 1943.[81]

On 11 January, Lemaire was dispatched to a reconnaissance regiment of the 6th Airborne Division, to serve as interpreter during the tactical questioning of German prisoners of war. Lemaire was a native of the German-speaking eastern region of Belgium that had been transferred from Germany after the First World War. Klein was also attached to a British reconnaissance regiment as an interpreter.

Information collected from a French patrol indicated that Saint-Hubert had been evacuated by the Germans, but that the area was covered with mines and booby traps.

Radino started the day trying to have his vehicles fixed. One had a problem with its fuel pump, and the other two had frozen radiators. Around 10 am, he received orders to leave with two vehicles, the third to follow later. After an hour, he reported to the HQ of 'A' Squadron in Aye and was ordered to report to Major Barnett on the road between Jemeppe (near Hargimont) and Champlon[82]. Shortly after noon, he linked up with the OC of 'A' Squadron at the T-junction where the road from Marche met the road between Harsin and Bande. One hundred yards to the southeast, a fallen tree was lying across the road. When trying to remove the obstacle, several Brits were injured by booby traps. Radino, Bogaert and four men of the 6th Airborne Armoured Reconnaissance Regiment proceeded on foot. Arriving at the crossroads leading to the villages of Bande and Grune, the patrol was informed by a civilian that thirty to forty civilians had been shot by the Nazis. The victims were found lying in a cellar close to the main road.[83]

On Christmas Eve, dozens of men had been rounded up in Bande and the nearby village of Grune by *Sicherheitsdienst* (and possibly including *Gestapo*) personnel and had been marched to the ruins of the Rulkin sawmill, where they had been interrogated. Together with the neighbouring houses on both sides of the main road from Marche to Bastogne, the building had been torched by the Germans as a reprisal for a Secret Army attack in which three Germans had been killed, days before the liberation in September 1944. From this group, thirty-three men aged between 17 and 32 had been selected and separated from the others. All but one had then been murdered, one by one, by a shot in the neck. One man had managed to hit his guard and escape in the dark. On Christmas Day, two others from the nearby village of Roy had also been murdered at the same spot.[84]

The village of Bande had been taken without German opposition by 'B' Company of the 1st Canadian Parachute Battalion, shortly after 9 am on 11 January.[85] Two weeks before, the battalion had sailed to Belgium with other units of the 6th Airborne Division and had reached the frontline at Rochefort on 2 January. Four days later, it had moved to Aye, 6 miles to the northeast. On the 9th, the battalion had moved again, 4 miles to the east, to Champlon-Famenne. Establishing OPs and conducting fighting patrols from defensive positions during the first week of January, it was the only Canadian ground combat unit to see action in the Ardennes.[86,87] Now, the Canadian paratroopers were advancing to the southeast, as part of the 3rd Parachute Brigade's attack, and the Germans seemed to withdraw faster than they could move forward.[88] At 10 am, hardly an hour after they had arrived, the Canadians in Bande had been relieved by the British 9th Parachute Battalion,[89] whose personnel would later assist the locals in recovering the bodies from the cellar and placing them in coffins.[90]

Disgusted by this Nazi cruelty, the day after the discovery, the 1st Canadian Parachute Battalion sent one man from each platoon to visit the site, so sufficient first-hand witnesses would be able to remember the event.[91] For the Canadian paratroopers, this seemed to be their first exposure to Nazi war crimes. The atrocity must have left a deep impression and may have altered their CO's view on taking German prisoners of war.[92]

Leaving the war crime site, Radino's party continued along the main road, finding another roadblock over a mile to the southeast of Bande. Around 3:40 pm, Radino was ordered to send a patrol to the crossroads west of the town of Champlon, to check if they were occupied by the Germans. Radino, Hendrick, Bogaert and Verfaillie were joined by eight Brits. Three more roadblocks were encountered on the main road over the next 2 miles and about a mile northwest of the crossroads, the road was found cratered, the hole being 15 feet deep and 12 feet wide, with mines laying around 100 feet behind. Closing in on the crossroads, civilians told the patrol that two enemies had left a mere ten minutes earlier. The patrol proceeded cautiously and observed the enemy some 200 yards from the crossroads. To assess their strength, the patrol conducted a reconnaissance by fire. The enemy opened up with rifle and light machine gun fire. Having located the enemy positions, the patrol returned, reaching its start point by 6:45 pm, after which orders were received to return to Marloie for the night, some 2 miles to the southwest of Marche-en-Famenne.

Early in the morning, Romnée was ordered to move to Forrières, a mile northeast of Wavreille. Due to the cold, a jeep motor was frozen, so departure had to be postponed until 1 pm. His patrol had to reconnoitre the same crossroads west of Champlon, using a different approach route. The road between Nassogne and Champlon was known to be mined since three jeeps of the 6th Airborne Division had been blown up just outside Nassogne. As ordered by Captain Oliver, OC of 'B' Squadron of the 61st, Romnée, with two jeeps and a scout car, reconnoitred the secondary road between Nassogne and Grune until halfway between both villages and continued on the track through the woods going southeast to the main road between Nassogne and Champlon. The forest track had deep ruts and before the patrol reached the top, the scout car and both jeeps became stuck. While the remainder of the crews tried to get the vehicles moving again, Romnée and Vijt continued south-south-east, but no enemy was seen. They joined the others and once the vehicles cleared, the patrol returned to Nassogne around 8 pm.[93]

On 12 January, a 'C' Squadron patrol with five Bren Carriers of the 61st Reconnaissance Regiment left Libin to conduct a recce to Saint-Hubert and to Champlon, to establish contact with 'A' Squadron. To avoid the mined road with blown-up bridges between Val de Poix and Hatrival, the patrol took a small track through the woods, but deep snow hindered their movement and one of the vehicles had to be left behind when it became stuck. Onboard the lead Bren Carrier were three Brits, Ryckx and de Changy – serving as interpreters – as well as two guides from the resistance. Around 11 am, about 1.5 miles from Hatrival (likely at the underpass at the railway west-south-west of the village), the lead vehicle hit a mine, wounding the two SAS men and both resistance fighters. They were immediately evacuated to the aid post at Redu, where they were treated by a doctor. de Changy had a fractured ankle, but Ryckx was severely wounded in both legs. In true SAS fashion, the brave NCO apologised to the squadron commander for not having been able to accomplish his mission.[94,95]

Ten miles to the north, Van Haezendonck and his jeep crew – part of Radino's team – conducted a recce with a troop from 'A' Squadron. Dismounting on the main road almost a mile southeast of Bande, the patrol continued to the area a few hundred yards east of the crossroads a mile west of Champlon and returned to Marloie.

To the southwest of this area, Romnée conducted a patrol with two jeeps and a half-track along part of the road from Nassogne to Champlon, and in the adjacent forest, finding several roadblocks and ammunition dumps all along the road, especially 37 mm rounds.

On 13 January, the SAS squadron's doctor and padre went to see the previous day's wounded and found Ryckx at Ciney, but de Changy had been moved further down the medical evacuation chain, while the resistance fighters had been taken to another hospital. With both legs amputated and his back burned, it was far from sure Ryckx would survive. The doctor and the padre continued their journey towards Bure to collect the bodies of Renkin's crew, but two attempts failed, hindered by the presence of mines and snow.

In Radino's sector, a mixed patrol went to Ramont, over a mile southeast of Champlon, finding out the enemy had left the same morning. Champlon was also found free of the enemy, but four prisoners of war were handed over by the French SAS and were evacuated to the HQ in Marloie.

On 14 January, the squadron received a warning order from the 6th Airborne Division to return to Brussels the next day and to prepare for future operations near Antwerp. Orders were issued for the return to Tervueren and for the advance party – Thonard and Klein – to leave for Antwerp the next day and for Van der Heyden to have the sections and interpreters attached to the British reconnaissance units to be brought back.[96]

On 15 January, the Belgian SAS Squadron ceased to be under command of the 6th Airborne Division.[97] Having received the order to start the move back, the squadron returned on a slippery road in clear but bitterly cold weather – it was -15°C. Despite numerous mechanical failures, Tervueren was reached shortly before 6 pm.[98]

In the Ardennes, the Allies continued their attacks from both flanks in the direction of Houffalize, where the 1st and 3rd American armies linked up on 16 January. The advance had been slow and heavily opposed by the Germans, who succeeded in withdrawing most of their troops from the closing gap. Upon reaching Houffalize, the two armies turned in an eastward direction to drive the Germans back beyond their initial lines.[99] At the same time, command of the American 1st Army was reverted to Bradley, but the American 9th Army remained under the operational control of Montgomery.[100]

Rear area security operations in Antwerp

Having spent a night at its barracks, Blondeel's squadron was sent to Antwerp to conduct rear area security operations. There was a fear that the Germans, having failed to reach the harbour by land, would attempt an airborne operation aimed at destroying the harbour installations that were vital for the Allied resupply. The squadron was installed in a girls' boarding school in Berchem and patrolled an area up to the Dutch border. During one of the missions, a jeep ended up in a canal but, fortunately, the crew could be rescued, and the vehicle could be recovered.

Concerned that the danger of a single incoming rocket might take out his whole unit at once, Blondeel eventually managed to have some of his troops billeted in private houses, to disperse them over a wider area. On 2 February, the perceived danger was gone and the unit returned to Tervueren.[101]

In the aftermath of the Ardennes campaign, the squadron lost a valuable member. Wladimir Aksakow, whose parents had settled in Belgium after the Russian Revolution but who still had Russian nationality, had been accepted for training, which he completed in time to join the squadron in the Ardennes. One day, however, Blondeel received the order from the Belgian Ministry of Defence to demobilise Aksakow, since the ministry wanted to avoid any conflict with the Soviets. Blondeel, who did not understand why the Soviets would have an issue with this, proposed to pay him with his own money and give him the regimental number of a fallen trooper. The ministry replied that the time had long passed when colonels of a regiment owned their soldiers and that he might face civil liability in case anything happened to Aksakow. Quite a convincing argument... When Aksakow heard the news, he was extremely sad about having to leave his friends and considered the ministry's decision unjust. However, during the visit of a British SAS major, Blondeel managed to recommend he enlist a good trooper, a native Polish speaker who also spoke French, Dutch, Russian, English and German but who could not be kept in his squadron since he was not a Belgian national. The British officer immediately accepted the offer and provided Blondeel with a document confirming that Trooper Aksakow had been accepted for service in His Majesty's forces. Happy with this twist of fate, Aksakow continued his service with the British SAS until the end of the war, after which he would eventually become a Belgian citizen.[102]

Chapter Eight

THE BELGIAN SAS REGIMENT SPEARHEADING THE LIBERATION OF THE NETHERLANDS

STILL DURING THE BATTLE in the Ardennes, the supreme Allied command had been continuing to plan for the final offensive to defeat Nazi Germany. The first phase of Eisenhower's plan consisted of the destruction of enemy forces west of the Rhine,[1] thereby breaching large parts of the *Weststellung*.[2] Once the Rhine was reached along the frontline, Eisenhower's 'broad front' strategy aimed at developing operations across the river with a main emphasis on the industrial heartland of the Ruhr.[3]

On 8 February, the Canadian 1st Army launched Operation 'Veritable', attacking from the Nijmegen bridgehead to the southeast, to clear the partly inundated area between the Maas and the Rhine, including the Reichswald Forest, to the general line Geldern – Xanten.[4] Although the objectives of Operation 'Veritable' had not been reached, the operation was concluded with the capture of Goch. On 26 February, a renewed offensive, Operation 'Blockbuster', was launched, reaching the objectives by 11 March.[5]

On 23 February, the American 9th Army started Operation 'Grenade', crossing the Roer[6] river and attacking northeast to the Rhine, after flooding of the Roer had been delaying the operation since 10 February. To the south of the 21st Army Group, Bradley's 12th Army Group launched Operation 'Lumberjack'. The American 1st Army protected the American 9th Army's right flank and quickly subdued Cologne, before turning south along the Rhine to converge with the American 3rd Army's attack through the Eifel to the Rhine. Confusion, including unclear command relationships, on the German side resulted in the American 9th Armored Division being able to cross the near-intact bridge at Remagen and establish a bridgehead east of the Rhine on 7 March. Further south, the Colmar pocket was reduced by early February. Around mid-March, Operation 'Undertone' had the Saar – Rheinpfalz area cleared, with the American 3rd US Army attacking across the Moselle to the southeast and east and the American 6th Army Group (American 7th Army and French 1st Army) further south attacking to the north and northeast.[7] During the night of 22-23 March, another bridgehead was established at Nierstein and nearby Oppenheim after a surprise night crossing by the American 5th Division.[8]

That same night, the 21st Army Group started operations 'Plunder' and 'Flashpoint', the assault crossings of the Rhine between Rees and Dinslaken by the British 2nd Army and the American 9th Army respectively. Supported by a massive airborne operation the next morning (Operation 'Varsity'), the bridgehead over the Rhine was secure by midnight on the 22nd. Within days, Allied formations were breaking out of the bridgehead and began the final advance into Germany and the Netherlands. Among them was the Canadian II Army Corps, which was heading for the Netherlands.[9]

Opposite the 21st Army Group was *Generaloberst* Blaskowitz's Army Group H. This army group had been established in November 1944 and was initially commanded by *Generaloberst* Student. It contained the 1st Parachute Army and the 15th Army. The latter's HQ was transferred to Army Group B in January 1945 and replaced by a new 25th Army HQ, which took over command of the 15th Army's two army corps. By the end of January 1945, Blaskowitz had replaced Student.[10]

Expansion to regiment

After conducting operations in the Ardennes and the province of Antwerp for over a month, Blondeel now faced new challenges. In Tervueren, he had to deal with several administrative issues, such as personnel not receiving their pay or having no access to welfare benefits. Annoying as they were, he nevertheless believed that officers needed to tackle them in a detailed and accurate matter, especially when the morale of troops depended on them. On the organisational side, having obtained approval to expand his squadron to regimental size, he needed to restructure his unit.[11] Blondeel was promoted to major on 15 January 1945.[12] His unit would be renamed 'Belgian Special Air Service Regiment', also known as the 5th SAS. Fortunately, since the liberation of Belgium, recruits had been in training all along. At the No. 1 Parachute Training School in Ringway, fifty-two men were awarded their parachute wings on 4 February and seventy-four more on 9 March,[13] but operational needs would also result in personnel being accepted who had undergone SAS training short of completing their parachute course, especially as the anticipated role for future operations would be similar to the last. Apart from the increase in manpower as such, the reorganisation of the unit also incorporated the lessons learned in the Ardennes. The campaign had shown the requirement for assault troops on foot (transported in lorries), 3-inch mortars, mainly to support the assault troops, improved wireless telegraphy sets for communications between the sections and the unit's HQ, engineers to facilitate bridging and demining, intelligence personnel trained for tactical questioning of prisoners of war, and increased organic logistical capabilities, especially sufficient transport for field kitchens, stores and workshops.

The new regiment had an HQ, an HQ squadron and two fighting squadrons. The HQ Squadron was commanded by Captain Robert Merchiers and grouped a squadron HQ, a signals troop (commanded by Canadian Captain Wallace Donnelly, on loan from Phantom), a mortar troop (initially commanded by Schils, later by Kirschen, and equipped with 3-inch mortars), an engineer troop (commanded by Radino), a motor transport section (commanded by Captain Paul Leyder), a quartermaster branch (commanded by Captain J. Cosyns) and an administrative troop (commanded by Warrant Officer Martin). 'A' Squadron was commanded by Van der Heyden and 'B' Squadron by Ghys. Each had a squadron HQ, a reconnaissance troop (equipped with jeeps, aka 'jeep troop') and an assault troop (equipped with a jeep and 15-cwt lorries).[14]

In the early days of March, the regiment again experienced the hazardous nature of special operations training. On 3 March, Trooper Nicolas Polys sustained a severe concussion following a backward landing after a parachute jump from a Dakota[15] and died at the Winwick emergency hospital three days later. It was the forty-fifth recorded training death involving static-line parachuting at RAF Ringway.[16,17] On 4 March, Mathijs, a veteran of several operations, was killed when he was hit in the head during a live fire exercise in Leopoldsburg.[18]

Around early March, changes also occurred at the higher level: McLeod was appointed Director of Military Operations in India and regretted he had to relinquish command of the SAS Brigade.[19]

Some of the old hands who had distinguished themselves under McLeod's command were presented awards for gallantry. Van der Heyden received the Military Cross, Debuf received the Distinguished Conduct Medal and Regner and Petit received the Military Medal. They had the honour of having their medals pinned to their chest by none other than Montgomery during a parade on the Grand-Place in Brussels on 10 March.[20]

In a personal letter to Blondeel, in which he thanked him for his leadership and loyalty and his regiment's performance, McLeod specifically expressed his disappointment of not having been able to welcome Kirschen – who was still behind enemy lines – and see him decorated with the award he so richly deserved.[21]

Looking back much later at his command of a multinational brigade with unorthodox units, McLeod shared his view on his subordinates:

> Paddy Mayne and the 1st SAS were straightforward. They said "Yes" to everything they were asked to do [...], they were always cheerful and welcoming, and they regarded my HQ as an unnecessary evil who should be humoured providing it did not interfere with what the Regiment thought should be done. [...] The French were "formidable". The powers that be, in their wisdom, had put the two battalions into one hutted camp in which the cookhouse, messes, etc., were all shared. Unfortunately, one battalion was composed of men who had escaped from France, many of whom had suffered in Spanish prisons on the way, and they were staunch Gaullists. They had come the hard way. The other battalion had been recruited in North Africa after the Allied landings and had come the easy way. The two units did not mix easily. [...] They took their training somewhat light heartedly. It was difficult to persuade these splendid characters that the local salmon river should not be used as a grenade range and their highly successful demolition of the branch line leading to the local colliery caused considerable umbrage in high places. [...] The Belgians were splendid. They all spoke English, indeed some who had been enlisted in Canada spoke little French or Flemish. They did what they were told, their discipline was admirable and my staff loved them. Their CO — Eddie Blondeel, was one of the best COs I have ever had to deal with. As may be imagined any order was received very differently by these three elements. Broadly speaking the Belgians did what they were told, the British did what they were told if it suited them, the French usually lost the order or professed never to have had it! After a bit we began to settle down and at HQ we all developed suitable techniques for dealing with our ill-assorted and highly individual team of units. Then 2nd SAS arrived from the Mediterranean and we had to start all over again to persuade them

> that unfortunately service in the UK was not as "free and easy" as overseas. [...] Any difficulties were, however, entirely mitigated by the character and enthusiasm of the officers and men whom I had the honour to command. They were all imbued with one single purpose and that was to get to France and to win the war.[22]

On 14 March, McLeod was succeeded by Brigadier Michael 'Mad Mike' Calvert,[23] a highly experienced special operations leader who had commanded the 77th Indian Infantry Brigade of the Special Force, which had been conducting prolonged long-range penetration operations behind Japanese lines in the jungles of Burma.[24]

Operation 'Larkswood'

On 28 March, Calvert was asked by the 21st Army Group HQ to discuss the possibility of operations by SAS troops in conjunction with the 1st Canadian Army in the Netherlands. During staff meetings in the following days, Calvert explained how SAS troops could be used advantageously by using small parties asserting their influence over a wide area and preventing the retreating enemy from forming a new defensive line, adding that in the circumstances of that moment, parties dropped by parachute should be overrun by friendly ground forces after no longer than three days. Calvert drafted a plan, which was approved with slight modifications and subject to any air considerations after he met Crerar. A warning order was sent out, and Calvert returned to his HQ in Essex and briefed his deputy, Colonel Guy Prendergast, former CO of the Long-Range Desert Group in North Africa.[25]

On 1 April, following the breakout from the Rhine bridgehead, the Canadian II Army Corps, commanded by Lieutenant General Guy Simonds, returned from the British 2nd Army to Crerar's Canadian 1st Army. The latter also included the Canadian I Army Corps that had recently returned from Italy, while the British army corps under Crerar's command returned to the British 2nd Army shortly afterwards. The day after, Crerar directed his II Corps to continue his northward advance, crossing the IJssel river south of Deventer up to the Apeldoorn – Otterlo line, while I Corps had to capture Arnhem.[26]

On 3 April, a second planning meeting was held at the HQ of the 1st Canadian Army, to go through the details of Calvert's plan. Prendergast attended on behalf of the SAS Brigade, while Squadron Leader Smith, the British liaison officer attached to the Belgian SAS Regiment, was also present. After additional coordination with No. 38 Group RAF, approval was given by the 1st British Airborne Corps, which had been closely involved throughout the planning process.

In Calvert's plan, the Belgian SAS Regiment was to be placed at once under the command of the Canadian II Corps to operate as a mounted reconnaissance unit, to penetrate through enemy lines and harass rear areas and to contact the SAS parties that would be parachuted in at the earliest opportunity. The operation would be called 'Larkswood'. One squadron of the British 2nd SAS was to execute Operation 'Keystone', being dropped – possibly with jeeps – in the Apeldoorn area at the time the 1st Army was about to cross the IJssel river. The squadron was to boost the Dutch resistance, to harass German communications, and if, possible, to prevent the destruction of bridges across the Apeldoorn canal. The French 3rd and 4th SAS would execute Operation 'Amherst'. They were to be dropped in the Drenthe province, about two days before the anticipated arrival of Canadian ground forces, to harass the enemy rear area, prevent demolitions, report information and raise whatever resistance movement that would be found in its area. One squadron from the 1st SAS was to remain in reserve, ready to conduct opportunity tasks.[27]

The same day, the 21st Army Group ordered Blondeel to send an advance party to the HQ of the Canadian II Army Corps at Huize Zelle, southwest of Ruurlo.

On 4 April, Blondeel, his regimental sergeant major, intelligence staff and one representative of each troop moved to the Canadian HQ. Blondeel conferred with Lieutenant Colonel Rothschild, operations officer of the II Corps. Intelligence showed that the enemy was only resisting at the canal crossings and Blondeel was informed that the Belgian SAS would be used as soon as a breakthrough was effected.

The next day, the regiment's main body joined the advance party. The chief of staff of the II Corps informed the Belgians that the regiment would be detached to the 4th Canadian Armoured Division to screen the division's left flank and to conduct recce operations. By the end of the day, the regiment had assembled fourteen officers and 254 other ranks.[28]

The same day, Calvert set up a tactical HQ at the Canadian 1st Army HQ. Originally intended to help facilitate the launch of the operation, once operations were ongoing, it would act as an interface for message traffic with the deployed SAS patrols, ensuring the staff at the 1st Canadian Army was confident at getting first-hand information providing complete and near-real-time updates of the developing situation.[29]

On 6 April, the regiment received an additional 3-ton lorry and two armoured 15-cwt lorries to render it fully mobile. The II Corps issued orders to move to Coevorden the next day. The day was spent making logistical preparations for the coming operations, maintaining vehicles and weapons and distributing supplies.[30] Meanwhile, fighting patrols from the 4th Canadian Armoured Brigade's infantry regiment approached Coevorden from the southwest and encountered heavy opposition, but by noon the infantry regiment, augmented by two infantry companies from the 10th Canadian Infantry Brigade and armour of the 4th Armoured Brigade (all part of the 4th Armoured Division), had cleared the town. Following the capture of Coevorden, there was some confusion as to whether the advance would continue to the north, or the east towards Meppen, across the German border. Shortly afterwards, the 4th Brigade was directed to proceed towards Meppen.[31]

The Canadian advance and Hitler's refusal to give up the Netherlands resulted in part of Blaskowitz's force being cut-off. To deal with the new reality, the command of Army Group H was transformed into the North-West High Command under *Generalfeldmarschall* Ernst Busch, on 7 April. Blaskowitz became commander of 'Fortress Holland', commanding the cut-off forces in the western part of the country, essentially consisting of the 25th Army, subordinate to Busch. Apart from the 1st Parachute Army (shortly known as 'Army Group Student'), Busch also commanded the North Coast Command and (from 9 April) the so-called Army Group Blummentritt, a weak formation made up of remnants from various units.[32,33,34]

On 7 April, the 4th Brigade regrouped before its advance to Meppen and handed over Coevorden to the Belgian SAS Regiment.[35] The 65th Battery of the 5th Canadian Antitank Regiment remained in support of the Belgians.[36] 'B' Squadron took up positions on the northern perimeter and sent out a patrol further north. An enemy concentration was reported in a small wood 6 miles north of Coevorden, about a mile west of Wachtum. Mortar fire was directed to disperse the enemy, two of whom, both wounded, were taken prisoner.[37] Likely these were men from a German parachute regiment, their capture being reported in a message sent to the 4th Canadian Division HQ very early the next morning, which also mentioned the presence of both German parachute units and Dutch SS personnel in the area north of Dalen.[38]

'A' Squadron was responsible for defending the western and southwestern part of the town perimeter. Half its personnel took up defensive positions, while the other half-squadron conducted patrols towards Hardenberg (about 7 miles to the southeast) and up to some 5 miles west of Coevorden. Reports on German troops included concentrations of Wehrmacht and SS in a wood 3 miles southwest of Hardenberg and stragglers on their way to Zwolle to augment the defence of the city. In the evening, the Dutch resistance in Hardenberg asked for help, as German troops were trying to cross the Vecht river. 2nd Lieutenant d'Oultremont's section was sent out to assist and received reliable information from the resistance by telephone from enemy-occupied territory. In Coevorden itself, the regimental HQ had to deal with several civil affairs issues and a curfew was enforced for the safety of the residents.[39]

On the night of 7-8 April, forty-six Stirling aircraft inserted close to 700 men from the 3rd and 4th SAS and a four-man Jedburgh team. One Stirling did not take off; its stick would be inserted the next night instead. The French SAS sticks mostly contained fifteen and some twelve men each and were intended to be dropped on up to twenty different DZs in the area between Meppel, Assen and Emmen. Low cloud cover over the area resulted in higher than usual drop altitudes, which, in addition to the obvious problem of identifying the DZs, caused most sticks to land miles from their planned location, while the planned drop of eighteen jeeps had to be cancelled at the very last moment.[40]

On 8 April, a message came in from the resistance that eleven Frenchmen[41] had been dropped near Dedemsvaart by mistake. Acting upon the initial information that the French team was encircled and had a wounded, a patrol of four jeeps and a 15-cwt lorry was sent out to assist. Contact with the French was established. They were not encircled and decided to stay to lay ambushes. The wounded man was evacuated to Coevorden.

An 'A' Squadron patrol with six jeeps was sent to Hardenberg and took a prisoner. Tactical questioning revealed no changes in the German dispositions, but incoming reports indicated that a breakthrough would be attempted at Hardenberg, while the enemy was regrouping at Hoogeveen and troops were being sent by train to Assen further north. A mortar section was sent to Hardenberg and kept the enemy at bay.

'B' Squadron's assault troop maintained its defensive positions, while the squadron's jeep sections conducted patrols, going north up to the Verlengde Hoogeveense Vaart, a canal flowing from east to west some 5 miles north of Coevorden. Krolikowski's section was ambushed on the road to the north, a mile northwest of Wachtum. The section managed to drive to a nearby farm and establish an all-round defence. Seeing the Germans were preparing to attack the farm, the section broke contact, withdrawing its jeeps one by one, without any casualties or loss of matériel. Based on the section's information, a mortar section shelled German positions.

In the afternoon, the CO of a Polish armoured regiment arrived to coordinate future operations and asked the Belgians to conduct a reconnaissance of and capture the Oosterhesseler bridge across the Verlengde Hoogveense Vaart, south of the Oosterhesselen village, as his regiment would follow soon and would need to cross the canal with its tanks.[42] The Polish 1st Armoured Division had come under command of the II Corps with effect of 8 am that morning.[43] The armoured regiments of the division's armoured cavalry brigade were mainly equipped with Sherman Mk IIA tanks, with 76 mm guns.[44,45] To check whether the 30-ton[46] tanks would be able to cross the bridge, contacts in the Dutch resistance facilitated bringing in an engineer from the *Rijkswaterstaat*, the Dutch governmental agency responsible for the development and maintenance of the national transportation infrastructure, with whom a conference was organised at the Belgian HQ. The conclusion was that the bridge could not carry the weight of the tanks and needed to be reinforced. The Dutch engineer suggested using the rails from a nearby steam tram depot, which could be transported by tram close to the bridge, after which Captain Radino made arrangements for implementing this option.

In the evening, Thonard's section reinforced the Allied positions in Hardenberg, close to a standing patrol of the 18th Armoured Car Regiment (12th Manitoba Dragoons), following reports of increased enemy activity in the area.[47]

Earlier in the day, Prendergast flew from the UK to Brussels with a small party and joined Calvert's forward HQ at the 1st Canadian Army HQ near Grave. The day after, the party was to go to Coevorden to set up an HQ to receive French personnel after their link-up with advancing Canadian forces.[48]

On 9 April, an 'A' Squadron jeep patrol went westwards in the morning, up to Slagharen, but met no organised resistance. Only scattered enemy troops were reported in this area by the resistance, while the enemy was still resisting at Hardenberg. 'B' Squadron's assault troop and a mortar section under Déom assisted in containing the situation, knocking out a German mortar.[49]

In the afternoon, Blondeel visited the HQ of the II Canadian Corps. Calvert also passed by the corps HQ which lived a somewhat hectic day.[50]

The Belgian SAS captured an enemy dump at Dalen in the early afternoon.[51] The village was on the route taken by Krolikowski's section, which moved north towards the Oosterhesseler bridge, having been tasked to reconnoitre and capture the bridge. Protected by a smoke screen put up by mortars, two small, wooded areas on both sides of the road, less than a mile south from the bridge, were cleared. The area north of these being open with hardly any cover or concealment, part of the section continued on foot, covered by the static jeeps. Reaching a spot 300 yards short of the bridge, the patrol discovered three enemy light machine gun positions. After reporting the enemy sighting, the patrol was ordered to stay put and wait for reinforcements. At 4 pm, six Polish Bren Carriers arrived.[52] A little more than two hours later, the bridge was assaulted, captured intact, and a firm bridgehead was established on the far side. Meanwhile, the engineer troop had been preparing the construction materials needed and moved them by steam tram to the bridge. At 8 pm, the troop started reinforcing the bridge, completing the task by 9:30.[53]

The 3rd Squadron of the *10 pułk strzelców konnych* (10th Mounted Rifle Regiment), the Polish division's armoured reconnaissance regiment equipped with Cromwell and A30 Challenger tanks,[54] moved to the far side and established defensive positions for the night.[55] By that time, the Belgian SAS Regiment was relieved at Coevorden and its forward elements had reached the Verlengde Hoogeveense Vaart between the Oosterhesseler bridge and the bridge near Holsloot, 3 miles further east.[56,57]

A jeep section from 'B' Squadron continued north and positioned itself in the village of Oosterhesselen, allowing an 'A' Squadron patrol with three[58] jeeps and a motorcycle to pass through and move further north. The latter was looking for a French SAS party that had reportedly been surrounded in a wood at Witteveen, over 4 miles north-north-west from Oosterhesselen. The French could be contacted without incident, so the report of them being surrounded proved false, but they had three killed and one man missing. They told their Belgian comrades that other French SAS personnel were closer to Westerbork, where some 100 German paratroopers were present. Since the French party did not need any help, the Belgian patrol returned to Oosterhesselen. At the crossroads a mile southeast of Mantinge, the patrol was attacked by German paratroopers, who quickly withdrew once the jeeps returned fire. The motorcycle and a jeep were put out of action and Becquet was wounded in the hand.[59] Back in friendly lines, Dr Sevens dressed his wound. Sadly for Becquet, this not-so-serious wound spelled the end of his career as a pianist.[60]

That night, the farms situated in front of the Oosterhesselen bridgehead were ablaze. Coming from the rear, a group of soldiers emerged from the darkness. Challenged by a Belgian sentry, it turned out to be Poles, who insisted on crossing the bridge. Shortly afterwards, echoes of intense gunfire resounded from the direction in which they had disappeared. The group returned, each man carrying multiple ducks. How they had found out about the duck farm remained a mystery. Blondeel watched them passing by when he noticed Padre Jourdain seemingly keeping watch in front of a barn. He asked: "What's going on there?" "Oh, nothing unusual, Sir", the priest replied. Somewhat curious, Blondeel pushed open the door and noticed two suspended pigs being butchered. The Belgians were also supplementing their rations, the pigs having been kindly offered by the Dutch from the neighbourhood.[61]

By the end of the day, the 4th Canadian Armoured Division was already operating on the eastern bank of the Ems river, while the 1st Polish Armoured Division was gradually arriving in Coevorden, the left flank being secured by the Canadian 18th Armoured Car Regiment, conducting patrols up to the outskirts of Meppel, 26 miles west of Coevorden.

On 10 April, 'A' Squadron sent out patrols in a westerly direction to Steenwijksmoer and brought back some prisoners of war.[62] 'B' Squadron was still stretched from Oosterhesselen to Hardenberg. Having to hold the line between Coevorden and Hardenberg – 16 miles from Oosterhesselen – was considered an ongoing burden,[63] but the SAS detachment in Hardenberg was relieved,[64] as the Polish 9th Rifle Battalion (*9 batalion strzelców*) took over the left flank protection from the 18th Canadian Armoured Car Regiment in the morning.[65] Units of the Polish armoured division moved over the Oosterhesseler bridge from the morning, advancing towards Emmen. The bridge over the Oranjekanaal (Orange canal) about a mile west of Emmen had been blown, so dismounted patrols entered the town, which was found empty of the enemy.[66] In the evening situation report from the Polish division, the Belgian SAS Regiment was now listed as one of the units under its command.[67]

On 11 April, 'B' Squadron moved to Wachtum, a mile southeast of the Oosterhesseler bridge. Hoogeveen was reconnoitred by 'A' Squadron and reported clear of enemy. To assist the French SAS, Thonard's and d'Oultremont's jeep sections, two assault sections, an engineer detachment and a medical detachment were sent out to the flax factory at Orvelte, on the north side of the Oranjekanaal. Without interference by the enemy, the detachment reached the site and linked up with the French. With the help of Mr Reijntjes, director of the factory, an improvised bridge was built so that jeep patrols could cross the narrow canal. A Belgian jeep section managed to recover French SAS personnel in contact with the enemy in the Schoonloo wood, a few miles to the north. Elp, to the west of the wood, was reported free of enemy. In the meantime, the regimental doctor treated six French casualties. Ten wounded prisoners of war were also taken care of. On the southern side of the canal, reconnaissance patrols to the west showed that Westerbork was free of the enemy, the first known enemy defensive positions now being at Beilen. Shortly after 8 pm, the regiments' subunits were back in Coevorden, preparing for their next move.[68]

On 12 April, the 1st Polish Armoured Division continued its advance north, its lead brigade group having reached the area west of Ter Apel and its armoured reconnaissance regiment having found Odoorn and Exlo – 8 miles further west – clear of the enemy the previous day.[69]

The SAS Regiment went north as well. At 7 am, it moved squadron by squadron to Ter Wisch, via Oosterhesselen, Meppen, Zweeloo, Emmen, Weerdinge, Valte, Osdoorn, Valthermond and Eksloërmond. By 10:30, the regimental HQ was established in Laude, with the squadrons taking all-round defensive positions.

With Polish armour advancing along the road between Tweede Eksloërmond and Onstwedde, more or less parallel to the Mussel-Aa canal, 'A' Squadron was tasked to reconnoitre the feasibility of crossing the canal east of Mussel and advancing on the road going to the northeast, while 'B' Squadron had to patrol northwards on the eastern side of the water.

d'Oultremont's section advanced to Sellingen, while Romnée's section, supported by Doome's mortar section, took a parallel road less than a mile to the west.

Romnée's section probably destroyed a German OP and noticed withdrawing enemy troops. The assault sections commanded by Goffinet and – now lieutenant – Tinchant were sent to consolidate Sellingen, took positions near the Ruiten-Aa canal east of the village and killed two Germans.

At 2 pm, Radino found himself in Sellingen when a civilian warned him that the enemy was moving to the village from the east. Radino went to the destroyed bridge with one of his engineer sections. Spotting enemy movement on the road and in the field, Bren guns were brought to bear and scattered the enemy, probably not more than half a dozen men. A jeep from 'A' Squadron joined the fight. After some twenty minutes of sporadic fire, no further movement was noticed.

d'Oultremont's section continued north through Plaggenborg and reported an unobstructed road up to 2 miles southeast of Vlagtwedde, which itself was in German hands. The bridge over the Mussel-Aa canal at Veele – a mile further north – was reportedly destroyed and German defences extended further northeast from Veele to Veelerveen.

In the open area a mile west of the Sellingen – Plaggenborg road, Romnée met weak resistance, killed a Dutch SS member and captured a dozen prisoners when discovering and rounding up a Dutch SS camp 2 miles northwest of Sellingen. The prisoners taken in this area that day included a member of the hated *Landwacht*,[70] who was carrying a list with names and addresses of important Dutch Nazis in the region. The traitor and the list were handed over to the Dutch police.

Further west, Thonard's section conducted a recce on the eastern bank of the Mussel-Aa canal. While seeing no enemy positions, the firing of a light machine gun was noticed and since a Polish unit had been reported at Mussel, Thonard wisely decided to withdraw to avoid a blue-on-blue incident.

Déom's section ran into the enemy at the crossroads east of Vlagtwedde. The assault sections were brought forward one by one and took up all-round positions a mile southeast of the village.

Goffinet's section took the wrong road, bypassed Vlagtwedde and came into contact with the retreating enemy near the Veele bridge. After taking three prisoners, the section returned to the main body.

'A' Squadron's assault troop and Déom's jeep section occupied Vlagtwedde, where the regiment halted and reorganised.

Blondeel conducted a recce of the ground ahead. The enemy in Veele was believed to consist of naval forces in defensive positions, their strength assessed as company-sized, probably without indirect fire support. A few isolated firing positions[71] were observed along the road from Vlagtwedde to Veele. Having made his appreciation, Blondeel formulated his plan – conducting a frontal attack, clearing the southern side of the bridge with two squadrons in line and establishing positions on the southern bank of the canal – and issued orders.[72]

Subordinate commanders gave their orders and prepared their units for combat. Having gone through this process numerous times before, it had become a well-rehearsed routine. To some, it looked no different from a training exercise, but then reality set in when a chilling "Fix bayonets!" was shouted. A frontal dismounted assault was not the usual way the regiment operated, nor had it been designed for these types of operations, but the situation left no other option. Even the original members had never experienced this.

The direction of attack followed the road from Vlagtwedde to Veele. 'B' Squadron attacked on the left of the road and 'A' Squadron on the right. Both squadrons deployed their assault troops in front, supported by the covering fire from the jeeps. They contained many of the young men who had been badged only weeks before and were now to receive their baptism of fire.

On the left, two sections of 1st Lieutenant Van Cauwelaert's assault troop, Sergeant Hubert de Mûelenaere's 1st section and 2nd Lieutenant Adelin Slosse's 2nd section, conducted a frontal assault, clearing the cemetery and the area north of it and occupying positions on the south bank of the canal. At the start of the attack, Trooper Jacques De Cooman was hit in the lip, resulting in a slight wound that would take him out of his section for only a day. A few Germans resisting from their position at the cemetery's mortuary were quickly eliminated, but a child was killed when a group of civilians hiding in a ditch at the fringe of the graveyard were caught in the crossfire. Sporadic fire from houses on their right flank was dealt with by Sas' 3rd section, who killed a German carrying a *Panzerfaust*[73] while taking several others prisoner.

On the right, Heilporn's assault troop moved by bounds to the south bank of the canal bank. The sections took defensive positions along the canal, using the cover provided by buildings, the inhabitants of which were sheltering in a basement. Goffinet's 2nd section was positioned near the bridge and the narrow lock footbridge parallel to the destroyed bridge. To his right, Sergeant Andre Jeukens' 4th section was located in a farm, Tinchant's section was in between the sections of Jeukens and Sergeant Philippe Rolin's 3rd section, which was sited behind a burning farm a bit further east. All were under heavy fire and 'A' Squadron's assault troop took the brunt of the casualties.

During the intense firefight, Rolin was hit in the abdomen and the head. Trooper Etienne Hazard retrieved the mortally wounded Rolin but was seriously wounded himself when returning to his position. Trooper Jean Louis Breuer was reloading Bren magazines when he suddenly fell, hit in the chest, abdomen and arm. Jacques Levaux, the troop sergeant, ran the gauntlet of enemy fire when going back to find stretchers. He managed to have the three wounded evacuated, concealed by a smoke screen provided by the mortar troop. Despite all efforts to save them, none survived their wounds.

Meanwhile, on the left flank, a small boat and some barges were discovered moored on the far side of the canal. Two troopers of the assault troop's 3rd section, Andy Segelaer and Jean Bastin, volunteered to swim across, bring back the small craft and drag one of the barges across. They doffed their kit and entered the water covered by heavy suppressive fire from their comrades. In no time, they had accomplished their dangerous task. de Mûelenaere and part of his section crossed the canal with the small craft, covered by the 2nd section near the bridge and by Thonard's jeep section, which had been brought forward to provide additional firepower. George Buysse was injured in the foot and fell into the water but could be rescued. Van Cauwelaert followed with his 2nd and 3rd sections and established a troop-sized foothold north of the canal, his 1st section positioned to the left, the 3rd section in the centre and the 2nd section to the right.

The engineer troop enlarged the crossing by putting additional barges alongside the first, so more men could cross simultaneously, but the plan to adapt it to allow vehicles to cross proved impractical.

Van Cauwelaert's troop took almost a dozen prisoners. Corporal Jef Heylen, commanding the 2nd section's support group with two light machine guns, was covering the assault group that was clearing the corner houses when he suddenly saw movement in a trench between the houses and the canal. He jumped in the trench and confronted four Germans. Knowing his Sten magazine was empty, he bluffed the enemy, took the submachine gun from one of them and took them prisoner.

Back on the right flank, jeeps were also rushed forward. Supported by a jeep section and the other sections of the assault troop, Goffinet, acting on his initiative, rushed forward with his section, crossed the footbridge and occupied the house at the corner on the far side of the canal, taking close to a dozen prisoners. Jeukens' section followed suit.

Assault sections from both squadrons cleared the houses along the Veele – Wedde road north of the canal. Accompanied by Heilporn, Jeukens' section cleared the buildings up to some 300 yards to the east, then turned north advancing parallel to the Veele – Wedde road. Some two dozen Germans were rounded up.

The two lead sections clearing the houses on both sides of the road to Wedde were under unrelentless enemy fire when reaching the crossroads some 500 yards north of the bridge. They took two prisoners but were kept at bay by two machine guns.

A few hundred yards east of the crossroads, Jeukens' section was also under constant fire when reaching a farm and forced the Germans to withdraw in a northwesterly direction. Goffinet went back to the bridge to request indirect fire support from the mortar troop, while the two sections under Tinchant on the southern bank of the canal maintained their positions to cover the eastern flank and their back. Déom's jeep section was replaced by Romnée's to allow the former to have his magazines reloaded. Romnée's crew located two shooters in trees who were assumed to have killed their comrades. Both were eliminated.

To prepare for the night, Blondeel ordered tighter dispositions to be taken up, reducing the bridgehead which was 300 yards wide and 400 yards deep to a 200-yard radius.

During the reorganisation, troopers Ligot and Odilon Fagnard, who had performed extremely well as a Bren team, were wounded. Ligot's helmet was penetrated by a round, causing a scalp wound, while Fagnard had an open arm fracture caused by shrapnel.

The engineer troop, assisted by civilians and 'A' Squadron personnel not on guard duty, built an improvised bridge using local materials. The bridge was ready by 6 am the following morning.[74,75,76,77,78]

On 13 April, the regiment advanced towards Wedde, over a mile to the north. The village was taken without much opposition. Vijt's and Déom's jeep sections reconnoitred the road bridge over the Westerwoldsche Aa river some 200 yards west of Wedde. When crossing the bridge, they were fired upon by machine guns and 20 mm cannons. Déom's jeep was hit by 20 mm rounds, one of which pierced the armoured glass windshield and another smashing the Vickers K mount. Déom had just jumped out of his jeep, probably to fix a stoppage with his gun, and was lucky to be hit by shrapnel in the knee only. Thévissen, his driver, was slightly wounded in the face and Boch, the rear gunner, was wounded in the eye, the abdomen and the legs. Vijt immediately returned fire and mortar fire was brought down on the 20 mm gun positions along the road to Blijham.

d'Oultremont replaced Déom and around 10:30 am, tanks were heard on the left flank. Romnée organised an all-round defence, positioning anti-tank weapons, both PIATs and bazookas. The moment Polish tanks were recognised, the Belgians were fired upon by machine gun fire from the Poles. Despite the fire from both friend and foe, Vijt managed to contact them and eventually, the Germans fled in disorder, leaving behind four 20 mm guns. Two were taken for potential future use, together with their ammunition supply. At the crossroads 400 yards west of the bridge, Polish tanks joined the main road to the north. Vijt was ordered to provide flank protection to the Polish armour on their way to Blijham and to reconnoitre secondary roads. Blijham was liberated without interference from the Germans and the regiment took up defensive positions for the night.

On 14 April, the assault and jeep sections positioned at the crossroads a mile west of Blijham (where the road from Oude Pekela joined the main road) were relieved around 7:30 am. Tinchant's section positioned itself 120 yards east of the Blijham church, at the crossroads where the road going northeast towards the Pekel-Aa river joined the main road, providing overwatch for Romnée's section who would conduct a recce up to 1.25 miles away. Around 9:30 am, while many were having breakfast, some forty Germans were reported moving from the south towards the eastern edge of Blijham. A Bren opened up when the enemy closed in within effective range, but jammed, resulting in the now-alerted enemy taking cover near a house. Romnée's section realised what was happening and conducted a pincer movement towards the building. d'Oultermont noticed the sound of fire and sent out Jeukens' section, which cleared the houses north of the main road at the eastern edge of the village. Two hours later, the enemy ceased fire. Tinchant's section attacked eastwards, while Romnée's section cleared the houses south of the main road. The Germans fled towards Friescheloo, 3 miles to the southwest, leaving behind five dead. A few Germans were taken prisoner, five of whom were wounded. According to the prisoners, they were part of a group of about forty coming from Veele and Wedde, trying to reach the town of Winschoten, 2 miles further to the northwest.

On the road from Winschoten to Blijham, a six-man bicycle patrol was intercepted. One German was killed and another was taken prisoner. The interrogation of the prisoners made that day allowed the intelligence officer to find out who the regiment had been facing during the recent fights. They belonged to the 359th and 361st *Marine-Festungs-Bataillone* (naval fortress battalions). The prisoners had been sent to the Netherlands only days before, while the main body was still close to the border at Nieuwe-Schans, 7 miles northeast of Blijham.

Between 11:30 am and 1 pm, the aforementioned crossroads west of the village were shelled by indirect fire systems, but many projectiles failed to explode. Afterwards, the shelling became more sporadic. Almost a mile further north, reconnaissance and aerial pictures revealed very strong defensive positions at the Winschoterhoogebrug, the bridge over the Pekel-Aa river on the southeastern approach route to Winschoten. A recce by Blondeel himself, joined by Calvert, the brigade commander, who happened to be in the area, confirmed that the open ground favoured the defender and resulted in an air strike request through the tactical HQ of the SAS Brigade.[79] Air support was approved for 4 pm but shifted as the aircraft had to wait for the mist to clear. At 6:15 pm, twelve Hawker Typhoon ground attack aircraft from No. 164 Squadron RAF equipped with 60-pound rockets took off from airfield B91 Kluis, near Nijmegen.[80,81] Flak being absent, they conducted three attack runs, strafing the area around the bridge[82] and boosting the Belgians' morale. After further artillery preparations and under cover of a smoke screen provided by artillery and supported by 3-inch mortars, Vijt tried to approach the bridge via a road along the canal but came under heavy shelling and machine gun fire and had to withdraw.

On 15 April, Winschoten was reported clear of the enemy, but mines had been laid near the Winschoterhoogebrug. Once removed by Ghys' party, 'B' Squadron's assault troop entered the town. Its No. 1 section discovered two Germans close to the road bridge leading to Oostereinde, northeast of the town. A malfunction of their Bren – caused by lack of time for proper maintenance – allowed the Germans to get away. A party from the engineer troop was brought forward to inspect the bridge and remove demolition charges if present, but was fired upon. Friendly fire was suspected to be at the origin, so Donnelly, the signals officer, sent a message to inform the Poles that Allied forces had already reached the bridge. The reply mentioned that the Poles had been assuming this to be the case indeed, but that they "just wanted to make sure…"[83]

The division reported that Winschoten was liberated between 10 and 11 am, by a combined force of Belgian SAS and a Polish infantry battalion,[84] the latter referring to the 1st Podhale Rifles Battalion (*1 batalion strzelców podhalańskich*), operating as part of the 3rd Infantry Brigade Group,[85] commanded by Lieutenant Colonel Władysław Dec, the 3rd Infantry Brigade's commander.[86]

The long-awaited liberators brought immense enthusiasm to Winschoten, as they were greeted with exuberant cheers, surpassing even the most glorious days of Orange celebrations. National tricolour and orange banners adorned the city's houses and official buildings. The entire town embraced the festive atmosphere, donning the beloved colours of the House of Orange. The indescribable joy marked the end of a repressive German occupation.[87]

A Belgian jeep section continued to reconnoitre ahead as far as 2 miles north of Finsterwolde, a mere 1.5 miles from the sea. Thonard noticed an enemy position and immediately attacked it, taking five prisoners after a short firefight. A coastal artillery battery in concrete emplacements, protected by minefields and machine gun positions, was sighted near the dyke of the Dollard Bay, at the river Ems estuary.

In Winschoten, 'A' Squadron joined the remainder and three groups were organised: Romnée's jeep section with Tinchant's assault section, d'Oultremont's jeep section with Jeukens' assault section and Crèvecœur's jeep section with Goffinet's assault section. They advanced north in the direction of the sea towards Beerta and Finsterwolde.

At around 2:30 pm, contact was made with a bicycle-mounted rear guard, which occupied positions in a lone farm east of the road on the southern edge of Beerta. Tinchant's and Jeukens' assault sections deployed to assault the farm, supported by Romnée's and Van Broekhuizen's jeep crews. The enemy fled and the village was rapidly cleared. Eight Germans had been killed, two were mortally wounded and over two dozen others taken prisoner.

North of the village, the bridge over the Beertster Diep river on the way to Finsterwolde was found destroyed. It was now around 4:30 pm. Van der Heyden and Romnée went forward to determine a new axis of advance when they came under artillery and mortar fire. Van der Heyden was hit in the forearm and leg. The vehicle crews were ordered to disperse and organise a hasty defence, expecting a counterattack from Nieuwe-Beerta, a village less than 3 miles to the northeast. The Polish liaison officer returned to Winschoten to request counterbattery fire support. By 6 pm, he was back and requested a section to join him to advance to Oostwolde, a mile west of Finsterwolde, and the sea. d'Oultremont was assigned the task and received orders not to commit himself to any heavy fight. Six tanks were due to arrive to support the Belgians during their advance to the sea, but until they arrived, Van der Heyden refused to be evacuated, despite some of his officers insisting on doing so.

Around 7 pm, Devignez and Robert Feremans were also hit by German fire. Feremans, a signaller, was wounded in the abdomen. Devignez was hit in the right flank, shrapnel entering his liver and lungs, and would later die in hospital.

Half an hour later, the tanks arrived. Assuming the Belgians had already continued towards the sea, the Polish colonel who arrived at the scene seemed surprised to find the Belgians still in Beerta, as had been requested by the liaison officer. The plan was now to try advancing through Finsterwolde along an alternate route. The tank commander appeared eager to reach the sea, on the condition that the Belgian jeeps would lead the way, and the assault troop would be carried on the tanks' hull. To Heilporn, this was unacceptable.

Romnée, who had taken over command of 'A' Squadron, took the lead of the tank column toward Finsterwolde, where Blondeel was met. A conference was held and now it seemed the Polish officer wanted a mixed force of some Polish tanks and Belgian dismounted jeep crews, to seize the coastal artillery position.

A heated discussion ensued and Blondeel, well informed about the artillery battery, thanks to information provided by a Dutch civilian who had been involved in its construction, refused to execute a pointless order. Advancing through minefields in open terrain without any cover and under enemy fire was close to suicidal. He agreed to obey, on the condition that the remaining tank crews not earmarked for the attack would dismount as well, and the Polish colonel would join Blondeel and his men in the attack, which the Pole refused.[88]

The German battery was the *Dollart-Süd* heavy air defence artillery battery equipped with four 105 mm air defence guns and manned by a battery of the 276th Naval Air Defence Battalion, part of the 6th Naval Air Defence Regiment, which defended the German harbour city of Emden, just across the Dollard Bay. Since the afternoon of 13 April, the battery had also been used in a ground role against Allied armour in the area around Winschoten and was still reported to be engaged against armour concentrations on 24 April, remaining in German hands for a few more days afterwards.[89,90]

By 8 pm, orders were received to move the complete regiment to Finsterwolde.

Meanwhile, d'Oultremont had led a patrol further north and had managed to reach the sea at Dollard Bay. He brought back a water bottle filled with seawater and presented it to the Polish colonel, who congratulated him.[91] Pleased with the achievement, the Polish 1st Armoured Division legitimately reported that at 4:30 pm, forward elements of the 3rd Polish Infantry Brigade Group had reached the sea.[92]

Returning to the rear area, d'Oultremont's patrol was shelled at Beerta. Trooper J.J. Dubois was hit in the chest but was saved by the body armour[93] he was wearing. Around 10 pm, two others were not so lucky. Troopers Jean Bernard and Joseph Wathelet were occupying an anti-tank position when they were fired upon by two

Germans they had mistakenly taken for Dutch civilians. Wathelet did not survive the encounter, his chest being rippled with bullet holes, the projectiles having gone straight through his Bren magazines.

To reduce the risk of heavy shelling, the decision was taken to clear Finsterwolde at dawn and withdraw with the bulk of the force, leaving only outposts in the village. A Polish artillery battery and 3-inch mortars positioned themselves south of the village to provide counterbattery fire.

At 6:20 am on 16 April, all houses were searched, but no enemy was found. Around 100 yards east of the crossroads near the church, on the eastern part of Finsterwolde, heavy shelling resumed and Jeukens was slightly wounded.

The main body of the regiment withdrew to Oostereinde, leaving No. 2 and No. 3 sections of 'B' Squadron's assault troop to guard the western and eastern approaches to Finsterwolde.

At 10 am, Van Broekhuizen's jeep section reconnoitred the bridge over the Buiskooldiep canal on the road between Beerta and Nieuwe-Beerta. The latter was found occupied by the enemy and the section returned to Beerta to take up defensive positions.[94]

Around 1:15 pm, enemy infiltrations were reported in Finsterwolde, and Van Cauwelaert called his reserve assault sections forward and attacked the enemy who had entrenched themselves at the cemetery. Some twenty Germans equipped with submachine guns, machine guns and *Panzerfauste* were seen fleeing in disorder, taking two wounded with them. Again, the Belgians came under heavy artillery attack.[95,96]

By 4:30 pm, the two sections were relieved by the No. 3 section and Thinard's jeep section and at 7, a section from the engineer troop took over positions at Finsterwolde. An hour later, the Belgian positions were shelled once more and Trooper Henri Tondreau was bit by shrapnel in his shoulder.

On 17 April, orders were received that the regiment was to leave the Polish division and that Polish troops would take over the Belgians' positions at Finsterwolde and Beerta from noon. The engineer troop was again under heavy artillery fire and left Finsterwolde by 3 pm without further casualties. At 5 pm, the regiment left Oostereinde and had to move to Tinnen, in Germany, via Wedde, Ter Apel and Haren, for four days of rest and refitting.[97]

With most of the Netherlands liberated, Operation 'Larkswood' would continue on German soil.

Chapter Nine

ADVANCE FORCE IN THE FINAL DEFEAT OF NAZI GERMANY

BY THE TIME THE Belgian SAS Regiment arrived in Germany, the Allies had been making significant progress on German territory. The Ruhr area – the industrial importance of which had already been severely degraded by the Allied air forces – had been encircled. The American 1st and 2nd armies advancing out of the Frankfurt area on the southern arm of the pincer movement, having met less resistance than Simpson's 9th Army in the north (on the right of Montgomery's 21st Army Group), had swung the eastern and northeastern flanks of the Ruhr to meet Simpson's army in the vicinity of Lippstadt, completing the encirclement of Model's Army Group B by 1 April. By mid-April, the Ruhr pocket had been reduced by Bradley's 12th Army Group and was on the verge of collapse. At the same time, Bradley's forces were advancing across Germany's central plateau, with Simpson's 9th Army in the north, Hodges' 1st Army in the centre and Patton's 3rd Army in the south, having reached or closing in on the Elbe and Mulde rivers, the general junction line agreed with the Soviets, whose forces were firmly established at the Oder river some 30 miles from Berlin and preparing for the final push over a front of more than 200 miles, in the general direction of Denmark, Berlin and the Dresden area. Further south, Devers' 6th Army Group had been protecting Bradley's right flank from early April, conducting a methodical advance with Patch's 7th Army and de Lattre's French 1st Army. On the north of Bradley's left flank, Montgomery's 21st Army Group was advancing toward Bremen and Hamburg. Its Canadian Army's I Corps had captured Arnhem on 15 April and was advancing further north, west of the IJssel river, while II Corps was continuing to clear the coastal belt eastward toward the Elbe, on the northwestern flank of the British 2nd Army.[1]

On 18 April, the regiment mustered for a morning parade on their first day in Germany. Having no tentage, the men had to be billeted on farms, so were given clear non-fraternisation rules for dealing with the German population.[2]

Major Blondeel visited the Canadian II Corps HQ to provide an overview of his regiment's operations under the command of the Polish 1st Armoured Division in the Netherlands and to discuss its probable future role under the command of the Canadian 2nd Armoured Brigade.[3] Meanwhile, the unit spent the day conducting maintenance of vehicles and other equipment.

During the night, the regimental HQ guard caught two civilians, who were interrogated and handed over to the Canadian field security section (FSS),[4] who had them on their wanted persons list. They turned out to be the *Ortsgruppenleiter*[5] from Meppen and his assistant.

While equipment maintenance continued, the officers were also busy conducting exercises to improve their radio communication skills using No. 22 sets.[6]

The regiment saw an increase in its number of officers: Marcel Demery, Barette, Krolikowski, Crèvecœur, Slosse, Tinchant, Klein and Devignez (killed a few days earlier) had been commissioned as 2nd lieutenants. Following a short well-deserved leave after their return from six months behind enemy lines, Kirschen's and Debefve's teams returned to the frontline. Debefve took command of 'B' Squadron and Kirschen took command of the mortar troop.[7]

On 21 April, Brigadier Robinson, commander of the Canadian 2nd Armoured Brigade, was called to the II Corps HQ to find out his future role. The tentative plan included a recce of the Emden – Wilhelmshaven area north of the Küstenkanal waterway, with the 1st Canadian Armoured Car Regiment (Royal Canadian Dragoons), a squadron from the 18th Canadian Armoured Car Regiment, the Belgian SAS and a British SAS unit under command. The brigade was to conduct a fast recce northwards to the Ems-Jade canal once the 4th Canadian Armoured Division had broken out of the bridgehead over the Küstenkanal. This was not expected to happen for several days, since the wet ground precluded off-road movement, which favoured the fanatical resistance by units of the 7th and 8th Parachute Division, assisted by naval units from Emden and Wilhelmshaven.[8] The British and Belgian SAS came under the brigade's command at 11:59 pm on the 22nd.[9]

The British SAS unit under the command of the 2nd Canadian Armoured Brigade – an independent brigade[10] within II Corps – was a reorganised squadron of the 1st SAS under the command of Major Marsh. The force, previously consisting of 'B' and 'C' squadrons and commanded by Lieutenant Colonel Mayne, the regiment's CO, had been infiltrating the German lines under the command of the Canadian 4th Armoured Division. During these operations, Mayne had once again displayed supreme leadership and bravery for which he would be recommended the Victoria Cross, eventually being downgraded to a third bar to his DSO. Meanwhile, the other half of Mayne's regiment ('A' and 'D' squadrons, under Major Poat) had been spearheading the advance of British and American units further east as part of Frankforce, commanded by the CO of the 2nd SAS, Lieutenant Colonel Franks.[11]

Since the bridgehead could only be expanded slowly, the Belgian SAS Regiment was forced to wait in Lorup and used the time to conduct live fire training. The medical section also treated some ten wounded from the 1st SAS, whose squadron did not have access to the unit's own regimental medical officer.[12]

On 27 April, a new regrouping came into effect at 3:30 pm: the Canadian 2nd Armoured Brigade, less its 10th Armoured Regiment and 27th Armoured Regiment, and with the Canadian 1st Armoured Car Regiment (Royal Canadian Dragoons), the British SAS squadron and the Belgian SAS Regiment under its command, came under command of the Canadian 4th Armoured Division. Its tasks included the capture of Godensholt, Ocholt, Apen and Barssel and once this area was under control, patrolling towards Torsholt and Rostrup (east of Ocholt) and establishing contact with the Polish 1st Armoured Division at Bollingen, 4 miles southwest of Barssel.[13] The Polish 1st Armoured Division had been advancing to the west of the Canadian 4th Armoured Division, having crossed the Ems near Heren on the 14th, continuing north along its eastern bank, crossing the Küstenkanal on the 19th, capturing Papenburg and clearing the area south of the Leda river while moving east.[14]

At 7 pm, the Belgian SAS Regiment suddenly received orders to move and Blondeel visited the HQs of the 4th Armoured Division and the 2nd Armoured Brigade.[15] The divisional main HQ and the brigade HQ had moved during the day to a location near Osterscheps, 2 miles north of the Küstenkanal.[16,17] 'B' Squadron and the regimental HQ followed soon afterwards.

On 28 April, with daylight well underway, a combined Canadian-Belgian force started its move to Godensholt to seize the town. An armoured car troop took the lead, followed by a jeep section of the Belgian SAS Regiment's 'B' Squadron, a tank troop, 'B' Squadron's two other jeep sections and its assault troop. The Belgian engineer troop was attached for the anticipated clearing of mines and booby traps and a bulldozer was kept at the Canadian 6th Armoured Regiment's 'B' Squadron HQ for removing felled trees blocking the roads. The number of waterways and the marshy ground limited the use of all vehicles to the few roads in the area.

Successive roadblocks a short distance apart on the road between Westerscheps and Rothenmethen slowed the column's advance. The first one was encountered near a bend in the road almost 1.5 miles northwest of Westerscheps. Assault troops with engineer personnel were called forward and cleared the obstacle and continued to clear the next, which was held under fire. The enemy opened up and shrapnel – possibly from mortar fire – killed Trooper Albert Bechet and wounded Trooper Willy Hendrikx and Lance Corporal Victor Jacobs van Merlen. Supported by tank fire, a reserve section attacked the enemy position, bypassing the obstacle, which was cleared by a bulldozer tank.[18,19]

Radino interrogated five prisoners of war taken by 'B' Squadron. They were identified as members of the 7th Parachute Division[20] and revealed that some 500 enemy troops were scattered in the area, operating in small groups and armed only with small arms. The information was incomplete; 'B' Squadron soon found out heavier guns were being used by the enemy.

In the meantime, the regiment's tactical HQ had moved to Westerscheps. Shortly before noon, it was visited by Lieutenant Colonel Frank White DSO, CO of the 6th Canadian Armoured Regiment (1st Hussars) and Major Cecil Mills, his 'B' Squadron's OC.[21]

White had been appointed commander of a new battle group, becoming effective at noon and was tasked with clearing the area towards Godensholt and Apen. Named 'Frankforce' (not to be confused with the abovementioned similarly named British SAS task force operating further east), it was composed of White's own regiment, 'D' Squadron of the Canadian 18th Armoured Car Regiment (12th Manitoba Dragoons) and the British and Belgian SAS assigned to the Canadian 2nd Armoured Brigade.[22,23,24]

The Belgian regimental medical officer and the padre went to 'B' Squadron's forward positions and oversaw the evacuation of the wounded to a medical treatment facility.

By 1:30 pm, 'A' Squadron and HQ Squadron had also arrived at Westerscheps, and around 2:20, shooting started from the south and a jeep section from 'A' Squadron was sent out to take defensive positions near the river bridges southwest and south of Westerscheps.

The advance to Godensholt – under German small arms fire – encountered further tree obstacles a few hundred yards from the previous ones, which were dealt with by the bulldozer. At around 2:45, the armoured car unit reported a crater in the road about a mile south of Rothenmethen. It was assessed to be 30-50 feet wide and a stream that crossed the road at the same spot prevented vehicles from circumventing the obstacle. A German self-propelled gun hit the suspension of the leading Canadian tank from a position 200 yards further north along the road, but the tank returned fire and knocked out the gun.[25,26,27]

Polain's jeep section was sent out to check a river bridge to access the parallel road on the left flank, but found it destroyed.

Around 4 pm, the engineer troop, which was waiting for further orders near the crater site, found itself under sporadic but accurate mortar fire. The roof of an isolated house in the marshlands east of the road was identified as a likely OP and one of the 20 mm guns captured in the Netherlands was put to good use. Although no enemy could be seen, as soon as the roof had been destroyed, the German mortar fire ceased. Half an hour later, 'B' Squadron also found itself at the receiving end of mortar fire and was ordered to withdraw and report the mortars' position. Shortly before 5 pm, no more mortar fire was observed and the SAS squadron could return to its forward positions near the crater. Around 5:30 pm, the squadron received a warning order to withdraw its main body to a firm base for the night. Half an hour later, the engineer troop rounded up eight more prisoners sitting in foxholes near the location of the fighting earlier that morning.

At 7 pm, White arrived with new orders from the brigade. The divisional engineers were to bridge the crater during the night and the Belgian SAS was to protect the site. An hour later, Blondeel went forward to 'B' Squadron's HQ and the site of the crater. Returning to his HQ, he met the Canadian engineers' recce party, who informed him of their intent to start the bridging operation immediately. The Belgians at once established a bridgehead on the far side of the crater without enemy interference. By 10 pm, a forward observation officer arrived and established an OP on the north side of the crater, ready to direct artillery fire if needed. Half an hour later, the Canadian engineers arrived and started clearing the approaches before the bridging materiel arrived.[28] By midnight the bridging was completed and soon afterwards, the four tanks of the 1st Troop from the 6th Armoured Regiment's 'B' Squadron crossed the bridge and took up defensive positions.

Around 4:30 am on 29 April, White decided to resume the advance and half an hour later, the 3rd Troop from the 6th Armoured Regiment's 'B' Squadron passed through the 1st Troop and continued with the armoured cars and the SAS. The tanks were now taking the lead instead of the armoured cars. No opposition was encountered by either the tanks or the SAS, until the area near Rothenmethen was reached, about 1.5 miles on the main road southeast of Godensholt, when the armoured troop sergeant's tank was knocked out by a self-propelled gun. Its crew got away unscathed and the threat was eliminated by the troop leader's tank, killing three among the German weapon system's crew. Infantry and small arms fire were also reported and several prisoners were taken shortly afterwards. Two were underage navy personnel who had been told by their officers they would be shot by the Allies if they surrendered.[29,30,31]

Shortly before noon, the Canadian 2nd Armoured Brigade sent out a message to

Frankforce stating the British SAS was to relieve the Belgian SAS by noon.[32] By mid-afternoon, the information arrived at the Belgian SAS HQ, around which time Bechet was buried alongside the main road. Around 4 pm, the Belgian regimental medical officer was called upon to treat a casualty from the 1st SAS but was unable to save him. Two wounded German civilians were also taken care of. For the remainder of the day, the regiment took some rest, to be ready again the next morning.[33] Meanwhile, Frankforce continued its advance towards Godensholt. Due to the soaked ground and the mined road, Marsh's British SAS squadron was forced to operate on foot at first, but later managed to use its jeeps.[34] No opposition was encountered, but another road crater less than a mile from Godensholt once again halted the advance. Around 6 pm, the 6th Armoured Regiment's 'B' Squadron was relieved by its 'A' Squadron. The latter's 3rd Troop took defensive positions protecting the engineers who bridged the gap and continued the advance with the British SAS at around 8:30 pm. Being fired upon from buildings along the road, the enemy positions were burned down by tank fire and at last light, the force consolidated its position for the night. Plenty of enemy movement was noticed at night, but artillery support kept the Germans at bay. Meanwhile, options were also considered to move through the right flank, to reach the road between Godensholt and Ocholt, 3 miles further northeast. A tank troop from 'B' Squadron and two armoured car troops moved off to the north at 5 am on the 30th. The advance was now being conducted in driving rain and snow, which seriously hampered the use of the armoured vehicles' optics. Half a mile southeast of Godensholt, the column ran into a heavy roadblock which was covered by machine gun fire, but Canadian tanks proved no match for the defenders. Some sixty Germans – mainly young sailors – were taken prisoner.

That morning, warning orders were issued to the Belgian SAS manoeuvre squadrons, to be ready at 10 am. Before noon, command meetings were held and 'A' Squadron was tasked with linking up with tanks, moving through the 1st SAS positions, occupying the southern edge of Godensholt and clearing the village, short of the road forming its eastern boundary, which had to be cleared by 'B' Squadron's assault troop, while 'A' Squadron's jeep troops had to cover the crossroads and western approaches to the village.[35] In the afternoon, the Belgians started to push forward, linking up with the Canadian tanks and relieving the British SAS. The combined force moved into Godensholt and cleared the village, disabling a self-propelled gun and taking over a dozen prisoners. By 7 pm, the village was under Canadian control.[36,37]

On 1 May, around 10 am, Heilporn and Romnée found themselves at the southeastern edge of the village and requested the engineer troop to remove mines and grenades from the houses occupied by Jeukens' section, when they were surprised by German indirect fire. Heilporn and Trooper Paul Ruscart were heavily wounded and evacuated. Ruscart, a member of the engineer troop, did not survive his wounds. Two others, troopers Eugene Huybrechts and Prosper Van Den Reym, were slightly wounded.

In heavy rain, limited activity was conducted throughout the day, during which contact was established with patrols from the Canadian 1st Armoured Car Regiment. The medical section treated liberated Russian and Yugoslav ex-prisoners, as well as a couple of German women who were injured during the shelling of Godensholt.[38]

Early in the morning of 2 May, the Canadian 2nd Armoured Brigade issued an operation instruction covering the new situation. German forces were reportedly withdrawing from the Canadian 4th Armoured Division's front to Wilhelmshaven, to be ferried across the water so they could be engaged in the defence of Hamburg. The Canadian 2nd Infantry Division was closing in on Oldenburg, on the 4th Division's right flank, while the latter was enveloping the enemy toward the north and east to cut off his retreat from Oldenburg. The Canadian 2nd Armoured Brigade was now to provide left flank protection to the 4th Division. The 1st Armoured Car Regiment, with the Belgian SAS Regiment under its command and supported by a squadron from the 6th Armoured Regiment, was tasked with retaining control of the Godensholt area with one armoured car squadron while moving the remainder to Rostrup. They should also be prepared to seize and maintain a firm base in Westerstede and seize road centres on the road between Torsholt and Groß-Garnholt (all to the northeast of Godensholt) and afterwards exploit towards Moorburg, Neuengland, Eggeloge and Spohle, a few miles further north.[39]

At 8 am, a meeting was held at the brigade HQ. Blondeel was informed that his regiment would move by 3:30 pm and warning orders were issued. The actual move proved more complicated than anticipated in the plan. A recce party went to Rostrup but was unable to find sufficient billets. 'B' Squadron and the engineer troop moved to Rostrup, but the remainder of the regiment had to stay near Westerscheps.

From 10 am on 3 May, patrols were conducted to the northwest from Rostrup by Thonard's and Vijt's sections. They located several mines and craters along the road but, bypassing the obstacles, they managed to reach Westerstede, which was also being entered from the west by troops of the Polish 1st Armoured Division. At the nearby Hüllstede, accommodation was found and preparations were made for the regiment to occupy the new billets. At 1 pm, additional jeep patrols were conducted by Ghys with two sections and Krolikowski's section. At 2:30 pm, 'A' Squadron moved to Rostrup.[40]

On 4 May, starting about a mile east of Eggeloge, 'B' Squadron of the 1st Armoured Car Regiment had orders to push north towards Zetel and advanced together with 'B' Squadron of the Belgian SAS Regiment. Progress was difficult, owing to multiple obstacles. At a crossroads 1.5 miles north, the road had been cratered, but a route to the left was found. Back on the main road just over a mile further north, a demolition charge was discovered connected to a remote activation mechanism in a field 50 yards to the right. The wires were cut and the advance continued. Movement again came to a halt when a crater 35 feet in diameter was encountered 2 miles to the southwest of Grabstede, 200 yards northeast of the Y-junction with the road to Neuenburg. The crater was filled and at 1 pm, two armoured car troops moved towards Grabstede, stopping 300 yards short of the railway crossing to the west of the village centre. Heavy shelling had to be endured. Further behind on the main road, over 1.5 miles southwest of Grabstede, a Staghound armoured car ran onto a mine killing all members of its crew. Enemy infantry at the railway crossing were attacked by Canadians and an SAS troop, but the attack had to be called off since a message was received that the Polish 1st Armoured Division intended to shell the area heavily, which occurred before the withdrawal could be completed.

Further east, the SAS Regiment's 'A' Squadron, which in the meantime had moved to Hüllstede, together with the regimental HQ, conducted patrols to the northeast of this village and met stiff resistance by German forces including armour. Trooper André Schaller was accidentally hit in the chest by a .45" bullet.

On the road from Linswege (2 miles northeast of Hüllstede) to Altjührden, a Belgian recce patrol was stopped when it came under fire 3 miles northeast of Linswege. A Canadian troop from the 1st Armoured Car Regiment's 'C' Squadron less than 2 miles further north on the same road was also fired upon by an anti-tank gun at short range, but returned fire and could break contact without casualties, hiding behind a smoke screen.

A mile east of this road, on a secondary road a mile northwest of Spohle, Polain, with four jeeps and an armoured car, came under tank fire and heavy and accurate indirect fire.

On the road to Spohle, another armoured car troop reached Petersfeld where a roadblock including mines and held under small arms, mortar and artillery fire was encountered, forcing the troop to withdraw. Alternate minor roads also proved blocked and under fire, precluding any further progress. Canadians and Belgians established harbours for the night, anticipating renewed operations from daylight the next morning, but the BBC reported Germany would soon surrender and later that evening, a message was sent by the II Army Corps to the 4th Armoured Division ordering an immediate cancellation of all offensive operations and announcing a ceasefire.[41,42,43,44]

A few hours earlier, the German high command had agreed to an unconditional surrender to the 21st Army Group of all forces under their control in the Netherlands, northwest Germany and Denmark with effect from 8 am on 5 May, the instrument of surrender having been signed by *Generaladmiral* Hans-Georg von Friedeburg in the presence of Montgomery.[45]

On 5 May, 'A' Squadron moved to billets in Linswege, less than 2 miles northeast of Hüllstede, where the regimental HQ remained. German prisoners were being rounded up, which would continue for the next few days.

On 6 May, Blondeel and Smith went to Lüneburg, to visit the British 2nd Army HQ. Blondeel returned on the evening of the next day, with orders to conduct counterintelligence operations in the British sector.[46] Earlier in the morning of 7 May, a surrender instrument had been signed by *Generaloberst* Alfred Jodl at Eisenhower's HQ in Reims, accepting an unconditional capitulation of the German armed forces as a whole, to become effective close to midnight on 8 May, while formal ratification of surrender was later to be signed again in Berlin.[47,48,49]

A war of unprecedented magnitude had come to an end in Europe, but operations in the Far East continued relentlessly. Anticipating the employment of SAS troops in the war against Japan, David Stirling had been planning future operations while still in captivity at Colditz Castle, and had discussed his plan with Prime Minister Churchill after his liberation in April. The war would eventually end before the plan could be implemented, but other tasks were waiting for the British and Belgian SAS in the months following the German surrender. The 1st and 2nd SAS soon found themselves on their way to Norway, where they were to supervise the disarming of German forces and to carry out internal security duties, while a team under the 2nd SAS intelligence officer started investigations on war crimes against captured SAS personnel.[50,51]

Meanwhile, the 5th SAS stayed in Germany, where they were to contribute to the British 2nd Army's occupational duties under the British military government. On 8 May, preparations were made to disperse the regiment over the VIII, XII and XXX army corps. A day later, an advance party moved to Oldenburg, Bremen, Hamburg, Lübeck and Kiel, passing through the HQs of the aforementioned army corps, while the regimental HQ directly drove to Kiel, to reach Rotenhahn a day later, some 7 miles south of Kiel.[52]

Chapter Ten

COUNTERINTELLIGENCE OPERATIONS IN OCCUPIED GERMANY

DURING CONFERENCES STARTING in 1943, the British prime minister, the president of the United States and the chairman of the Council of Peoples' Commissars of the Union of Soviet Socialist Republics had agreed to divide Germany into occupation zones and, two years before the end of hostilities, planning for a military government in post-war occupied Germany had already been initiated.[1] In 1945, the final agreement resulted in four zones, to be occupied by the United States, the United Kingdom, France and the Soviet Union and to be administered through a central Control Council consisting of the supreme commanders of the occupying powers with its HQ in Berlin, the German capital, which would also be divided between the four Allied nations.[2]

In the area it occupied, the 21st Army Group faced major problems. The population had to be fed, housed and kept healthy, but industrial and agricultural production had almost come to a standstill, while transportation and communication services were no longer functional. More than a million refugees had fled into the area under British control, in front of the advancing and vengeful Red Army troops. Around a million German wounded were in hospitals in the area without sufficient medical supplies and more than 1.5 million German military personnel still fit to bear arms were prisoners of war.

Responsibilities in the British sector would reside in Montgomery's hands following his appointment – announced on 22 May – as commander-in-chief of the British forces of occupation and British member of the Allied Control Council in Germany, whose signing ceremony and inaugural meeting occurred in Berlin on 5 June.[3]

While trying to avoid economic chaos, measures had to be taken at the same time to implement the disarmament, demilitarisation and denazification of Germany as agreed between the heads of government of the United Kingdom, the United States and the Soviet Union. The denazification process, including the intent to bring all war criminals to just and swift punishment, was an activity in which the Belgian SAS Regiment was to become actively involved. To Blondeel, it did not come as a surprise. Already in February, his unit had received some basic counter-espionage training, learning how to neutralise enemy agents left behind by withdrawing enemy forces. The knowledge of the German language by some thirty of his men was also a skill that would prove invaluable.[4]

On 9 May, the Belgian SAS Regiment came under command of the British 2nd Army and was to provide detachments to reinforce FSSs for counter-intelligence operations. Three sections had to be detached to the XXX Corps at Bremervörde, four to the XII Corps at Hamburg and eight to the VIII Corps at Kiel. The remainder of the regiment had to move with the regimental HQ near Kiel and was to be held in reserve. The same day, all groups reached their destination and the next day, the sections were decentralised towards British units subordinate to the three army corps.[5]

Originally, plans for the organisation of the British occupation zone included the establishment of four corps districts but these were reduced to three during later planning. The 21st Army Group had to redeploy its forces so the British I, VIII and XXX army corps could assume responsibility for their respective districts, while at the same time adjusting the external boundaries of the area occupied by the Army Group to bring these in line with the zones agreed between the Allies. The HQ of the 21st Army Group was to become the HQ for the entire British zone. The British 2nd Army HQ was to disappear as the corps districts were to come under the direct control of the 21st Army Group HQ. In a gradual transfer, I Corps passed to direct control by the 21st Army Group on 21 May, XXX Corps on 8 June and VIII Corps on 16 June, after which the British 2nd Army was absolved of all responsibility for military government.[6]

Following this reorganisation when XII Corps was withdrawn, a reshuffle resulted in three detachments being assigned to XXX Corps (operating from Göttingen, Goslar and Hildesheim) and fourteen sections being detached to VIII Corps (operating from Tønder (in Denmark), Flensburg, Wismar, Schwerin, Hamburg and Blankenese). The regimental HQ stayed in Rotenhahn and saw the arrival of an additional group that had been training in Tervueren and was now also to be trained in this new role and would afterwards be posted to the British VIII Army Corps.

Their main activities, which will be covered in more detail by geographical area below, included area patrolling, conducting raids, house and camp searches, making arrests, conducting interrogations and transporting prisoners. Each section took care of its own daily administration, but the regimental HQ kept in touch with all sections to assist them with administrative issues as required. In the early days, armoured jeeps were often used, as some resistance was to be expected, but the quick transition and back-to-back operations had resulted in a lack of proper vehicle maintenance after weeks of intensive field use, especially affecting the armoured jeeps, given the additional strain caused by the heavy armour plating. The British Royal Electrical and Mechanical Engineers (REME) were generally very helpful in repairing Belgian vehicles, but a major overhaul of armoured jeeps by REME workshops proved unfeasible. When their jeeps had broken down completely, some detachments eventually obtained requisitioned cars to allow them to continue their activities.[7]

Rotenhahn

In Rotenhahn, the regimental HQ was installed in conditions of unprecedented comfort, but soon found itself struggling with all kinds of administrative tasks that so far had been postponed to deal with more pressing operational issues. Mombel, Pécher and de Merkline could hardly leave their desk, trying to manage a unit deployed over an area larger than Belgium and subject to both British and Belgian regulations.

Merchiers was pleasantly surprised to discover a German military workshop, which he immediately used to his advantage for having the regiment's vehicles repaired, until a higher authority claimed the workshop for its exclusive use.

1st Lieutenant Pierre De Bluts stayed in touch with a delegation of the Belgian Red Cross in Lübeck to search for Belgian prisoners of war and one day, found three compatriots that had been liberated but abandoned in a hospital. Via the base in Tervueren, messages were sent to reassure their families and arrangements were made to have them repatriated by aeroplane.[8]

Despite the food shortage in Schleswig-Holstein, there existed a perception that sufficient food was available, at least locally.[9,10] Blondeel attributed the ability of his cook to obtain flour, sugar and butter without any problem to the presence of food stocks unable to be distributed further south for several months. Whatever the real situation, the cook managed to bake tasty biscuits, but another factor contributed to the reputation soon to be achieved by the Belgian mess. The Belgians had discovered a stock containing an estimated 10,000 bottles of *Moulin à Vent*, a French wine from the Beaujolais area, so meals were often accompanied by abundant wine. Once this became known, many senior officers showed an interest in visiting the regimental HQ to see how things were going, hoping to leave with some bottles.[11]

Hamburg

Two sections commanded by Crèvecœur operated from Hamburg, initially in the XII Corps district, with the 26th and 30th FSSs.

During an investigation in the Neuengamme concentration camp,[12] documents of interest were recovered.

A raid on an SS camp resulted in the arrest of six men, including a major, while an arms cache was discovered in a garden and the bodies of an SS family which had committed suicide were found.

During an operation on a cemetery, a resistance group leader and his assistants were arrested.

Many other small operations were conducted and a section which originally had been operating from Albensdorf joined Hamburg and started field security duties in support of a French security office.[13]

d'Oultremont joined the Hamburg office and took over from Crèvecœur on 15 May.[14]

The section under Van Broekhuizen worked with the 41st FSS. Its principal area of operations was the Pinneberg *Kreis*,[15] some 10 miles northwest of Hamburg. Daily routine included arrests, house searches and interrogations, using at least two jeeps for each mission.

The Itzehoe sector, some 20 miles further northeast, also had to be covered by this section. Many personnel files were found and exploited, which led to the arrest of *Obergruppenführer* Herbert Fust, chief of the Hamburg *Sturmabteilung*,[16] a female leader from the Buchenwald concentration camp,[17] two other concentration camp leaders and a dozen SS and *Gestapo* personnel.

Lance Corporal Hendrickx's initiative and cleverness led to the discovery of highly important documents, allowing the Brits to dismantle a large spy ring.

Van Broekhuizen also detached a jeep and its crew to conduct similar operations in support of French counter-intelligence personnel and by the end of June, his section had contributed to 300 arrests.[18]

On the morning of 15 June, Goffinet reported to the 26th FSS office to receive orders as part of his daily routine. Waiting outside the building were two German civilians who conveyed crucial information. They claimed to know where Joachim von Ribbentrop, Nazi Germany's Minister of Foreign Affairs during the war, was hiding and gave him the address of an apartment in Hamburg where he was said to be living under the alias 'Von Riese'. Although somewhat sceptical, Goffinet, accompanied by British Lieutenant Adams and a few colleagues, went to the specified location. Arriving at the apartment on the fourth floor, the men encountered a locked door and rang the doorbell a couple of times, without success. Goffinet attempted to open the lock using his dagger. He had hardly finished his attempt when, to the team's surprise, the door was answered by a beautiful blonde woman in a nightdress. Upon entering the bedroom, Goffinet and his team caught von Ribbentrop off guard, finding him asleep in silk pyjamas. Realising the futility of escape, von Ribbentrop did not attempt to flee. Goffinet removed von Ribbentrop's false teeth and searched the buccal cavity for the presence of a cyanide capsule to prevent his captive from taking his own life. When searching the apartment, 200,000 German marks were found, as well as envelopes containing letters addressed to Churchill and Montgomery. The war criminal was arrested and would be trialled at Nuremberg, found guilty and hanged in 1946.[19,20,21]

The section of Tinchant was made available to support the 40th FSS under Captain Harrison. During the first days, several investigations were conducted and multiple arrests were made of SS and *Nationalsozialistisches Kraftfahrkorps*[22] leaders, but after a week, the tempo somewhat slackened. For this reason, Tinchant received approval to start independent enquiries and build a network of informants. This eventually allowed him to clean up the Wellingsbüttel quarter in Hamburg and to identify prominent Nazis such as the right hand of Hermann Okraß, editor of the *Hamburger Tageblatt*, a Nazi Party newspaper.[23,24] During a larger operation against a hospital that was a hotbed of SS activity, reinforcements by armoured vehicles were required and searches led to the arrest of several suspects.

After the departure of the 40th FSS, Tinchant's section worked for the 265th FSS. A major and difficult task the men had to deal with was the investigation into the *Werwolf Abschnitt Nordsee*[25] resistance group, which eventually allowed the team to uncover the activities of *SS-Obersturmbannführer* Dr Specht and many other members, although the enquiry was still ongoing when the section's operation came to an end. Tinchant was also able to discover an SS officer's yearbook from 1938, the exploitation of which proved useful in finding further information.[26]

Bremerhaven

From 12 May to 2 June, Barette, with a section of the mortar troop, was attached to an FSS in Bremerhaven, in the district of the XXX Corps. The section routinely had two jeeps on the road and one jeep on stand-by at the HQ. Each vehicle had two men, one of whom was usually a German speaker. The section's 15-cwt lorry was used for administrative purposes and to transport prisoners. On average, some fifteen to twenty persons were rounded up for interrogation each day, which sometimes required driving over 30 miles and exceptionally even up to 100 miles to find a specified individual. In total, over 100 arrests were made, which included war criminals or other persons of interest, usually officers and NCOs from military or paramilitary organisations.[27]

On 20 May, a handover ceremony was held in the presence of the commanders of the British XXX Corps, the British 51st (Highland) Division and the American 29th Infantry Division to mark the handover of Bremerhaven to American forces.[28] At the time of the Yalta conference, the British and American governments had agreed to create enclaves under American control in the British occupation zone at Bremen and Bremerhaven and grant transit rights to allow American shipping to access and resupply the otherwise landlocked American occupation zone.[29]

For Barette, it was a smooth transition. After the handover, the Belgians worked with a team of the 970th Counterintelligence Corps Detachment[30] until 2 June but could still rely on British administrative support.[31]

Zeven

In Zeven, two other detachments, commanded by Kirschen and Radino respectively, were assigned to the XXX Corps. Their primary task was to assist in the demobilisation of German forces. In the beginning Kirschen perceived the presence of Belgian personnel as a burden for the overworked British intelligence staff, who had not prepared any tasks for them. After three days, work slowly started without knowing what the next day would bring, which affected the men's morale. In addition, the relaxed dress standards of the SAS were the cause of some friction when dealing with other HQs, where the peacetime spit and polish policy had been reverted to.[32]

When arriving in Zeven on 11 May, to work with the 45th FSS, Radino was surprised to see that German military authorities were releasing a large number of officers and other ranks from the forces, despite the unconditional surrender terms that required the German forces to remain in the positions occupied at the time of surrender. A justified fear existed that many war criminals and party leaders would try to escape.

From 12 May, Radino's team conducted patrols, arresting dozens of Germans, who were subsequently interrogated and sent to a prisoner camp. A few days into this business, German uniforms were disappearing from the street, requiring a change of procedures; from then on, every person in civilian clothes would have to be stopped to check his identity. Those released from the forces carried an *Entlassungsschein*, a document confirming their dismissal, many of which were dated before 4 May, to give the impression they had been relieved from their military duties on a legal basis. However, the systematic checks became known to the Germans and after a while, hardly any traffic at all could be noticed on the roads. An alternate German plan to avoid Allied controls in Hamburg (30 miles to the northeast) was quickly discovered. Blankenese (to the west of Hamburg) was used as a rallying location, after which the fleeing Germans crossed the Elbe river with all types of craft. Radino's men could just wait on the southwestern bank to arrest them in numbers.

Although each countermeasure eventually became known to the Germans, many still tried to pass through unnoticed, assisted by the local population. The *Entlassungsscheine* became useless, and new forged documents started appearing.

These included meticulously crafted counterfeit forms from German civilian authorities and release documents from concentration camps, sometimes written in English, complete with stamps. Some false identity papers were provided by the *Kriminalpolizei* of Hamburg. No matter the quality of the forgery, a search of an individual's luggage often revealed his true identity, as many kept a *Soldbuch* (a booklet containing various data of military personnel, which also served as identification document), letters, diaries or pictures hidden in their bags.

Between 12 and 29 May, some 650 men were caught by Radino's detachment. The success of the operations was limited mainly by the transportation capacity. Radino had only five jeeps at his disposal and whenever a load of prisoners had to be brought back to Zeven, the general area where arrests were being made by his team became easier to cross.

Among those arrested were some Nazi Party leaders, but mainly minor officials, as well as the commander of one of the prisoner camps from Fallingbostel. Under interrogation, a Pole captured with forged documents revealed that three days earlier, he had seen former *Reichsführer*-SS Heinrich Himmler, until recently chief of the SS and German police.[33]

No longer wanted at Dönitz's HQ, Himmler had been moving south, crossing the Elbe by boat and trying to cross the guarded bridge over the Oste river on the east of Bremervörde, 13 miles north of Zeven, together with more than a dozen others. On 22 May, Himmler and two companions were arrested by a patrol before reaching the bridge; the others of his group had passed the bridge two days earlier but, unbeknownst to Himmler, had been arrested immediately afterwards. The checkpoint manned by the 51st (Highland) Division served as a screening point for the 45th FSS. Just like the other members of his group, Himmler – travelling under the name of 'Hizinger' – had false papers carrying a stamp from the *Geheime Feldpolizei*, which triggered the interest of the intelligence staff working near the checkpoint.[34] Members of the *Geheime Feldpolizei* were considered German intelligence service personnel and belonged to the automatic arrest and detention category as devised by the Western Allies.[35] Furthermore, known German intelligence personnel were included in this category thanks to information from the comprehensive files of MI5 and the SIS and by the beginning of June, some 3,000 of those were detained.[36]

On 23 May, Himmler was first transported to Zeven, then to the civil internment camp at Westertimke (7 miles to the southwest) and afterwards to the civil internment camp at Kolkhagen, near Barnstedt (45 miles east of Zeven). There he admitted his true identity, after which he was finally taken to the HQ of the British 2nd Army in Lüneburg (some 7 miles north from Barnstedt), where he committed suicide by crushing a cyanide phial during his medical examination.[37]

Radino regretted that his detachment did not catch the much-wanted Nazi criminal of the highest order,[38] although Petit apparently claimed Belgian SAS personnel had been part of the routine patrol that had arrested him, which, according to the cited interview, included two Brits.[39]

Radino's detachment also had to end the reign of terror, rape and plunder imposed by former Soviet prisoners of war at Zeven. During raids to disarm them, occasional shootings occurred but without any casualties or significant damage.

On 29 May, the 45th FSS left for Nienburg, 45 miles to the south. The Belgians' activities were suspended and on 5 June, they also left Zeven. The mortar section (commanded by Doome), with which Radino had been working, went to Hildesheim (85 miles south of Zeven), while the engineer troop went to Göttingen (40 miles further south).[40,41]

Goslar

The area of Goslar, Hildesheim and Göttingen had initially been occupied by units of the American 1st and 9th armies,[42,43] but were located inside the XXX Corps district of the British occupation zone.[44,45]

Upon concluding its activities in Bremerhaven, Barette's detachment went to Goslar under the command of Schils, Barette being on leave at the time. It was attached to the 12th FSS and had a somewhat different role from their previous job, now mainly being confined to office work. Split over several *Kreise*, the small teams needed to deal with plenty of logistical issues themselves, in addition to their paperwork, since they found little to fall back on after the Americans had left the area.

Operational tasks in the town were limited to the most important cases, resulting in over forty arrests. These included *Generalmajor* Gerhard Triepel, a few *Oberführer* of the SS and two men being suspected of torture. Some members of underground organisations, SA and SD were being tracked down, but these cases could not be completed at the time the detachment had to end its activities in Goslar.[46]

Göttingen

Following the move from Zeven, Radino's detachment was attached to the 1003rd Field Security Reserve Detachment and started operating in its new area of operations on 6 June.

The tasks were quite similar to those of its previous assignment: arresting suspects, such as party leaders, SA and SS members, house searches to find documents and weapons, etc. Between 6 June and 1 July, Radino's men arrested 200 persons in an area of approximately a 30-mile radius around Göttingen. Some persons who had been arrested had to be released when it turned out that informers were out on revenge for private matters.

On 10 June, acting upon information from the XXX Corps HQ, the Belgian SAS detachment arrested a badly wanted presumed spy during a quite spectacular cordon and search operation in the town of Klein Lengden, 3 miles southeast of Göttingen.

In Radino's view, not many important arrests were made. In his assessment, high-ranking Nazi officials either had left the town or had gone into hiding.

On 2 July, the engineer troop and the two mortar troop sections in Goslar and Hildesheim left Germany.

Flensburg

On 10 May, the British 11th Armoured Division (part of VIII Corps) arrived in the northern part of Schleswig-Holstein. Its 159th Infantry Brigade became responsible for the Flensburg area, where thousands of fully armed German troops were wandering around.[47] The same day, Acting Captain Van Cauwelaert arrived in Flensburg as the advance party for two jeep and two assault sections from 'B' Squadron that had been detached to the British HQ in Flensburg. A few hours later, the main body arrived. A house was commandeered and the inhabitants were given two hours to vacate the building. Van Cauwelaert's detachment was expected to conduct patrols along the German-Danish border to ensure that no German military personnel or civilians would enter Germany except at the border control stations southeast of Tønder in the west and north of Flensburg in the east. The Danish and German sides of the Flensburg fjord also had to be patrolled as far south as Eckernförde. In addition, they had to provide armed escorts for FSSs when arresting Nazis and all kinds of other suspects. Given the size of the area to be patrolled, Vijt was permanently posted with a jeep section in Tønder, from where a standing patrol was to be sent to the border control point each day, while the remainder of the section conducted mobile border patrols to the west. Van Cauwelaert kept the three other sections at Flensburg, from where each day at least one long-range patrol was conducted with a complete section and a shorter patrol with one or two jeeps along the border, while the remainder stayed in the HQ on guard duty and providing escorts for arrests. Arrests were made at any time throughout the day but mostly at night.[48]

The Flensburg fjord, to the northeast of the city, contained several military facilities, including the naval academy at Mürwik, where *Großadmiral* Karl Dönitz had arrived and set up his HQ on 3 May, having been appointed by Hitler as head of state and supreme commander of the German armed forces to succeed him after his death. Dönitz's government was not recognised by the Allies but was initially left alone in an enclave along the shore which also included Glücksburg Castle.[49,50]

On 18 May, Van Cauwelaert's men contributed to the arrest of *Reichsleiter* Alfred Rosenberg, a Nazi ideologist and author and former minister for the civil administration of the occupied East, who would be trialled at Nuremberg, found guilty and hanged in 1946.[51,52,53] He had been hiding in the part of the Mürwik naval academy that was used as a hospital.[54]

On 23 May, Belgian SAS personnel were involved in the arrest of the Dönitz government, which had been ordered shortly before, after much debate within the British and American governments.[55,56] Operation 'Blackout', which involved several battalions, resulted in nearly 6,000 Germans being taken into custody in a few hours' time.[57]

Others arrested included *Abwehr* (German armed forces intelligence service) personnel, such as Dr Karl Heinz Krämer, who had been posted in Stockholm (Sweden) between 1942 and 1945, his secretary, Nina Anna Siemsen, and SS-*Obergruppenführer* Günther Pancke, former head of the German police in Denmark.[58,59,60]

On 29 May, a tragic accident struck the detachment. During a transport, a bouncing lorry ejected Trooper François Magriet, who landed on his skull and died shortly afterwards.[61]

On 3 June, part of the assault section working with Slosse in Wismar was sent to reinforce Van Cauwelaert's detachment.[62]

A patrol commanded by Corporal Michel van Strydonck on the Danish Isle of Kegnæs, to the northeast of the Flensborg fjord, proved uneventful but confirmed the

Germans could easily join or leave the island. Along the coast, which was intermittently watched by Danish patrols, a few fishing and leisure boats could be observed, as well as many stranded dinghies.[63] During patrols on the east coast between Kappeln and Eckernförde, locations for possible guard posts were identified, but no significant activity seemed to have occurred in this sector.[64] Patrols along the fjord's coastline revealed the presence of some German military personnel at Holnis (9 miles northeast of Flensburg), though without perceived threat, and the continued presence of many refugees at Birk Nack (11 miles east of Flensburg).[65] Several weeks after the surrender, the German-Danish border also seemed to be quiet. Most border crossing posts had been closed by the Danes, but even those remaining open seemingly did not see a lot of traffic.[66]

At the end of June, the officers commanding the 65th FSS and 335th FSS regretted seeing the Belgians leave and acknowledged in a letter to Blondeel the valuable assistance Van Cauwelaert and Thonard and their men had been providing.[67]

Mölln – Ratzeburg – Lübeck – Geesthacht

An assault section from 'A' Squadron and a jeep section from 'B' Squadron commanded by Debefve were detached to the British FSS at Mölln, 25 miles east of Hamburg. Debefve and Jeukens' section stayed at this location, while Krolikowski was sent to Ratzeburg (6 miles northeast of Mölln), Maréchal and three others to Lübeck (11 miles further north) and three men to Geesthacht (18 miles southwest of Mölln).

In addition to assisting the British intelligence staff to arrest Nazis, the detachment had to contribute to prevent the local population from fleeing from the East, since the adjacent area would soon be occupied by Soviet forces. To this end, road patrols were conducted while surveilling communication nodes, checking identity documents and arresting suspects.[68]

Wismar – Grevesmühlen – Schwerin – Ludwigslust

During the final campaign in Germany, British and American forces had advanced far beyond the zonal boundaries that had been agreed upon by the Allies and would have to withdraw from the areas assigned to the Soviets in due time.[69] The British push to the Baltic coast had resulted from the fear that Soviet forces would advance into Denmark.[70] On 1 May, Brigadier James Hill, commander of the British 3rd Parachute Brigade, had been given oral orders to rapidly advance to Wismar (a city on the Baltic Sea coast) to deny access to the Danish peninsula by Soviet troops.[71] With the Canadian 1st Parachute Battalion as its lead unit, the brigade had been advancing in front of the 6th Airborne Division through an area congested with thousands of terrified Germans retreating from the advancing Soviets. With one company transported by Sherman tanks of the Royal Scots Greys (2nd Dragoons) and two others by tactical troop transport vehicles, the Canadian parachute battalion had reached Wismar on 2 May, having arrived mere hours before Soviet forces.[72,73] Further west, a T-Force[74] of several hundred men commanded by Colonel Tony Hibbert, working with elements of the 30th Assault Unit[75] and the 1st SAS,[76,77,78] had been acting under similar orders to capture Kiel.[79]

Due to a reorganisation, the FSSs to which Debefve's detachment was attached in the Mölln area moved further east in the VIII Corps district to Wismar and Grevesmühlen (10 miles west of Wismar). Debefve's detachment also moved to the new locations. Debefve, Jeukens' section and half a jeep section went to Grevesmühlen while Krolikowski and half a jeep section went to Wismar, where they were reinforced by Slosse and an assault section, who had arrived in Wismar on 18 May and had been attached to the 17th FSS.[80,81]

In a seven-day period between 24 and 31 May, the group at Grevesmühlen arrested some seventy Nazis, including *Kreisleitern, Ortsgruppenleitern* and SS personnel. Debefve was full of praise for the efficiency of the British field security personnel and regretted having to move once again after hardly a week of interesting activities.

From 1 to 30 June, the new locations for his detachment – whose mission remained unchanged – were Wismar, Schwerin and Ludwigslust. Debefve joined Slosse in Wismar, Krolikowski (probably with Jeukens' assault section) and half a jeep section went to Schwerin, and 1st Lieutenant Jean Henrard and half a jeep section were based in Ludwigslust, 38 miles south of Wismar.[82]

Meanwhile, the section working under Slosse's command arrested at least thirty persons, including *Ortgruppenleitern* and *Gestapo* members between 18 May and 3 June. On 3 June, this section was split with one part sent to Schwerin (under the command of Krolikowski) and the remainder to Flensburg (under the command of Van Cauwelaert).[83]

On 7 June, a column with four sections of newly trained personnel under the command of 2nd Lieutenant Henri Williot left the regimental HQ in Rotenhahn, each section driving an armoured jeep and a 15-cwt lorry. For months, they had been training hard and had been disappointed multiple times for not being able to join their regiment in combat operations. Now they were happy to participate in an active military task after all and had meticulously prepared their vehicles, arms and equipment, trying to compensate for their lack of experience.

Two sections, accompanied by Squadron Sergeant Major Bertie Woodin, on loan from the RAF, drove to Schwerin to replace the section working with Krolikowski and came under his command. Williot and the other two sections went to Wismar, replacing the section that had worked under Slosse and had left Wismar a few days earlier. The new sections operated under the overall command of Debefve.

Those at Wismar worked with an FSS consisting of two British sergeants who arrived when Williot was already in Wismar, replacing their predecessors only after the latter's departure, with one of both positions being replaced twice in less than a month.

Each day, the senior British intelligence NCO presented the list of persons to be arrested, and the number of men and vehicles required, after which one of both Belgian section commanders assigned the men to each mission, ensuring a rotational system allowed all men to participate. A board providing an overview of all missions was kept up to date and after each mission, one participant was tasked with providing Williot with a concise written report. Between 7 and 22 June, twenty-six missions were assigned.[84]

During the first mission, five Belgians drove to a village 6 miles from Wismar together with a British major and two French officers to obtain information.[85] Twelve missions involved the arrests of Nazis. Many arrests were uneventful,[86,87,88,89,90] but not all arrested Nazis were looking forward to the likely prospect of being trialled. An *Ortsgruppenleiter* was found in the possession of poison[91] and another committed suicide in his cell.[92] Sometimes a more extended search was required when the wanted person was not at his domicile.[93,94] On one occasion, the suspect could not be found[95] and on another, the wanted person turned out already having been arrested.[96] One suspect, an SS member in Wismar, was not arrested in the end, since he provided lists of his SS men who lived in the city, information on a general officer of the SS in Rostock, and pictures of an *SS-Obersturmführer*. He was left at liberty, this way being more useful as an intelligence source.[97] Several days before the area would be handed over to the Soviets, orders were received to suspend all arrests.[98]

Another common task was the transport of prisoners. Seven transports were conducted to transfer detainees to the prison of Schwerin.[99,100,101,102,103,104,105] During two other missions, prisoners were picked up at Grevesmühlen[106,107] and the last one involved the pick-up of Nazi Party members in Rehna, 18 miles southeast of Wismar.[108] Often, documents related to accompanying prisoners were carried, but also a single mission in which files were transported, was executed.[109]

Nazis were not the only object of the hunt. On 20 June, five men with two jeeps started the search for a German scientist and his four associates, presumedly refugees in Wismar, aiming at recovering them before they fell into Soviet hands. They did not find their names on the refugee list with the police in Wismar, while an engineer from Stettin, who was a refugee in Wismar, could not provide any useful information either. Next, they contacted the director of a technical school at Wismar, who had met the scientist several weeks earlier for laboratory-related activities, but he had no information on his current whereabouts. The laboratory's concierge, however, knew that he was a refugee in Schwerin and that he visited the lab every week. She was able to provide the name of the hotel where he was accommodated in Wismar, but the Belgians found out he had left the hotel without leaving an address.

The search being unsuccessful so far, Sergeant Louis Fauconnier decided to continue on his own with Trooper Joseph De Man as an interpreter and went to Schwerin, where they found his address in the refugee register, after which he was quickly recovered.[110]

During his stay in Wismar, personal interactions with the Soviets left a lasting impression on Williot. Finding them sometimes cordial, sometimes inhuman, two incidents stayed in his mind. When bringing back a Soviet soldier who had wandered into the British sector while drunk, the receiving officer told Williot he should not have bothered but should have shot him. During another encounter, Belgians and Soviets were displaying their weapons to each other when a Soviet soldier demonstrated his submachine gun's capabilities by simply shooting a passing German woman.[111] Incidents like those were not the exception and were well known at the highest command levels. Montgomery did not hide his disdain for the Russians. He found their approach to every problem different from the western Allies', and although he found them good fighters, he also noted they were barbarous Asiatics who had never enjoyed a civilisation comparable to that of the rest of Europe, being especially repulsed by their treatment of women.[112]

In Schwerin, Krolikowski conducted similar missions with his detachment, which was assigned to the 1021st Field Security Reserve Detachment. While limited in numbers, the Belgians spared no effort hunting down suspects, no matter the time of day, and were responsible for most of the 300 physical arrests conducted in the area.[113] During a mission on 21 June, Krolikowski was driving a jeep at about 25 miles per hour when some 5 yards from the corner of an adjacent road, a young boy suddenly crossed the street. Krolikowski slammed on his brakes, but, unfortunately, these failed, and the boy was knocked down. He rushed the child to the hospital and returned later in the day to check on his condition but found he had died of his wounds. A post-incident inspection revealed a very rare defect in the rear brakes.[114]

Henrard, was detached with three men to the 39th FSS in Ludwigslust. Their area of operations covered the area south of Schwerin (20 miles to the north), delineated by the Elbe river (18 miles to the south), the boundary between British and Soviet forces in the east and the north-south line going through Boizenburg (30 miles to the west).

Between 10 and 29 June, 118 arrests were made, with sixty-five suspects remaining in custody. Much time was devoted to inquiries which proved fruitless in the end.

On 29 June, responsibilities for the area were handed over to the Soviets.[115] By 4 July, a smooth handover of the Wismar area to Soviet forces was completed.[116]

Conclusion of operations

On 30 June, the operations in occupied Germany came to an end for the Belgian SAS. Most wanted Nazis having been arrested and in need of another reorganisation, the regiment returned to its barracks in Tervueren.[117]

In a letter to Calvert, Brigadier Edgar Williams of the 21st Army Group who had been serving as intelligence officer on Montgomery's staff since North Africa,[118] expressed his appreciation for the very great assistance that Blondeel and his men had rendered to the 21st Army Group during the counterintelligence operations, noting that all ranks, and especially the junior leaders, had shown commendable initiative despite the short preparation time for their task and acknowledging the keenness, willingness, discipline and bearing which had won the admiration of all with whom they had come into contact.[119]

EPILOGUE

A FEW WEEKS AFTER the return of the Belgian SAS Regiment to Belgium, the war in the Far East was also concluded and it was only a matter of time before the multinational SAS Brigade was dissolved.

In a letter from August 1945, Brigadier Calvert conveyed his brigade's gratitude to the Belgian SAS Regiment, expressing his hope that the unity of purpose between Great Britain and Belgium, which had been realised in war, would be maintained in peace.[1] On 8 September, the Belgian SAS Regiment was assembled for a parade in the La Cambre Abbey in Brussels. It was the last time the regiment was lined up for inspection by Calvert, who presented colours to the Belgian SAS, handing them over to Blondeel as a token of appreciation and friendship between the two nations' SAS communities.[2]

On 2 October, a ceremony in Tarbes (southern France) marked the handover of the French SAS to the French army.[3,4] Two days later, on 4 October, the War Office sent a memorandum giving authority to disband the 1st and 2nd SAS, to commence the following day, with the notification that formal authority for the complete disbandment of the SAS Regiment would be issued subsequently,[5] but the effective disbandment of the British SAS did not occur immediately and was short-lived, as the requirement for such troops would become clear soon enough during post-war counterinsurgency campaigns.[6]

On 10 October, the regiment came under the administrative command of the 2nd Infantry Division of the newly-established post-war Belgian army, a temporary arrangement in view of further reorganisations.[7]

On 20 October, a medal parade was held on the Grand-Place in Brussels, where Major General George Surtees decorated fourteen members of the Belgian SAS, including Blondeel, who received a DSO.[8] It served as a visible conclusion of the unit's wartime achievements, in which the regiment had made its contribution to the defeat of Belgium's eastern neighbour.

After more than eight decades, German imperialism had been contained, never to re-emerge again. But during the next eight decades, the free world would face another formidable opponent trying to destabilise Western Europe. The SAS and their successor units in Britain, France and Belgium would adapt to contribute to the effort to counter the threat from the aspirational Russian empire and to confront its proxies on several continents.

After demobilisation, the renewed national service provided sufficient personnel, allowing the regiment to expand its strength and continue its rigorous training programme under the supervision of battle-hardened instructors. Even though it was now peacetime, the realistic training involved high-risk activities, which sadly became tangible when troopers Leo Schepers, Raymond Kahn and Mathieu Wuytjens, all veterans of the campaign in the Netherlands and Germany, were killed in training.[9]

On 22 October 1946, Blondeel – promoted to lieutenant colonel at the end of

1945 – was presented the regimental colours by H.R.H. the Prince Regent during a ceremony in Brussels. That same year, the regiment received its regimental march, which would later be adopted by the British SAS as well.

Blondeel was demobilised in 1947.

In 1948, the Belgian SAS Regiment moved to Leopoldsburg.

In 1951, the regiment was re-named '1st Parachute Battalion' and integrated into the newly formed Para-Commando Regiment, together with the Commando Regiment, the descendant of the wartime Belgian troop in the No. 10 (Inter-Allied) Commando. In 1953, the 1st Parachute Battalion moved to Diest, where it would remain until its disbandment.

As the new Para-Commando Regiment's tasks were shifting towards a primarily conventional role as airborne light infantry, mainly focused on operations in colonial Central Africa, as well as contributing to NATO's Allied Command Europe Mobile Force, the need to have special operations reconnaissance capabilities similar to those developed during the Second World War was identified by the 1st Belgian Army Corps, based in the Federal Republic of Germany.

An organic corps-level long-range reconnaissance unit was created in 1956 and remained in existence under different names until the disbandment of the army corps when the unit's remnants were transferred to become the Long-Range Reconnaissance Patrol Detachment of the Para-Commando Brigade, the latter being the successor to the Para-Commando Regiment.

This small detachment became the nucleus of the Special Forces Company, established in 2000 and re-named 'Special Forces Group' three years later.

Following the decision for its disbandment, the 1st Parachute Battalion handed over the regimental colours to the Special Forces Group during a parade in Diest on 10 December 2010.[10]

No longer being the sole special operations unit after the inauguration of the Special Operations Regiment in 2018, the Special Forces Group – still carrying the traditions of the Second World War Belgian SAS – became the regiment's premier special operations unit, serving next to two para-commando battalions which had been re-roled into the special operations role, the three core units being supported by two training centres, a signals unit and a regimental HQ.

APPENDIX 1[1]

ROLL OF HONOUR

Belgian Independent Parachute Company

Private Etienne Battaille	Killed in training, Withington, England, 19 April 1943
Private Florent Depauw	Killed in training, Withington, England, 19 April 1943

Belgian Special Air Service Squadron/Regiment, August 1944 – May 1945

Trooper Albert Bechet	KIA, Westerscheps, Germany, 28 April 1945
Trooper Jean Breuer	DOW, the Netherlands, 14 April 1945 (WIA 12 April 1945, Veele, the Netherlands)
Lance Corporal Roger Carrette	KIA, La Chartre-sur-le-Loir, France, 9 August 1944
Trooper Claude de Villermont	KIA, Bure, Belgium, 31 December 1944
2nd Lieutenant Denis Devignez	DOW, Ootmarsum, the Netherlands, 17 April 1945[2] (WIA 15 April 1945, Beerta, the Netherlands)
Lance Corporal Etienne Hazard	DOW, Brussels, Belgium, 27 August 1945 (WIA 12 April 1945, Veele, the Netherlands)
Corporal Raymond A. Holvoet	Executed in Zwolle, the Netherlands, 10 April 1945
Captain[3] Freddy Limbosch	KIA, Peer, Belgium, 8 September 1944
Trooper Emile Lorphèvre	KIA, Bure, Belgium, 31 December 1944
Trooper Jean Lox	KIA, Chabrehez, Belgium, 10 September 1944
Trooper François Magriet	DOW, Flensburg, Germany, 29 May 1945 (wounded on operation, Flensburg, 29 May 1945)
1st Lieutenant Charles Mathijs	Killed in training, Leopoldsburg, Belgium, 4 March 1945
Sergeant Jean Melsens	KIA, Meeuwen, Belgium, 10 September 1944
Trooper Nicolas Polys	DOW, Winwick, England, 6 March 1945 (wounded in training, Ringway, England)
1st Lieutenant Paul Renkin	KIA, Bure, Belgium, 31 December 1944
Sergeant Philippe Rolin	KIA, Veele, the Netherlands, 12 April 1945
Trooper Paul Ruscart	DOW, Friesoythe, Germany, 2 May 1945[4] (WIA, Godensholt, Germany, 1 May 1945)
Trooper Joseph Wathelet	KIA, Finsterwolde, the Netherlands, 15 April 1945

Key:

DOW died of wounds
KIA killed in action
WIA wounded in action

APPENDIX 2[1]

RECORD OF BELGIAN PARACHUTE COMPANY AND SPECIAL AIR SERVICE PERSONNEL IN THE SECOND WORLD WAR

Key to campaigns & operations:

Ard	Ardennes from December 1944	Hag	Haggard
Ben	Benson	LNe	Larkswood – Netherlands
Ber	Bergbang	LGe	Larkswood – Germany
Bru	Brutus	Noa	Noah
Bun	Bunyan	Fab	Regan/Fabian
Cal	Caliban	Sha	Shakespeare
Cha	Chaucer	Tim	Timon
CI	Counterintelligence - Germany May-June 1945	Tru	Trueform
Gob	Portia/Gobbo		

Key to casualty status

DOW died of wounds • **KIA** killed in action • **WIA** wounded in action

	Name (last, first)	Cover name	Service number	Parachute qualification	Operations	Remarks
1	Adan Pierre		9002	04/02/1945	LNe, LGe	
2	Aelter André		0501	11/07/1942		
3	Aksakow Wladimir		12043	12/10/1944	Ard	
4	Alliet O.		1643	09/08/1942		
5	Amand Germain		F5/533	27/08/1945	LNe, LGe, CI	
6	Antoine Alex		F6/96		CI	
7	Arcq Jacques		1501	11/07/1942	Ard, LNe, LGe, CI	
8	Arents Joseph		2549			
9	Artielle F.		F5/281		LNe, LGe, CI	
10	Artois Joseph		F9/645		CI	
11	Aszenfarb David		3234	11/02/1943	Ard	
12	Badts Eduard		0505			Jump refusal 1942
13	Baert Robert		9003	04/02/1945	LNe, LGe, CI	WIA 16/04/1945
14	Baines Georges		9004	04/02/1945	LNe, LGe, CI	
15	Balsat René		3626	17/04/1944	Bun, Ber, Ard, LNe, LGe, CI	
16	Barette Constant Raymond	Burnett	0583	17/01/1942	Bun, Bru, Ard, LNe, LGe, CI	
17	Bastin Jean		9162	09/03/1945	LNe, LGe, CI	

	Name (last, first)	Cover name	Service number	Parachute qualification	Operations	Remarks
18	Battaille Etienne		3427			Killed in training 19/04/1943
19	Baut Gaston		9005	04/02/1945	LNe, LGe, Cl	
20	Bechet Albert		9136	09/03/1945	LNe, LGe	KIA 28/04/1945
21	Beckers		1154			Jump refusal 1942
22	Becquet Alfred	Berger	2540	09/08/1942	Cha, Noa, Ard, LNe	WIA 09/04/1945
23	Beels			02/05/1942		
24	Bellery Richard		F6/255			Cl
25	Berckmans Maurice		5878	1944	LNe, LGe, Cl	
26	Berger François		1646	11/07/1942		
27	Bernard Jean		9054	04/02/1945	LNe	WIA 15/04/1945
28	Bernard P., J.		0205	20/03/1942	Noa, LNe, LGe, Cl	
29	Beyens François		9006	04/02/1945	LNe, LGe, Cl	
30	Blanpain P.		2122	20/03/1942		
31	Blondeel Edouard	Blunt	32547	02/05/1942	Noa, Ard, LNe, LGe, Cl	
32	Blondeel Jacques		9203		LNe, LGe, Cl	
33	Boch Laurent	Berry	2911	08/08/1942	Bun, Noa, Ard, LNe	WIA 15/04/1945
34	Boden Florent		1431			
35	Bogaert Albert	Bossey	2757	09/08/1942	Noa, Ard, LNe, LGe, Cl	
36	Bondroit Hubert		9007	04/02/1945	LNe, LGe, Cl	
37	Bonne Henri		1649	02/05/1942	Tru, Noa, Ard, LNe, LGe, Cl	
38	Boonen Jacques		9008	04/02/1945	LNe, LGe, Cl	
39	Borremans Julien		3053	06/06/1942		
40	Bosny Louis		5763	09/11/1944	Ard, LNe, LGe, Cl	
41	Boudoux Roger		9132	09/03/1945	LNe, LGe, Cl	
42	Bouillon André	Bayeux	3741	17/04/1944	Ben, Ard, LNe, LGe, Cl	
43	Brasseur Ivo		1870	28/02/1942	Bun, Ard, LNe, LGe, Cl	WIA 08/08/1944
44	Breuer Jean Louis		9074	09/03/1945	LNe	WIA 12/04/1945 DOW 14/04/45
45	Breuze Hector		3436	04/06/1943	Bun	WIA 08/08/1944
46	Broothaerts Petrus		9141	09/03/1945	LNe, LGe	Wounded 30/04/1945
47	Broucke Johannes Cammilius		3240			
48	Brouckxon		1902	28/02/1942		
49	Bruneel		0676	05/10/1942		
50	Bruylandts Jean Marie		F9/13		Cl	
51	Budts John		0508	17/01/1942		
52	Buffin		5879	1944	Ard	
53	Bury		F10/418		LNe, LGe, Cl	
54	Buysse Georges		9114	09/03/1945	LNe, LGe, Cl	WIA 12/04/1945
55	Carmes Jean-Pierre		3209	11/02/1943		Transferred to SOE, KIA 05/1944

	Name (last, first)	Cover name	Service number	Parachute qualification	Operations	Remarks
56	Carpentier Emile		9122	09/03/1945	LNe, LGe, Cl	
57	Carrette Marcel		9010	04/02/1945	LNe, LGe, Cl	
58	Carrette Roger	Owen	3286	11/02/1943	Sha	KIA 09/08/1944
59	Casier G.		3928	17/04/1944	Noa	
60	Cassart Jean	Courtoy / Cederwell		1941	Ber	
61	Catoul Gerard		9011	04/02/1945	LNe, LGe, Cl	
62	Cattier Edmond		9066	09/03/1945	LNe, LGe	Wounded 02/05/1945
63	Cerfontaine		3503			
64	Chauvaux Marcel	Clervoix	2467	11/07/1942	Cha, Noa, Ard, LNe, LGe	
65	Claes Albert		9133	09/03/1945	LNe, LGe, Cl	
66	Claesen Albert		1153	20/03/1942	Tru	
67	Claessens		2272	11/07/1942		
68	Clamot Théo	Clavier	3028	06/06/1942	Cha, Noa, Ard, LNe, LGe, Cl	
69	Clasen Albert	Clasen	0853	20/03/1942	Tru, Bru, LNe, LGe, Cl	WIA 05/09/1944
70	Clement François		9048	04/02/1945	LNe, LGe, Cl	
71	Cock Stan		9123	09/03/1945	LNe, LGe, Cl	
72	Coetsier Kamiel		9173	09/03/1945	LNe, LGe, Cl	Mental injury 14/04/1945
73	Collard Adrien		9012	04/02/1945	LNe, LGe, Cl	
74	Colle Jean Pierre		9175	09/03/1945		
75	Colleyn H.		F4/291		Cl	
76	Compere René		9139	09/03/1945	LNe, LGe, Cl	
77	Cornez Lucien		9094	09/03/1945	LNe, LGe, Cl	
78	Cosyns Jozef		6118		LNe, LGe, Cl	
79	Coucke Gustaaf		F1/290		LNe, LGe, Cl	
80	Cougnet Andre		9137		LNe, LGe, Cl	
81	Craeghs Rik		9149	09/03/1945	LNe, LGe, Cl	
82	Crèvecœur Jules	Curry	2440	09/08/1942	Bun, Ber, Ard, LNe, LGe, Cl	
83	Croquet Paul		3876	1944	Ard, LNe, LGe, Cl	
84	Cruybeke Robert		9065	09/03/1945	LNe, LGe, Cl	
85	Cruyt Georges		9158	09/03/1945	LNe, LGe, Cl	WIA 14/04/1945
86	Curtis Robert		9107	09/03/1945	LNe, LGe, Cl	
87	Daemen Jaak		9163	09/03/1945	LNe, LGe, Cl	
88	Daems François		5474	12/10/1944	Ard, LNe, LGe, Cl	
89	Daenen Marcel		9183	09/03/1945	LNe, LGe, Cl	
90	Damas Georges		9197	28/08/1945	LNe, LGe, Cl	
91	Dasy François		2490			
92	Daubioulle		9060		Ard	
93	Dauw Louis		F9/24		LNe, LGe, Cl	
94	De Bakker Roger		9159	09/03/1945	LNe, LGe, Cl	
95	De Becker Karl		1667	11/07/1942	Tru, Cal, Ard, LNe, LGe, Cl	
96	De Belser August		1666	02/05/1942	Tru, Cal, Ard, LNe, LGe, Cl	

	Name (last, first)	Cover name	Service number	Parachute qualification	Operations	Remarks
97	De Belser Karel		1667	11/07/1942	Tru, Cal, Ard, LNe, LGe, CI	
98	de Bergeyck Hubert		9117	09/03/1945	LNe, LGe, CI	
99	De Block A.		1648	06/06/1942		
100	De Block Frank					
101	De Block Georges		4159	17/04/1944	Tru, Ber, Ard, LNe, LGe, CI	
102	De Bluts Pierre		36189	19/02/1945	Ard, CI	
103	De Bruyn		9103	07/03/1945	LNe, LGe, CI	
104	De Bruyn Joseph		9128	09/03/1945	LNe, LGe, CI	
105	De Busser		0598			
106	de Changy André		9130	07/03/1945	LNe, LGe, CI	
107	de Changy Renaud		5418	12/10/1944	Ard	WIA 12/01/1945
108	De Clerq Cosmo		1672		Ard, LNe, LGe, CI	
109	De Coene Eddy		4954			
110	De Cooman Jacques		9118	09/03/1945	LNe, LGe, CI	WIA 12/04/1945
111	De Groote Désiré		9092	09/03/1945	LNe, LGe, CI	
112	De Halleux J.		9069	09/03/1945	LNe, LGe, CI	
113	de Hemptinne Christian		9112	09/03/1945	LNe, LGe, CI	
114	De Jonghe Guy		2566	09/11/1944	Ard, LGe, CI	WIA 30/12/1944
115	De Jonghe Robert		9015		LNe, LGe, CI	
116	De Lison Arthur		3478	07/05/1944	Tru, Dru, Ard, LNe, LGe, CI	Wounded 13/04/1945
117	De Louvain J.		F4/15		CI	
118	de Maere Marcel		9019		LNe, LGe, CI	
119	De Man Joseph		9202		CI	
120	de Merkline Laurent		6154	24/11/1944	Ard, LNe, LGe, CI	
121	de Montpellier Arnaud		5449	1944	Ard, LNe, LGe, CI	
122	de Mûelenaere Hubert		5760	24/02/1945	LNe, LGe, CI	
123	De Neef Roger		1681	02/05/1942	Noa	
124	De Rechter André	Clarke	0522	21/03/1942	Tru, Cal, LNe, LGe, CI	
125	De Saedeleer Karel		F2/311	28/08/1945	CI	
126	de Saint-Guillain		4326	17/04/1944	Tru, Ber	
127	De Serrano Maurice	Surrey	1682	28/02/1942	Sha, Cal, Ard, LNe, LGe, CI	
128	De Temmerman		2442	11/1942		
129	de T'Serclaes Charles		5657	12/10/1944	Ard, LNe, LGe, CI	
130	de Villermont Claude	Villers	3556	17/04/1944	Noa, Ard	KIA 31/12/1944
131	De Vos		9164	09/03/1945	LNe, LGe, CI	
132	De Vulder Maurice		1684	28/02/1942	Tru, Cal, Ard, LNe, LGe, CI	
133	De Waele Oscar		F2/244		CI	
134	De Witte Albert		9020	04/02/1945	LNe, LGe, CI	
135	de Wykerslooth Regner		5424	05/1944	Ard, LNe, LGe, CI	
136	Debecker August		1666	02/05/1942	Tru, Cal, Ard, LNe, LGe, CI	
137	Debefve Emile	Mac Bef	39382	05/10/1942	Sha, Noa, Gob, LGe, CI	WIA 04/12/1944
138	Debuf Victor	Bush	2538	11/07/1942	Sha, Cal, Ard, NI, LGe, CI	

	Name (last, first)	Cover name	Service number	Parachute qualification	Operations	Remarks
139	Decorte		9016			
140	Degen Jacques		9091	09/03/1945	LNe, LGe, Cl	
141	Dehaes M.		0686	09/08/1945		
142	Deheusch Willy	Dens	2493	11/07/1942	Cha, Ber, LNe, LGe, Cl	
143	Dehopré A.		0127	20/03/1942		
144	Delagaye Arthur	Wright	2130	02/05/1942	Tru, Bru, Ard, LNe, LGe, Cl	
145	Delbart		F10/16		Cl	
146	Delcourt Jean Louis		9071	9/03/1945	LNe, LGe, Cl	
147	Delelienne Etienne	Delaing	26144	21/05/1944	Tru	
148	Delhez Jean		9017	04/02/1945	LNe, LGe, Cl	
149	Delhez René		9018	09/03/1945	LNe, LGe, Cl	
150	Deloge J.		F4/512	28/08/1945	LNe, LGe, Cl	
151	Delsaer Alphonse	Dale	4912	17/04/1944	Tru, Cal, Ard	WIA 05/09/1944
152	Delvigne Emile		0943	17/04/1944	Tru, Ber, Ard, LNe, LGe, Cl	
153	Demery Jean	Daneghan	4061	17/04/1944	Cha, Ber, Ard, LNe, LGe, Cl	WIA 09/09/1944
154	Demery Marcel	Dubois	2246	02/05/1942	Cha, Bru, LNe, LGe, Cl	
155	Demoor Daniel	Durbin	3248	11/02/1943	LNe, LGe, Cl	
156	Denys Jacques		9177	09/03/1945	LNe, LGe, Cl	
157	Déom Joseph	Dorsey	2788	11/02/1943	Bun, Noa, Ard, LNe	WIA 13/04/1945
158	Depauw Florent		3434			Killed in training 19/04/1943
159	Depourque Jean		9084	09/03/1945	LNe, LGe, Cl	
160	Deprez Robert		9061		LNe, LGe, Cl	
161	Deprez Urbain	Dubois	2465	06/06/1942	Cha, Noa, Ard, LNe, LGe, Cl	WIA 28/08/1944
162	Depue Ch.		F4/206		LNe, LGe, Cl	
163	Depyper Jan		9099	09/03/1945	LNe, LGe, Cl	
164	Derath Henri	Dorcas	0603	09/08/1942	Sha, Ber, Ard	
165	Desamblanx Rene-Pierre		0900			Jump refusal 1942
166	Devignez Denis		3307	11/02/1943	Cha, LNe	WIA 15/08/1944 DOW 17/04/1945
167	Dhooge Pierre		9190		LNe, LGe, Cl	
168	Dierck Julien		1686			
169	Dierckx Robert		2775	09/08/1942		
170	Diericx		1686			
171	Dirix Maurice		9155	09/03/1945	LNe, LGe, Cl	
172	Donnely Wallace McClung				LNe, LGe, Cl	Detached from GHQ Liaison Regt
173	Doome Jacques Griffith		0136	05/10/1942	Tru, Bru, Ard, LNe, LGe, Cl	
174	Dooremont Albert		0813			
175	Dopchie		2423			
176	d'Oultremont Georges		3468	03/08/1943	Noa, Ard, LNe, LGe, Cl	WIA 31/12/1944

	Name (last, first)	Cover name	Service number	Parachute qualification	Operations	Remarks
177	Dubois A.		9078	07/03/1945	Ard	
178	Dubois Jean-Jacques		5903	04/02/1945	LNe, LGe, CI	
179	Dubois Paul Emil		F4/527	28/08/1945	CI	
180	Dubois Raymond		9021	04/02/1945	LNe	Wounded 09/04/1945
181	Dulait Jean	Dill	35903	17/04/1944	Tru, Bru	
182	Dumont		F6/31		LNe, LGe, CI	
183	Duriau		1682	02/05/1942		
184	Dusausoir Louis		F10/674	28/08/1945	LNe, LGe, CI	
185	Eeckeleers Henri					
186	Emonts-Pohl Freddy		2937	03/01/1943	Tru, Ber	
187	Engelen L.		3443	1943		
188	Engelen Marcel	Johnson	1179	21/03/1942	Tru, Cal, LNe, LGe, CI	
189	Etienne		3049	11/07/1942		
190	Fagnard Odilon		9022	04/1945	LNe	WIA 12/04/1945
191	Falleur		F5/578		CI	
192	Fassin Robert		0189			Jump refusal 1942
193	Fauconnier Louis		9192		CI	
194	Fauconnier Willy		F4/529	04/02/1945	CI	
195	Feremans Robert		2803		Ard, LNe	WIA 15/04/1945
196	Fierens Carlo		9191		LNe, LGe, CI	
197	Flameng A.		4912			
198	Flasschoen Gustave	Frank	3292	11/02/1943	Tru, Ber, Ard, LNe, LGe, CI	WIA 19/08/1943
199	Flasschoen Maurice	Frank	3429	04/06/1943	Tru, Ber, Ard	WIA 09/09/1944
200	Flips Henri	Frost	3830	17/04/1944	Bun, Ben, Ard, LNe, LGe, CI	
201	Forceville Pierre Joseph		2752	05/10/1942		
202	Fraipont		0701			
203	Fraix Jules	Franklin	2491	11/07/1942	Tru, Bru, Ard, LNe, LGe, CI	
204	Francotte				LNe, LGe, CI	
205	Franssen Jacques		F3/430	28/08/1945	LNe, LGe, CI	
206	Freson Noel		0702	04/1942		
207	Fries		2176	28/02/1942		
208	Frison Dieudonné	Fraser	1691	06/06/1942	Tru, Noa, Ard, LNe, LGe, CI	
209	Frognet Maurice		5875	1944	Ard, LNe, LGe, CI	
210	Fromes Armand		5866	04/02/1945	LNe, LGe, CI	
211	Gailly Etienne		4785	04/02/1945	LNe, LGe, CI	
212	Geelhand Francis		9023	04/02/1945	LNe, LGe, CI	
213	Geeraers Jozef		1152	20/02/1942		
214	Geldof Rene-Gaston	Gauvin	4308	10/03/1942	Sha, Bru, Ard	
215	Gendebien Olivier		5772	12/10/1944	Ard, LNe, LGe, CI	
216	Genis Roger		2885	04/06/1943		
217	Genot				LNe, LGe, CI	

	Name (last, first)	Cover name	Service number	Parachute qualification	Operations	Remarks
218	Genyn		1694			
219	Gerard Philippe		3463	04/06/1943	Noa, Ard, LNe, LGe, Cl	
220	Geysens Jean		0612	09/08/1942	Bun, Ber, Ard, LNe, LGe, Cl	
221	Gheuens A.		1019	20/03/1942		
222	Ghyckiere R.		9166	09/03/1945	LNe, LGe, Cl	
223	Ghys Joseph	Gordon	1205	02/05/1942	Cha, Cal, LNe, LGe, Cl	
224	Gigot Jean	Baron	2600	1944	Tru, Bru	
225	Gilson Jacques	Galland	2896	09/08/1942	Cha, Noa, LNe, LGe, Cl	
226	Glaude Georges		9100	09/03/1945	LNe, LGe, Cl	
227	Godfroid R.		3.153	11/02/1943		
228	Godichal					
229	Goessens Lucien	Gautier	1700	02/05/1942	Sha, Cal, Ard, LNe, LGe, Cl	
230	Goffinet Jacques	Goffin	3046	10/03/1941	Cha, Noa, LNe, LGe, Cl	
231	Gouzée Christian	9087		09/03/1945	LNe	Wounded 15/04/1945
232	Govaerts Henri			09/03/1945	LNe, LGe, Cl	
233	Greban de St. Germain		35261	20/03/1942		
234	Grétry Florent		3031	11/1940	Noa, Ard, LNe, LGe, Cl	
235	Grimee Armand		2754	09/08/1942		Transferred to SOE
236	Groenewout Rudolphus	Greenwood	1525	28/02/1942	Tru, Bru, Friesland	
237	Grondelaers Pieter		9145	09/03/1945	LNe, LGe, Cl	Wounded 28/04/1945
238	Guelton Marco		9076	09/03/1945	LNe, LGe, Cl	
239	Guerisse Jean (Johnny)		9068	09/03/1945	LNe, LGe, Cl	
240	Guillemyn Maurits		9024	04/02/1945	LNe, LGe, Cl	
241	Guinotte Freddy		9025	04/02/1945	LNe, LGe, Cl	
242	Haegemans Marcel		9199		LNe, LGe, Cl	
243	Hambursin Jacques	Harris	2525	11/07/1942	Cha, Noa, LNe, LGe, Cl	
244	Hazard Etienne Marie Joseph		9090	09/03/1945	LNe	WIA 12/04/1945 DOW 27/08/1945
245	Hébette Jean	Harrison	0710	09/08/1942	Tru	WIA 17/08/1944
246	Heilporn Jean Claude	Davies	1703	06/06/1942	Tru, Ber, Ard, LNe, LGe	WIA 01/05/1945
247	Hellegards François		1704	06/06/1942	Tru, Cal, Ard, LNe, LGe, Cl	
248	Hendrick Johny		4382	17/04/1944	Ber, Ard, LNe, LGe, Cl	
249	Hendrickx Ferdinand	Hardy	3012	06/06/1942	Cha, Noa, Ard, LNe, LGe, Cl	
250	Hendrickx Leo		3515	09/03/1945		Transferred to SOE
251	Hendrikx Willy		9125	09/03/1945	LNe, LGe	WIA 28/04/1945
252	Henrard Jean		0070	19/02/1945	LNe, LGe, Cl	
253	Heylen Gaston	Harris	1194	11/02/1943	Noa, Gob, LGe, Cl	

	Name (last, first)	Cover name	Service number	Parachute qualification	Operations	Remarks
254	Heylen Jef		9188	09/03/1945	LNe, LGe, Cl	
255	Heynderickx		1333			
256	Hollants Marcel		9033	04/02/1945	LNe, LGe, Cl	
257	Hollemans A.				Cl	
258	Holvoet Raymond	Vermarcke - Henderson	2478	11/09/1942	Hag, Tim	Executed 10/04/1945
259	Houdevelt Joseph		2655			
260	Houet André		3775	07/05/1944	Tru, Ard, LNe, LGe, Cl	
261	Humblet					
262	Huybrecht Franciskus	Hubby	0543	20/03/1942	Tru, Ard	
263	Huybrechts		9113			
264	Huybrechts Eugene		9027	24/02/1945	LNe, LGe	WIA 01/05/1945
265	Ingeveld P.		9089	09/03/1945		
266	Irtou Charles		3006	06/06/1942		
267	Jacobs Fançois		9195		LNe, LGe, Cl	
268	Jacobs van Merlen Victor		9026	04/02/1945	LNe, LGe	WIA 28/04/1945
269	Janne Raymond		9120	09/03/1945	LNe, LGe, Cl	
270	Jansegers G.		F7/800		LNe, LGe, Cl	
271	Janssens		F8/54		LNe, LGe, Cl	
272	Janssens				Cl	
273	Janssens van der Maelen M.		9083	07/03/1945		
274	Janssens van der Maelen Pierre		5775	12/10/1944	Ard, LNe, LGe, Cl	
275	Jeukens Andre		5758	04/02/1945	LNe, LGe, Cl	WIA 16/04/1945
276	Joakim Georges-Emile		1613	28/02/1942		
277	Jonckheere Jean		9072	09/03/1945	LNe, LGe, Cl	
278	Jottrand Georges-Emile		9201	28/08/1945	Cl	
279	Jourdain Robert	Rolain	12625	05/1941	Noa, Ard, LNe, LGe, Cl	
280	Kahn Raymond		9079	09/03/1945	LNe, LGe, Cl	Killed in training 11/09/1945
281	Keldermans E.				LNe, LGe, Cl	
282	Keyeux		2157			
283	Kirschen Gilbert-Sadi	King	105GB	06/06/1942	Bun, Ben, Fab, LGe, Cl	
284	Klein Walter		1711	28/02/1942	Cha, Cal, Ard, LNe, LGe, Cl	
285	Kowarski Bernard	Kelly	1847	02/05/1942	Tru, Cal, Ard, LNe, LGe, Cl	
286	Kowarski David	Kelly	1848	02/05/1942	Tru, Cal, Ard, LNe, LGe, Cl	
287	Krins René		2978	04/06/1943	Sha, Ber, Ard, LNe	WIA 15/04/1945
288	Krolikowski Jacques	Kipling	1246	04/06/1943	Noa, Ard, LNe, LGe, Cl	

	Name (last, first)	Cover name	Service number	Parachute qualification	Operations	Remarks
289	Lalot		2908	05/10/1942		
290	Lambillon Arthur		5502	12/10/1944	Ard, LNe, LGe, Cl	
291	Lament R.		4114	12/04/1944	Tru, Ber	
292	Lameys H.		54GB			
293	Lamiroy Alexander	Law	3428	04/06/1943	Tru, Ber, Ard, LNe, LGe, Cl	
294	Lams Leon		3298			
295	Laurent Robert		4414	17/04/1944	Tru, Ber	
296	Laureys H.		51GB			
297	Leblud Robert		9109	09/03/1945	LNe, LGe, Cl	
298	Lecaille August		4815	09/02/1944	Ard, LNe, LGe, Cl	
299	Leclef Marcel			17/01/1942		
300	Lecluse Henri		1913			
301	Lecoq		4172	17/04/1944		
302	Lecrenier Robert		1716		LNe	
303	Ledant Georges Roland		9097	09/03/1945	LNe, LGe, Cl	
304	Ledoyen Julien		3294	11/02/1943	Transferred to SOE	
305	Lefèvre Jules		3613			
306	Lemaire Charles	Lavache	2970	05/10/1942	Cha, Noa, Ard, LNe, LGe, Cl	
307	Lemal		4143			
308	Lepage Guillaume		1790			
309	Leroy Jacques		5668	12/10/1944	Ard, LNe, LGe	
310	Lesage Albert		0026	17/01/1942		
311	Levaux Jacques	Lewis	4139	17/04/1944	Bun, Tru, Ard, LNe, LGe, Cl	
312	Levaux Joseph	Larry	3315	11/02/1943	Bun, Noa, Gob, LGe, Cl	WIA 16/03/1945
313	Leveque Willy		9194			
314	Leyder Paul			06/04/1945	LNe, LGe, Cl	
315	L'Hoir Georges		1722			
316	Libotte Jean-Louis		5850	04/02/1945	LNe	Wounded 05/04/1945
317	Libotte Raymond		5848	04/02/1945	LNe, LGe, Cl	
318	Lierman Jules		1914			
319	Lietard Jean		9051	04/02/1945	LNe, LGe, Cl	
320	Ligot Rene		9028	04/02/1945	LNe	WIA 12/04/1945
321	Limborg Achille		2758	09/08/1942		Transferred to SOE
322	Limbosch Freddy	McLean	10413	28/02/1942	Sha, Cal	KIA 08/09/1944
323	Limbosch Jean	Monro	40507	08/01/1943	Noa	
324	Limbourg		1723	28/02/1942		
325	Logie Henri		F7/327			
326	Longfils		2203			
327	Lorphèvre Emile		2502	09/08/1942	Sha, Ber, Ard	KIA 31/12/1944
328	Lox Jean		3068	06/06/1942	Tru, Bru	KIA 10/09/1944
329	Luyckx Jacques		0626			

	Name (last, first)	Cover name	Service number	Parachute qualification	Operations	Remarks
330	Luyens		3280			
331	Machiels Philippe	Martin	4378	17/04/1944	Tru, Ber	
332	Magriet François		9205		LNe, LGe	DOW 29/05/1945
333	Mal Jean	Malet	4376	17/04/1944	Noa, Ard, LNe, LGe, Cl	
334	Maréchal Armand	Marshall	0632	09/08/1942	Noa, LNe, LGe, Cl	
335	Marginet Andre	Morgan	1726	11/07/1942	Sha, Cal, Ard, LNe, LGe, Cl	
336	Marinis L.		9029	04/02/1945	LNe, LGe, Cl	
337	Markey Walter		9052	04/02/1945	LNe, LGe, Cl	
338	Marquet Paul		9063	07/03/1945		
339	Martens		F6/263		Cl	
340	Martin				LNe, LGe, Cl	
341	Mas Michel	Maurice	3573	17/04/1944	Tru, Ber, Ard, LNe, LGe, Cl	
342	Masquelier Florian		4042			
343	Massin		3403	17/04/1944		
344	Mastyn		0727	09/08/1942		
345	Mathy Lionel		9198		Cl	
346	Mathys Charles	Martin	9422	20/03/1942	Sha, Bru, Ard	Killed in training 04/03/1945
347	Meerpoel Alfons		9102	09/03/1945	LNe, LGe, Cl	
348	Meisch Albert	Morris	3435	04/06/1943	Tru, Noa, Ard, LNe, LGe, Cl	
349	Melsens Jean	Foster	0630	30/03/1942	Cal, Sha	KIA 10/09/1944
350	Mercatoris Emile		9030		Ard, LNe, LGe, Cl	
351	Merchiers Robert		2563	29/03/1945	Ard, LNe, LGe, Cl	
352	Mérenne		0165			Jump refusal 1942
353	Mertens Louis		0166	09/08/1942		
354	Mestdagh Albert		3318	11/02/1943	Sha, Ber, Ard, LNe, LGe, Cl	
355	Meunier Jean		9196	28/08/1945	LNe, LGe, Cl	
356	Meuwese		9096			
357	Michel V.		F6/264	28/08/1945	Cl	
358	Moeren J.L.					
359	Mombel René	Sylvain	2516	07/08/1944	Tru, Bru, Ard, LNe, LGe, Cl	
360	Mommen Joseph		9080	09/03/1945	LNe, LGe, Cl	
361	Moors F.		F3/50	28/08/1945	Cl	
362	Moreau Louis		9129	07/03/1945	LNe, LGe, Cl	
363	Moreau Marcel		3574	17/04/1944	Bun, Ber, Ard, LNe, LGe, Cl	
364	Moreels		1730	09/08/1942		
365	Morel Jean		2492	05/10/1942		Transferred to SOE
366	Mouchart		F6/63		Cl	
367	Moyse Joseph	John Saville	0088	20/03/1942	Bun, Ben, Fab, LGe, Cl	
368	Munster					
369	Natengel Roger	Nasier	2987	11/02/1943	Tru, Ber, Ard	
370	Nelissen Willy		F10/229		LNe, LGe, Cl	
371	Nicaise A.		F5/485		Cl	

	Name (last, first)	Cover name	Service number	Parachute qualification	Operations	Remarks
372	Nicolas		1735	28/02/1942		
373	Nieman A.		F8/608			
374	Nieuwenhuyse Henri		2547	05/10/1942		
375	Nizet Roger	Nicholson	1090	09/08/1942	Tru, Ber, Ard, Cl	
376	Noel Fernand		3149	04/06/1943	Noa, LNe, LGe, Cl	
377	Nolf		1736			
378	Nopère Paul		2917	09/08/1942		Transferred to SOE
379	Ongena Maurice		1737	06/06/1942	Tru, Noa, Ard, LNe, LGe, Cl	
380	Oosters Jacques		3615	07/05/1944	Tru, Ber, Ard, LNe, LGe, Cl	
381	Orban J.		5808	09/11/1944	LNe, LGe, Cl	
382	Ortmans Jacky		9031	04/02/1945	LNe, LGe, Cl	
383	Pallemans Alfons		5164	09/11/1944	Ard, LNe, LGe, Cl	
384	Papeleu R.		F7/321		Cl	
385	Paps Henry		5471	12/10/1944	Ard, LNe, LGe, Cl	
386	Parmentier Roger		1739	02/05/1942	Bun, Ber, LNe, LGe	
387	Patyn Georges	Paterson	0637	09/08/1942	Tru, Ber, Ard, LNe, LGe	
388	Pécher Daniel	Pechey	3127	04/06/1943	Tru, Bru, LNe, LGe	
389	Peemans Jacques		9059	04/02/1945	LNe, LGe	
390	Peere Alphons	Perry	0552	20/03/1942	Sha, Ber, Ard, LNe, LGe	
391	Peeters A.		F8/206	28/08/1945	Cl	
392	Petit Albert	Pajol	1273	11/02/1943	Cha, Cal, LNe, LGe, Cl	Wounded 21/04/1945
393	Philippe Adrien		9121	09/03/1945	LNe LGe Cl	
394	Phillips		0384			
395	Picavet L.		5523	12/10/1944	Ard, LNe, LGe, Cl	
396	Pietquin René		0554	17/01/1942	Bun, Ben, Fab, LNe, LGe, Cl	
397	Piron Robert		9032		LNe, LGe, Cl	
398	Pirotte Charles		2447	11/07/1942		Transferred to SOE
399	Pittoors		2471	11/02/1943		
400	Poeckers Marcel		9208		LNe, LGe, Cl	
401	Polain Etienne		9106	09/03/1945	LNe, LGe, Cl	
402	Polain Pierre		4492	17/04/1944	Cha, Ber, Ard, LNe, LGe, Cl	
403	Polys Nicolas		9135			DOW 06/03/1945
404	Posteau		4115	07/05/1944		
405	Pus Pierre	Parson	0559	17/01/1942	Tru, Ber, Ard, LNe, LGe, Cl	
406	Quirain Jean	Quinet	2976	05/10/1942	Bun, Ber, Ard, LNe, LGe, Cl	
407	Radino Charles		25144		Ard, LNe, LGe, Cl	
408	Ramackers Marcel		9209	28/08/1945	LNe, LGe, Cl	
409	Raquez J.		9138	09/03/1945	LNe, LGe, Cl	
410	Raskin Emile		9131	09/03/1945	LNe, LGe, Cl	
411	Ratinckx Georges	Riviere	3035	06/06/1942	Cha, Noa, Ard, LNe, LGe, Cl	

	Name (last, first)	Cover name	Service number	Parachute qualification	Operations	Remarks
412	Ravet Albert	John	2992	04/06/1943	Tru, Ber, Ard, LNe, LGe, CI	Wounded 16/04/1945
413	Regner Jules	Robinson	2104	09/08/1942	Bun, Fab, Ard, LNe, LGe, CI	WIA 03/08/1944
414	Renkin Jules		9034	04/02/1945	LNe	WIA 15/04/1945
415	Renkin Paul	Rankin	0642	28/02/1942	Noa, Ard	KIA 31/12/1944
416	Reynkens Annibal-François		F3/57		CI	
417	Rielens Pierre-François		F3/567	28/08/1945	CI	
418	Ries		4464			
419	Rivers		1749			
420	Robert		F12/573	28/08/1945	CI	
421	Roeckx J.		0095	28/02/1942		
422	Roegist Leonard	Rogers	1750	28/02/1942	Sha, Ard, LNe, LGe, CI	WIA 09/08/1944
423	Roels Jacques		9204		CI	
424	Roiseux J.		R1/461	28/08/1945		
425	Rolin Philippe		5761	04/02/1945	LNe	KIA 12/04/1945
426	Romnée José		38890	09/11/1944	Ard, LNe, LGe, CI	
427	Roqueplo J.		9095	09/03/1945	LNe, LGe, CI	
428	Rossius Daniel	Robinson	3560	17/04/1944	Bun, Noa, Ard	
429	Rotschild Roger		2192	11/02/1943		
430	Rozenfeld		2559			
431	Rubant		1754	11/07/1942		
432	Ruffato		3465	04/06/1943		
433	Ruscart Paul		5820	09/03/1945	LNe, LGe	DOW 02/05/1945
434	Ryckx Emanuel		5774	12/10/1944	Ard	WIA 12/01/1945
435	Saen				LNe, LGe, CI	
436	Saint Victor				LNe, LGe, CI	
437	Salaets Arnold		9179	09/03/1945	LNe, LGe, CI	
438	Salaets Lambert		9180	09/03/1945	LNe, LGe, CI	
439	Salpetrier J.				CI	
440	Sas Charles	Bickford	1755	28/02/1942	Sha, Cal, Ard, LNe, LGe, CI	WIA 10/08/1944
441	Schaller André		9081	09/03/1945	LNe, LGe	Wounded 04/05/1945
442	Schepers Leo		9035	04/02/1945	LNe, LGe, CI	Killed in training 11/09/1945
443	Schils Robert	Steward	0278	17/01/1942	Tru, Bru, Ard, LNe, LGe, CI	Wounded 13/09/1944
444	Scoriels Jean		9053	04/02/1945	LNe, LGe, CI	
445	Segelaer Andy		9161	09/03/1945	LNe, LGe, CI	
446	Segers Jozef		9115	09/03/1945	LNe, LGe, CI	
447	Servais Gaston					

	Name (last, first)	Cover name	Service number	Parachute qualification	Operations	Remarks
448	Sevens Frank		0493	06/12/1944	Ard, LNe, LGe, Cl	
449	Siffert François	Whineheart	0045	18/02/1942	Sha, Cal, Gob, LGe, Cl	
450	Slosse Adelin		4154	09/03/1945	LNe, LGe, Cl	
451	Smets A.		9036		Ard, LNe, LGe, Cl	
452	Smeyers Armand		1758			
453	Smeyers Paolo		9037	24/02/1945	LNe, LGe, Cl	
454	Sougné Henri	Warburton	2589	11/02/1943	Tru	
455	Speler		2223			
456	Stas J.		4424			
457	Steinbach Leon		9038	04/02/1945	LNe, LGe, Cl	
458	Stessel		9067			
459	Stevens Andre		1762	02/05/1942	Tru, Ard	
460	Stichnot Louis		0852	09/08/1942		
461	Stoops L.		551/ 20037	28/08/1945	Cl	
462	Streel		0046	20/03/1943		
463	Stroobants Gilbert		1763	02/05/1942	Ber, Ard, LNe, LGe, Cl	
464	Swaters Jacques		0891	09/03/1945		
465	Switters Jean	Charter	0891	20/03/1942	Sha, Cal, Ard, LNe, LGe, Cl	
466	Tack Robert		9077	09/03/1945	LNe, LGe, Cl	
467	Tampère Arthur		F1/622		LNe, LGe, Cl	
468	Temmerman Jean	Govaerts	2725	04/06/1943	Hag	
469	Thévissen Jean	Terling	3296	11/02/1943	Bun, Ber, Ard, LNe, LGe, Cl	WIA 13/04/1945
470	Thise Jules					
471	Thonard Paul	Thompson	1765	06/06/1942	Tru, Ard, LNe, LGe, Cl	
472	Timmermans Joseph		9039	04/02/1945	LNe	Wounded 09/04/1945
473	Tinchant José	Tyne/Tine	3251	04/06/1943	Tru, LNe, LGe, Cl	WIA 10/09/1944
474	Tondreau Henri		9075	09/03/1945	LNe	WIA 15/04/1945
475	Valentin Paul		9093	09/03/1945	LNe, LGe, Cl	WIA 01/05/1945
476	Van Broekhuizen Jacques		4474		Noa, Ard, LNe, LGe, Cl	
477	Van Campenhout		1952			
478	Van Caubergh Philipp		9040	04/02/1945	Cl	
479	Van Cauter Josse		9041	04/02/1945	LNe, LGe, Cl	
480	Van Cauwelaert H.		1545			
481	Van Cauwelaert Leo		1773	06/06/1942	LNe, LGe, Cl	
482	Van Cauwenberghe Denis		9050	04/02/1945	LNe, LGe, Cl	
483	Van Cauwenberghe Jacques				Ard	
484	Van Damme Jacques		2972	05/10/1942		
485	Van De Ginste Roger		5722	04/02/1945	LNe, LGe, Cl	

elgian SAS jeeps
ıd a 15-cwt lorry at
•osterhesselen. Note the
AS insignia painted on
ıe armour plates in front
f the drivers.
'egasus Museum Diest)

eele bridge, where the
elgian SAS Regiment
›nducted a two-
ıuadron frontal attack
› cross the canal and
:cure the passage.
Daemen)

Belgian SAS jeep with one man behind the forward-mounted twin Vickers K machine guns and another in a kneeling position with an M1 carbine.
(F. Van Haezendonck)

Winschoterhoogebrug, the bridge over the Pekel-Aa river on the southeastern approach route t Winschoten. *(H. Strating)*

Belgian SAS jeep in Winschoten, with troopers André Bouillon, Moreau, Ferdinand Hendrickx Marcel Chauvaux and Lance Corporal Jean Quirain. Note the Bren gun on a mount on the driver side and the body armour worn by Quirain. *(A. d'Oultremont)*

elgian SAS jeeps in Winschoten. *(Van Haezendonck)*

A' Squadron jeep in the area around Winschoten. *(A. d'Oultremont)*

Belgian SAS jeeps with Sergeant Van Broekhuyzen in the back of the rear jeep. Note the bazook anti-tank rocket launcher visible behind the rear Vickers K machine gun. *(A. d'Oultremont)*

Belgian SAS jeep crossing a column of German prisoners of war. *(J. Temmerman)*

From: Brigadier E.T. WILLIAMS, C.B.E., D.S.O.,

GSI
Headquarters, 21 Army Group
BLA

21 A Gp/INT/2025/3

6 Jul 45

Dear Calvert,

I should be most grateful if you would convey to Major BLONDEL, O.C. Belgian SAS Regt, my appreciation for the very great assistance which he and the officers and men of his unit rendered to 21 Army Group when they were engaged on counter-intelligence duties.

They had previously had only a very short period of training in this work, but in spite of this all ranks, and particularly the junior leaders, showed commendable initiative. Their keenness, willingness, discipline and bearing won the admiration of all with whom they came into contact.

This unit proved a most welcome addition to our resources at a time when we were stretched to the limit. It was a great pleasure for us to work with them, and we hope that the future may bring us an opportunity to do so again. In the meantime we send them all our warmest thanks and very best wishes.

Yours sincerely,

E.T. Williams

Brigadier J.M. CALVERT, D.S.O.,
Commander SAS Troops,
APO, England

REGISTERED
SDS/APO/SDR

RS

Herewith letter received since I wrote mine to you.
JMC

Letter from Brigadier Williams to Brigadier Calvert. *(Pegasus Museum Diest)*

Building occupied by the Belgian SAS Regiment during counterintelligence operations in Germany. In front of the gate are troopers Jaak Daemen and Maurice Dirix. *(J. Daemen)*

Troopers Maurice Dirix (underneath jeep) and Jaak Daemen (with beret) conducting vehicle maintenance during counterintelligence operations in Germany. *(J. Daemen)*

Trooper Marcel Chauvaux sitting on a jeep in Germany. *(F. Van Haezendonck)*

Corporal Rene Van Haezendonck and Trooper Lucien Goessens in their jeep during counterintelligence operations in Germany. *(F. Van Haezendonck)*

Corporal Rene Van Haezendonck overseeing German prisoners of war during counterintelligence operations in Germany. Note the captured German leather pistol holster on his belt. *(F. Van Haezendonck)*

Trooper Marcel De Maere (wearing a leather jerkin) and Corporal Rene Van Haezendonck (with a beret without a cap badge) during counterintelligence operations in Germany. *(F. Van Haezendonck)*

Column of 2nd Lieutenant Henri Williot during counterintelligence operations in Germany. *(F. Van Haezendonck)*

Troops during counterintelligence operations in Germany. *(F. Jacobs)*

Rounding up German troops during counterintelligence operations in Germany. *(SAS Veterans News)*

15-cwt lorry during counterintelligence operations in Denmark. Trooper François Jacobs, the lorry driver, is sitting on the bonnet. *(B. Otté)*

Troopers Maurice Dirix, Freddy Vanderveken, Jaak Daemen and Albert Claes with a capture German car during a halt on the return to Belgium following counterintelligence operations i Germany. *(J. Daemen)*

rigadier Calvert handing over colours bearing the SAS insignia to Major Blondeel during a parade n the La Cambre Abbey in Brussels, 8 September 1945. It was the last time the Belgian SAS Regiment was assembled for inspection by Calvert. *(A. d'Oultremont)*

Now that the war has been victoriously ended, I wish to express to you something of the gratitude which all the officers and men of the Special Air Service Brigade who took part in the campaign of Belgium, 1944, feel towards you for the selfless devotion and memorable courage with which you aided them in the accomplishment of their tasks. The help you gave contributed in a large measure to any success we achieved, and we are full of admiration for the disregard of danger and the generosity of spirit with which that help was given.

All men who were involved in the bitter conflict of 1939-1945 grew to recognise the importance to victory of civilian loyalty, steadfastness and determination. We realise that in no country and at no time did the practise of those virtues demand greater firmness than in Belgium under German occupation, and that nowhere was that firmness more abundantly forthcoming. Your individual acts of patriotism as they affected our operations have been brought to the notice of the British Government and will be preserved in the official records of the British War Office.

Those of our men who had known Belgium before, returned to England with renewed faith in the destiny of your country to which the civilisation of the world owes so much: those who had not known Belgium before have now an impression of a great people of indomitable spirit. All the British troops under my command have been most deeply touched by the sentiments of comradeship with England which their allies of Belgium have expressed to them in words, and so valiantly proved in deeds. It is our fervent hope that the unity of purpose and ideals between Great Britain and Belgium which we have realised in war will be maintained triumphantly in peace.

On behalf of the Special Air Service Brigade, I wish all good fortune to you personally and to Belgium and offer you our most sincere thanks.

J. M. Calvert.
Brigadier.

Letter from Brigadier Calvert to the Belgian SAS Regiment. *(Pegasus Museum Diest)*

ieutenant Colonel Blondeel, wearing post-war Belgian rank insignia on his collar.
'egasus Museum Diest)

'Manneken Pis', a famous statue near the Grand-Place in Brussels, stands just under 22 inches ta and the original dates back over six centuries. Throughout the years, he has worn more than thousand different outfits. The one shown here represents a lance corporal of the SAS, donated b the Belgian SAS Regiment in October 1945. *(A. d'Oultremont)*

ketch by Jules Regner
howing an SAS patrol
perating along a railway
ne. *(J. Regner)*

Portrait of Brigadier Roderick McLeod by Marco Guelton. *(M. Guelton)*

Portrait of Brigadier Mike Calvert by Marco Guelton. *(M. Guelton)*

)rawing by Paul Renkin showing the many potential hazards during parachute operations. As the ;reen light goes on, paratroopers squeeze themselves through the bottom hatch of the bomber. Care ıad to be taken not to smash one's face on the opposite side of the floor opening and jumping too oon after each other was not without risk either. *(Renkin familiy)*

Painting by Rudolphus Groenewout.
(Jaak Daemen family)

Humorous drawing by Jacques Oosters depicting the ambushing of a German lorry. Oosters ha been an illustrator for Belgian cartoonist Hergé, author of *The Adventures of Tintin*. *(A. d'Oultremont*

	Name (last, first)	Cover name	Service number	Parachute qualification	Operations	Remarks
486	Van De Moortele Alphonse		1774			
487	Van De Spiegle Jacques		2533	09/08/1942		Transferred to SOE
488	Van Den Bempt		F3/168		CI	
489	Van Den Bergh		2984	11/02/1943		
491	Van Den Reym Prosper		9042	04/02/1945	LNe, LGe	WIA 01/05/1945
492	Van der Heyden Raymond	Hazel	38403	02/05/1942	Cha, Ber, Ard, LNe	WIA 15/04/1945
493	Van Der Mensbrugge Marc		9186	09/03/1945	LNe, LGe, CI	
494	van Doosselaere Guy		5771	12/10/1944	Ard, LNe, LGe, CI	Wounded 25/04/1945
495	Van Driessche Gerard		5773	12/10/1944	Ard, LNe, LGe, CI	
496	Van Durme Marcel		F7/488		CI	
497	Van Eetvelde		5776	12/10/1944	Ard, LNe, LGe, CI	
498	Van Gastel Jacques		0460	02/05/1942		Transferred to SOE
499	Van Haezendonck Rene	Van Huyze	1783	28/07/1942	Noa, Ard, LNe, LGe, CI	
500	Van Hantsaeme Leo		1784		LNe, LGe	
501	Van Haverbeke		2076			
502	Van Hecke Christian		9171	09/03/1945	LNe, LGe, CI	
503	Van Homwegen Jean		9044	04/02/1945	LNe, LGe, CI	
504	Van Lerberghe		1925			
505	Van Melle Christian		9046	04/02/1945	LNe, LGe, CI	WIA 16/04/1945
506	Van Melle Guy		9049	04/02/1945	LNe, LGe, CI	
507	Van Mierlo		0954			
508	Van Oost G.		1368			
509	Van Ruymbeke Emile		F1/677		CI	
510	Van Schoonlandt F.		F3/291	28/08/1945	CI	
511	Van Stratum Thierry		9047	04/02/1945	LNe, LGe, CI	
512	van Strydonck Michel		9116	09/03/1945	LNe, ID, CI	
513	Van Tuyckom Paul		9073	09/03/1945	LNe, LGe, CI	
514	Van Uffelen Franciscus		2197	28/02/1942	Tru, Noa, Ard, LNe, LGe, CI	
515	Van Vlierberghe		1841			
516	van de Put Gilles				CI	
517	Vanderlinden Marcel		9043	04/02/1945	LNe, LGe, CI	
518	Vandermeeren Alexander		1778	02/05/1942	Sha, Cal	
519	Vanderoost Raoul		9200	28/08/1945	CI	
520	Vandersmissen P.		3810			
521	Vanderstecken		3155	06/01/1943		

	Name (last, first)	Cover name	Service number	Parachute qualification	Operations	Remarks
522	Vanderstock Bob		9057	24/02/1945	LNe, LGe, Cl	
523	Vanderveken Freddy		9126		LNe, LGe, Cl	
524	Vandevoir Gérard		9070	09/03/1945	LNe, LGe, Cl	
525	Vanhoren Tony		9045	04/02/1945	LNe, LGe, Cl	
526	Verberckmoes Georges	Jefferson	1795	28/02/1942	Cal, Sha, Ard, LNe, LGe, Cl	
527	Vercruysse		9162	09/03/1945		
528	Vereecken Raymond		3456			
529	Verelst		0766	17/01/1942		
530	Verfaillie Camiel	Wilson	4354	17/04/1944	Tru, Ber, Ard, LNe, LGe, Cl	
531	Verfaillie R.		F8/236	28/08/1945	Cl	
532	Vergauwen Jos		9127	09/03/1945	LNe	
533	Verhulst Roger		9058		LNe, LGe, Cl	
534	Vermeulen		1295	09/08/1942		
535	Veroft Jean	Williams	1871	06/06/1942	Sha, Cal, Ard, LNe, LGe	
536	Verschuere Henry	Grant	1800	02/05/1942	Tru, Ber	
537	Verslijken W.		1801		LNe, LGe	
538	Vertongen		5800	09/11/1944	Ard, LNe, LGe	
539	Vervaet		1802			
540	Vervroegen Louis		1803			
541	Vieuxtemps Edgard		4396	07/08/1944	Noa, Ard, LNe, LGe	
542	Vilain		1076	20/03/1942		
543	Vincart Marcel		9206		Cl	
544	Visée Marcel	Vernon	0052	20/03/1942	Tru, Bru, Ard, LNe, LGe, Cl	
545	Vivey Victor		3496	04/06/1943	Tru, Cal, Ard, LNe, LGe, Cl	
546	Vlaeminck Julien		9168	09/03/1945	LNe, LGe	
547	Vlietinck		1804			
548	Vos Jan	Fox	4601	17/04/1944	Tru, Cal, Ard, LNe, LGe, Cl	Wounded 10/04/1945
549	Vuylsteke		1447			
550	Vyt Albert		9156	09/03/1945	LNe	15/04/1945
551	Vijt Charles		5751	09/11/1944	Ard, LNe, LGe, Cl	
552	Waem Jules		3504	04/06/1943		
553	Walhez		5793	1944	Ard, LNe, LGe, Cl	
554	Wanty Jacques					
555	Warnant		2755			
556	Wathelet Joseph		9108	09/03/1945	LNe	KIA 15/04/1945
557	Wauters Albert		0417			Jump refusal 1942
558	Webert		3015	06/06/1942		
559	Willemot Pierre		9090	09/03/1945	LNe, LGe, Cl	
560	Willems G.		F9/508		Cl	

	Name (last, first)	Cover name	Service number	Parachute qualification	Operations	Remarks
561	Willems P.		1809	1/07/1942		
562	Williot Henri		42957	22/04/1945	CI	
563	Wilmotte		3304			
564	Wilssens Edgard		1869			
565	Windels		1812			
566	Wuytjens Mathieu		9055	04/02/1945	LNe, LGe, CI	Killed in training 11/09/1945

APPENDIX 3

RECIPIENTS OF BRITISH AWARDS FOR EXPLOITS WHILE SERVING IN THE BELGIAN SPECIAL AIR SERVICE

Companion of the Distinguished Service Order (DSO)

Major Edouard Blondeel[1]
Captain Emile Debefve[2]
1st Lieutenant Gilbert-Sadi Kirschen[3]

Member of the Order of the British Empire (MBE)

Warrant Officer Maurice Berckmans[4]
Captain Josef Cosyns[5]
Captain Laurent de Merkline[6]
Captain Robert Merchiers[7]
Captain Charles Radino[8]

Military Cross (MC)

1st Lieutenant Jean Heilporn[9]
2nd Lieutenant José Romnée[10]
1st Lieutenant Frank Sevens[11]
1st Lieutenant Paul Thonard[12]
1st Lieutenant Leo Van Cauwelaert[13]
1st Lieutenant Raymond Van der Heyden[14]

Distinguished Conduct Medal (DCM)

Trooper Victor Debuf[15]
Sergeant Josef Déom[16]
Lance Corporal Joseph Moyse[17]
Sergeant François Siffert[18]
Warrant Officer Charles Vijt[19]

Military Medal (MM)

Trooper Jean Bastin[20]
Sergeant Georges d'Oultremont[21]
Sergeant Jacques Goffinet[22]
Trooper Albert Petit[23]
Corporal Pierre Polain[24]
Lance Corporal Jules Regner[25]

British Empire Medal (BEM)

Staff Sergeant Guillaume Lepage[26]
Staff Sergeant René Mombel[27]
Staff Sergeant Marcel Visée[28]

APPENDIX 4[1]

BELGIAN SPECIAL AIR SERVICE REGIMENT BATTLE HONOURS

Normandy

"The Belgian Parachute Unit was the first of the Belgian units to participate in operations in Normandy, where it was dropped behind enemy lines from 27 July 1944. During numerous battles, it contributed to causing confusion among the German units, notably in the Falaise pocket."

Belgium

"The Belgian Parachute Unit was the first Allied unit to operate on Belgian territory. Dropped behind enemy lines from 15 August 1944, in the regions of Limburg, Gedinne, and the Fens, it inflicted heavy losses on the enemy, by putting numerous units out of action and destroying an artillery battery. It worked closely with the Secret Army in these regions."

Ardennes

"The Belgian Parachute Unit participated in the offensive operations conducted by Anglo-American armies during the von Rundstedt offensive, despite extremely adverse weather conditions and the particularly difficult and mine-infested terrain. Specifically, it participated in the deadly battle for the liberation of Bure."

Emden

"The Belgian Parachute Regiment participated in the final offensive in Friesland. Attached to the Polish Armoured Division, this Regiment was always forming the spearhead throughout the fighting, inflicted heavy losses on the enemy, and was the first unit to reach the North Sea during a daring raid southwest of the port of Emden."

Oldenburg

"The Belgian Parachute Regiment participated in the final offensive in Oldenburg. Attached to the 2nd Canadian Armoured Brigade, this regiment was highly valued by the Allied Command for its boldness in combat until the end of the campaign, despite the heavy losses inflicted on it by the enemy."

APPENDIX 5

BELGIAN SAS ARTISTS

A few members of the Belgian SAS used their graphic artistic talents during their stay in the unit to keep a visual record of their adventures or everyday events.

Jules Regner made black-and-white sketches often related to operational employment, in a rather sombre style.

Marco Guelton created a variety of black-and-white and colour drawings, including highly detailed and often dramatic action scenes, as well as several portraits of Belgian and British SAS personnel.

Paul Renkin used a much lighter style in his drawings representing the unit's training and daily routine, integrating a lot of humour in his colourful artwork, which did not avoid self-mockery when visualising the less glorious aspects or the hazards of their vocation.

Rudolphus Groenewout made drawings and colour paintings.

Jacques Oosters was the author of many humorous cartoons. Already having a great deal of drawing experience before the war, he had been working as an illustrator for the world-renowned Belgian cartoonist Hergé (pen name of Georges Remi), author of *The Adventures of Tintin* comics. During his service with the SAS, Oosters always carried a drawing book in which he recorded his experiences, often full of humour and sometimes very realistic. His closest comrades in arms, Georges d'Oultremont and Michel Mas were the usual subjects of his illustrations. His drawing book also contained drawings from the comics *Tintin in the Land of the Soviets*, *Tintin in America*, *The Blue Lotus* and *The Broken Ear.*

Several creations of the above artists are shown in the plates sections.

SOURCES

Published books

Éric Alary, *La ligne de démarcation 1940-1944*, Presses universitaires de France, Paris, 1995

Amicale Belgian SAS Vriendenkring, *Des SAS au "Special Forces Group" – 75 ans de forces spéciales belges*, Kortrijk, 2016

James R. Arnold, *Ardennes 1944, Hitler's last gamble in the West*, Osprey Publishing, London, 1990

Stephen Badsey, *Operation 'Market Garden'*, Osprey Publishing, London, 1993

Bryton Barron (editor), *Foreign Relations of the United States: Diplomatic Papers, Conferences at Malta and Yalta, 1945*, United States Government Printing Office, Washington, 1955

Pier Paolo Battistelli, *Panzer Divisions 1944–45*, Osprey Publishing, Oxford, 2009

Antony Beevor, *Ardennes 1944: The Battle of the Bulge*, Viking, New York, 2015

Christer Bergström, *The Ardennes 1944-1945 - Hitler's Winter Offensive*, Casemate, Oxford, 2014

Henri Bernard, *La Résistance 1940-1945*, La Renaissance du Livre, Brussels, 1968

Freddy Bernier, *La résistance et l'Armée secrète en Condroz Namurois 1940-1945*, partie I - généralités, 2017

Perry Biddiscombe, *The Last Ditch: An Organizational History of the Nazi Werwolf Movement, 1944-45*, ProQuest, Ann Arbor, 2014

Rudy A. Blatt, *To Live...You Fight – A War Diary*, New York, 1960

Theodoor Alexander Boeree, *De Kroniek van Ede en omgeving gedurende de vijf jaren van de Duitsche bezetting*, Ede, June 1946

Thomas Boghardt, *Covert Legions – U.S. Army Intelligence in Germany, 1944-1949*, Washington, D.C., 2022

Omar N. Bradley and Clay Blair, *A General's Life, An Autobiography by General of the Army Omar N. Bradley*, Simon & Schuster, New York, 1983

W. D. Brown, Royal Aircraft Establishment, *X Type Parachutes: A Review of the Fatal Accidents at No. 1 P and G.T.S and their Causes*, Farnborough (undated)

Ben Buunk (junior), *Ben Buunk alias "Fopkonijn"*, Breda, 2018

Craig Cabell, *The History of 30 Assault Unit – Ian Fleming's Red Indians*, Pen & Sword, Barnsley, 2009

Peter Caddick-Adams, *Snow and Steel - Battle of the Bulge 1944-45*, Oxford University Press, Oxford, 2015

Michael Calvert, *Prisoners of Hope*, Jonathan Cape, London, 1952

Elsa Caspers, *To Save a Life – Memoirs of a Dutch Resistance Courier,* Deirdre McDonald Books, London, 1995

Klaas Castelein & Michel Wenting, *The Dutch Resistance 1940–45 - World War II Resistance and Collaboration in the Netherlands*, Osprey Publishing, Oxford, 2022

Winston S. Churchill, *The Second World War, Volume VI – Triumph and Tragedy*, Houghton Mifflin, Boston, 1953

Comité scientifique Mook 1944, 1944 - *La Wehrmacht insaisissable*, Editions Weyrich, Brussels, 2022

Commission des crimes de guerre, Ministère de la Justice, Royaume de Belgique, *Les Crimes de Guerre commis pendant la contre-offensive de von Rundstedt dans les Ardennes - Décembre 1944 - Janvier 1945 - Bande*, George Thone, Liège 1945

Terry Crowdy, *SOE Agent, Churchill's Secret Warriors*, Osprey Publishing, Oxford, 2008

Stephen Cullen, *World War II Vichy French Security Troops*, Osprey Publishing, Oxford, 2018

Wolfgang Curilla, *Die deutsche Ordnungspolizei im westlichen Europa 1940-1945*, Schöningh/Brill, Paderborn, 2019

Dr. L. De Jong, *Het Koninkrijk der Nederlanden in de Tweede Wereldoorlog, Deel 10b, eerste helft*, Martinus Nijhoff, 's Gravenhage, 1981

Eddy de Roever, *Zij sprongen bij maanlicht – De geschiedenis van het Bureau Bijzondere Opdrachten en de agenten, Londen 1944-1945*, Hollandia, Baarn, 1986

Guy de Pierpont en André Lefèvre, *Historique des Régiments Parachutistes, SAS, Commando et Para-Commando, tome II*, Groupe G.O. & Co., Brussels, 1977

Emmanuel Debruyne, *Un service secret en exil - L'Administration de la Sûreté de l'Etat à Londres, novembre 1940 - septembre 1944*, in: Centre d'Etudes et de Documentation Guerre et Societes Contemporaines, *Journal of Belgian History - Vol. 15*, Brussels, 2005

H. M. Denham, *Inside the Nazi Ring: A Naval Attaché in Sweden, 1940-1945*, John Murray, London, 1984

Richard Doherty, *The British Reconnaissance Corps in World War II*, Osprey Publishing, Oxford, 2007

F.S.V. Donnison, *Civil affairs and military government, North-West Europe 1944-1946*, Her Majesty's Stationary Office, 1961

Jeremy Duns, *Need to Know, An Archive of Journalistic Pursuits*, 2020

Simon Dunstan, *Flak Jackets - 20th-century military body armour*, Osprey Publishing, London, 1984

Dwight D. Eisenhower, *Crusade in Europe*, Doubleday & Company, Baltimore, 1948

Colonel Roger Flamand, *Paras de la France libre*, Presses de la Cité, Paris, 1976

Roger Flamand, *Amherst : les parachutistes de la France libre, 3e et 4e SAS, Hollande 1945*, Saint-Cloud, 1998

David Fletcher, *Universal Carrier 1936–48*, Osprey Publishing, Oxford, 2005

David Fletcher & Richard Charley, *Cromwell Cruiser Tank 1942-50*, Osprey Publishing, Oxford, 2006

Roger Ford, *Fire from the Forest – The SAS Brigade in France, 1944,* Cassell, London, 2003

Jo Gérard, Hervé Gérard & Gustave Rens, *Se battre pour la Belgique 1940 – 1945*, Editions J.M. Collet, Brussels, 1984

Ken Ford, *Operation Market-Garden 1944 (2) - The British Airborne Missions*, Osprey Publishing, Oxford, 2016

Ken Ford, *The Rhineland 1945*, Osprey Publishing, Oxford, 2000

Ken Ford, *The Rhine Crossings 1945*, Osprey Publishing, Oxford, 2007

M.R.D. Foot, *SOE in France, An Account of the Work of the British Special Operations Executive in France 1940–1944*, Frank Cass & Co, London, 2004

William M. Franklin and William Gerber (editors), *Foreign Relations of the United States: Diplomatic Papers, The Conferences at Cairo and Tehran, 1943*, United States Government Printing Office, Washington, 1961

Helen Fry, *MI9 – A History of the Secret Service for Escape and Evasion in World War Two*, Yale University Press, New Haven and London, 2020

Emile Genot, *Bérets Rouges, Bérets Verts, 50000 Para-Commandos*, Gutenberg Editions, Brussels, 1986

Emile Genot, *Chesty George, Captain Blunt - Deux personnages hors du commun,* Claes Printing, Brussels, 2000

Emile Genot, *Humour en rouge et vert – Témoignages au travers d'anecdotes et de faits divers*, Brussels, 2014

George Gerolimatos: *Structural Change and Democratization of Schleswig-Holstein's Agriculture, 1945-1973*, University of North Carolina, Chapel Hill, 2014

Lambert Grailet, *Première mondiale pour le V-2 sur Paris,* auto-édition, Liège, 1996

Neil Grant, *The Bren Gun*, Osprey, Oxford, 2013

Christian Gruslin, *Du Mercator à la capture d'Himmler*, Editions J. M. Collet, Braine-l'Alleud, 1992

Major Robert G. Gutjahr, *The Role of Jedburgh Teams on Operation Market Garden*, U.S. Army Command and General Staff College, Fort Leavenworth, 1990

General Sir John Hackett, *I was a stranger*, Pimlico, London, 1999

Alan W. Hall, *Vickers Wellington*, Hall Park Books Ltd., Husborne Crawley, 1997

Alan W. Hall, *Westland Lysander*, Warpaint Books Ltd, Luton, 2000

Stephen A. Hart, *Panther Medium Tank 1942–45*, Osprey Publishing, Oxford, 2003

Leo Heaps, *The Grey Goose of Arnhem - The Story of the Most Amazing Mass Escape of World War II*, Sapere Books, Leeds, 1976

F. H. Hinsley & C. A. G. Simkins, *British Intelligence in the Second World War – Volume 4, Security and Counter-Intelligence*, Her Majesty's Stationery Office, London, 1990

Jelle Hooiveld, *Operatie Jedburgh – Geheime geallieerde missies in Nederland 1944-1945*, Boom, The Hague, 2014

Bernd Horn & Michel Wyczynski, *Canadian Airborne Forces since 1942*, Osprey Publishing, Oxford, 2006

Lieutenant-Colonel Bernd Horn and Michel Wyczynski, *Paras Versus the Reich: Canada's Paratroopers at War, 1942-1945*, The Dundurd Group, Toronto, 2003

George Hutchinson, *The Nazi Ideology of Alfred Rosenberg*, University of Oxford, 1977

Infantry Journal Press, *Conquer, The Story of Ninth Army 1944-1945,* Washington, D.C., 1947

J. Israël, *Jean Melsens 1922-1944 – Het verhaal van een Belgische parachutist die stierf voor onze vrijheid*, Valkenswaard, 1996

Robert Jackson, *The Secret Squadrons – Special Duty Units of the RAF and USAAF in the Second World War*, Robson Books Ltd., London, 1983

Malcolm James, *Born of the Desert: With the SAS in North Africa*, Collins, London, 1945

Dietrich Janßen, *Flak um Emden - Chronik der Marine-Flak-Abteilung 236*, Emden

Jeffrey Jarkowsky, *German Special Operations in the 1944 Ardennes Offensive*, U. S. Army Command and General Staff College, Fort Leavenworth, Kansas, 1994

Benjamin F. Jones, *Eisenhower's Guerillas - The Jedburghs, the Maquis, and the Liberation of France*, Oxford University Press, New York, 2016

Tim Jones, *SAS: The First Secret Wars – The Unknown Years of Combat and Counter-Insurgency,* London, 2005

Cécile Jouan, *Comète – Histoire d'une ligne d'évasion*, Editions du Beffroi, Furnes, 1948

Marvin D. Kays, *Weather effects during the battle of the Bulge and the Normandy invasion*, US Army Electronics Research and Development Command, White Sands Missile Range, 1982

James L. Kennedy Jr., *The Failure of German Logistics during the Ardennes Offensive of 1944*, U. S. Army Command and General Staff College, Fort Leavenworth, Kansas, 2000

Robert J. Kershaw, *'It never snows in September' – The German View of Market-Garden and The Battle of Arnhem*, Ian Allan Publishing, September 1944, Hersham 2004

Gilbert-Sadi Kirschen, *Six amis viendront ce soir*, Presses de Belgique, Brussels, 1983

Damien Lewis, *The Nazi Hunters – The Ultra-Secret SAS Unit and the Quest for Hitler's War Criminals*, Quercus Publishing, London, 2015

Damien Lewis, *SAS Forged in Hell: From Desert Rats to Dogs of War: The Mavericks who Made the SAS*, Quercus Publishing, London, 2023

S. J. Lewis, *Jedburgh Team Operations in Support of the 12th Army Group*, August 1944, US Army Command and General Staff College, Fort Leavenworth, Kansas, 1991

Eugène Liptak, *Office of Strategic Services 1942-45, The World War II Origins of the CIA*, Osprey Publishing, Oxford, 2009

Oliver Lock, *British Airborne Insignia*, Military Mode Publishing, Hitchin, 2015

Oliver Lock, *British Airborne Insignia Volume 2*, Military Mode Publishing, Hitchin, 2017

Sean Longden, *T-Force - The Race for Nazi War Secrets, 1945*, Constable & Robinson, London, 2009

Robin Lumsden, *The Allgemeine-SS*, Osprey Publishing, Oxford, 1993

Charles B. MacDonald, *The Last Offensive*, Center of Military History, United States Army, Washington, D.C., 1993

Fitzroy Maclean, *Eastern Approaches*, Penguin Books, London, 1991

Colonel Victor Marquet, *Entre Bocq et Semois, l'Armée Secrète, Zone V – Secteur 5*, Remy éditeurs, Beauraing, 1984

Colonel Victor Marquet, *Contribution à l'histoire de l'Armée Secrète 1940-1944, deuxième partie – Armée de Belgique - Armée Secrète 1943-1944, fascicule V –* l'organisation, Pygmalion, Brussels

Colonel Victor Marquet, *Contribution à l'histoire de l'Armée Secrète 1940-1944, deuxième partie – Armée de Belgique - Armée Secrète 1943-1944, fascicule VI –* l'action, Pygmalion, Brussels

Evan McGilvray & Janusz Jarzembowski, *First Polish Armoured Division 1938-47: A History*, Pen & Sword, Barnsley, 2022

Chris McNab, *MG 34 and MG 42 Machine Guns*, Osprey Publishing, Oxford, 2012

Richard Mead, *The Men Behind Monty*, Pen & Sword, Barnsley, 2015

Samuel W. Mitcham Jr., *Panzers in Winter: Hitler's army and the Battle of the Bulge*, Praeger Security International, Westport, 2006

Jon Lake, *Halifax Squadrons of World War 2*, Osprey Publishing, Oxford, 1999

David Littlejohn, *The SA 1921–45: Hitler's Stormtroopers*, Osprey Publishing, Oxford, 1990

Martin Middlebrook, *Arnhem 1944 – The Airborne Battle, 17-26 September*, Pen & Sword, Barnsley, 2009

Kriegstagebuch der Seekriegsleitung 1939-1945 – Teil A – Band 68 – 1. bis 20. April 1945, Verlag E.S. Mittler & Sohn, 1989

Gavin Mortimer, *The SAS in Occupied France - 1 SAS Operations, June to October* 1944, Pen & Sword, Barnsley, 2020

Matthew Moss, *The PIAT - Britain's anti-tank weapon of World War II,* Osprey Publishing, Oxford, 2020

Bernard Law Montgomery, *The Memoirs of Field-Marshal the Viscount Montgomery of El Alamein, K.G.*, The World Publishing Company, Cleveland, 1958

Field Marshal The Viscount Montgomery of Alamein, *Normandy to the Baltic – A personal account of the conquest of Germany*, Printing and Stationery Service British Army of the Rhine, 1946

Tim Moreman, *Chindit 1942-45*, Osprey Publishing, Oxford, 2009

Robert Moulié, *Des SAS au 1er RPIMA*, Editions LBM, Paris, 2010

Airey Neave, *Little Cyclone*, Hodder and Stoughton, London, 1954

Airey Neave, *They Have Their Exits*, Pen & Sword, Barnsley, 2002

Airey Neave, *Saturday at M.I.9: The Classic Account of the WW2 Allied Escape Organisation*, Pen & Sword, Barnsley, 2010

Dr. Philipp Neumann-Thein & Sandra Siegmund (editors), *Wegweiser durch die Gedenkstätte Buchenwald*, Stiftung Gedenkstätten Buchenwald und Mittelbau-Dora, Weimar, 2023

Robert Oulds, *Counterattack, Montgomery and the Battle of the Bulge*, The Bruges Group, 2023

Jean-Paul Pallud, *Ardennes 1944 - Peiper & Skorzeny,* Osprey Publishing, London, 1987

Danny S. Parker, *Hitler's Ardennes Offensive: The German View of the Battle of the Bulge*, Skyhorse Publishing, New York, 1997

Martin Peeters, *Oorlog op en rond 't Lin – Belgische S.A.S-operatie Caliban*, Heemkundige Kring Peer, Peer, 1995

Martin Pegler, *The Thompson Submachine Gun - From Prohibition Chicago to World War II*, Osprey, Oxford, 2010

André Pioger, *Le Mans et la Sarthe pendant la 2de guerre mondiale*, La Province du Maine, Le Mans, 1976

Bruce Quarrie, *The Ardennes Offensive, VII Panzer Armee, Northern Sector*, Osprey Publishing, Oxford, 1999

Bruce Quarrie, *The Ardennes Offensive, V Panzer Armee, Central Sector*, Osprey Publishing, Oxford, 2000

Bruce Quarrie, *The Ardennes Offensive, I Armee and VII Armee, Southern Sector*, Osprey Publishing, Oxford, 2001

Bruce Quarrie, *The Ardennes Offensive, US VII & VIII Corps and British XXX Corps, Central Sector,* Osprey Publishing, Oxford 2000

Bruce Quarrie, *The Ardennes Offensive, US III & XII Corps, Southern Sector,* Osprey Publishing, Oxford, 2001

Nicholas Rankin, *Ian Fleming's Commandos – The Story of 30 Assault Unit in WWII*, Faber & Faber, London, 2011

Heemkring De Reengenoten - Meeuwen, *De oorlogsjaren in Ellikom, Gruitrode, Meeuwen, Neerglabbeek, Wijshagen, 1940-1945*, Meeuwen, 2004

Der Reichsorganisationsleiter der NSDAP, *Organisationsbuch der NSDAP*, Franz-Eher-Verlag, München, 1936

Guy Richards, *World War II Troop Type Parachutes – Allies: U.S., Britain, Russia, An Illustrated Study*, Schiffer Publishing, Atglen, 2003, pp. 21-43

Russ Rodgers, *Nierstein and Oppenheim 1945 - Patton Bounces the Rhine*, Osprey Publishing, Oxford, 2020

Hamish Ross, *Paddy Mayne – Lt Col Blair 'Paddy' Mayne, 1 SAS Regiment,* The History Press, Stroud, 2014

Gordon L. Rottman, *The Bazooka,* Osprey Publishing, Oxford, 2012

Gordon L. Rottman, *The Hand Grenade,* Osprey Publishing, Oxford, 2015

Gordon L. Rottman, *Panzerfaust and Panzerschreck*, Osprey Publishing, Oxford, 2014

Daniel Ryelandt, *Chasseurs Ardennais dans le Maquis, La vie et l'action d'un groupe de l'A.S. 43-44*, Editions de « La Dryade », Vieux-Virton, 1969

Peter Schrijvers, *The Unknown Dead: Civilians in the Battle of the Bulge*, The University Press of Kentucky, Lexington, 2005

Karin Schawe (editor), *Die KZ-Gedenkstätte Neuengamme – Ein Überblick über die Geschichte des Ortes und die Arbeit der Gedenkstätte,* KZ-Gedenkstätte Neuengamme, Hamburg, 2010

Peter R. Senich, *The German Sniper: 1914-1945*, Paladin Press, Boulder, 1982

Colonel C.P. Stacey, *Official History of the Canadian Army in the Second World War, Volume III, The Victory Campaign, The Operations in North-West Europe 1944-1945*, The Queen's Printer and Controller of Stationery, Ottawa, 1960

Gene B Stafford, *P-38 Lightning in Action,* Squadron Signal Publications, Ellijay, 1976

Special Air Service Regimental Association, *SAS War Diary 1941-1945*, London, 2011

Supreme Headquarters Allied Expeditionary Force – Office of the Assistant-Chief-of-Staff, G2, Counter-Intelligence Sub-division, Evaluation & Dissemination Section, *Arrest Categories Handbook – Germany*

John Tanner, *RAF Airborne Forces Manual – The official Air Publications for RAF Paratroop Aircraft and Gliders, 1942-1946*, Hippocrene Books, New York, 1979

Oliver Tapper, *Armstrong Whitworth Aircraft Since 1913*, Putnam & Company, London, 1973

Major Digby Tatham Warter, DSO, *Dutch Courage and "Pegasus"*, Nabyuki, 1991

Jean Temmerman, *Les Paras belges dans l'action*, J. M. Collet, Brussels, 1987

Jean Temmerman, *Les parachutistes belges 1942-1945 - Acrobates sans importance*, Edition DVB, Liège, 1999

Chris Thomas, *Typhoon Wings of 2nd TAF 1943–45*, Osprey Publishing, Oxford, 2010

Nigel Thomas, *Wehrmacht Auxiliary Forces*, Osprey Publishing, Oxford, 1992

Leroy Thompson, *The Colt 1911 Pistol,* Osprey, Oxford, 2011

Leroy Thompson, *Fairbairn-Sykes Commando Dagger*, Osprey, Oxford, 2011

Leroy Thompson, *The M1 Carbine*, Osprey, Oxford, 2011

Leroy Thompson, *The Sten Gun,* Osprey, Oxford, 2012

United States Forces European Theater (USFET) Interrogation Center, *BATTLE OF THE ARDENNES – Interview with Lieutenant Colonel OTTO SKORZENY, Commanding Officer for Operation "Greif"*, European Theater Historical Interrogation (ETHINT) Series #12, Oberusel, 12 August 1945

Wouter van den Brandhof, *Hitlers parachutistengeneraal - Kurt Student (1890-1978): een militaire biografie*, Uitgeverij Verloren, Hilversum, 2019

Nicholas van der Bijl, *Sharing the Secret: The History of the Intelligence Corps, 1940–2010*, Pen & Sword, Barnsley, 2013

Jean Vigile, *1944 – La Libération du Perche*, Fédération des Amis du Perche, France, 1997

War Department, *Technical Manual No. 9-754, Medium Tank M4A4*, Washington, 1943

The War Office, *The tactical employment of Armoured Car and Reconnaissance Regiments, Military Training Pamphlet No. 60, Part 4 – Reconnaissance Regiment*, March 1944

Guy Weber, *Les précurseurs - 13 janvier 1942*, Editions L. Bourdeaux-Capelle, Dinant, 1991

Ian Wellsted, *With the SAS across the Rhine – Into the Heart of Hitler's Third Reich*, Frontline Books, Yorkshire, 2020

Peter Wilkinson & Joan Bright Astley, *Gubbins & SOE*, Leo Cooper, London, 1997

Dennis Williams, *Stirlings in Action with the Airborne Forces – Air Support for SAS and Resistance Operations During* WWII, Pen & Sword, Barnsley, 2008

Gordon Williamson, *German Military Police Units 1939–45*, Osprey Publishing, Oxford, 1989

Gordon Williamson, *German Special Forces of World War II*, Osprey Publishing, Oxford, 2009

Robert K. Wittman & David Kinney, *The Devil's Diary: Alfred Rosenberg and the Stolen Secrets of the Third Reich*, HarperCollins Publishers, London, 2017

Steven J. Zaloga, *Sherman Medium Tank 1942–45*, Osprey Publishing, London, 1993

Steven J. Zaloga, M4 (76mm) *Sherman Medium Tank 1943–65*, Osprey Publishing, Oxford 2003

Steven J. Zaloga, *Battle of the Bulge 1944 (1): St Vith and the Northern Shoulder*, Osprey Publishing, Oxford, 2003

Steven J. Zaloga, *Battle of the Bulge 1944 (2): Bastogne*, Osprey Publishing, Oxford, 2004

Steven J. Zaloga, *German V-weapon sites 1943-45*, Osprey Publishing, Oxford, 2007

Steven J. Zaloga, *Defense of the Rhine 1944-45*, Osprey Publishing, Oxford, 2011

Steven J Zaloga, *Downfall 1945 - The Fall of Hitler's Third Reich*, Osprey Publishing, Oxford, 2016

Steven J. Zaloga, *Tanks in the Battle of the Bulge*, Osprey Publishing, Oxford, 2020

Earl F. Ziemke, *The U.S. Army In the Occupation of Germany*, Center of Military History, United States Army, Washington, D.C., 2003

Unpublished manuscripts

Edouard Blondeel, *Mémoires*, Brussels, 1995

Willy Deheusch, *Recueil des sauts effectués par les parachutistes belges à l'entraînement et en opérations*

Hubert de Mûelenaere, *Souvenirs d'événements*, Brussels, 1994

Georges d'Oultremont, *Mémoires*

Jules Regner, *Sélection d'oeuvres – Uitgekozen kunstwerken*, Ecaussines, 1985

Jean Temmerman, *Le singe parachutiste Emile*

Charles Vijt, *Mémoires*

Journals

Special Air Service Regimental Association, *Mars and Minerva – The Journal of the Special Air Service*, London

S.A.S. Veterans News, Brussels

Amicale Nationale Para Commando Vriendenkring, *Para-Commando*, Brussels

Société Royale deş Officiers Retraités - Koninklijke Vereniging van de Oprustgestelde Officieren, *La Belgique militaire – Militair België*, Brussels

The International Guild of Battlefield Guides, *Despatches – the magazine of the International Guild of Battlefield Guides*, Derby

Cambridge University Press, *Central European History*, Cambridge

Cambridge University Press, *The Historical Journal*, Cambridge

Battle of Britain International, *After the Battle*, Essex

Wojskowe Biuro Historyczne [Military History Office], *Przegląd Historyczno-Wojskowy* [Military History Review], Warsaw

Le-Livre, *Armes-Militaria-Info* (AMI), Sablons

Zeitverlag Gerd Bucerius GmbH & Co. KG, *Die Zeit*, Hamburg

Miscellaneous publications from the following archives

General Intelligence and Security Service - Classified Archives Section (SGRS-S/CA), Evere, Belgium

Study and Documentation Centre for War and Contemporary Society, State Archives, Brussels, Belgium

Pegasus Museum Archives, Diest, Belgium

Musée des Commandos, Flawinne, Belgium

National Archives, Kew, United Kingdom

Imperial War Museums, London, United Kingdom

National Army Museum, Chelsea, United Kingdom

Airborne Assault (ParaData) Archives, The Museum of the Parachute Regiment and Airborne Forces, Duxford, United Kingdom

Carpetbagger Aviation Museum, Harrington, England

Library and Archives Canada

National Archives, College Park, Maryland, United States

The Library of Congress, Washington, DC, United States

Nederlands Instituut voor Militaire Historie, the Netherlands

Erfgoedcentrum Achterhoek en Liemers, Doetinchem, the Netherlands

Gelders Archief, the Netherlands

City of Winschoten online archives, the Netherlands (https://www.winschoterarchief.nl)

Federal Archives, Federal Republic of Germany

Maps

War Office, *G.S.G.S. No. 4464, Europe 1:2,000,000*, London 1944, Lloyd Reeds Map Collection, McMaster University Library, Hamilton, Ontario, Canada

War Office, *G.S.G.S. No. 4369, 1:500,000 RAF* (War), London, 1945, McMaster University Library

War Office, *G.S.G.S. No. 4072, 1:500,000 Europe (Air)*, London, 1942, McMaster University Library

Army Map Service, *A.M.S. M404 (GSGS 4072) 1:500,000 Europe (Air)*, U.S. Army, Washington, D.C., 1944, University of Texas Libraries

War Office, *G.S.G.S. No. 4249, France 1:100,000*, London, 1943-1944, McMaster University Library

Army Map Service, *A.M.S. M661 (G.S.G.S. 4249), France 1:100,000,* U.S. Army, Washington, D.C., 1943, McMaster University Library

War Office, *G.S.G.S. No. 4336, France 1:100,000*, London, 1943, McMaster University Library

War Office, *G.S.G.S. No. 4336, Belgium and N.E. France, 1:100,000*, London, 1943, McMaster University Library

Army Map Service, *A.M.S. M641 (G.S.G.S. 4416), Germany 1:100,000*, U.S. Army, Washington, D.C., 1944-1952, McMaster University Library

War Office, *G.S.G.S. No. 4416 (AMS M641), Germany 1:100,000*, London 1944-1952, McMaster University Library

War Office, *G.S.G.S. No. 4081, Germany 1:100,000*, London, 1943, McMaster University Library

War Office, *G.S.G.S. No. 4416, Central Europe 1:100,000*, London 1943-1944, McMaster University Library

War Office, *G.S.G.S. No. 4210, Denmark 1:100,000*, London, 1944, McMaster University Library

War Office, *G.S.G.S. No. 4040, France and Belgium, 1:50,000*, London, 1942-43, McMaster University Library and University of Texas Libraries

Army Map Service, *A.M.S. M832 (G.S.G.S. 4414), Eastern Holland 1:25000*, U.S. Army, Washington, D.C., 1944, McMaster University Library

Footnotes

Chapter 1 – The Formation of the Belgian Independent Parachute Company

1 Edouard Blondeel, *Mémoires* (unpublished), Brussels, 1995.

2 Eighteen Days' Campaign: the campaign fought by the Belgian armed forces between 10 May 1940 (invasion by Nazi Germany) and 28 May 1940 (capitulation by King Leopold III as commander-in-chief of the Belgian armed forces).

3 Emile Genot, *Jules Regner... SAS et Artiste*, in: *Revue Para-Commando*, No 79, Brussels, 1998.

4 Jules Regner, *Sélection d'oeuvres – Uitgekozen kunstwerken*, ANPCV, Ecaussines, 1985 (preface by Kirschen).

5 The demarcation line between the German-occupied northern part of France (covering over half the French territory) and the non-occupied southern part (with the 'capital' of the collaborating regime in the town of Vichy) was instituted by the Franco-German armistice agreement signed on 22 June 1940, coming into effect shortly afterwards. The demarcation line started in the west at the Spanish border, running northwards and then to the east, joining the Swiss border. This arbitrary boundary, some 750 miles long, was under surveillance and crossing was only authorised at designated crossing points on presentation of an identity card and a pass issued by the authorities of the occupying power. From the summer of 1940, crossing routes were established to smuggle goods and persons across the border. The demarcation line was abolished in February 1943, after the Germans had occupied the whole of France in November 1942. See: Éric Alary, *La ligne de démarcation 1940-1944*, Presses universitaires de France, Paris, 1995.

6 Godfroid also joined the Belgian Independent Parachute Company, obtained his parachute wings on 12 February 1943, but left the company afterwards.

7 Miss Freda Moore was a secretary at the British embassy in Madrid when the war broke out. When she learned of the fate that awaited the escaped Allies, specifically the Belgians in the camps and prisons of Franco's Spain, she committed herself with moral and material help to alleviate their suffering. This earned her the nickname 'Angel of Miran' or 'Godmother of Miran'.

8 Emile Genot, *J'avais 20 ans en 1945... Mon évasion 1941-1942*, in: *Revue Para-Commando*, No 108, Brussels, 2008.

9 Emile Debefve, interview with Emile Genot, 1980.

10 Polain was the son of a Belgian diplomat in Tangier. His fiancée died in a traffic accident. Grief and guilt prompted him to join the Foreign Legion in 1940. In 1943, he was awarded the French War Cross for his conduct in the fights from Sidi Bel Abbes during the Tunisian Campaign. He joined the Belgian SAS in 1944 and later returned to the Foreign Legion. In 1946 he was part of the *3ième Régiment Etranger d'Infanterie* in Indochina, a regiment which consisted largely of Germans, but also Poles, Frenchmen, Spaniards, Swiss and a few Belgians. He was killed on 25 July 1948 during a fight against Vietnamese insurgents in French Indochina. (Interview with Jaak Daemen, 2015)

11 Emile Genot, *L'Adjudant de 1ère Classe Charles Vijt*, in: Revue Para-Commando, No 91, Brussels, 2002.

12 Dagger: referring to the Fairbairn-Sykes commando dagger developed for the British

commandos by William Fairbairn and Eric Sykes, both retired from the Shanghai Municipal Police and commissioned in the British Army to train the newly formed commandos and SOE operatives. The dagger was designed for both thrusting and slashing and existed in various models; it was issued to British (and hence Belgian) commando, airborne and SAS units; see: Leroy Thompson, *Fairbairn-Sykes Commando Dagger*, Osprey, Oxford, 2011.

13 Charles Vijt, *Mémoires* (unpublished).

14 Emile Genot, *Cassart: un personnage étonnant*, in: Revue Para-Commando, No 88, Brussels, 2001, p. 16.

15 Westland Lysander: a high-winged monoplane with a very heavy-duty fixed undercarriage able to sustain landing on rough fields, used in a variety of roles, including clandestine sorties to occupied Europe. The aircraft dedicated to support SOE were assigned to No. 138 (Special Duties) Squadron and No. 161 (Special Duties) Squadron RAF. They were modified, having a stepladder at the port side, an extended-range fuel tank and two seats in the rear cockpit, but could carry up to four passengers in an emergency. Depending on the number of passengers carried, the aircraft could take off from an unprepared strip between 300 and 600 yards long. See: Alan W. Hall, *Westland Lysander*, Warpaint Books Ltd, Luton, 2000, pp. 6, 29-30, 32.

16 Genot, op. cit.

17 The *Geheime Feldpolizei* (Secret Field Police) were Germany's 'plain clothes' military police. Formed in 1939, their functions included counter-espionage, counter-sabotage, detection of treason, counter-propaganda and assisting the military legal system in investigations for court martials. Their personnel were largely recruited from the criminal police. See: Gordon Williamson, *German Military Police Units 1939–45*, Oxford, 1989, pp. 13-14.

18 *Guardia Civil*: Spanish gendarmerie.

19 Jean Temmerman, interview with Emile Genot, 1986.

20 *Cantine Suédoise*: Swedish Canteen, a canteen sponsored by the Swedish embassy in Brussels on Rue Ducale, where soup was served each noon and clothing distributed to poor children, aided by Madame Scherling, a Swedish national who happened to be a friend of Alexander von Falkenhausen, the military governor of Belgium and Northern France. Clothing was supplied from Stockholm, the capital of neutral Sweden, and the benevolent activities were inspired by the pre-war actions of Astrid of Sweden, the beloved Queen of Belgium, who tragically died in a car accident in 1935. The director of the canteen was Baron Jean Greindl, the head of the *Comète* evasion line from April 1942, to which the canteen served as a cover for its headquarters. See: Helen Fry, *MI9 – A History of the Secret Service for Escape and Evasion in World War Two*, Yale University Press, New Haven and London, 2020, pp. 87-8; Cécile Jouan, *Comète – Histoire d'une ligne d'évasion*, Editions du Beffroi, Furnes, 1948, pp. 43-4; Airey Neave, *Little Cyclone*, Hodder and Stoughton, London, 1954, pp. 66-7.

21 Arnould d'Oultremont, interview with Lieutenant Colonel Tom B., March 2016.

22 The Belgians who arrived in England left for Tenby where the 1st Fusiliers Battalion was formed. Later, after the arrival of Belgians from Canada, the 2nd Fusiliers Battalion was formed in Malvern.

23 Guy de Pierpont en André Lefèvre, *Historique des Régiments Parachutistes, SAS, Commando et Para-Commando, tome II*, Groupe G.O. & Co., Brussels, 1977, p. 17.

24 Willy Deheusch, *Recueil des sauts effectués par les parachutistes belges à l'entraînement et en opérations* (unpublished), pp. 14-15.

25 Guy Richards, *World War II Troop Type Parachutes – Allies: U.S., Britain, Russia, An Illustrated Study*, Schiffer Publishing, Atglen, 2003, pp. 21-43.

26 Deheusch, op. cit., p. 15.

27 Armstrong Whitworth A.W.38 Whitley: twin-engine heavy bomber developed in the mid-1930s. In 1940, this aircraft type was chosen for parachute training by the Central Landing School (later renamed Parachute Training School and No. 1 Parachute Training School) at Ringway. See: Oliver Tapper, *Armstrong Whitworth Aircraft Since 1913*, Putnam & Company, London, 1973, pp. 255-76.

28 Robert Schils, interview with Emile Genot, 1956.

29 Guy Weber, *Les précurseurs de janvier 1942*, Dinant, 1991, p. 74.

30 2nd Lieutenant M. Leclef, *Rapport sur Cours de Parachutistes*, dated 18 January 1942, Temmerman archives, Study and Documentation Centre for War and Contemporary Society, Brussels.

31 Blondeel, op. cit.

32 Deheusch, op. cit, pp. 21-2.

33 Office of the Minster of Defence, Letter of the Undersecretary of State for Defence, London, 27 April 1942, Pegasus Museum archives.

34 Amicale Belgian SAS Vriendenkring, *Des SAS au "Special Forces Group" – 75 ans de forces spéciales belges*, Kortrijk, 2016, p. 37.

Chapter 2 – Training for War

1 Jean Temmerman, *Le singe parachutiste Emile* (unpublished).

2 Willy Deheusch, *Recueil des sauts effectués par les parachutistes belges à l'entraînement et en opérations* (unpublished), pp. 25-8.

3 Daily orders No. 400 dated 11 July 1944, in: Parachute Company, *O.J. – No 384 du 12 Juin 1942 au No 691 du 21 Août 1943*, Belgian SAS archives, General Intelligence and Security Service - Classified Archives Section (SGRS-S/CA), Evere.

4 Edouard Blondeel, Mémoires (unpublished), Brussels, 1995.

5 At that time, the maroon beret with a metal Belgian lion cap badge was worn without permission of the British, who had assigned this colour to their own airborne forces. This led to negative reactions from the British, who officially asked the Belgians to stop wearing the berets. When in early 1943 it became clear that the Belgian company would not be integrated into a British airborne division, an official request was submitted to wear a dark brown beret. The issue persisted until early 1944. From 1 April 1944, when the SAS Brigade became part of the Army Air Corps (AAC), an overarching administrative organisation for airborne forces (including the Glider Pilot Regiment and the Parachute Regiment), the dress regulations applicable to the SAS mandated a maroon beret to be worn (with a waiver (or at least a tolerated non-compliance) for the originals in the British SAS who still had a tan one). The controversy over the berets was resolved even before the official integration into the AAC. On 21 February 1944, Blondeel informed the Belgian Ministry of Defence that the maroon beret was still to be worn, referring to instructions issued by the SAS Brigade HQ several days earlier. In accordance with the AAC regulations, SAS personnel now also wore blue-on-maroon Pegasus & Bellerophon sleeve patches (commonly known as 'Pegasus patches' or 'Pegasus flashes') on their battle dress uniforms (but not on camouflage

smocks). Later on, also blue-on-maroon 'S.A.S.' shoulder flashes were worn by some, while the previously worn 'BELGIUM' shoulder flashes were no longer to be worn once the unit was part of the SAS. The metal Belgian lion badge on the beret was replaced with the cloth SAS badge from the spring of 1944, when the SAS parachutist qualification badge was also introduced for parachute-trained personnel, replacing the British Army parachutist badge that had been approved by the Army Council in 1940. In the Belgian SAS, both types of parachute qualification insignia (commonly known as 'parachute wings', 'jump wings' or just 'wings') were worn, especially from 1945, possibly due to a shortage of SAS wings. For details on these insignia, see: Oliver Lock, *British Airborne Insignia*, Military Mode Publishing, Hitchin, 2015, pp. 15-16, 47, 50, 168-82, 222; Oliver Lock, *British Airborne Insignia Volume 2*, Military Mode Publishing, Hitchin, 2017, pp. 244-5.

6 Daily orders No. 571 dated 28 February, No. 575 dated 7 March and No. 605 dated 17 April 1943, in: Parachute Company, op. cit.

7 Padre Robert Jourdain was parachuted with a radio operator but the latter's parachute remained attached to the aircraft and Jourdain was on his own on the ground. His radio operator died of exposure before the plane reached England. Padre Jourdain completed his mission but was betrayed and had to flee. He reached England via Miranda de Ebro.

8 Lieutenant General Victor Jean Clément van Strydonck de Burkel, in some sources also written as 'Van Strijdonck'. He was first commander (1940-41) and then inspector general (1941-44) of the Belgian forces in the United Kingdom. In 1944 he became head of the Belgian military mission at the Supreme Headquarters Allied Expeditionary Force.

9 Blondeel, op. cit.

10 Daily orders No. 593 dated 30 March 1943 and No. 650 dated 15 June 1943, in: Parachute Company, op. cit.

11 Deheusch, op. cit., pp. 43-4.

12 Vickers Wellington: twin-engine bomber developed in the early 1930s and entering RAF service from the end of 1938. It was used in a variety of roles, including as an operational training aircraft and for the dropping of paratroops. See: Alan W. Hall, *Vickers Wellington*, Hall Park Books Ltd., Husborne Crawley, 1997, pp. 1, 4, 25.

13 NO. 22 O.T.U., *Report on Flying Accident or Forced Landing not Attributable to Enemy Action P.403161*, dated 21 April 1943, RG 24 Volume 28305, Library and Archives Canada.

14 Daily orders No. 606 dated 19 April 1943, in: Parachute Company, op. cit.

15 Daily orders No. 676 dated 23 July 1943, in: Parachute Company, op. cit.

16 Daily orders No. 687 dated 13 August 1943, in: Parachute Company, op. cit.

17 Blondeel, op. cit.

18 *Aide-memoire of meeting at 117, Eaton Square, S.W.1*, dated 20 Februray 1942, The National Archives of the UK (TNA): HS6-232.

19 Peter Wilkinson & Joan Bright Astley, *Gubbins & SOE*, Leo Cooper, London, 1997, p. 104.

20 Daily orders No. 731 dated 14 November 1943, in: Parachute Company, *O.J. – Compagnie. A partir du No 692 du 22/8/1943 au No 830 du 11.5.44,* Belgian SAS archives, SGRS-S/CA, Evere.

21 Blondeel, op. cit.

22 Emile Genot, *Bérets Rouges, Bérets Verts, 50 000 Para-Commandos*, Gutenberg Editions, Brussels, 1986, p. 17.

23 Temmerman, op. cit.

24 Daily orders No. 563 dated 15 February and No. 565 dated 17 February 1943, in: Parachute Company, op. cit.

25 Temmerman, op. cit.

26 Guy de Pierpont en André Lefèvre, *Historique des Régiments Parachutistes, SAS, Commando et Para-Commando, tome II*, Groupe G.O. & Co., Brussels, 1977, p. 37; Emmanuel Debruyne, *Un service secret en exil - L'Administration de la Sûreté de l'Etat à Londres, novembre 1940 - septembre 1944*, in: Centre d'Etudes et de Documentation Guerre et Societes Contemporaines, *Journal of Belgian History - Vol. 15*, Brussels, 2005, p. 339.

27 Blondeel, op. cit.

28 Jean Temmerman, *Les Paras belges dans l'action*, J. M. Collet, Brussels, 1987, p. 6.

29 de Pierpont, op. cit., p. 47.

Chapter 3 – Joining the Special Air Service Brigade

1 Daily orders No. 764 dated 8 February 1944, in: *O.J. – Compagnie – A partir du No 692 du 22/8/1943 au No 830 du 11.5.44*, Belgian SAS archives, SGRS-S/CA, Evere.

2 Colonel Roger Flamand, *Paras de la France libre*, Presses de la Cité, Paris, 1976, p. 303.

3 Daily orders No. 768 dated 17 February 1944, in: *O.J. – Compagnie – A partir du No 692*, op. cit.

4 From 21 April on, the postal address was to be changed to '1st Belgian Parachute Squadron, HQ SAS Troops, Army Post Office, England', still without any indication related to the unit's location (see daily orders No. 810, in: *O.J. – Compagnie – A partir du No 692, op. cit.*).

5 Daily orders No. 777 dated 29 February 1944, in: *O.J. – Compagnie – A partir du No 692*, op. cit.

6 Daily orders No. 784 dated 14 March 1944, in: *O.J. – Compagnie – A partir du No 692*, op. cit.

7 Eureka: lightweight transponder used as a navigational aid for aircraft equipped with the Rebecca system, used mainly by ground parties allowing aircraft to home in and accurately locate drop zones.

8 Edouard Blondeel, *Mémoires* (unpublished), Brussels, 1995.

9 Emile Genot, *Bérets Rouges, Bérets Verts, 50 000 Para-Commandos,* Gutenberg Editions, Bruxelles, 1986, p. 18.

10 Short Stirling: four-engine heavy bomber with a relatively low service ceiling and hence vulnerable to air defences, which, after having been withdrawn from the RAF's main bomber force at the end of 1943, was used by No. 190, No. 196, No. 299 and No. 620 Squadron of the RAF's No. 38 Group. This group, together with No. 46 Group, was responsible for insertion and resupply missions in support of the SAS, SOE and conventional airborne forces. See: Dennis Williams, *Stirlings in Action with the Airborne Forces – Air Support for SAS and Resistance Operations During WWII,* Pen & Sword, Barnsley, 2008.

11 Armstrong Whitworth A.W.41 Albemarle: twin-engine aircraft developed at the start of the war as a medium bomber but, being obsolete in the bomber role by the time it came into production, was used by the RAF to conduct airborne forces insertions from 1943. See: Oliver Tapper, *Armstrong Whitworth Aircraft Since 1913*, Putnam & Company, London, 1973, pp. 276-85.

12 Handley Page Halifax: four-engine heavy bomber developed at the end of the 1930s, used by the RAF's 'special duties' squadrons in support of SOE from the end of 1941 and later by the RAF No. 38 Group's No. 298 and 644 Squadron in support of the SAS, SOE and conventional airborne forces. It was capable of dropping jeeps. See: Jon Lake, *Halifax Squadrons of World War 2*, Osprey Publishing, Oxford, 1999, pp. 72-6, 80-4, 99.

13 Daily orders No. 789 dated 24 March and No. 790 dated 25 March 1944, in: *O.J. – Compagnie – A partir du No 692* op. cit.

14 Daily orders No. 790 dated 25 March 1944, in: *O.J. – Compagnie – A partir du No 692* op. cit.

15 Jean Temmerman, *Les parachutistes belges 1942-1945 - Acrobates sans importance*, Edition DVB, Liège, 1999, p. 384.

16 Daily orders No. 793 dated 29 March 1944, in: *O.J. – Compagnie – A partir du No 692* op. cit.

17 Blondeel, op. cit.

18 Hence his cover name 'Blunt'.

19 Jean Temmerman, *Le singe parachutiste Emile* (unpublished).

20 Jean Delhez was a member of a Belgian resistance organisation. He later joined the Belgian SAS and had a career in the Belgian army after the war. He retired as warrant officer, serving with the clandestine operations division of the military intelligence service.

21 Emile Genot, *Chesty George, Captain Blunt - Deux personnages hors du commun*, Claes Printing, Brussels, 2000, p. 86.

22 Imperial War Museums, records H 37831, H 37832, H 37833, H 37834, H 37835, H 37836.

23 Amicale Belgian SAS Vriendenkring, *Des SAS au "Special Forces Group" – 75 ans de forces spéciales belges,* Kortrijk, 2016, p. 56.

24 Blondeel, op. cit.

25 Ibid.

26 'Pilou', as his friends called him, later became CO of the 3rd Para-Commando Battalion (later the 3rd Parachute Battalion) in the Congo from 1957-1960. He ended his career as a colonel commanding the clandestine operations division of the military intelligence service.

27 The narrative referring to these officers covers a period starting prior to the integration of the unit in the SAS Brigade. For this reason, the term 'platoon' is used, which was the correct term when the unit was a company. In a squadron, the name 'troop' is used to designate the immediately subordinate level, the size of which might be quite similar.

28 As a major, lieutenant colonel and colonel, Van der Heyden became CO of the 3rd Para-Commando Battalion in Kamina, from 1955-1957, and later commanded the Para-Commando Regiment from 1960-1963.

29 Jean Temmerman, *Les Paras Belges dans l'action*, J. M. Collet, Brussels, 1987.

Chapter 4 – The Belgian SAS in Normandy

1 Edouard Blondeel, *Mémoires* (unpublished), Brussels, 1995.

2 Ibid.

3 Gilbert-Sadi Kirschen, *Six amis viendront ce soir,* Presses de Belgique, Brussels, 1982, pp. 11-12.

4 Ibid., p. 71.

5 Jean-Pierre Chantrain & René Smeets, *Les Para-Commandos belges – I. La Deuxième Guerre mondiale, in: Armes-Militaria-Info no.* 7, Le-Livre, Sablons, 1980, p. 67.

6 Initially, the code names for these operations were 'Haft 105', 'Haft 205' and 'Haft 305' respectively; see SAS Brigade operation instruction no. 39 in Belgian SAS archives, SGRS-S/CA, Evere.

7 Gilbert-Sadi Kirschen, op. cit., pp. 21-4.

8 1st Lieutenant Ghys, operating under the cover name 'Gordon', was promoted to captain for the duration of this mission, hence his reports by 'Captain Gordon'.

9 Conflicting sources mention different airfields, either Fairford or Keevil.

10 The parachutist jumped out of the plane with the kitbag attached to his leg. Once the parachute canopy properly opened, he released the bag, which remained attached to the parachute harness through a 5-metre-long sling. Provided the extension sling properly unfolded, the kitbag hit the ground first upon landing. Because of the lateral movement of the parachute (unless there was no wind at all), the parachutist landed

next to his kitbag. The moment the kitbag touched the ground, the total weight under the canopy was reduced, slightly slowing down the parachutist during the final metres of his descent and hence lowering the chance on injury. In addition, it allowed the parachutist to hear when he was about to hit the ground on a dark night.

11 Guy de Pierpont & André Lefèvre, *Historique des Régiments Parachutiste SAS, Commando et Para-Commando belges, tome II*, Groupe G.O. & Co., Brussels, 1977, p. 60.

12 Blondeel, op. cit.

13 Captain Gordon, Operation 'Chaucer' reports, Belgian SAS archives, SGRS-S/CA, Evere.

14 Jean Temmerman, *Les parachutistes belges 1942-1945 - Acrobates sans importance*, Edition DVB, Liège, 1999, p. 34-5.

15 Captain Gordon, op. cit.

16 Temmerman, op. cit., p. 35.

17 de Pierpont, op. cit, p. 61.

18 Ibid., p. 61.

19 The use of civilian clothing by military personnel was not prohibited by the law of armed conflict. However, under article 23 of the annex to Convention IV of The Hague (1907), the perfidious use of civilian clothes, such as killing or wounding an unsuspecting enemy, was prohibited. Although intelligence-gathering activities while wearing civilian clothing were not forbidden, military personnel engaged in such activities risked being considered spies under article 29 and could face punishment, provided this resulted from a formal trial, as stipulated by article 30 of the same treaty.

20 Captain Gordon, op. cit.

211st Lieutenant Debefve, operating under the cover name 'Mac Bef', was promoted to captain for the duration of this mission, hence his reports by 'Captain Mac Bef'.

22 Sometimes spelled 'Mathys'. It was not unusual to replace 'ij' with 'y' in names, especially in less official writings.

23 André Pioger, *Le Mans et la Sarthe pendant la 2de guerre mondiale*, La Province du Maine, Le Mans, 1976, p. 275.

24 TNA: AIR-27-2583, pp. 238-240, and TNA: AIR-27-1644, operations record book – July 1944, p. 5.

25 Likely an Albemarle from No. 297 Squadron, RAF, whose operations record book listed a mission with one person and one package dropped around the same time mentioned in Debefve's reports; see: TNA: AIR-27-2575, p. 15-16.

26 *Milicien:* member of the *Milice française* ('French Militia'), usually called '*Milice*' in short, a paramilitary armed security organisation of Vichy France, established in January 1943 and collaborating with the German occupier; see: Stephen Cullen, *World War II Vichy French Security Troops*, Osprey Publishing, Oxford, 2018, pp. 24-47.

27 de Pierpont, op. cit., p. 62.

28 Loir: on contemporary Allied maps sometimes misspelt 'Loire', which is another river, some 20 miles further south.

29 Kirschen, operating under the cover name 'King', was promoted to captain for the duration of this mission.

30 TNA: AIR-27-2575, pp. 12-14.

31 Jean Vigile, 1944 – *La Libération du Perche*, Fédération des Amis du Perche, France, 1997, p. 184.

32 According to Kirschen's after-action report and post-war book, the insertion happened on the night of 2-3 August. In the description of events in the following paragraphs, Kirschen's reported timings of events have been used from Saturday, 5 August onwards.

33 Gilbert-Sadi Kirschen, op. cit., p. 34.

34 Vigile, op. cit, p. 184.

35 Portable radio device used to broadcast during the final phase before a drop, to make a connection between the crew of the plane and the reception committee on the ground.

36 Alternate spelling forms include 'Chérencey' and 'Charencey'.

37 Gilbert-Sadi Kirschen, op. cit., pp. 34-9.

38 Gilbert-Sadi Kirschen, op. cit., p. 40.

39 Lieutenant Kirschen, *Operation "Bunyan"*, Belgian SAS archives, SGRS-S/CA, Evere.

40 In the Belgian SAS reports, his name was spelled as 'Levêque'.

41 Gilbert-Sadi Kirschen, op. cit., pp. 39-45.

42 Tyre buster (sometimes also called 'tyre burster' in British and Belgian SAS reports): a device to damage vehicle tyres. The SAS used explosive tyre busters. Although throughout the text, the generic designation 'tyre buster' is used, it is not always clear whether this may have included caltrops, which are mechanical four-spiked devices laid upon the ground to disable horses, puncture tyres, etc.

43 Temmerman, op. cit., pp. 54-60.

44 1st Lieutenant Van der Heyden, operating under the cover name 'Hazel', was promoted to captain for the duration of this mission, hence his reports by 'Captain Hazel'.

45 Stick: a number of parachutists organised inside an aircraft to jump as one entity in sequence during a single aircraft pass over a drop zone.

46 Temmerman, op. cit., pp. 39-41.

47 TNA: AIR-27-1167-4, August 1944, p. 151.

48 Captain Hazel, Operation 'Chaucer' reports, Belgian SAS archives, SGRS-S/CA, Evere.

49 Captain Gordon, op. cit.

50 Captain Hazel, op. cit.

51 Captain Gordon, op. cit.

52 Captain Hazel, op. cit.

53 Captain Gordon, op. cit.

54 Temmerman, op. cit., pp. 46-7.

55 Captain Hazel, op. cit.

56 Likely Stirling LK 556 of No. 196 Squadron, RAF; the operation's record books mentioned five Stirling aircraft taking off at intervals between five and fifty-five minutes apart, dropping at the same DZ; while all were listed as an SOE mission (likely to supply the resistance), four aircraft dropped twenty-four containers each, and three of those a few additional panniers or other packages, while LK 556, although also listed as an SOE mission, dropped fifteen troops (specified as 'Belgian' in pen or pencil above the typed text) with ten containers listed as cargo, one of which was brought back; this correlates with the nine dropped containers for the Belgian SAS party, as Limbosch's report mentioned eighty containers for the resistance and Debefve's report mentioned eighty-nine containers in total, the order of magnitude being similar even if the resupply for the resistance consisted of ninety-six containers; also the encounter with an enemy fighter was reported by both Limbosch and the operations record books; see: TNA AIR-27-1167, p. 150.

57 Captain Mac Lean, *Report on Operation 'Shakespeare'*, Belgian SAS archives, SGRS-S/CA, Evere.

58 Temmerman, op. cit., p. 61

59 1st Lieutenant Limbosch was promoted to captain for the duration of this mission, hence his reports by 'Captain Mac Lean'.

60 Captain Mac Bef, Operation 'Shakespeare' reports, Belgian SAS archives, SGRS-S/CA, Evere.

61 After the liberation of Belgium, Marcel Carrette, a lieutenant in the Kortrijk resistance, enlisted in the Belgian SAS squadron to 'replace' his deceased cousin.

62 Airey Neave later became a Member of Parliament and advisor to Margaret Thatcher. He was assassinated by Irish National Liberation Army terrorists in 1979.

63 Airey Neave, *Saturday at M.I.9: The Classic Account of the WW2 Allied Escape Organisation*, Pen & Sword, Barnsley, 2010.

64 Mac Lean, op. cit.

65 Captain Mac Bef, op. cit.

66 *Forces Françaises de l'Intérieur* ('French Interior Forces'): name used in 1944 to refer to the majority of armed resistance groups in occupied France.

67 Neave, op. cit.

68 Mac Lean, op. cit.

69 Gilbert-Sadi Kirschen, op. cit., pp. 45-6.

70 TNA: AIR-27-1167-4, August 1944, p. 151.

71 Gilbert-Sadi Kirschen, op. cit., pp. 46-50.

72 Lieutenant Kirschen, *Operation "Bunyan"*, op. cit.

73 *Opération Shakespeare – Rapport du sergent Parmentier*, Belgian SAS archives, SGRS-S/CA, Evere.

74 de Pierpont & Lefèvre, op. cit., p. 73.

75 Temmerman, op. cit., p. 73.

76 Sgt Parmentier, *Rapport sur l'operation "Bunyan"*, Belgian SAS archives, SGRS-S/CA, Evere.

77 Benzedrine: a brand name for amphetamine sulfate, a chemical stimulant.

78 Gilbert-Sadi Kirschen, op. cit., p. 50-3.

79 De Pierpont, op. cit., p. 74.

80 American pistol in 0.45-inch calibre.

81 de Pierpont & Lefèvre, op. cit., p.70-1.

82 Gilbert-Sadi Kirschen, op. cit., pp. 53-5.

83 *Opération Shakespeare – Rapport du sergent Parmentier*, op. cit., and Sgt Parmentier, op. cit.

84 No. 82 grenade or 'Gammon bomb', named after its inventor: British hand grenade adopted from mid-1943, consisting of an impact-detonating fuse assembly and collar riveted to a textile bag that could be filled with up to almost 2 pounds of plastic explosives, for use against personnel, field fortifications or lightly-armoured vehicles. See: Imperial War Museums, IWM MUN 205; Gordon L. Rottman, *The Hand Grenade*, Osprey Publishing, Oxford, 2015, p. 60.

85 Sten gun: British submachine gun made primarily from stamped components, using thirty-two round side-mounted magazines with 9 mm × 19 mm cartridges; developed in 1941, different models existed, with a tubular, skeleton or wooden stock, including versions with a suppressor and an airborne version with front and rear pistol grips, which was also used by the Belgian SAS; tens of thousands were dropped to European resistance groups; see: Leroy Thompson, *The Sten Gun*, Osprey, Oxford, 2012.

86 Gilbert-Sadi Kirschen, op. cit., pp. 62-3 and Lieutenant Kirschen, *Operation "Bunyan"*, op. cit.

87 Bren gun: British light machine gun using curved thirty-round top-mounted magazines with .303" (7.7 mm × 56 mm) cartridges and used as the standard infantry section machine gun having been introduced shortly before the Second World War; see: Neil Grant, *The Bren Gun*, Osprey, Oxford, 2013.

88 *Opération Shakespeare – Rapport du sergent Parmentier*, op. cit., and Sgt Parmentier, op. cit.

89 Spelled as 'Miserey' in the Belgian SAS reports. The castle was situated near clearings in the southern part of the Cherencey Forest, just south of the road between Marchainville and La Ventrouze and east of l'Onglée.

90 Lieutenant Kirschen, *Operation "Bunyan"*, op. cit.

91 *Opération Shakespeare – Rapport du sergent Parmentier*, op. cit., and Sgt Parmentier, op. cit.

92 Gilbert-Sadi Kirschen, op. cit., pp. 66-67 and Lieutenant Kirschen, *Operation "Bunyan"*, op. cit.

93 Temmerman, op. cit., pp. 80-1.

94 Also spelled as 'Yvoy'.

95 Major Lepine, *Report on Operation 'Haggard'*, Belgian SAS archives, SGRS-S/CA, Evere.

96 Consolidated B-24 Liberator: American four-engine long-range heavy bomber developed at the end of the 1930s. Four US Army Air Forces 'Carpetbagger' squadrons dedicated to supporting special operations were equipped with modified all-matte black B-24 aircraft. See: Robert Jackson, *The Secret Squadrons – Special Duty Units of the RAF and USAAF in the Second World War,* Robson Books Ltd., London, 1983, pp. 112-19.

97 From a B-24 Liberator, the paratroopers had to exit the aircraft through a trap door, which served as an emergency exit for the aircrew.

98 Temmerman, op. cit., pp. 82-3

99 Major Lepine's report mentioned the night of 10-11 August but plenty of confusion exists when comparing the conflicting reports from different actors involved in the operation, including but not only related to the starting date. See: Gavin Mortimer, *The SAS in Occupied France - 1 SAS Operations, June to October 1944*, Pen & Sword, Barnsley, 2020, chapter 5; Roger Ford, *Fire from the Forest – The SAS Brigade in France, 1944*, Cassell, London, 2003, p. 122.

100 Some sources reported eight SAS jumpers. The SAS advance party was inserted together with Jedburgh team Alec (see below) by three B-24s (serial numbers 42-40992, 42-50600 and 42-63801) of the 801st Bomb Group (assigned to Operation 'Carpetbagger') of the American Army's 8th Air Force. The aircraft mission reports listed four jumpers in one aircraft, while the other two initially listed four but were changed to three each, totalling ten jumpers between the three B-24s. Retracting the three jumpers from the Jedburgh team, the seven remaining jumpers correlate to the number reported by Temmerman. See: aircraft # 801, 406th Bombardment Squadron, mission report 1521; aircraft # 922, 36th Bombardment Squadron, mission report 1522; aircraft # 0600, 850th Bombardment Squadron, mission report 1523.

101 Temmerman, op. cit., p. 84.

102 Ibid., p. 84.

103 'Jedburgh' was a combined programme run by the British Special Operations Executive, the American Office of Strategic Services – Special Operations branch,

and the Free French *Bureau Central de Renseignements et d'Action* (BCRA) ('Central Intelligence and Action Bureau'). It employed uniformed three-person teams, consisting, in principle, of a Brit, an American, and an inhabitant of the country in which they were deployed. Usually, two were officers and the third an NCO wireless operator. They were trained in guerrilla tactics and leadership and in demolition work and were to provide a general staff for the local resistance, to coordinate the local efforts in the best interests of Allied strategy, and to arrange further supplies for the resistance. Thirteen teams were dropped into France in June 1944, and eighty more followed in the ten weeks thereafter. See: M.R.D. Foot, *SOE in France, An Account of the Work of the British Special Operations Executive in France 1940–1944*, Frank Cass & Co, London, 2004; Eugène Liptak, *Office of Strategic Services 1942-45, The World War II Origins of the CIA*, Osprey Publishing, Oxford, 2009; *Terry Crowdy, SOE Agent, Churchill's Secret Warriors*, Osprey Publishing, Oxford, 2008.

104 According to team Alec's report, the Jedburgh team was dropped 60 miles east of its intended DZ and was tasked with providing a link between the SAS operating against the Vierzon-Tours and Vierzon-Orléans railway lines (i.e. west of the Operation 'Haggard' area of operations) and the local resistance, but the air mission reports confirmed that all three aircraft found the exact DZ, identified by code letters signalled by flashlight. Possibly, team Alec had been attached to the wrong SAS team. See: aircraft # 801, 406th Bombardment Squadron, mission report 1521; aircraft # 922, 36th Bombardment Squadron, mission report 1522; aircraft # 0600, 850th Bombardment Squadron, mission report 1523; Alec team report, 801/492nd Bomb Group Association archives; Ford, op. cit., pp. 122-13.

105 Temmerman, op. cit., pp. 88-9.

106 Ibid., pp. 99-107.

107 Ibid., p. 110.

108 Benjamin F. Jones, *Eisenhower's Guerillas - The Jedburghs, the Maquis, and the Liberation of France*, Oxford University Press, New York, 2016, pp. 228-37.

109 Ibid, p. 121.

110 Ibid., p. 123.

111 *Report on Operation 'Haggard' commanded by Major Lepine, "B" Squadron, 1st SAS Regt.*, Temmerman archives, Study and Documentation Centre for War and Contemporary Society, Brussels, p. 5.

112 *SAS Brigade operation instruction no. 43* dated 15 August 1944, Belgian SAS archives, SGRS-S/CA, Evere.

113 'La Bossière' according to Temmerman, but 'Boisseret' according to the report written by Heilporn; a typo and actually referring to the village of Boisset-les-Prévanches is a possibility.

114 Lieutenant Davies, *Rapport sur l'operation "Trueform"*, Belgian SAS archives, SGRS-S/CA, Evere.

115 de Pierpont & Lefèvre, op. cit., p. 90.

116 TNA: AIR-27-2134-26, p. 12; Operation Noah load manifests, Belgian SAS archives, SGRS-S/CA, Evere.

117 *Report on Operation Trueform*, Belgian SAS archives, SGRS-S/CA, Evere

118 Sergeant De Vulder, *Report on Operation "Trueform"*, Belgian SAS archives, SGRS-S/CA, Evere.

119 TNA: AIR-27-2134-26, August 1944, p. 7, and passenger manifest – party 3, Belgian SAS archives, SGRS-S/CA, Evere.

120 Spelled 'Fresny' on contemporary War Office maps.

121 Lance Corporal de Saint-Guillain, *Report on Operation Trueform*, Belgian SAS archives, SGRS-S/CA, Evere.

122 Gigot was a Catholic priest who, after his parachute training, served as stretcher bearer. On Catholic holidays, he performed his priestly duties for the benefit of his SAS comrades.

123 Warrant Officer Groenewout, *Report on Operation "Trueform"*, Belgian SAS archives, SGRS-S/CA, Evere.

124 TNA: AIR-27-2585, p. 205, and AIR-27-1654-10.

125 de Pierpont, op. cit., p. 92.

126 *Oflag:* German abbreviation for '*Offizierslager*', denoting a (prisoner-of-war) camp for officers.

127 Written declaration extracted from Delelienne's personnel files, Belgian SAS archives, SGRS-S/CA, Evere.

128 Groenewout, op. cit.

129 Temmerman, op. cit., pp. 133-4.

130 .45" pistol: American automatic pistol developed by Colt using .45" 'Automatic Colt Pistol' cartridges, normally in standard seven-round magazines; it was the primary pistol used by American military forces during the Second World War but both the Colt 1911 and the (improved) 1911A1 were also used by British forces during the war, especially special operations units; see: Leroy Thompson, *The Colt 1911 pistol*, Osprey, Oxford, 2011.

131 Tinchant, *Rapport d'opération – Trueform*, Belgian SAS archives, SGRS-S/CA, Evere.

132 TNA: AIR-27-1167-4, August 1944, p. 153.

133 The Belgian SAS archives contain conflicting reports. Pus reported the drop took place on 17 August at 00:20 hours, but De Rechter refers to the night of 17-18 August. The 196th Squadron's operations record book (see reference in the previous note) states 17 August as the mission (start) date and correlates with the load manifest, which is also dated 17 August. Load manifests were completed before the flight, and most night insertions started after dark, with the actual drops happening shortly after midnight, i.e. the next day.

134 M1: American short, lightweight semi-automatic carbine, using fifteen-round magazines with 7.62 mm × 33 mm cartridges; initially intended to replace pistols, it was issued to American troops from mid-1942 and used by the SAS after 1943 and tens of thousands were dropped to the French resistance; the M1A1 version, with folding stock, later became the standard individual weapon of American paratroops; see: Leroy Thompson, *The M1 Carbine*, Osprey, Oxford, 2011.

135 *Operation Trueform, Relation des faits par le Sgt.* Pus, Belgian SAS archives, SGRS-S/CA, Evere.

136 Sgt De Rechter, *Report on "Trueform" Operation*, Belgian SAS archives, SGRS-S/CA, Evere.

137 *Operation Trueform, Relation des faits par le Sgt. Pus*, op. cit.

138 TNA: AIR-27-2585, pp. 203-204, and TNA: AIR-27-1654-10, August 1944.

139 Capt Dill [Dulait] and Lt Thompson [Thonard], *Report on Operation 'Trueform'*, Belgian SAS archives, SGRS-S/CA, Evere.

140 Lieutenant Thompson, *Report on Operation 'Trueform'*, Belgian SAS archives, SGRS-S/CA, Evere.

141 Temmerman, op. cit., pp. 140-1.

142 Lockheed P-38 Lightning: American twin-engine, multi-role, long-range fighter aircraft characterised by its distinctive twin-boom design and separate central compartment containing the cockpit and armament. It entered service just before the Second World War and was used as an escort fighter for bombers to provide top cover for naval and ground assets, and to conduct air-to-ground attacks. See: Gene B Stafford, *P-38 Lightning in Action*, Squadron Signal Publications, Ellijay, 1976.

143 Thompson, op. cit.

144 S/Sgt R. Sylvain, *Report on Operation Trueform I*, Belgian SAS archives, SGRS-S/CA, Evere.

145 Dill, op. cit.

146 Temmerman, op. cit., p. 141-2.

147 Dill, op. cit.

148 *SAS Brigade Operation Instruction no. 48* dated 25 August 1944, Belgian SAS archives, SGRS-S/CA, Evere.

149 *Rapport Benson*, Belgian SAS archives, SGRS-S/CA, Evere.

150 TNA: AIR-27-2585, pp. 328-329, and Operation Benson load manifest, Belgian SAS archives, SGRS-S/CA, Evere.

151 It was likely almost double that distance between the planned and actual DZ when comparing the descriptions of the team's movement in Kirschen's after-action report and post-war book with the location of the planned DZ mentioned in the aircraft's post-mission report. The pilot indeed reported an unusually weak ground signal on what he believed to be the correct DZ; see TNA: AIR-27-2585, pp. 328-9.

152 Lieutenant Kirschen, *Report on Operation 'Benson'*, Belgian SAS archives, SGRS-S/CA, Evere.

153 Gilbert-Sadi Kirschen, op. cit., p. 77.

154 Ibid., p. 78.

155 Temmerman, op. cit., p. 127.

156 Gilbert-Sadi Kirschen, op. cit., pp. 84-6.

157 Emile Genot, *Humour en rouge et vert,* Brussels, 2013, p. 30.

Chapter 5 – Vanguard of the Allied Advance into Belgium

1 TNA: AIR-27-2134-26, August 1944, p. 6, and Operation 'Noah' load manifests, Belgian SAS archives, SGRS-S/CA, Evere. The aircraft number and mission details are missing in the squadron's operations record book, but the crew names correlate to those on the load manifest.

2 Capt Blondeel, *Report on Operation 'Noah'*, Belgian SAS archives, SGRS-S/CA, Evere.

3 Jean Temmerman, *Les parachutistes belges 1942-1945 - Acrobates sans importance*, Edition DVB, Liège, 1999, p. 145.

4 *Operation Noah – Rapport de Lieutenant Renkin (traduction de l'anglais)*, Belgian SAS archives, SGRS-S/CA, Evere.

5 S. J. Lewis, *Jedburgh Team Operations in Support of the 12th Army Group, August 1944*, US Army Command and General Staff College, Fort Leavenworth, Kansas, 1991, p. 31.

6 Temmerman, op. cit., p. 146.

7 A career officer trained at the Saint-Cyr military academy, de Bollardière would later command the 3rd SAS during Operation Amherst and become a brigadier after the war.

8 M.R.D. Foot, *SOE in France, An Account of the Work of the British Special Operations Executive in France 1940–1944*, Frank Cass & Co, London, 2004, pp. 322 and 354.

9 Temmerman, op. cit., pp. 148-9.

10 *Operation Noah – Rapport de Lieutenant Renkin*, op. cit.

11 Temmerman, op. cit., p. 149.

12 Colonel Victor Marquet, *Entre Bocq et Semois, l'Armée Secrète, Zone V – Secteur 5*, Remy éditeurs, Beauraing, 1984, p. 172.

13 The Secret Army (*Geheim Leger* in Dutch and *Armée secrète* in French), originally known as the 'Belgian Legion' (*Het Belgisch Legioen* in Dutch and *Légion belge* in French), later renamed 'Army of Belgium' (*Leger van België* in Dutch and *Armée*

de Belgique in French), before adopting its final name on 1 June 1944, was one of many resistance organisations in Belgium between 1940 and 1944. All but one of the organisations sanctioned by the Belgian government in exile in London were controlled by the Ministry of Justice through the Belgian State Security in coordination with British agencies such as the SOE. The Secret Army was controlled by the Belgian Ministry of Defence. It was designed to operate as uniformed lawful belligerents as defined by the regulations respecting the laws and customs of war on land, according to which the laws, rights, and duties of war apply not only to armies but also to militia and volunteer corps fulfilling the following conditions: to be commanded by a person responsible for his subordinates; to have a fixed distinctive emblem recognisable at a distance; to carry arms openly; and to conduct their operations in accordance with the laws and customs of war. Although both Belgium and Germany had ratified the IV Convention of The Hague of 1907, German forces generally did not respect the legal status of the Secret Army. Since February 1944, the organisation had been under the command of Lieutenant General Pire. In early 1944, following the latest territorial reorganisation for its operations, Belgium was divided into five zones, which in turn were subdivided into sectors and groups. Zone I comprised the Province of Hainaut and the adjacent area of the Province of Namur between the rivers Sambre and Meuse. Zone II consisted of the provinces of Antwerp and Limburg. Zone III consisted of the provinces of West Flanders and East Flanders. Zone IV comprised the Province of Brabant (which included the capital, Brussels), part of the Province of Liège on the left bank of the Meuse river and part of the province of Namur north of the Sambre and Meuse rivers. Zone V comprised the Province of Luxembourg and part of the provinces of Liège and Namur east of the Sambre and Meuse and was divided into seven sectors. In Sector 5, a staff and four 'groups' ('A', 'B', 'C' and 'D') were active. See: Colonel e.r. Victor Marquet, *Contribution à l'histoire de l'Armée Secrète 1940-1944, deuxième partie – Armée de Belgique - Armée Secrète 1943-1944, fascicule V – l'organisation,* Pygmalion, Brussels, pp. 230-1, 306; Henri Bernard, *La Résistance 1940-1945*, La Renaissance du Livre, Brussels, 1968, p. 108; Freddy Bernier, *La résistance et l'Armée secrète en Condroz Namurois 1940-1945, partie I - généralités, 2017, pp. 2-5; Convention (IV) respecting the Laws and Customs of War on Land and its annex: Regulations concerning the Laws and Customs of War on Land,* The Hague, 18 October 1907.

14 *Operation Noah – Rapport de Lieutenant Renkin*, op. cit.

15 Temmerman, op. cit., p. 152.

16 Patchett: commonly used name for the British Sterling submachine gun, named after its designer, George Patchett; introduced into service in 1944 and incorporating improvements over the Sten gun such as a more comfortable stock, pistol grip and full-length ventilated handguard; very few Sterlings were used in combat during the war; see: Leroy Thompson, *The Sten Gun,* Osprey, Oxford, 2012, pp. 73-4; Hugues Wenkin, *Un objet: la mitraillette Patchett*, in: *Comité scientifique Mook 1944, 1944 - La Wehrmacht insaisissable*, Editions Weyrich, Brussels, 2022, pp. 38-9.

17 After the war, Renkin's weapon, marked with the number '032', was added to the collection of the Royal Museum of the Armed Forces and Military History in Brussels.

18 *Operation Noah – Rapport de Lieutenant Renkin*, op. cit.

19 Louis Barthélemy, letter dated 16 November 1970, Belgian SAS archives, SGRS-S/CA, Evere.

20 *Operation Noah – Rapport de Lieutenant Renkin*, op. cit.

21 Daniel Ryelandt, *Chasseurs Ardennais dans le Maquis, La vie et l'action d'un groupe de l'A.S. 43-44*, Editions de « La Dryade », Vieux-Virton, 1969, p. 90.

22 Marquet, *Entre Bocq et Semois*, op. cit., p. 185.

23 *Operation Noah – Rapport de Lieutenant Renkin*, op. cit.

24 Louis Barthélemy, letter dated 22 November 1971, Belgian SAS archives, SGRS-S/CA, Evere.

25 Daniel Ryelandt, letter dated 19 November 1970, Belgian SAS archives, SGRS-S/CA, Evere.

26 Edouard Blondeel, *Mémoires* (unpublished), Brussels, 1995.

27 The DZ was located some 1,300 yards north of Rienne. Its previous names were 'Grenadier' and 'Géranium'. Although most DZ names in the area had been changed twice by August 1944, the original DZ names were still used in many accounts. See: Marquet, Contribution à l'histoire de l'Armée Secrète 1940-1944, deuxième partie, fascicule V, op. cit., pp. 288-93; Colonel e.r. Victor Marquet, *Contribution à l'histoire de l'Armée Secrète 1940-1944, deuxième partie – Armée de Belgique - Armée Secrète 1943-1944, fascicule VI – l'action*, Pygmalion, Brussels, p. 540.

28 TNA: AIR-27-2583, pp. 397-399, and TNA: AIR-27-1644, p. 108.

29 d'Oultremont, Van Broekhuyzen and Van Haezendonck had been transferred from the SOE shortly before.

30 Blondeel, op. cit.

31 The *Gendarmerie* was a Belgian police force which existed from the independence of Belgium in 1830 as a military organisation. During the German occupation of 1940-44, its activities – under German control – were severely limited, mainly to maintain law and order in accordance with existing Belgian civil law. Many gendarmes actively supported the resistance or were active members of a resistance movement. In 1992, the *Gendarmerie* was transformed into a civilian police force, and in 2001, it was disbanded, its personnel being absorbed in the newly established integrated police (with a federal and a local level).

32 Georges d'Oultremont, *Mémoires* (unpublished).

33 Visible but not named on War Office 1:50000 and 1:100000 maps and spelled 'Daucis' by Marquet (Marquet, *Entre Bocq et Semois*, op. cit., p. 160).

34 Capt Blondeel, op. cit.

35 The DZ's centre was located some 1,400 yards south-south-west of the church of Bourseigne-Neuve. See: Marquet, *Entre Bocq et Semois*, op. cit., p. 156 ; Marquet, *Contribution à l'histoire de l'Armée Secrète 1940-1944, deuxième partie – fascicule VI*, op. cit., p. 540.

36 TNA: AIR-27-1651, pp. 421-4 and TNA: AIR-27-2159-10, p. 79.

37 Capt MacBef (Lieutenant Debefve), *Report on Operation 'Noah'*, Belgian SAS archives, SGRS-S/CA, Evere.

38 TNA: AIR-27-1651, pp. 421-4.

39 TNA: AIR-27-2159-10, p. 36.

40 Capt Blondeel, op. cit.

41 Capt MacBef, op. cit.

42 Capt Blondeel, op. cit.

43 Capt MacBef, op. cit.

44 *Operation Noah – Rapport de Lieutenant Renkin,* op. cit.

45 Capt Blondeel, op. cit.

46 PIAT: acronym for 'projector, infantry, anti-tank', a British man-portable spring-action anti-tank weapon system which launched a hollow charge anti-tank projectile, with an effective range of around 100 yards. See: Matthew Moss, *The PIAT - Britain's anti-tank weapon of World War II*, Osprey Publishing, Oxford, 2020.

47 Bazooka: common name for different variants of American portable recoilless rocket launchers which fired 3.26-inch rockets for the models issued during the Second World War, including high-explosive anti-tank rockets, with an effective range of about 250 yards. See: Gordon L. Rottman, *The Bazooka*, Osprey Publishing, Oxford, 2012.

48 *Operation Noah – Rapport de Lieutenant Renkin*, op. cit.

49 Hand grenade No. 75, aka 'Hawkins grenade': a British anti-vehicle grenade with a volume of about a pint and a flat rectangular can shape with rounded corners, intended to be used as a hasty mine that could be laid or thrown and activated by the pressure caused by the vehicle running over the grenade; see: Gordon L. Rottman, *The Hand Grenade*, Osprey Publishing, Oxford, 2015, pp. 58-60.

50 Capt MacBef, op. cit.

51 Capt Blondeel, op. cit.

52 Capt MacBef, op. cit.

53 Marquet, *Contribution à l'histoire de l'Armée Secrète 1940-1944, deuxième partie – fascicule VI*, op. cit., p. 541.

54 1st lieutenant, acting captain.

55 Capt MONRO (Lt LIMBOSCH), MO [medical officer], *Report on Operation "NOAH"*, Belgian SAS archives, SGRS-S/CA, Evere.

56 TNA: AIR-27-1652, p. 31-33 and TNA AIR-27-2159-12, p. 87. Note that the RAF report mentioned a troop load of five persons between both aircraft.

57 Capt MacBef, op. cit.

58 *Emile Debevfe ou la grande épopée des SAS*, in: Jo Gérard, Hervé Gérard &

Gustave Rens, *Se battre pour la Belgique 1940 – 1945*, Editions J.M. Collet, Brussels, 1984, p. 352.

59 Capt MacBef, op. cit.

60 *Operation Noah – Rapport de Lieutenant Renkin*, op. cit.

61 MG 34: crew-served and belt or drum-fed German medium machine gun using 7.92 mm x 57 mm rounds and used as section-level machine gun during the war; see: Chris McNab, *MG 34 and MG 42 Machine Guns*, Osprey Publishing, Oxford, 2012.

62 Sir Hugh Fraser was commissioned into the Lovat Scouts before the Second World War and served with E Squadron, GHQ Liaison Regiment (aka Phantom), Royal Armoured Corps in 1943 and with F Squadron (attached to the SAS Brigade) of the same regiment in 1944. Later in the war, he joined MI9 and was awarded an MBE. He was the younger brother of Simon Fraser, 15th Lord Lovat, who commanded the 1st Special Service Brigade on D-Day. He became a Member of Parliament for the Conservative Party after the war and survived an IRA assassination attempt in 1975.

63 Bois de Saint-Jean (as spelled on War Office maps) is also known as Bois Saint-Jean. Currently, Bois Saint-Jean is the name of an entire area of private property, including forest, ponds, clearings, pastures and a castle. The latter was marked as a farm on War Office maps.

64 Capt Blondeel, op. cit.

65 Special Force Headquarters (SFHQ) was the new name of SOE/SO, from May 1944. For their operations in northwestern Europe, the British Special Operations Executive (SOE) and the Special Operations (SO) Branch of the American Office of Strategic Services (OSS) had been working as a fused headquarters in London, under the formal title of 'SOE/SO'. Given its important role in the upcoming D-Day operations and beyond, it was decided that the headquarters needed a new (cover) name which could be used openly, SOE's name and existence still being classified at the time. SFHQ was directly subordinate to Eisenhower's Supreme Headquarters Allied Expeditionary Force (SHAEF). Note that 'Force' was used in its singular form.

66 *SAS Brigade Operation Instruction No. 51* dated 31 August 1944, Belgian SAS archives, SGRS-S/CA, Evere.

67 Lieutenant Martin (2nd Lieutenant Mathijs), *Report on Operation "Brutus"*, Belgian SAS archives, SGRS-S/CA, Evere.

68 Lambert Grailet, *Première mondiale pour le V-2 sur Paris,* auto-édition, Liège, 1996, pp. 16-42.

69 Steven J. Zaloga, *German V-weapon sites 1943-45*, Osprey Publishing, Oxford, 2007, p. 55.

70 TNA: AIR-27-1167-6, September 1944, p. 161. The operations record book of the 196th Squadron mentions thirteen troops to be dropped by Stirling LJ888. It also mentions another mission, by Stirling LJ272, on the same DZ during the same time frame, which was unsuccessful as the DZ could not be located. In his report, Delagaye mentioned that Heilporn had to be dropped fifteen minutes before and would have

to provide a recognition signal for Delagaye's party. Eventually, Heilporn would be parachuted a few days later as part of Operation 'Bergbang'.

71 Operation 'Brutus' load manifests, Belgian SAS archives, SGRS-S/CA, Evere.

72 Lewes bomb: an innovative lightweight explosive device that combined high-explosive and incendiary properties, invented by Lieutenant John 'Jock' Lewes, one of the original members of L Detachment SAS.

73 CSM Delagaye, *Report on Operation 'Brutus'*, Belgian SAS archives, SGRS-S/CA, Evere.

74 Lieutenant Martin, op. cit.

75 CSM Delagaye, op. cit.

76 Conflicting sources exist about the location of German units, which is hardly surprising as the reports on a rapidly changing situation during the hasty German withdrawal likely resulted in much confusion on both sides. According to the daily situation maps of the Allied 12th Army Group, the 1st SS Armoured Division's location was assessed as being north of Tongeren, 38 miles north of Amonines, on the 9th at noon, and in the Maastricht area, 40 miles north of Amonines, on the 10th at noon. According to German situation maps, parts of the division were in the La Gleize – Stoumont area, 15 miles northeast of Amonines, on the 9th, while a battle group from the 12th SS Armoured Division likely had Amonines in its sector, its map position being (up to) 10-12 miles east of Amonines, which according to the map was now lying on the forward edge of the (more or less north-south oriented) German defensive lines, which had moved 10 miles further east on the 10th. Both armoured divisions were part of the I SS Armoured Corps. See: Library of Congress Geography and Map *Division, HQ Twelfth Army Group situation maps*, 9 and 10 September 1944, Library of Congress control numbers 2004629134 and 2004629135, Washington, D.C.; Lage Frankreich, Stand 9.9.44 and 10.9.44, Federal Archives, Federal Republic of Germany (BArch) RH 2-KART/11001 and RH 2-KART/11004.

77 Lieutenant Martin, op. cit.

78 CSM Delagaye, op. cit.

79 TNA: AIR-27-2159-12, September 1944, p. 5.

80 TNA: AIR-27-1652, pp. 68-69 and TNA: AIR-27-1649, September 1944, p. 4.

81 Operation 'Brutus' load manifests, op. cit.

82 Capt Dulait, *Report on Operation "Brutus"*, Belgian SAS archives, SGRS-S/CA, Evere.

83 SSM Schils, *Report on Operation "Brutus"*, Belgian SAS archives, SGRS-S/CA, Evere.

84 Capt Dulait, op. cit.

85 Lieutenant Martin, op. cit.

86 Capt Dulait, op. cit.

87 CSM Delagaye, op. cit.

88 Lieutenant Martin, op. cit.

89 SSM Schils, op. cit.

90 Lieutenant Martin, op. cit.

91 Spelled 'Hardwick' in the Belgian report, but most likely 'Hardwicke'. See note in chapter 7.

92 CSM Delagaye, op. cit.

93 Lieutenant Martin, op. cit.

94 Major H. Fraser, *Report on Operation BRUTUS, Belgian ARDENNES, 2-18 Sep 44*, Belgian SAS archives, SGRS-S/CA, Evere.

95 SAS Brigade operation instruction No. 47 dated 25 August 1944, Belgian SAS archives, SGRS-S/CA, Evere.

96 Temmerman (op. cit., p. 190) mentioned Geysens instead. The official reports used either first names or cover names, and both men had the same first name. On the French version of Cassart's report in the Belgian SAS archives, Quirain's name was added in pencil, while his name and the corresponding regimental number had been typed on the original parachute manifest.

97 This refers to the interstate border between Germany and Belgium after the annexation of the eastern part of Belgium into the Greater German Reich. This was mainly German-speaking territory that had been transferred to Belgium after the First World War.

98 Captain P. Courtoy [Major Cassart], *Report on Operation 'Bergbang'*, Belgian SAS archives, SGRS-S/CA, Evere.

99 Captain John Hazel, article in FM – No. 36, 4 September 1969, Belgian SAS archives, SGRS-S/CA, Evere.

100 Captain Hazel, *Report on Operation BERGBANG*, Belgian SAS archives, SGRS-S/CA, Evere.

101 Srgt. Parson (Srgt. Pus), *Report on Operation "Bergbang"*, Belgian SAS archives, SGRS-S/CA, Evere.

102 Temmerman, op. cit., p. 201.

103 Marquet, *Contribution à l'histoire de l'Armée Secrète 1940-1944, deuxième partie – fascicule VI*, op. cit., p. 543.

104 Captain Hazel, op. cit.

105 Srgt. Parson, op. cit.

106 Captain Hazel, op. cit.

107 Captain P. Courtoy, op. cit.

108 Ibid.

109 Wouter van den Brandhof, *Hitlers parachutistengeneraal - Kurt Student (1890-1978): een militaire biografie*, Uitgeverij Verloren, Hilversum, 2019, pp. 218-25.

110 *Verslagen van besprekingen van Sectie G8 (krijgsgeschiedenis) der generale Staf met Generaloberst Kurt Student en Generalleutnant Von Wülisch in het Bewarings- en Verblijfskamp Avegoor betreffende de inzet van het Luftlandekorps in Holland 1940*, Nederlands Instituut voor Militaire Historie, Den Haag, 'Von Sponeck' papieren, toegang 505, inventarisnummer 84.

111 Special Air Service Regimental Association, *SAS War Diary 1941-1945*, London, 2011.

112 2nd lieutenant, acting captain.

113 1st lieutenant, acting captain.

114 2nd Lieutenant Ghys, *Report on Operation "CALIBAN"*, Belgian SAS archives, SGRS-S/CA, Evere.

115 While Vandermeeren was listed (misspelt 'Vandermeren') on the passenger manifest, with an assigned parachute number, some post-war accounts questioned his participation in this operation. Neither the SAS reports nor the No. 196 Squadron's operations record book mentioned any occurrence of a person planned to jump who didn't, while one account reported he assisted in operating the radio. To add to the confusion, some sources also spelled his name 'Van der Meersch' or 'Vandermeersch'. See: Heemkring De Reengenoten - Meeuwen, *De oorlogsjaren in Ellikom, Gruitrode, Meeuwen, Neerglabbeek, Wijshagen, 1940-1945*, Meeuwen, 2004, pp. 277-9.

116 Operation Caliban load manifests, Belgian SAS archives, SGRS-S/CA, Evere.

117 TNA: AIR-27-1167-6, September 1944, p. 161. In the operations record book of No. 196 Squadron, the number of troops carried was listed as thirteen for each aircraft.

118 Post-war accounts listed varying numbers and different names in each aircraft. See: *Martin Peeters, Oorlog op en rond 't Lin – Belgische S.A.S-operatie Caliban*, Heemkundige Kring Peer, Peer, 1995, pp. 23-4, J. Israël, *Jean Melsens 1922-1944 – Het verhaal van een Belgische parachutist die stierf voor onze vrijheid*, Valkenswaard, 1996, p. 39, and Heemkring De Reengenoten, op. cit., pp. 276-7.

119 In the operations record book of No. 196 Squadron, the planned DZ mentioned for both aircraft was located some 12 miles south of the planned DZ mentioned in the SAS after-action report. The crews of both aircraft reported having difficulty finding the DZ, one specifying approximately an hour was spent on finding the DZ.

120 Serg-Maj. Jefferson [Verberckmoes], *Operation Caliban*, Belgian SAS archives, SGRS-S/CA, Evere.

121 Ghys, op. cit.

122 Not many details are provided in Verberkckmoes' after-action report, but he mentioned that all those Russians had been armed with Tommy guns and no. 36 grenades. Temmerman mentioned the escaped Russian prisoners of war had been working in the coal mines [several of which were present in the Province of Limburg] and, having escaped, requested to be armed by the SAS party, which, according to him, was refused, however. See: Temmerman, op. cit., p. 205.

123 Jefferson, op. cit.

124 Ghys, op. cit.

125 Jefferson, op. cit.

126 The White Brigade, renamed 'White Brigade (Fidelio)' during the liberation of Belgium, was one of the resistance organisations recognised by the Belgian Government. It had been created in Antwerp in 1940 but later expanded its activities to many other areas in the country, mainly in Flanders.

127 One-time pad: document containing an encryption key to be used only once, which, if generated and used correctly, cannot be broken.

128 Ghys, op. cit.

129 Bernard Kowarski, *Notes on Operation Caliban,* Belgian SAS archives, SGRS-S/CA, Evere, and Temmerman, op. cit., p. 207.

130 Temmerman, op. cit., pp. 209-10 .

131 Marc Daemen, *Interview with Martinus Loos,* dated 24 February 2020.

Chapter 6 – Working in Nazi-Occupied Territory in the Netherlands

1 Dwight D. Eisenhower, *Crusade in Europe*, Doubleday & Company, Baltimore, 1948, pp. 306-307.

2 Stephen Badsey, *Operation 'Market Garden'*, Osprey Publishing, London, 1993, pp. 27-9.

3 Notes from Gilbert-Sadi Kirschen, Belgian SAS archives, SGRS-S/CA, Evere.

4 Gilbert-Sadi Kirschen, *Six amis viendront ce soir,* Presses de Belgique, Brussels, 1982, pp. 90-3.

5 Lt G.S. Kirshen, *Report on Operation REGAN – FABIAN* (15 Sep 44 – 14 Mar 45), Belgian SAS archives, SGRS-S/CA, Evere.

6 Steven J. Zaloga, *German V-weapon sites 1943-45*, Osprey Publishing, Oxford, 2007, p. 55.

7 The RBZ was a portable receiver, introduced in 1943 by the Emerson Radio and Phonograph Corporation for the US Navy, but was also used by other organisations, including SOE, OSS and resistance groups for the reception of BBC broadcasts. The set contained two main elements, the actual receiver and a battery case, made from Bakelite.

8 Thompson: American submachine gun using .45" Automatic Colt Pistol cartridges; the M1928 Thompson was used by British forces from 1941 until it was replaced by the much cheaper Sten; the M1928A1 model featured a nearly vertical frontal grip and could be used with a fifty-round drum magazine or with straight twenty- or thirty-round magazines; later models (the M1 and M1A1) had a simpler construction, featuring a horizontal forward grip, and could no longer be used with a drum magazine;

see: Martin Pegler, *The Thompson Submachine Gun - From Prohibition Chicago to World War II,* Osprey, Oxford, 2010.

9 Lt G.S. Kirschen, op. cit.

10 Kirschen, op. cit., p. 95.

11 Notes from Kirschen, op. cit.

12 TNA: AIR-27-2586, pp. 119-21.

13 Dr. L. De Jong, *Het Koninkrijk der Nederlanden in de Tweede Wereldoorlog, Deel 10b, eerste helft*, Martinus Nijhoff, 's Gravenhage, 1981, p. 605.

14 Lt G.S. Kirschen, op. cit.

15 Martin Middlebrook, *Arnhem 1944 – The Airborne Battle*, 17-26 September, Pen & Sword, Barnsley, 2009, chapters 2, 11 and 12.

16 Liliane G. Maillard, *Sorn revisited, in: Mars and Minerva, The Journal of the Special Air Service*, Volume 3, No. 16, June 1978, pp. 9-10.

17 Lt G.S. Kirschen, op. cit.

18 Kirschen, op. cit., p. 104.

19 L/Cpl Regner, *Report on Operation 'Regan'*, Belgian SAS archives, SGRS-S/CA, Evere.

20 Robert J. Kershaw, *'It never snows in September' – The German View of Market-Garden and The Battle of Arnhem, September 1944,* Ian Allan Publishing, Hersham 2004, p. 78.

21 Ibid., p. 38.

22 Regner, op. cit.

23 Ken Ford, *Operation Market-Garden 1944 (2) - The British Airborne Missions*, Osprey Publishing, Oxford, 2016, pp. 84-5.

24 Kirschen, op. cit., p. 102-103.

25 Lt G.S. Kirschen, op. cit.

26 Kirschen, op. cit., p. 98.

27 Spelled 'Olyff' in Kirschen's report, but 'Olliff' in several other sources.

28 Lt G.S. Kirschen, op. cit.

29 Kirschen, op. cit., p.113.

30 Leo Heaps, *The Grey Goose of Arnhem - The Story of the Most Amazing Mass Escape of World War II,* Sapere Books, Leeds, 1976, p. 90.

31 Lt G.S. Kirschen, op. cit.

32 Heaps, op. cit., p. 146.

33 Intelligence School Number 9 (IS9): the more secret and executive branch of MI9, concerned with facilitating evasion and escape activities.

34 Heaps, op. cit., pp. 192-3.

35 Lt G.S. Kirschen, op. cit.

36 Major Digby Tatham Warter, DSO, *Dutch Courage and "Pegasus"*, Nabyuki, 1991, pp. 19-20.

37 Heaps, op. cit., p. 172.

38 Helen Fry, *MI9 – A History of the Secret Service for Escape and Evasion in World War Two*, Yale University Press, New Haven and London, 2020, p. 254.

39 Major Robert G. Gutjahr, *The Role of Jedburgh Teams on Operation Market Garden,* U.S. Army Command and General Staff College, Fort Leavenworth, 1990, p. 114.

40 Hawker Typhoon: single-seat, single-engine monoplane aircraft armed with four 20 mm cannons (for most models) originally introduced in 1941 as an interceptor, but transformed into a fighter-bomber from the end of 1942 and a rocket-equipped ground attack aircraft from 1943; the Typhoon could also carry supply containers for dropping supplies to SAS troops operating behind enemy lines; see: Chris Thomas, *Typhoon Wings of 2nd TAF 1943–45*, Osprey Publishing, Oxford, 2010, pp. 6-21, 45, 95.

41 Wouter van den Brandhof, *Hitlers parachutistengeneraal - Kurt Student (1890-1978): een militaire biografie,* Uitgeverij Verloren, Hilversum, 2019, pp. 253-6.

42 Kirschen, op. cit., pp. 125-7.

43 Beeldnummer 3714, oorlogsschade aan kasteel Wisch, Erfgoedcentrum Achterhoek en Liemers, Doetinchem, collectie 0946-3 (fotocollectie gemeente Wisch).

44 12 October 1944: seven Typhoons from No. 137 Squadron attacking Wisch Castle, Terborg, see: TNA: AIR 27/954/74, p. 209; 06 November 1944: twenty-seven Typhoons (twelve from No. 181 Squadron, eight from No. 182 Squadron (likely including one flown by the wing commander) and seven from No. 247 Squadron), see: TNA: AIR 27/1134/48, p. 159, TNA: AIR 27/1134/47, p. 156, TNA: AIR 27/1136/22, p. 168, TNA: AIR 27/148/30, p. 112 and TNA: AIR 27/1489/29, p. 107; 08 November: twelve Typhoons from No. 181 Squadron and eight from No. 182 Squadron (likely including one flown by the wing commander) (in addition, eight aircraft from No. 247 Squadron were mentioned in the No. 181 Squadron's records of events, but according to the No. 247 Squadron's operations record books, no operational missions were flown by the latter squadron on that day), see: TNA: AIR 27/1134/48, p. 159, TNA: AIR 27/1136/22, p. 168, TNA: AIR 27/1489/30, p. 113 and TNA: AIR 27/1489/29; 10 November 1944: eleven Typhoons from No. 181 Squadron, according to its operations record book's records of events, but omitted in the operations record book's summary of events of the same squadron (in addition, eight aircraft from No. 137 Squadron were mentioned in the No. 181 Squadron records of events, but according to the No. 137 Squadron's operations record books, no operational missions were flown by the latter squadron on that day, while this target was not mentioned in the No. 247 Squadron's operations record books for the same day), see: TNA: AIR 27/1134/47 p. 156, TNA: AIR 27/1134/48, p. 160, TNA: AIR 27/1489/29 p. 108, TNA: AIR 27/1489/30, p. 113, TNA: AIR 29/954/75 p. 214,

TNA: AIR 29/954/76 p. 219 and TNA: AIR 29/1489/29, p. 108; 11 November 1944: thirty-one Typhoons (eight from No. 137 Squadron, eleven from No. 181 Squadron and twelve from No. 247 Squadron), see: TNA: AIR 27/954/76, p. 219, TNA: AIR 27/1134/47 p. 156 and TNA: AIR 27/1489/29, p. 108; 15 December 1944: fifteen Typhoons (eleven from No. 181 Squadron, four from No. 182 Squadron), see: TNA: AIR 27/1134/49, p. 163, TNA: AIR 27/1134/50, p. 166, TNA: AIR 27/1136/23, p. 173, TNA: AIR 27/1136/24, p. 177.

45 Chris Thomas, *Typhoon Wings of 2nd TAF 1943–45*, Osprey Publishing, Oxford, 2010, p. 89.

46 Airey Neave, *Saturday at M.I.9: The Classic Account of the WW2 Allied Escape Organisation*, Pen & Sword, Barnsley, 2010, pp. 292-3.

47 Tatham Warter, op. cit., pp. 29-36.

48 Airey Neave, *They Have Their Exits,* Pen & Sword, Barnsley, 2002, p. 154.

49 Lt G.S. Kirschen, op. cit.

50 Elsa Caspers, *To Save a Life – Memoirs of a Dutch Resistance Courier,* Deirdre McDonald Books, London, 1995, p. 54.

51 Based on a comparison of conflicting sources, this was likely in Scherpenzeel.

52 *Sicherheitsdienst* (SD) ('Security Service'): political intelligence service of the German Nazi party, part of the *Allgemeine-SS*. See: Robin Lumsden, *The Allgemeine-SS*, Oxford, 1993, p. 39.

53 Lt G.S. Kirschen, op. cit.

54 Caspers, op. cit., p. 54.

55 Lt G.S. Kirschen, op. cit.

56 De Jong, op. cit., pp. 625-7.

57 Middlebrook, op. cit., p. 438.

58 Kirschen, op. cit., p. 150.

59 Gordon Williamson, *German Special Forces of World War II,* Osprey Publishing, Oxford, 2009, p. 53.

60 Lt G.S. Kirschen, op. cit.

61 Neave, *Saturday at M.I.9*, pp. 287.

62 Lt G.S. Kirschen, op. cit.

63 General Sir John Hackett, *I was a stranger*, Pimlico, London, 1999, pp. 96, 151-96.

64 Lt G.S. Kirschen, op. cit.

65 Eddy de Roever, *Zij sprongen bij maanlicht – De geschiedenis van het Bureau Bijzondere Opdrachten en de agenten, Londen 1944-1945,* Hollandia, Baarn, 1986, p. 105.

66 Frans Hals, *Report on the activities of Frans Hals from the 23rd of June 1943 till 18th April 1945*, 22 July 1945, National Archives, College Park, Maryland.

67 *Feldgendarmerie:* police unit belonging to the regular German army. See: Gordon

Williamson, *German Military Police Units 1939–45*, Osprey Publishing, Oxford, 1989, pp. 6-12.

68 Theodoor Alexander Boeree, *De Kroniek van Ede en omgeving gedurende de vijf jaren van de Duitsche bezetting, Ede*, June 1946, pp. 280-3.

69 Le 1er soldat Temmerman, *Mission en Angleterre du 18-11-44 au 19-2-1945*, 25 February 1945, Belgian SAS archives, SGRS-S/CA, Evere.

70 Kirschen, op. cit., pp. 154-5 .

71 de Roever, op. cit., pp. 106-107.

72 In one of his books, Temmerman noted 13 December as the insertion date. The report from the aircrew of a Stirling of No. 299 Squadron RAF stated 11 December as the date for a flight in support of Operation 'Fabian', mentioning a single passenger, bad weather preventing his insertion, and reporting the jumper was sick, details which correlate to Temmerman's description of events. See: TNA: AIR-27-2586, pp. 531-2.

73 Le 1er soldat Temmerman, op. cit.

74 Jean Temmerman, *Les parachutistes belges 1942-1945 - Acrobates sans importance,* Edition DVB, Liège, 1999, pp. 227-9.

75 Boeree, op. cit., p. 283.

76 de Roever, op. cit., p. 107.

77 Theodoor Alexander Boeree, *De Kroniek van Ede en omgeving gedurende de vijf jaren van de Duitsche bezetting*, Ede, June 1946, pp. 279-88.

78 *Sicherheitspolizei und Sicherheitsdienst:* the German police organisation established in 1939 under SS control combining the *Sicherheitspolizei* and the *Sicherheitsdienst.* The *Sicherheitspolizei* (security police, abbreviated '*Sipo*') consisted of the *Geheime Staatspolizei* (secret state police, abbreviated '*Gestapo*', the political police from Nazi Germany) and the *Kriminalpolizei* (criminal police, abbreviated '*Kripo*'). See: Robin Lumsden, *The Allgemeine-SS*, Oxford, 1993, pp. 39-40.

79 Wolter Noordman, *De vijftien executies - Liquidaties aan de IJsseloever, april 1945*, Utrecht, 2015, pp. 15, 30-1.

80 Lt Debefve, *Opération "Gobbo"*, Belgian SAS archives, SGRS-S/CA, Evere.

81 R.A. Blatt, *Report on Operation Gobbo in Holland from Sept 44 until April 45*, London 21 Apr 45, Belgian SAS archives, SGRS-S/CA, Evere.

82 Rudy A. Blatt, *To Live…You Fight – A War Diary*, New York, 1960.

83 While Debefve's and Blatt's accounts stated they were parachuted on 26 September, it is not excluded the insertion happened on the night of 26-27 September, with the actual drop early on 27 September. According to the No. 644 Squadron's records, Halifax LL301 executed a mission in support of Operation 'Portia', dropping six troops and two panniers. The location of the assumed DZ being erroneous, the final leg of the reported flight route pointed towards Westerbork. See TNA: AIR-27-2159-12, p. 107.

84 There are slight differences between Debefve's and Blatt's reports. Debefve

mentioned Dr Assen, but Blatt mentioned Van der Bosch instead. Blatt's war diary clarified that Dr Van den Bosch was living in the city of Assen.

85 De Jong, op. cit., p. 688.

86 Arthur Seyss-Inquart, an Austrian Nazi who was appointed *Reichskommissar für die besetzten niederländischen Gebiete* (Reich Commissioner for the Occupied Dutch Territories) and later trialled and hanged as a war criminal in Nuremberg.

87 *Ordnungspolizei* (law and order police), abbreviated '*Orpo*': national police force under the Ministry of the Interior in Nazi Germany, conducting police duties in Germany and rear area security duties in German-occupied territories. Also known by their nickname of *Grüne Polizei* (green police), because of their green uniforms. See: Gordon Williamson, *World War II German Police Units*, Oxford, 2006, pp. 4, 6-16; Gordon Williamson, *German Security and Police Soldier 1939-45*, Oxford, 2002, pp. 15-24. For a detailed study of *Ordnungspolizei* in the Netherlands, see: Wolfgang Curilla, *Die deutsche Ordnungspolizei im westlichen Europa 1940-1945*, Schöningh/Brill, Paderborn, 2019, pp. 165-302.

88 Debefve, op. cit.

89 Debefve's report mentioned 21 October, but Blatt's report and war diary mentioned 25 October. Since this was Blatt's birthday, it is not unreasonable to assume he would have remembered it accurately.

90 Debefve, op. cit.

91 R.A. Blatt, op. cit.

92 Rudy A. Blatt, op. cit., pp. 262-90.

93 Debefve, op. cit.

94 Ben Buunk (junior), *Ben Buunk alias "Fopkonijn"*, Breda, 2018, p.55.

95 Debefve, op. cit.

96 Jelle Hooiveld, *Operatie Jedburgh – Geheime geallieerde missies in Nederland 1944-1945*, Boom, The Hague, 2014, p. 7.

97 *Marechaussee*: Dutch military police force, which had been demilitarised by the Germans and integrated into the civil police during the occupation of the Netherlands. The Germans also changed its original name '*Koninklijke Marechaussee*', removing 'Koninklijke' ('Royal').

98 Rudolf Groenewout, *1st report about mission and weapons* instructions to the *underground movement in Friesland*, 24 April 1945 (main body) and 1 June 1945 (annex), Belgian SAS archives, SGRS-S/CA, Evere.

99 Different sources show different ranks.

100 Groenewout, op. cit.

Chapter 7 – The Belgian SAS Squadron in the Battle of the Ardennes

1 Dwight D. Eisenhower, *Crusade in Europe*, Doubleday & Company, Baltimore, 1948, pp. 326-40.

2 Edouard Blondeel, *Mémoires* (unpublished), Brussels, 1995.

3 A human performance programme developed by French Navy officer Georges Hébert.

4 Private 9046, *Er was eens...*, in: *SAS Veterans News*, 3/2002, pp. 23-4.

5 Willy Deheusch, *Recueil des sauts effectués par les parachutistes belges à l'entraînement et en opérations*, pp. 51-2 (unpublished).

6 Hamish Ross, *Paddy Mayne – Lt Col Blair 'Paddy' Mayne, 1 SAS Regiment*, Sutton Publishing, 2004, pp. 73-94.

7 Fitzroy Maclean, *Eastern Approaches*, Penguin Books, London, 1991, pp. 226-62.

8 Damien Lewis, *SAS Brothers in Arms – Churchill's Desperadoes: Blood-and-Guts Defiance at Britain's Darkest Hour*, Quercus, London, 2022, pp. 188-90.

9 Malcolm James, *Born of the Desert: With the SAS in North Africa*, Collins, London, 1945, pp. 319, 245-6.

10 TNA: WO 373/46/35.

11 Blondeel, op. cit.

12 *Ordre de bataille du 15 décembre 1944*, Belgian SAS archives, SGRS-S/CA, Evere.

13 Blondeel, op. cit.

14 James R. Arnold, *Ardennes 1944, Hitler's last gamble in the West*, Osprey Publishing, London, 1990, p. 31.

15 Sometimes referred to as the 6th SS Armoured Army, which seems to be an unofficial designation. See: Danny S. Parker, *Hitler's Ardennes Offensive: The German View of the Battle of the Bulge*, Skyhorse Publishing, New York, 1997, p. 21.

16 Bruce Quarrie, *The Ardennes Offensive, VII Panzer Armee*, Northern Sector, Osprey Publishing, Oxford, 1999, pp. 10, 21, 27, 63, 79.

17 Bruce Quarrie, *The Ardennes Offensive, V Panzer Armee, Central Sector,* Osprey Publishing, Oxford, 2000, pp. 11-12, 14-15, 58, 75, 90-1.

8 Bruce Quarrie, *The Ardennes Offensive, I Armee and VII Armee, Southern Sector*, Osprey Publishing, Oxford, 2001, pp. 10-12, 15-16, 51-2.

19 Marvin D. Kays, *Weather effects during the battle of the Bulge and the Normandy invasion*, US Army Electronics Research and Development Command, White Sands Missile Range, 1982, p. 10.

20 Omar N. Bradley and Clay Blair, *A General's Life, An Autobiography by General of the Army Omar N. Bradley*, Simon & Schuster, New York, 1983, pp. 356-63.

21 Steven J. Zaloga, *Battle of the Bulge 1944 (1): St Vith and the Northern Shoulder,* Osprey Publishing, Oxford, 2003, pp. 42-6, 92.

22 Steven J. Zaloga, *Battle of the Bulge 1944 (2): Bastogne*, Osprey Publishing, Oxford, 2004, pp. 33-4.

23 Bernard Law Montgomery, *The Memoirs of Field-Marshal the Viscount Montgomery of El Alamein, K.G.*, The World Publishing Company, Cleveland, 1958, pp. 276-7.

24 Robert Oulds, *Counterattack, Montgomery and the Battle of the Bulge*, The Bruges Group, 2023, p. 31.

25 Belgian sources often misspell his name as 'Hardwick'.

26 Captain Radino, *Report on operations PRE-REGENT*, Belgian SAS archives, SGRS-S/CA, Evere, p. 1.

27 Jean Temmerman, *Les parachutistes belges 1942-1945 - Acrobates sans importance*, Edition DVB, Liège, 1999, p. 253.

28 Radino, op. cit., pp. 1-2.

29 Montgomery, op. cit., p. 276.

30 Bruce Quarrie, *The Ardennes Offensive, US VII & VIII Corps and British XXX Corps, Central Sector*, Osprey Publishing, Oxford 2000, p. 10.

31 Eisenhower, op. cit., p. 355.

32 Radino, op. cit., p. 2.

33 Major Lepine, *Report on Operation 'Haggard'*, Belgian SAS archives, SGRS-S/CA, Evere, p. 4.

34 Antony Beevor, *Ardennes 1944: The Battle of the Bulge*, Viking, New York, 2015, p. 94.

35 Jean-Paul Pallud, *Ardennes 1944 - Peiper & Skorzeny*, Osprey Publishing, London, 1987, p. 3.

36 United States Forces European Theater (USFET) Interrogation Center, *BATTLE OF THE ARDENNES – Interview with Lieutenant Colonel OTTO SKORZENY, Commanding Officer for Operation "Greif"*, European Theater Historical Interrogation (ETHINT) Series #12, Oberusel, 12 August 1945, pp. 3-5.

37 Pallud, op. cit., p. 6.

38 Ibid., p. 8-9.

39 Stephen A. Hart, *Panther Medium Tank 1942–45*, Osprey Publishing, Oxford, 2003, p. 39.

40 USFET Interrogation Center, op. cit., pp. 3, 6-8.

41 Radino, op. cit., p. 2.

42 Georges d'Oultremont, *La Bataille des Ardennes*, in: *La Libre Belgique*, 26 December 1969.

43 Radino's report states these were part of the 'U.S. 84th Armd [Armored] Div[ision]'. It may have been the lead elements of the 84th Infantry Division, which were not

withdrawing, but on their way to Marche-en-Fammenne; see: Bruce Quarrie, *The Ardennes Offensive, US VII & VIII Corps and British XXX Corps*, p. 33.

44 Radino, op. cit., pp. 3-4.

45 Blondeel, op. cit.

46 Jeffrey Jarkowsky, *German Special Operations in the 1944 Ardennes Offensive*, U. S. Army Command and General Staff College, Fort Leavenworth, Kansas, 1994, pp. 19-20.

47 Peter Caddick-Adams, *Snow and Steel - Battle of the Bulge 1944-45*, Oxford University Press, Oxford, 2015, p. 353-4.

48 James L. Kennedy Jr., *The Failure of German Logistics during the Ardennes Offensive of 1944*, U. S. Army Command and General Staff College, Fort Leavenworth, Kansas, 2000, p. 92.

49 Samuel W. Mitcham Jr., *Panzers in Winter: Hitler's Army and the Battle of the Bulge*, Praeger Security International, Westport, 2006, p. 76.

50 Parker, op. cit., p. 42.

51 Zaloga, *Battle of the Bulge 1944* (2), op. cit., pp. 81-3.

52 Eisenhower, op. cit., pp. 358-60.

53 Bruce Quarrie, *The Ardennes Offensive, US III & XII Corps, Southern Sector*, Osprey Publishing, Oxford, 2001, p. 20.

54 *Report on Operation REGENT I*, Belgian SAS archives, SGRS-S/CA, Evere.

55 Zaloga, op. cit., p. 86.

56 Christer Bergström, *The Ardennes 1944-1945 - Hitler's Winter Offensive*, Casemate, Oxford, 2014, p. 303.

57 Beevor, op. cit., p. 314.

58 Tactical Investigation Directorate, War Office, *Operations of 30 (Br) Corps during the German Attack in the Ardennes, December 1944 – January 1945*, TNA: WO 205/1130, pp. 7-8.

59 *Report on Operation REGENT I*, op. cit.

60 Temmerman, op. cit., p. 263.

61 The report specifically mentioned "by one or two anti-tank guns or by two tanks with 88 mm guns". Since it is next to impossible to identify the calibre of rounds when fired upon by a gun that cannot be positively identified, this assumption was probably based on what was likely to be encountered. If it was an 88 mm gun, it was most probably either a towed 88 mm anti-aircraft gun (in the anti-tank role) from the divisional anti-aircraft artillery battalion, or a *Jagdpanther* (a specific type of tank destroyer, i.e. a self-propelled anti-tank gun) from the 559th Heavy Anti-Tank Battalion which was attached to the *Panzer Lehr* Division. The only tanks having an 88 mm gun were the Tiger I and Tiger II, none of which were found in units assigned to the 5th Armoured Army, so this possibility has to be excluded. See: Steven J. Zaloga,

Tanks in the Battle of the Bulge, Osprey Publishing, Oxford, 2020, p. 17; Pier Paolo Battistelli, *Panzer Divisions 1944–45*, Osprey Publishing, Oxford, 2009, pp. 13, 39.

62 In the overall after-action report, Romnée's patrol was covered twice, with one version (by an unspecified author) mentioning 30 December, and Romnée's own undated report being integrated after the events of 31 December. This confusion resulted in some authors reporting the events on 31 December. Since the reported timeline coincided with the actions of both the 'Lion' and 'Tiger' patrols in the same area, but neither of those made any reference to Romnée's patrol nor did Romnée mention having seen or heard any action by the other two patrols, it must be concluded that 30 December was the correct date.

63 Report on Operation REGENT I, op. cit.

64 d'Oultremont, op. cit.

65 Spelled as Tiène des Pôtis on War Office maps, but likely a phonetic transcription error of Tienne des Potis, as this area is known locally. In the local dialect in the southern part of the Belgian Ardennes and in the French Ardennes, 'tienne' means 'slope', 'hillock' or 'mound'.

66 TNA: WO 373/153/62.

67 Report on Operation REGENT I, op. cit.

68 Quarrie, *The Ardennes Offensive, US VII & VIII Corps and British XXX Corps*, op. cit., p. 91.

69 *Report on Operation REGENT I*, op. cit.

70 Field Marshal The Viscount Montgomery of Alamein, *Normandy to the Baltic – A personal account of the conquest of Germany*, Printing and Stationery Service British Army of the Rhine, 1946, p. 223.

71 Tactical Investigation Directorate, op. cit., p. 13.

72 13th (Lancashire) Battalion, The Parachute Regiment, *War Diary*, January 1945, in: S.A.S. Veterans News, No. 4/89, Brussels, 1989, p. 36.

73 Major Jack Watson, OC 'A' Company, 13th (Lancashire) Battalion, The Parachute Regiment, quoted in: Ralph Bennett, *Commemoration Tour to Bure, in: Despatches, the magazine of the International Guild of Battlefield Guides*, Derby, Summer 2018, p. 24.

74 Tactical Investigation Directorate, op. cit., p. 13.

75 The report mentioned 'assault sections of engineers'. It is unclear whether this was a reporting mistake since reconnaissance regiments had no organic engineers. The assault troop of each reconnaissance squadron was equipped with a jeep and five 15 cwt lorries, while their three scout troops each had two carrier sections, equipped with three carriers per section. These were 'Universal Carriers', one of the variants of a series of open-top tracked vehicles, although the names 'Bren Carrier' or 'Bren Gun Carrier' were often used as a more popular interchangeable designation. There are no indications that these vehicles were used by the divisional Royal Engineers companies or squadrons. See: Richard Doherty, *The British Reconnaissance Corps in World War*

II, Osprey Publishing, Oxford, Oxford, 2007, p. 12; David Fletcher, *Universal Carrier 1936–48*, Osprey Publishing, Oxford, 2005, pp. 38, 42; The War Office, *The tactical employment of Armoured Car and Reconnaissance Regiments, Military Training Pamphlet No. 60, Part 4 – Reconnaissance Regiment,* March 1944.

76 *Report on Operation REGENT I*, op. cit.

77 13th (Lancashire) Battalion, op. cit., p. 37. A post-war monument at the Bure church mentions that sixty-one of those were killed. Casualties of the company of the 2nd Battalion, Oxfordshire and Buckinghamshire Light Infantry, which had reinforced the 13th Para Battalion during the battle, are not included, nor are those from the armoured units, who lost sixteen Sherman tanks.

78 Peter Schrijvers, *The Unknown Dead: Civilians in the Battle of the Bulge*, The University Press of Kentucky, Lexington, 2005, pp. 257-327.

79 The after-action report stated that it was impossible to hold Bure, the surrounding heights being in enemy hands and that a new operation would be tried north of the village, during which the Belgian squadron would have to protect the right flank. This is probably a misunderstanding since the decision to evacuate Bure seems to have been based on the fact that German forces had left Bure and were withdrawing from the area.

80 *Report on Operation REGENT I*, op. cit.

81 Damien Lewis, *SAS Forged in Hell: From Desert Rats to Dogs of War: The Mavericks who Made the SAS*, Quercus Publishing, London, 2023, pp. 283-349.

82 Aka Champlon-en-Ardenne, to differentiate from Champlon-Famenne.

83 *Report on Operation REGENT I*, op. cit.

84 Commission des crimes de guerre, Ministère de la Justice, Royaume de Belgique, *Les Crimes de Guerre commis pendant la contre-offensive de von Rundstedt dans les Ardennes - Décembre 1944 - Janvier 1945 - Bande*, George Thone, Liège, 1945, pp. 7-30.

85 1st Canadian Parachute Battalion, *War Diary – 1 Jan to 21 Jan 45*, Government of Canada archives, Reference RG24-C-3, volume number 15299, file number 1351.

86 Bernd Horn & Michel Wyczynski, *Canadian Airborne Forces since 1942*, Osprey Publishing, Oxford, 2006, p. 13.

87 Army Headquarters Historical Section, *The 1st Canadian Parachute Battalion in the Low Countries and in Germany - Final Operations (2 January - 18 February and 24 March - 5 May 1945)*, 1947, p. 7.

88 Lieutenant Colonel Bernd Horn and Michel Wyczynski, *Paras Versus the Reich: Canada's Paratroopers at War, 1942-1945*, The Dundurd Group, Toronto, 2003, p. 183.

89 1st Canadian Parachute Battalion, op. cit.

90 Schrijvers, op. cit., p. 329.

91 1st Canadian Parachute Battalion, op. cit.

92 Lieutenant-Colonel Bernd Horn and Michel Wyczynski, op. cit., p. 183.

93 *Report on Operation REGENT I*, op. cit.

94 Ibid.

95 Sgt Ryckx, *REPORT ON TASK CARRIED OUT WHEN ATTACHED TO 'C' SQN – 61st RECCE REGT*, Belgian SAS archives, SGRS-S/CA, Evere, p. 2.

96 *Report on Operation REGENT I*, op. cit.

97 British 6th Airborne Division, War Diary – January 1945, TNA: WO 171

98 *Report on Operation REGENT I*, op. cit.

99 Eisenhower, op. cit., p. 364

100 Field Marshal The Viscount Montgomery of Alamein, op. cit, p. 224.

101 Blondeel, op. cit.

102 Emile Genot, *Humour en rouge et vert : Témoignages au travers d'anecdotes et de faits divers, Brussels*, 2014, pp. 35-6.

Chapter 8 – The Belgian SAS Regiment Spearheading the Libération of the Netherlands

1 Dwight D. Eisenhower, *Crusade in Europe*, Doubleday & Company, Baltimore, 1948, pp. 366-74.

2 The *Weststellung* was a German defensive belt that provided defence in depth and amplified the original core provided by the *Westwall*. While the latter covered about 535 miles of frontier, the *Weststellung* covered a front of about 1,550 miles. It included 6,000 miles of new trenches, while the construction programme added about 22,000 new bunkers and gun positions to the remaining 8,000 *Westwall* bunkers, as well as over 80,000 combat positions. Its value declined after the defeat of the Germans in the Ardennes, partly due to the drastically diminished combat effectiveness of remaining German formations, but also due to an increasing rigidity in defensive tactics imposed by Hitler. Often, the erroneous name 'Siegfried Line' was used to designate either the *Westwall* or the more extensive defensive positions built in 1944-45. See: Steven J. Zaloga, *Defense of the Rhine 1944-45*, Osprey Publishing, Oxford, 2011.

3 Ken Ford, *The Rhineland 1945*, Osprey Publishing, Oxford, 2000, p. 20.

4 Colonel C.P. Stacey, *Operation "Veritable": The Winter Offensive between the Maas and the Rhine, 8 - 25 Feb 45 (preliminary report)*, 1946, p. 13.

5 Colonel C.P. Stacey, *Official History of the Canadian Army in the Second World War, Volume III, The Victory Campaign, The Operations in North-West Europe 1944-1945*, The Queen's Printer and Controller of Stationery, Ottawa, 1960, pp. 489-522.

6 The Roer ('Rur' in German) is a tributary of the Meuse (Maas) river, not to be confused with the similarly pronounced Ruhr, which is a tributary of the Rhine.

7 Charles B. MacDonald, *The Last Offensive,* Center of Military History, United States Army, Washington, D.C., 1993, pp. 137-256.

8 Russ Rodgers, *Nierstein and Oppenheim 1945 - Patton Bounces the Rhine,* Osprey Publishing, Oxford, 2020

9 Ken Ford, *The Rhine Crossings 1945*, Osprey Publishing, Oxford, 2007, pp. 13-90.

10 BArch, RH 19-XIII.

11 Jean Temmerman, *Les parachutistes belges 1942-1945 - Acrobates sans importance,* Edition DVB, Liège, 1999, p. 281.

12 Eddy Blondeel file, Belgian Armed Forces personnel register.

13 Willy Deheusch, *Recueil des sauts effectués par les parachutistes belges à l'entraînement et en opérations*, pp. 52-3 (unpublished).

14 *Report on Operation Larkswood*, Belgian SAS archives, SGRS S/CA, Evere.

15 Dakota: British designation of the American Douglas C-47 transport aircraft. Originally designed as a civil transport aircraft before the war, it was used as a troop and cargo transport aircraft and easily modified for parachute drops and glider towing. The Dakota could carry twenty fully equipped parachute troops who jumped out of a side door on the port side near the back of the aircraft. See: John Tanner, *RAF Airborne Forces Manual – The official Air Publications for RAF Paratroop Aircraft and Gliders, 1942-1946*, Hippocrene Books, New York, 1979, pp. 34-9.

16 W.D. Brown, Royal Aircraft Establishment, *X Type Parachutes: A Review of the Fatal Accidents at No. 1 P and G.T.S and their Causes*, Farnborough (undated), pp. 1-3.

17 Polys personnel file, National Archives 2 - Joseph Cuvelier repository, State Archives, Brussels.

18 R[é]giment de Parachutistes S.A.S., *Etat des militaires accident[é]s au cours des op[é]rations,* part of: Jean Temmerman, Documentation de recherche concernant les paracommandos belges, BE-A0547 / FICINV_2865, Study and Documentation Centre for War and Contemporary Society, State Archives, Brussels.

19 HQ SAS Troops, *Order of the Day, War Diary – March 1945*, dated 05 March 1945, TNA: WO 218/117.

20 Imperial War Museums, records B 15503, B 15509, B 15521 and B 15522.

21 Brigadier R.W. McLeod, *HQ SAS Tps/TS/40/1/DO*, Halstead, 13 March 1945.

22 General Sir Roderick McLeod, KCB, CBE, *'On Taking Command',* in: *Mars and Minerva, The Journal of the Special Air Service*, December 1994, pp. 3-4.

23 HQ SAS Troops, *War Diary – March 1945,* TNA: WO 218/117.

24 For a quick overview of these operations and Calvert's role in them, see: Tim Moreman, *Chindit 1942-45*, Osprey Publishing, Oxford, 2009; for an in-depth view, see his own account: Michael Calvert, *Prisoners of Hope*, Jonathan Cape, London, 1952.

25 Brigadier J. M. Calvert, *Operation AMHERST, Report by Brigadier J.M, CALVERT, DSO, Comd SAS Troops, on an airborne operation in North HOLLAND*, Nederlands Instituut voor Militaire Historie (NIMH), Den Haag, Bevrijding van Nederland, toegang 447, inventarisnummer 67.

26 Stacey, *The Victory Campaign*, op. cit., p. 545-6.

27 Calvert, op. cit.

28 *Report on Operation Larkswood*, op. cit.

29 Calvert, op. cit.

30 *Report on Operation Larkswood*, op. cit.

31 Headquarters, 4th Canadian Armoured Brigade, *War Diary from 1 April 1945 to 30 April 1945*, p. 8, RG24-C-3, vol 14054, file 950, Library and Archives Canada.

32 BArch, RH 19-XIII.

33 BArch, RH 20-22.

34 Steven J Zaloga, *Downfall 1945 - The Fall of Hitler's Third Reich*, Osprey Publishing, Oxford, 2016, p. 78.

35 HQ, 4th Canadian Armoured Brigade, op. cit., p. 9.

36 Headquarters, 5th Canadian Antitank Regiment, Royal Canadian Artillery, *War Diary from 1 Apr 45 to 30 Apr 45*, sheet no. 4, RG24-C-3, volume 4568, file 1992, Library and Archives Canada.

37 *Report on Operation Larkswood*, op. cit.

38 Message from Belgian SAS to 4 Div HQ with time indication 080015B, Belgian SAS archives, SGRS-S/CA, Evere.

39 *Report on Operation Larkswood*, op. cit.

40 Calvert, op. cit.

41 Two French SAS teams landed close to Dedemsvaart: 1st Lieutenant Sriber's 15-man team (4th SAS) landed 2.5 miles southeast of Dedemsvaart, 28 miles from its intended DZ, and 1st Lieutenant Baratin's 15-man team (3rd SAS) landed to the southwest of Dedemsvaart, 7 miles from its intended DZ. (See: Calvert, op. cit.; *Amherst* – C.R 2e RCP, NIMH, Bevrijding, 447, inv. 67) One account mentioned that it was Sriber's stick that was contacted by the Belgian SAS on 08 April (Karel Margry, *Operation 'Amherst' – French SAS in Holland,* 1945, in: *After the Battle*, No. 185, Essex, 2019, p. 35). Temmerman mentioned that the wounded man was 'Hentschke', likely referring to Gilbert Henstchké (Temmerman, op. cit., p. 302) but according to Moulié, Hentschké (misspelled 'Hentke' in his account) was wounded during operations in the area of Schoonloo as a rear gunner in Moulié's jeep, which had been retrieved in Coevorden (Robert Moulié, *Des SAS au 1er RPIMA*, Editions LBM, Paris, 2010, pp. 88-90). Prendergast (in Calvert's report) mentioned that the French SAS jeeps only arrived in Coevorden on 10 April (Calvert, op. cit.), so as far as the treatment of French wounded was concerned, the mission to Dedemsvaart on 8 April was most likely confused with the one near the Schoonloo area on the 11th.

42 *Report on Operation Larkswood*, op. cit.

43 General Staff – 2 Canadian Corps, *sitrep number 555 for period up to 081200B*, RG24-C-3, volume 13716, file 1701/GS, Library and Archives Canada.

44 Evan McGilvray & Janusz Jarzembowski, *First Polish Armoured Division 1938--47: A History*, Pen & Sword, Barnsley, 2022.

45 The M4A1 with 76 mm gun was designated as Sherman IIA in British service. In northwest Europe, the Sherman IIA was not used by British or other Commonwealth units, but it was used to re-equip the Polish 1st Armoured Division in late 1944 when supplies of the previously issued M4A4 (Sherman V in British designation) ran out. See: Steven J. Zaloga, *Sherman Medium Tank 1942–45*, Osprey Publishing, London, 1993, pp. 39-40; Steven J. Zaloga, M4 *(76mm) Sherman Medium Tank 1943–65*, Osprey Publishing, Oxford 2003, pp. 38-9.

46 According to the after-action report, 30 ton was the planning yardstick used. The M4A4, the previous Sherman model used by the Polish 1st Armoured Division, had an empty weight of approximately 66000 pounds (29.93 ton). With the new turret and gun, the M4 (76 mm) series were heavier than the 75 mm versions and with the added weight of fuel, ammunition, crew and other equipment and supplies carried, the combat weight would be significantly higher. Also, it was common for Polish Sherman IIA tanks to have additional track sections welded to the hull and turret for added protection. While the real protective value of track sections and sandbags was debatable, it added weight which put excessive strain on the suspension and power train. See: War Department, *Technical Manual No. 9-754*, Washington, 1943, p. 8; *Zaloga, M4 (76 mm) Sherman Medium Tank 1943–65*, op. cit., pp. 11, 24, 38.

47 Report on *Operation Larkswood*, op. cit.

48 Calvert, op. cit.

49 *Report on Operation Larkswood*, op. cit.

50 Main HQ II Canadian Corps, *War Diary from 1 Apr 45 to 30 Apr 45*, page 3, RG24-C-3, volume 13716, file 1701/GS, Library and Archives Canada.

51 HQ 1st Canadian Army, Operations log – 9 April 45, serial 54, RG24-C-3, volume 13638, file 1150/GS, Library and Archives Canada.

52 McGilvray & Jarzembowski (op. cit.) mentioned that already by 3 pm, which differs from the Belgian after-action report, the bridge had been taken by (Polish) dragoons and the Belgians, and only afterwards, an armoured reconnaissance squadron was sent to the bridge. This seems to indicate that the Bren Carriers belonged to the *10 pułk dragonów zmotoryzowanych* (10th Dragoon Regiment), an armoured infantry battalion from the 10th Armoured Cavalry Brigade.

53 *Report on Operation Larkswood*, op. cit.

54 David Fletcher & Richard Charley, *Cromwell Cruiser Tank 1942-50*, Osprey Publishing, Oxford, 2006, p. 24.

55 McGilvray & Jarzembowski, op. cit.

56 HQ 1st Canadian Army, op. cit., 9 April 1945, serial 152.

57 The fact that the bridge had been seized and a bridgehead established at the Oosterhesseler bridge was recorded in the 1st Canadian Army's operations log in the late morning of 10 April, having been reported by the 1st Polish Armoured Division

shortly before and relayed by a Phantom detachment. The Polish message did not mention the (earlier) date or time of the event and only mentioned the involvement of the 10th Mounted Rifle Regiment, while the same message also mentioned the Belgian SAS was now under the command of the Polish division. A Belgian situation report was recorded later on the 10th and mentioned the bridge had been seized the day before. See: HQ 1st Canadian Army, op. cit., 10 Apr 45, serials 44 and 143.

58 While the Belgian after-action report mentioned three jeeps, a situation report recorded in the 1st Canadian Army's operations log mentioned four jeeps (but no motorcycles). See: HQ 1st Canadian Army, op. cit., 10 Apr 45, serial 143.

59 *Report on Operation Larkswood*, op. cit.

60 Temmerman, op. cit., p. 307.

61 Temmerman, op. cit., pp. 307-308.

62 *Report on Operation Larkswood*, op. cit.

63 HQ 1st Canadian Army, op. cit., 10 Apr 45, serial 143.

64 *Report on Operation Larkswood*, op. cit.

65 HQ 1st Canadian Army, op. cit., 10 Apr 45, serial 44.

66 *Report on Operation Larkswood*, op. cit.

67 Main HQ II Canadian Corps, *War Diary from 1 Apr 45 to 30 Apr 45, Appendix 3 (operations log)*, 11 Apr 45 - serial 11, RG24-C-3, volume 13716, file 1701/GS, Library and Archives Canada.

68 *Report on Operation Larkswood*, op. cit.

69 Main HQ II Canadian Corps, *War Diary from 1 Apr 45 to 30 Apr 45, Appendix 1 (Sitreps for month of Apr 45)*, 12 Apr 45, RG24-C-3, volume 13716, file 1701/GS, Library and Archives Canada.

70 *Nederlandse Landwacht*: a pro-German home guard militia founded in November 1943, composed of Dutch NSB party members and consisting of a full-time 'professional' wing and a part-time 'auxiliary' wing. The *Nationaal-Socialistische Beweging* (NSB, National Socialist Movement) was a fascist political party established in 1931. The *Nederlandse Landwacht* should not be confused with the *Landwacht Nederland*, a *Waffen-SS*-controlled military territorial defence force established in March 1943 and renamed *Landstorm Nederland* in October 1943. After several name changes, from February 1945 it used the name *34. SS-Freiwilligen-Grenadier-Division 'Landstorm Nederland'*. See: Klaas Castelein & Michel Wenting, *The Dutch Resistance 1940–45 - World War II Resistance and Collaboration in the Netherlands*, Osprey Publishing, Oxford, 2022, pp. 4, 19, 23.

71 The after-action report mentions 'snipers'. However, it seems this term was used liberally in the report since a sniper is supposed to operate from a concealed position, unlikely to be detected by quick visual reconnaissance. Nevertheless, the German Navy had some trained sharpshooters by the end of the war that could have been used in the sniper role. See: Peter R. Senich, *The German Sniper: 1914-1945*, Paladin Press, Boulder, 1982.

72 *Report on Operation Larkswood*, op. cit.

73 *Panzerfaust:* German-made lightweight easy to use single-shot portable anti-tank weapon-ammunition system consisting of a tube with a folding sight and trigger system and containing the booster and propellant charge to propel the attached hollow charge; different variants, ranging in size, were used. See: Gordon L. Rottman, *Panzerfaust and Panzerschreck,* Osprey Publishing, Oxford, 2014.

74 *Report on Operation Larkswood*, op. cit.

75 Temmerman, op. cit., pp. 314-19.

76 Jaak Daemen, *De Operatie Larkswood en de ontmoeting met de Geschiedenis*, mei 2012, in: Nationale Vriendenkring Para-Commando Vzw, *News Flash,* Nr. 38 September-December 2012, pp. 7-10.

77 LtGen (ret) Jozef Segers, *Larkswood*, in: Société Royale des Officiers Retraités - Koninklijke Vereniging van de Oprustgestelde Officieren, *La Belgique militaire – Militair België,* No. 2757, Brussels, September 1995, p. 32.

78 Hubert de Mûelenaere, *Souvenirs d'événements* (unpublished), Brussels, 1994, pp. 17-21.

79 *Report on Operation Larkswood,* op. cit.

80 TNA: AIR 27/1085/65, p. 157, AIR 27/1085/66, p. 162.

81 Chris Thomas, *Typhoon Wings of 2nd TAF 1943–45*, Osprey Publishing, Oxford, 2010, p. 91.

82 Flying Officer Harry Bletcher, 164 Sqn RAF, *personal flying logbook* (unpublished, private collection).

83 *Report on Operation Larkswood*, op. cit.

84 II Canadian Corps, *War Diary, Appendix 3,* op. cit., 16 Apr – serial 4.

85 A brigade group is a formation based on a brigade as its core but with an altered task organisation compared to the organic organisation based on its table of organisation and equipment. The 1st Polish Armoured Division at that time used two brigade groups, one based on its 10th Armoured Cavalry Brigade (*10 Brygada Kawalerii Pancernej*), and the other based on its 3rd Infantry Brigade (*3 Brygada Piechoty*). This allowed to mix infantry and tank units within a single brigade group, which could be further reinforced by adding divisional units such as reconnaissance, artillery, engineer and signal units. Within the brigade groups, battalion-size battle groups were used based on the same principle of task organising organic and non-organic infantry companies and armoured squadrons within a single battle group, to match their organisation with tactical requirements.

86 Juliusz S. Tym, *Zarys działań polskiej 1 Dywizji Pancernej w północno-wschodniej Holandii i we Fryzji w kwietniu i maju 1945 roku*, in: Przegląd Historyczno-Wojskowy 12 (63)/3 (236), pp. 130, 138.

87 City of Winschoten online archives, https://www.winschoterarchief.nl/cat-bevrijding-van-winschoten-15-april-1945/winschoten-tweede-wereldoorlog/, retrieved 03 January 2024.

88 *Report on Operation Larkswood,* op. cit.

89 Dietrich Janßen, *Flak um Emden - Chronik der Marine-Flak-Abteilung 236*, Emden, 1999, pp. 382-383, 393 on: https://bunkermuseum.de/en/die-marine-flak-abteilung-236, retrieved 01 January 2024.

90 *Kriegstagebuch der Seekriegsleitung 1939-1945 – Teil A – Band 68 – 1. bis 20. April 1945*, Verlag E.S. Mittler & Sohn, 1989, p. 382-A.

91 *Report on Operation Larkswood,* op. cit.

92 II Canadian Corps, *War Diary, Appendix 3*, op. cit., 16 Apr 45 - serial 4.

93 From 1944, the SAS, amongst some other units, had been issued body armour developed by the British Medical Research Council. The system consisted of three separate 1 mm-thick manganese steel plates that were slightly curved to conform to the body contours and were carried in canvas covers which were attached to each other by webbing straps. The chest plate measured 9" x 8" and was designed to protect the heart, great blood vessels and lung roots. The back plate was 14" wide and 4" high at both ends, with the centre part gradually protruding up to 5" upward, and was to be worn below the shoulder blades to protect the base of the lungs, the liver and a portion of the spine. The abdominal plate measured 8" by 6". The complete system with canvas covers and webbing weighed 3.5 lbs. In tests, it withstood a .38" handgun bullet at 5 yards, a .303 bullet at 700 yards, and a Tommy Gun .45" bullet at 100 yards. Although well padded, the plates tended to cut into the soft-skin areas of the body causing chafing and sometimes causing profuse perspiration. See: Simon Dunstan, *Flak Jackets - 20th-century military body armour*, Osprey Publishing, London, 1984, p. 9.

94 *Report on Operation Larkswood,* op. cit.

95 Ibid.

96 Temmerman, op. cit., p. 332.

97 *Report on Operation Larkswood,* op. cit.

Chapter 9 – Advance Force in the Final Defeat of Nazi Germany

1 Dwight D. Eisenhower, *Crusade in Europe,* Doubleday & Company, Baltimore, 1948, pp. 396-412.

2 *Report on Operation Larkswood,* Belgian SAS archives, SGRS-S/CA, Evere.

3 Main HQ II Canadian Corps, *War Diary from 1 Apr 45 to 30 Apr 45,* page 7, RG24-C-3, volume 13716, file 1701/GS, Library and Archives Canada.

4 Field security section: section with Intelligence Corps personnel whose duties included the compilation and issue of classified lists of military and civilian Nazi functionaries and collaborators and members of the SS, *Gestapo* and German Secret Field Police, conducting field interrogations of prisoners of special interest, contributing to the divisional HQ intelligence cycle by searching buildings, translating documents and briefing intelligence officers, contributing to the security of key points and conducting

security investigations prior to deployment. See: Nicholas van der Bijl, *Sharing the Secret: The History of the Intelligence Corps, 1940–2010*, Pen & Sword, Barnsley, 2013, pp. 119-20.

5 *Ortsgruppenleiter:* Nazi Party political official responsible for all expressions of the party's will and the political and ideological leadership and direction of the area under his authority. The *Ortsgruppe* was the smallest regional organisation with its own adminstrative support, usually within a town or a borough in larger cities. See: Der Reichsorganisationsleiter der NSDAP, *Organisationsbuch der NSDAP*, Franz-Eher-Verlag, München, 1936, p. 119,

6 *Report on Operation Larkswood*, op. cit.

7 Jean Temmerman, *Les parachutistes belges 1942-1945 - Acrobates sans importance*, Edition DVB, Liège, 1999, p. 334,

8 Headquarters 2nd Canadian Armoured Brigade, *War Diary from 1 Apr 45 to 30 Apr 45*, pp. 11-12, RG24-C-3, volume 14047, file 940, Library and Archives Canada,

9 1st Canadian Armoured Car Regiment (Royal Canadian Dragoons), *War Diary from 1 Apr 45 to 30 Apr 45*, Appendix 9, RG24-C-3, volume 14188, file 570, Library and Archives Canada,

10 An independent unit is a unit assigned to a command level higher than the next higher (theoretical) command level in a command structure. The 2nd Canadian Armoured Brigade depended directly from the II Corps. The brigade was not part of a division, which is the immediate subordinate level of an army corps and the next higher command level of a brigade.

11 Special Air Service Regimental Association, *SAS War Diary 1941-1945*, London, 2011,

12 *Report on Operation Larkswood*, op. cit.

13 G Branch, Headquarters 4th Canadian Armoured Division, *War Diary from 1 Apr 45 to 30 Apr 45*, p. 30, RG24-C-3, volume 13790, microfilm reel T-10547, file 900/GS, Library and Archives Canada,

14 Colonel C.P. Stacey, *Official History of the Canadian Army in the Second World War, Volume III, The Victory Campaign, The Operations in North-West Europe 1944-1945*, The Queen's Printer and Controller of Stationery, Ottawa, 1960, p. 561,

15 *Report on Operation Larkswood,* op. cit.

16 General Staff - II Canadian Corps, *War Diary from 1 Apr 45 to 30 Apr 45, Appendix 3* (Operations Log), 27 Apr 45, sheet 2, serial 4, RG24-C-3, volume 13716, file 1701/GS, Library and Archives Canada, General Staff - II Canadian Corps, op. cit.

17 HQ 2nd Canadian Armoured Brigade, op. cit., p. 13.

18 *Report on Operation Larkswood*, op. cit.

19 6th Canadian Armoured Regiment (1st Hussars, *War Diary from 1 May 45* to 31 May 45, Appendix 5 (*'B' Squadron, 6th Canadian Armoured Regiment (1st Hussars), Report on operations, 18 May 45*), RG24-C-3, volume 14214, microfilm reel T-12657, file 3, Library and Archives Canada.

20 18th Canadian Armoured Car Regiment (12th Manitoba Dragoons), *War Diary from 1st April to 30th April 1945*, Appendix 8 (Operational communications log), 28 Apr 45, RG24-C-3, volume 14248, microfilm reel T-12715, file 977, Library and Archives Canada.

21 *Report on Operation Larkswood*, op. cit.

22 HQ 2nd Canadian Armoured Brigade, op. cit., Appendix 1 (Events Log), p. 123. Note that this log entry did not mention the British SAS.

23 6th Canadian Armoured Regiment (1st Hussars, *War Diary from 1 Apr 45 to 30 Apr 45*, p. 10, RG24-C-3, volume 14214, microfilm reel T-12657, file 3, Library and Archives Canada. Confusingly, in the war diary, the designation 'RCD' for 'Royal Canadian Dragoons' was added between brackets after '18 Armd Car'. The Royal Canadian Dragoons were in fact the 1st Armoured Car Regiment, whereas the Canadian 18th Armoured Car Regiment were the 12th Manitoba Dragoons. See: Stacey, op. cit., pp. 231, 554.

24 18th Canadian Armoured Car Regiment, *War Diary*, op. cit., message from 2nd Canadian Armoured Brigade dated 28 April 1945, RG24-C-3, volume 14249, microfilm reel T-12715, file 977, Library and Archives Canada. Note that this message did not mention the British SAS.

25 *Report on Operation Larkswood*, op. cit.

26 6th Canadian Armoured Regiment, *War Diary, Appendix 5*, op. cit.

27 18th Canadian Armoured Car Regiment (12th Manitoba Dragoons), *War Diary*, op. cit., *Appendix 8, 28 Apr 45.*

28 *Report on Operation Larkswood*, op. cit.

29 6th Canadian Armoured Regiment, op. cit., Appendix 5.

30 *Report on Operation Larkswood*, op. cit.

31 II Canadian Corps, *War Diary from 1 Apr 45 to 30 Apr 45, Appendix 3*, op. cit., 29 Apr 45, sheet 2, serial 9.

32 HQ 2nd Canadian Armoured Brigade, op. cit., Appendix 1 (Events Log), p. 129. The command relationships and their timings are somewhat confusing, since the 28 April entry in the 6th Canadian Armoured Regiment's war diary already mentioned the (reorganised squadron of the) British 1st SAS as part of Frankforce, whereas this message from the 2nd Canadian Armoured Brigade stated the British SAS was to come under command of Frankforce on 29 April at 9 am.

33 *Report on Operation Larkswood,* op. cit.

34 SAS Regimental Association, op. cit.

35 *Report on Operation Larkswood*, op. cit.

36 6th Canadian Armoured Regiment, *War Diary, Appendix 5*, op. cit.

37 6th Canadian Armoured Regiment (1st Hussars), *War Diary from 1 May 45 to 31 May 45, Appendix 4 (Operation report of 'A' Squadron, 6th Canadian Armoured Regiment (1st Hussars) in Frankforce 29 Apr – 3 May 45*), 5 May 45, RG24-C-3,

volume 14214, microfilm reel T-12657, file 3, Library and Archives Canada.

38 *Report on Operation Larkswood,* op. cit.

39 1st Canadian Armoured Car Regiment (Royal Canadian Dragoons), *War Diary from 1 May 45 to 31 May 45, Appendix 3 (2 Cdn Armd Bde Op Instr No. 6)*, RG24-C-3, volume 14189, file 570, Library and Archives Canada.

40 *Report on Operation Larkswood,* op. cit.

41 1st Canadian Armoured Car Regiment, *War Diary from 1 May 45 to 31 May 45*, op. cit., p. 3.

42 Headquarters 2nd Canadian Armoured Brigade, *War Diary from 1 May 45 to 31 May 45*, p. 2, RG24-C-3, volume 14047, file 940, Library and Archives Canada.

43 *Report on Operation Larkswood,* op. cit.

44 G Branch, Headquarters 4th Canadian Armoured Division, *War Diary from 1 May 45 to 31 May 45*, Appendix 5, RG24-C-3, volume 13790, microfilm reel T-10548, file 900/GS, Library and Archives Canada.

45 Field Marshal The Viscount Montgomery of Alamein, *Normandy to the Baltic – A personal account of the conquest of Germany*, Printing and Stationery Service British Army of the Rhine, 1946, p. 276-7.

46 *Report on Operation Larkswood*, op. cit.

47 Eisenhower, op. cit., pp. 426-7.

48 Act of Military Surrender; 5/7/1945; Instruments of German Surrender, 5/4/1945 - 5/10/1945; Records of the U.S. Joint Chiefs of Staff, Record Group 218; National Archives at College Park, College Park, MD.

49 Act of Military Surrender; 5/8/1945; Instruments of German Surrender, 5/4/1945 - 5/10/1945; Records of the U.S. Joint Chiefs of Staff, Record Group 218; National Archives at College Park, College Park, MD.

50 SAS Regimental Association, op. cit.

51 For a vivid account of these operations, see: Damien Lewis, *The Nazi Hunters – The Ultra-Secret SAS Unit and the Quest for Hitler's War Criminals*, Quercus Publishing, London, 2015.

52 *Report on Operation Larkswood*, op. cit.

Chapter 10 – Counterintelligence Operations in Occupied Germany

1 William M. Franklin and William Gerber (editors), *Foreign Relations of the United States: Diplomatic Papers, The Conferences at Cairo and Tehran, 1943*, United States Government Printing Office, Washington, 1961.

2 Bryton Barron (editor), *Foreign Relations of the United States: Diplomatic Papers, Conferences at Malta and Yalta, 1945,* United States Government Printing Office, Washington, 1955.

3 Bernard Law Montgomery, *The Memoirs of Field-Marshal the Viscount Montgomery of El Alamein, K.G.*, The World Publishing Company, Cleveland, 1958, pp. 319, 323-4, 336.

4 Edouard Blondeel, *Mémoires* (unpublished), Brussels, 1995.

5 Report on CI work, *Belgian SAS Regiment,* Belgian SAS archives, SGRS-S/CA, Evere.

6 F.S.V. Donnison, *Civil affairs and military government, North-West Europe 1944-1946,* Her Majesty's Stationary Office, 1961, p. 225.

7 *Report on CI work, Belgian SAS Regiment*, op. cit.

8 Jean Temmerman, *Acrobates sans importance,* Edition DVB, Liège, 1984, pp. 200-201.

9 George Gerolimatos, *Structural Change and Democratization of Schleswig-Holstein's Agriculture, 1945-1973,* University of North Carolina, Chapel Hill, 2014.

10 Alice Weinreb, *"For the Hungry Have No Past nor Do They Belong to a Political Party": Debates over German Hunger after World War II,* in: *Central European History*, Volume 45, No. 1, March 2012, pp. 50-78.

11 Blondeel, op. cit.

12 The Neuengamme concentration camp and its more than eighty-five satellite camps had been housing more than 100,000 prisoners, who were used as slave labour for the war industry. After the war, it was used as a British internment camp. See: Karin Schawe (editor), *Die KZ-Gedenkstätte Neuengamme – Ein Überblick über die Geschichte des Ortes und die Arbeit der Gedenkstätte*, KZ-Gedenkstätte Neuengamme, Hamburg, 2010.

13 2nd Lieutenant Crèvecœur, *Report on CI work A Squadron Hamburg*, Belgian SAS archives, SGRS-S/CA, Evere.

14 2nd Lt d'Oultremont, *Report on CI work A Squadron Hamburg*, Belgian SAS archives, SGRS-S/CA, Evere.

15 *Kreis:* literally 'circle'; municipal association and a regional authority under German municipal law.

16 *Sturmabteilung* (SA): 'assault battalion', an organisation created to protect Nazi Party rallies and later expanded to serve as a propaganda and paramilitary organisation and preparatory school for the armed forces. See: David Littlejohn, *The SA 1921–45: Hitler's Stormtroopers,* Osprey Publishing, Oxford, 1990.

17 In the Buchenwald concentration camp and its 139 satellite camps, nearly 280,000 persons from more than fifty nations were held captive between 1937 and 1945. Many inmates were used as slave labour for the war industry and for others the camp was a departure point for transportation to extermination camps. After the war, it was used as a Soviet internment camp. See: Dr. Philipp Neumann-Thein & Sandra Siegmund (editors), *Wegweiser durch die Gedenkstätte Buchenwald*, Stiftung Gedenkstätten Buchenwald und Mittelbau-Dora, Weimar, 2023.

18 Sgt Van Broekhuizen, *Report on CI work Panther Section (from 9-5/45 to 31-6-*

45), Belgian SAS archives, SGRS-S/CA, Evere.

19 Temmerman, op. cit., pp. 203-204.

20 Jeremy Duns, *Need to Know, An Archive of Journalistic Pursuits*, 2020, p. 594.

21 Jacques Goffinet, letter to Jaak Daemen dated 25 April 1997, Jaak Daemen private archives.

22 *Nationalsozialistisches Kraftfahrkorps* (NSKK) ('National Socialist Motor Transport Corps'): a paramilitary organisation set up in 1931 to transport high-ranking Nazi officials and to control and promote motor transport, later expanded to support the war effort. See: Nigel Thomas, *Wehrmacht Auxiliary Forces*, Osprey Publishing, Oxford, 1992, pp. 3-8.

23 2nd Lt Tinchant, *Report on CI work A Squadron Hamburg*, Belgian SAS archives, SGRS-S/CA, Evere.

24 Benedikt Erenz, *Reines Wollen, heller Wahn*, in: *Die Zeit*, Ausgabe Nr. 17/2015, Hamburg, 23 April 2015.

25 The *Werwolf* (Werewolf) guerilla organisation was based on cells of four to six men (*Gruppen*), which were grouped into *Sektors* (sectors) aka *Züge* (platoons) consisting of some six to ten cells. Six to eight sectors formed an *Abschnitt* (section). See: Perry Biddiscombe, *The Last Ditch: An Organizational History of the Nazi Werwolf Movement, 1944-45*, ProQuest, Ann Arbor, 2014, pp. 7, 119.

26 Tinchant, op. cit.

27 2nd Lt Barette, *Report on CI work in German[y] (from 12-5-45 to 2-7-45)*, Belgian SAS archives, SGRS-S/CA, Evere.

28 Imperial War Museums, records BU 6563, BU 6564, BU 6565.

29 Earl F. Ziemke, *The U.S. Army In the Occupation of Germany*, Center of Military History, United States Army, Washington, D.C., 2003, pp. 124-5.

30 The 970th Counter Intelligence Corps Detachment was established on 10 May 1945, replacing and recovering the personnel of the 12th Army Group's 418th Counter Intelligence Corps Detachment, which was disbanded on the same day. Counter Intelligence Corps personnel in occupied Germany had wide-ranging powers and responsibilities, such as investigating potential threats to the military government and collecting information on political, social, economic, and military issues. Special agents had the authority to arrest suspects and often operated in uniform wearing armbands with the letters 'CIC' and carrying handguns. In May 1945, the 970th had an authorised strength of 1,400 persons. See: Thomas Boghardt, *Covert Legions – U.S. Army Intelligence in Germany, 1944-1949*, Washington, D.C., 2022, pp. 145-8.

31 Barette, op. cit.

32 Captain Kirschen, *Activities of Detachment, Detached to 30th Corps*, dated 12 May, Belgian SAS archives, SGRS-S/CA, Evere.

33 Captain Radino, *Report on CI Work in Germany*, Belgian SAS archives, SGRS-S/CA, Evere.

34 Winston G. Ramsey (editor), *Himmler's Suicide*, in: *After the Battle*, No. 14, London, 1976, pp. 29-31.

35 Supreme Headquarters Allied Expeditionary Force – Office of the Assistant-Chief-of-Staff, G2, Counter-Intelligence Sub-division, Evaluation & Dissemination Section, *Arrest Categories Handbook – Germany*, April 1945, p. 4.

36 F. H. Hinsley & C. A. G. Simkins, *British Intelligence in the Second World War – Volume 4, Security and Counter-Intelligence,* Her Majesty's Stationery Office, London, 1990, p. 268.

37 Ramsey, op. cit., pp. 30-5.

38 Radino, op. cit.

39 Christian Gruslin, *Du Mercator à la capture d'Himmler*, Editions J. M. Collet, Braine-l'Alleud, 1992, p. 169.

40 Radino, op. cit.

41 Barette, op. cit.

42 Charles B. MacDonald, *The Last Offensive,* Center of Military History, United States Army, Washington, D.C., 1993, pp. 389-91 .

43 Infantry Journal Press, *Conquer, The Story of Ninth Army 1944-1945*, Washington, D.C., 1947, p. 297

44 *Map Showing Occupation Zones in Germany and Austria, July 1945* [Cartographic Record], Record Group 226, National Archives at College Park, MD.

45 *Map of Germany, 1942, customised to show the borders of the different zones of occupation in 1945*, National Army Museum, Chelsea, Accession Number NAM. 2018-03-6-5-1.

46 Barette, op. cit.

47 Karel Margry, *The Flensburg Government,* in: *After the Battle*, *No. 128*, Essex, 2005, p. 10.

48 Van Cauwelaert, *10.5.45 to 1.7.45*, Belgian SAS archives, SGRS-S/CA, Evere.

49 Margry, op. cit., pp. 6-11.

50 Montgomery, op. cit., p. 318.

51 George Hutchinson, *The Nazi Ideology of Alfred Rosenberg*, University of Oxford, 1977, pp. 11-18.

52 Robert K. Wittman & David Kinney, *The Devil's Diary: Alfred Rosenberg and the Stolen Secrets of the Third Reich*, HarperCollins Publishers, London, 2017.

53 Van Cauwelaert, op. cit.

54 Margry, op. cit., p. 11.

55 Van Cauwelaert, op. cit.

56 Marlis G. Steinert, *The Allied Decision to arrest the Dönitz government*, in: *The Historical Journal, 1988;* 31(3):651-63.

57 Margry, op. cit., pp. 13-16.

58 Van Cauwelaert, op. cit.

59 H. M. Denham, *Inside the Nazi Ring: A Naval Attaché in Sweden, 1940-1945*, John Murray, London, 1984, pp. 50-1.

60 TNA: KV 2/144 – KV 2/157.

61 Temmerman, op. cit., p. 206.

62 S/Lt Slosse, *Rapport CI de Wismar (du 18 Mai au 3 Juin 1945)*, Belgian SAS archives, SGRS-S/CA, Evere.

63 M. van Strydonck, *Patrol on 11/6/45 to Isle of Kegnæs (Denmark)*, Belgian SAS archives, SGRS-S/CA, Evere.

64 B Squadron, *Patrol on the East Coast between Kappeln and Eckernförde*, dated 18 June, Belgian SAS archives, SGRS-S/CA, Evere.

65 Cpl Heylen, *Patrol-report by the 2nd Assault section*, dated 19 June 1945, Belgian SAS archives, SGRS-S/CA, Evere.

66 Sgt de Mûelenaere, *Patrol along the German-Danish border*, dated 20 June 1945, Belgian SAS archives, SGRS-S/CA, Evere.

67 OCs 65 and 335 F.S. Sections, letter to CO, Belgian SAS, dated 28 June 1945, Belgian SAS archives, SGRS-S/CA, Evere.

68 Capitaine Debefve, *Rapport C.I. dans le Secteur Est*, Belgian SAS archives, SGRS-S/CA, Evere.

69 Montgomery, op. cit., pp. 337-40.

70 Winston S. Churchill, *The Second World War, Volume VI – Triumph and Tragedy*, Houghton Mifflin, Boston, 1953, pp. 449, 469.

71 *Operation Eclipse – The "C" Enigma*, Airborne Assault (ParaData) Archives, The Museum of the Parachute Regiment and Airborne Forces, Duxford, undated, p. 3.

72 *History 3 Para Bde*, Airborne Assault (ParaData) Archives, The Museum of the Parachute Regiment and Airborne Forces, Duxford, undated, p. 7.

73 1st Canadian Parachute Battalion, *War Diary from 1 May 1945 to 31 May 1945*, G24-C-3, RG24M 912011 volume 15300, file 1351, Library and Archives Canada.

74 In July 1944, a directive was sent by Eisenhower's supreme HQ to their army groups, announcing the forthcoming issue of special target lists and recommending the formation of 'T' (target) forces. The general concept was to place troops under a single 'T' force commander to seize and guard intelligence targets of interest to different agencies. See: *History of 'T' Force*, TNA, FO 1031/49; Sean Longden, *T-Force - The Race for Nazi War Secrets, 1945*, Constable & Robinson, London, 2009.

75 An inter-service commando unit established in 1942 upon request from the Director of Naval Intelligence of the Royal Navy as '30 Commando Unit', using the cover name 'Special Engineering Unit' and later renamed '30 Assault Unit'. The unit was designed to collect and exploit items of high intelligence value and was initially placed under

the Chief of Combined Operations and later under the Allied Naval Commander-in-Chief Expeditionary Force. See: Craig Cabell, *The History of 30 Assault Unit – Ian Fleming's Red Indians*, Pen & Sword, Barnsley, 2009; Nicholas Rankin, *Ian Fleming's Commandos – The Story of 30 Assault Unit in WWII*, Faber & Faber, London, 2011.

76 Special Air Service Regimental Association, *SAS War Diary 1941-1945*, London, 2011.

77 Robert 'Bob' Bennett, *Oral history*, Imperial War Museums, record 18045, reel 5.

78 Ian Wellsted, *With the SAS across the Rhine – Into the Heart of Hitler's Third Reich*, Frontline Books, Yorkshire, 2020, pp. 99-100.

79 *Operation Eclipse*, op. cit., pp. 4-6.

80 Slosse, op. cit.

81 Debefve, op. cit.

82 Ibid.

83 Slosse, op. cit.

84 Sous-Lieutenant Williot, *Rapport sur l'activité du détachement de Belgian S.A.S. Regiment en mission de C.I. à Wismar (Allemagne occupée) du 7 au 25 juin 1945*, dated 17 July 1945, Belgian SAS archives, SGRS-S/CA, Evere. Note that the report occasionally mentioned 'July', whereas this should have been 'June'.

85 Poeckers, Mission C.I. n 1. – *Rapport de mission du 7 juin 1945*, Belgian SAS archives, SGRS-S/CA, Evere.

86 Trooper Marcel Vincart, *Mission C.I. n 3.*, dated 08 June 1945, Belgian SAS archives, SGRS-S/CA, Evere.

87 Trooper Armand Germain, *Mission C.I. n 5.*, dated 11 June 1945, Belgian SAS archives, SGRS-S/CA, Evere.

88 Trooper Jacques Blondeel, *Mission C.I. n 6.*, dated 12 June 1945, Belgian SAS archives, SGRS-S/CA, Evere.

89 Trooper Gilles van de Put, *Mission C.I. n 7.*, dated 12 June 1945, Belgian SAS archives, SGRS-S/CA, Evere.

90 Trooper Richard Bellery, *Mission C.I. n 19.*, dated 18 June 1945, Belgian SAS archives, SGRS-S/CA, Evere.

91 Trooper Jacques Blondeel, *Mission C.I. n 15.*, dated 16 June 1945, Belgian SAS archives, SGRS-S/CA, Evere.

92 Trooper Alex Antoine, *Mission C.I. n 20.*, dated 19 June 1945, Belgian SAS archives, SGRS-S/CA, Evere.

93 Lance Corporal Jacques Roels, *Mission C.I. n 2.* – Rapport de mission du 7 juin 1945, Belgian SAS archives, SGRS-S/CA, Evere.

94 Trooper Georges Damas, *Mission C.I. n 12.*, dated 14 June 1945, Belgian SAS archives, SGRS-S/CA, Evere.

95 Trooper Richard Bellery, *Mission C.I. n 26.*, dated 22 June 1945, Belgian SAS archives, SGRS-S/CA, Evere.

96 Trooper Jacques Blondeel, *Mission C.I. n 16.*, dated 16 June 1945, Belgian SAS archives, SGRS-S/CA, Evere.

97 Trooper Gilles van de Put, *Mission C.I. n 4.*, dated 11 June 1945, Belgian SAS archives, SGRS-S/CA, Evere.

98 Debefve, op. cit.

99 Trooper Alex Antoine, *Mission C.I. n 8.*, dated 12 June 1945, Belgian SAS archives, SGRS-S/CA, Evere.

100 Trooper Germain Armand, *Mission C.I. n 10.*, dated 13 June, Belgian SAS archives, SGRS-S/CA, Evere.

101 Trooper Joseph De Man, *Mission C.I. n 11.*, dated 13 June 1945, Belgian SAS archives, SGRS-S/CA, Evere.

102 Trooper Emil Van Ruymbeke, *Mission C.I. n 13.*, dated 14 June, Belgian SAS archives, SGRS-S/CA, Evere.

103 Trooper Marcel Poeckers, *Mission C.I. n 17.*, dated 16 June 1945, Belgian SAS archives, SGRS-S/CA, Evere.

104 Jacques Roels, *Mission C.I. n 22. – Rapport de mission*, dated 19 June 1945, Belgian SAS archives, SGRS-S/CA, Evere.

105 Trooper Marcel Poeckers, *Mission C.I. n 24.*, dated 20 June 1945, Belgian SAS archives, SGRS-S/CA, Evere.

106 Trooper Georges Damas, *Mission C.I. n 9.*, dated 13 June 1945, Belgian SAS archives, SGRS-S/CA, Evere.

107 Trooper Lionel Mathy, *Mission C.I. n 14.*, dated 15 June 1945, Belgian SAS archives, SGRS-S/CA, Evere.

108 Trooper Georges-Emile Jottrand, *Mission C.I. n 18.*, dated 18 June 1945, Belgian SAS archives, SGRS-S/CA, Evere.

109 Trooper Georges Damas, *Mission C.I. n 21.*, dated 18 June 1945, Belgian SAS archives, SGRS-S/CA, Evere.

110 Lance Corporal Jacques Roels, *Mission C.I. n 23. – Rapport de mission*, dated 20 June 1945, Belgian SAS archives, SGRS-S/CA, Evere.

111 Temmerman, op. cit., p. 213.

112 Montgomery, op. cit., p. 319.

113 OC 39 FSS, letter dated 22 June 1945, Pegasus Museum Archives, Diest.

114 Traffic accident report dated 21 June 1945, Pegasus Museum Archives, Diest.

115 Lt. Henrard, *Report on CI Work Det Ludwigslust (Mecklenburg-Schwerin) from 10-6-45 to 29-6-45*, Belgian SAS archives, SGRS-S/CA, Evere.

116 Montgomery, op. cit., p. 344.

117 *Report on CI work*, op. cit.

118 Richard Mead, *The Men Behind Monty*, Pen & Sword, Barnsley, 2015, chapters 4, 7, 9-13, 16-22, 24, 26-8.

119 Brigadier E. T. Williams, O.B.E., D.S.O., letter 21 A Gp/INT/2025/3 to Brigadier J. M. Calvert dated 6 July 1945, Pegasus Museum Archives, Diest.

Epilogue

1 Letter from Brigadier Calvert dated August 1945, Pegasus Museum archives, Diest.

2 Annotated pictures, Pegasus Museum archives, Diest, and personal collection Arnould d'Oultremont.

3 Roger Flamand, *Amherst: les parachutistes de la France libre, 3e et 4e SAS, Hollande 1945*, Saint-Cloud, 1998, p. 187.

4 Imperial War Museums, records B 15783, B 15785, B 15786, B 15793.

5 Special Air Service Regimental Association, *SAS War Diary* 1941-1945, London, 2011.

6 Tim Jones, *SAS: The First Secret Wars – The Unknown Years of Combat and Counter-Insurgency*, London, 2005.

7 MDN/IGT/1e Don n° O/24799, dated 25 September 1945, SGRS-S/CA, Evere.

8 IWM, records BU 11280, BU 11283.

9 Guy de Pierpont and André Lefèvre, *Historique des Régiments Parachutiste SAS, Commando et Para-Commando, tome II*, Groupe G.O. & Co., Brussels, 1977, p. 204.

10 Amicale Belgian SAS Vriendenkring, Des SAS au *"Special Forces Group" – 75 ans de forces spéciales belges*, Kortrijk, 2016, pp. 264-372.

Appendix 1 – Roll of Honour

1 Primary sources: R[é]giment de Parachutistes S.A.S., *Etat des militaires accident[é]s au cours des op[é]rations*, part of: Jean Temmerman, Documentation de recherche concernant les paracommandos belges, BE-A0547 / FICINV_2865, Study and Documentation Centre for War and Contemporary Society, State Archives, Brussels; individual personnel files, National Archives 2 - Joseph Cuvelier repository, State Archives, Brussels.

2 The headstone of his grave states 15 April.

3 1st lieutenant, acting captain.

4 The headstone of his grave states 4 May 1945.

Appendix 2 – Record of Belgian Parachute Company and Special Air Service Personnel in the Second World War

1 The list is not complete but is based on the best available information. Other names circulate as having been part of the unit, but some non-badged personnel were officially transferred pending their qualification (and being returned to their unit in case of failure), while it is likely that on other occasions, personnel were temporarily attached and only officially transferred upon passing qualification training. This situation, combined with different ways to spell names of the same persons, clerical errors and the dispersal of personnel files over different archives, some of which have been confirmed lost, make it next to impossible to accurately reconstruct a complete list of all personnel having been officially assigned to the unit. Primary sources: Jean Temmerman, *Les parachutistes belges 1942-1945 - Acrobates sans importance*, Edition DVB, Liège, 1999, pp. 370-81; Guy Weber, *Les précurseurs - 13 janvier 1942*, Editions L. Bourdeaux-Capelle, Dinant, 1991, pp. 33-5; Robert Tabary, *Belgian Forces in the United Kingdom 1940-1945*, Comité 44-94, Brussels, 1994, pp. 158-63.

Appendix 3 – Recipients of British Awards for Exploits While Serving in the Belgian Special Air Service

1 TNA: WO 373/153/60.
2 TNA: WO 373/153/97.
3 TNA: WO 373/153/45.
4 TNA: WO 373/153/161.
5 TNA: WO 373/153/159.
6 TNA: WO 373/153/.
7 TNA: WO 373/153/380.
8 TNA: WO 373/153/381.
9 TNA: WO 373/153/113.
10 TNA: WO 373/153/61.
11 TNA: WO 373/153/162.
12 TNA: WO 373/153/114.
13 TNA: WO 373/153/112.
14 TNA: WO 373/153/41.
15 TNA: WO 373/153/42.
16 TNA: WO 373/153/115.
17 TNA: WO 373/153/46.
18 TNA: WO 373/153/98.
19 TNA: WO 373/153/116.
20 TNA: WO 373/153/117.
21 TNA: WO 373/153/62.
22 TNA: WO 373/153/118.
23 TNA: WO 373/153/44.
24 TNA: WO 373/153/119.

25 TNA: WO 373/153/43.
26 TNA: WO 373/153/384.
27 TNA: WO 373/153/382.
28 TNA: WO 373/153/383.

Appendix 4 – Belgian Special Air Service Regiment Battle Honours

1 The battle honours were embroidered on the colours of the Belgian SAS Regiment, in Dutch on one side, and in French on the other. Their associated citations were translated from the original authentic texts in French and Dutch.

Index